ISSUES IN NEW INFORMATION TECHNOLOGY

COMMUNICATION AND INFORMATION SCIENCE
Edited by
BRENDA DERVIN
The Ohio State University

Recent Titles

ISSUES IN NEW INFORMATION TECHNOLOGY

edited by

Benjamin M. Compaine

ABLEX PUBLISHING CORPORATION
NORWOOD, NEW JERSEY

Chapters 2, 3, 4, 5, and 7 are reprinted with permission of the Program on
Information Resources Policy, Harvard University; copyright © by the Program on
Information Resources Policy in years as follows: Chapter 2 (1984), Chapter 3
(1985), Chapter 4 (1985), Chapter 5 (1984). Chapter 8 is abridged from a publication
of the same name (1986).

Chapter 6 is reprinted with permission from *Telecommunications Policy,* 10:3,
March 1986, pp. 5–12, Buttreworth Scientific, PO Box 63, Guildford, GU2 5BH,
United Kingdom.

Library of Congress Cataloging-in-Publication Data

Compaine, Benjamin M.
    Issues in new information technology.

    Bibliography: p.
    Includes index.
    1. Information technology—Economic aspects.   2. Information technology—
Social aspects.   3. Information technology—Political aspects.   4. Information
resources management.   I. Title.
HC79.I55C65   1988   303.4'83   87-37443
ISBN 0-89391-500-9
ISBN: 0-89391-468-1

Ablex Publishing Corporation
355 Chestnut Street
Norwood, New Jersey 07648

Table of Contents

In loving memory of my Father

ABOUT THE AUTHORS

ABOUT THE EDITOR

Benjamin M. Compaine is a partner in Samara Associates, a research and consulting firm in Cambridge, Mass. He is also president of Nova Systems Inc., a firm which develops and markets specialized management information software. From 1979 to 1986 he was executive director at Harvard University's Program on Information Resources Policy, where he directed research projects that resulted in most of the studies published in this volume. At other times he has been a book and newspaper publisher and has taught management, marketing and mass communication. His books include *Understanding New Media* (1984), *Who Owns the Media?* (2nd ed., 1982) and *Business: An Introduction (1984)*. A graduate of Dickinson College, he received an M.B.A. from Harvard's Graduate School of Business Administration and a Ph.D. from Temple University.

ABOUT THE CONTRIBUTORS

Gladys Ganley has been a writer for 20 years, much of that with the National Institute of Health. She received her M.A. from Harvard University.

Oswald Ganley is executive director of the Program on Information Resources Policy, with primary responsibility for international issues. Previously he was a career foreign service officer in the State Department, where he became Deputy Assistant Secretary of State for Science and Technology. He is the author of *To Inform or Control? The New Communications Networks.* He earned his M.P.A. from Harvard and his Ph.D. from the University of Michigan.

Richard Hooper is managing director of Super Channel, Ltd. in the U.K. At the time he wrote his chapter he was chief executive, Value Added Services, British Telecom. In this capacity he was responsible for Prestel, the original videotex service. He has an MA from Oxford University.

Erwin Krasnow is a partner in the Washington law firm of Verner, Liipfert, Bernard & McPherson, where he specializes in broadcast regulation. Previously he was senior vice president and general counsel, National Association of Broadcasters. He is co-author of *The Politics of Broadcast Regulation.* He received his J.D. from Harvard Law School.

Meredith Mendes received her J.D. in 1983 from Harvard Law School. She is currently an attorney specializing in public finance with Hopkins & Sutter, Chicago.

Jill Abehouse Stern is a partner in the Washington law firm of Miller, Young & Holbrooke, where she specializes in satellite and broadcast matters. She is a graduate of Smith College and received her J.D. with high honors from George Washington University Law School.

PREFACE

THE PROGRAM ON INFORMATION RESOURCES POLICY

This book is mostly a collection of research reports and incidental papers previously published by the Program on Information Resources Policy at Harvard University. This Program has a unique method of operation, aimed at providing research for policymakers that is different from other, similar-sounding research efforts. For that reason, a short description of the goals and methods of the Program will help put this work in context.

To accomplish its research mission, the Program was established in 1972 with a unique funding mechanism. Because it would be dealing in areas of high stakes and corporate and political self-interest, it set out to establish a broad base of financial support. (A list of contributors current to publication of this book is provided in Appendix A.) The Program made a conscious effort to have participants from all segments of the information business, as well as organizations that are consumers of information. Competing industries and competitors within industries are represented. The Program does no proprietary research for these contributors nor for anyone else. All the research in this book, as well as the Program's other publications, was undertaken on its own initiative and on its own terms. None was paid for exclusively by any vested interest in the issues.

To ensure the accuracy of the facts, most of the studies in this book have undergone the Program's review process. This involves sending drafts of works in progress to knowledgeable reviewers at the organizations who contribute to the Program as well as to others who can lend some specific expertise. The Program asks these reviewers if the paper has the facts right, if it is asking the right questions, if it has identified issues, and if it has correctly represented the interest of the contending parties.

This process is intended to ensure accuracy as well as objectivity. It also means that even papers written by authors who work for an organization with a stake in the outcome of some issue can be reviewed by opposing stakeholders. The result is typically a report to which all parties can stipulate to the facts, though ultimately with varying interpretation of what the facts mean. Some of the chapters in this volume are "incidental paper." In this case, they were not reviewed externally, but are included because of their general interest and applicability.

The introduction and final chapters were written specifically for this book and do not necessarily reflect the views of the Harvard Program.

INFORMATION AS A RESOURCE

The Program's premise at its inception was the early observation that the traditional telephone business was becoming increasingly intertwined with the computer world. As the former was a highly regulated industry and the latter was young, entrepreneurial and quite unregulated, there was going to be a period of confusion and destabilization both in corporate executive suites and in public policy. Moreover, the Program foresaw that the stakes in the outcome of this merging of computer and telecommunications (or "compunications") technologies were greater than for each of those two industries alone. Compunications was part of an infrastructure that included physical delivery of goods, via the U.S. Postal Service and other private carriers. In addition, numerous other industries, the media among them, had a stake in the outcome of the regulatory battles that could present these industries with new opportunities as well as threats to their existing franchises.

At an even more global level, the Program's underlying theology is that the stakes in the broadly described information business touch on nearly all business and government organizations. Information has always been a resource, but only recently have we seen the first glimmers of understanding of information in the same context as economists describe materials or energy as resources. Information is a resource of similar magnitude. Increasingly,information is being substituted for these other resources. Today, microprocessors in automobile engines improve fuel efficiency, thus exchanging information for energy. Financial institutions are becoming more conscious that information – on interest rates, gold prices, crop size, political instability around the world – is their real raw material. Information resources include expenditures on capital equipment, such as a word processors, or labor, such as a researcher.

In translating information as a resource into a working agenda, the Program has been looking at the issues facing those who are in the information business. *Issues in New Information Technology* is a continuation of that agenda.

An exhaustive list of acknowledgments for those who have aided with this book would include the dozens of reviewers of the individual chapters as well as the many who have provided guidance and insights. They will therefore go unnamed here, but their assistance over the years has been crucial to the Program's goal of accuracy and objectivity. Having left the Program about a year ago, I feel it appropriate to thank my former colleagues there, Tony Oettinger, John LeGates, John McLaughlin and Ossie Ganley, for their guidance and insights over the years.

Ben Compaine
Cambridge, Mass.
October 1987

APPENDIX A:
PROGRAM ON INFORMATION
RESOURCES POLICY

Harvard University   Center for Information Policy Research

Affiliates

Action for Children's Television
American Telephone & Telegraph Co.
Ameritech Publishing
Anderson, Benjamin, Read & Haney, Inc.
Apple Computer, Inc.
Arthur D. Little, Inc.
Auerbach Publishers Inc.
Automated Marketing Systems
Bell South Corporation
Bell Atlantic
Booz-Allen & Hamilton, Inc.
Bull, S.A. (France)
Commission of the European Communities
Communications Workers of America
Computer & Communications Industry Assoc.
Copley Newspapers
Cowles Media Co.
Data Communications Corp. of Korea
Department of Communication (Australia)
Dialog Information Services, Inc.
Digital Equipment Corp.

Direction Generale des Telecommunications (France)
Dow Jones & Co., Inc.
Equifax Research
Gannett Co., Inc.
GTE Corporation
Hitachi Research Institute (Japan)
Honeywell, Inc.
IBM Corp.
Information Gatekeepers, Inc.
Information Industry Association
International Data Corp.
International Resource Development, Inc.
Invoco AB Gummar Bergvall (Sweden)
Knowledge Industry Publications, Inc.
Lee Enterprises, Inc.
John and Mary R. Markle Foundation
Martin Marietta Corp.
MCI Telecommunications, Inc.
McKinsey & Co., Inc.
Mead Data Central
MITRE Corp.
Motorola, Inc.
National Computer Board (Singapore)

National Telephone Cooperative Assoc.
The New York Times Co.
NEC Corp. (Japan)
Nippon Telegraph & Telephone Corp. (Japan)
Northern Telecom Ltd. (Canada)
Nova Systems Inc.
NYNEX
Ing. C. Olivetti & C., S.p.A. (Italy)
The Overseas Telecommunications Commission (Australia)
Pitney Bowes, Inc.
Public Agenda Foundation
Reader's Digest Association, Inc.
Research Institute of Telecommunications and Economics (Japan)
RESEAU (Italy)
Saint Phalle International Group
Salomon Brothers
Scaife Family Charitable Trusts
SEAT S.P.A. (Italy)
Southern New England Telecommunications Corp.
State of California Public Utilities Commission
State of Minnesota Funding
State of Nebraska Telecommunications and Information Center

TEKNIBANK S.p.A. (Italy)
Telecommunications Research Action Center (TRAC)
Telecom Plus International, Inc.
Third Class Mail Association
Times Mirror Co.
TRW Inc.
United States Government:
   National Telecommunications and Information Administration
   Department of Health and Human Services National Library of Medicine
   Department of State Office of Communications
   Federal Communications Commission
   Federal Emergency Management Agency
   National Aeronautics and Space Administration
   National Security Agency
   U.S. Army:
      Office of the Assistant Chief of Staff for Information Management
   United States Postal Rate Commission
US West
United Telecommunications, Inc.
The Washington Post Co.

Chapter 1

INTRODUCTION: THE INFORMATION "REVOLUTION" IS MORE THAN TECHNOLOGY

Benjamin M. Compaine

It was nearly 350 years before the first substantial improvement was made to Gutenberg's original printing press. That was when steam power replaced human muscle for its operation. But society has more than made up for that slow start. In the last 65 years—the span of a single lifetime—man has moved from essentially a one mass medium society—print—to a multi-media society.

The implications have been profound, not only in industrialized democracies but among totalitarian regimes and in third world backwaters. Whether it's grand thoughts of beaming radio signals across national boundaries by satellites 22,300 miles over the earth, or the proliferation of cheap and small audio and videocassettes found in all corners of the globe, or the more mundane revolution of the ubiquitous photocopying machine as everyman's printing press, it is impossible to overlook the changes that new media technologies have wrought in our cultural, economic, and political lives.

The media hold a special place in our thoughts, part passion, part practicality. The notion that the media are the primary conveyors of ideas, information, and culture elevates the media business into a sphere different from that of almost any other institution. We need only reflect on the difference in the emotional pitch reached in the 1986 case of Nicholas Daniloff, a reporter for *U.S. News and World Report,* from that of American businessman Francis Crawford in 1978. Following the arrest by the United States of two Soviets as spies. Crawford was arrested in Moscow on currency charges, tried, convicted, and sentenced to prison before having the sentence suspended and being expelled.[1]

The reason for this ardor is likely tied to a historical affinity for the promotion of ideas. It was Cardinal Newman who wrote, "Men will die for a dogma who will not even stir for a conclusion."

OBJECTIVES AND ASSUMPTIONS

Much of what has been written about the "information revolution" has focused on the technology itself, on the possibilities of new products or services the technology makes possible, and in some cases on predictions of how society will change. Some of the prognosticators see a gloomy future. Others in the predicting business see a rosy future.

The reality is that the outcomes of technology have never been very predictable. Short-term disruptions give way to long term stability, or vice versa. Some regulations may be quite robust despite changes in details, while others quickly become antiquated and require revision.

The chapters in this book address one or more facets of the following questions: Given that information technology is changing, what are the issues, what does it mean, for whom, and to what end?

This book does not provide a definitive answer these questions. Indeed, one objective is to raise additional questions, thereby raising the level of complexity. There are few easy policy decisions for complex issues.

A few years ago there was a revival of the music of Tom Lehrer. Lehrer, an erstwhile Harvard mathematician, had a following in the mid-1960s for his songs of political and social satire. At the time of the '80s revival he was asked (I believe in a *Wall Street Journal* article) why he didn't write songs anymore. His answer was that, as he grew older, he was less able to see issues in stark terms. "It's hard to fit 'on the other hand' into a song."

And so it is with the political, social, cultural, or economic issues arising from changing information technology. Whether privacy, ownership, copyright, equity, literacy, or whatever, the "right" answer is always subject to legitimate debate. Among the variables are:

- Are the debaters talking about short term (which might be a few years to a decade or more in some cases) or long term?
- Are they making spurious extrapolations from historic trends (see Chapter 5)?
- What assumptions are they using? Is there another set of reasonable assumptions that would yield different answers?

- If some groups are seen as losers, what groups are winners? Can everyone win or lose?
- Who are the stakeholders and how likely are they to fight for a particular end? Which stakeholders win under different scenarios?
- What is the agenda of the would-be policy makers? Do they state their agenda, or is there a hidden agenda?

Although this book does not set forth a recommended course of action, there are some assumptions that are at its foundation. One is that the existing political and economic systems in the Western democracies in general and the Untied States in particular are not likely to change. Thus, fundamental notions of private ownership and representative government will be the rule. A second assumption is that regulation is a function, not only of economics and rationality, but of political compromise as well. A third assumption is that cultural values, like other values, change over time. Values of right and wrong, good and bad, and so on, are candidates for incremental evolution.

Thus, *Issues in New Information Technology* is about describing the terrain. It is *not* about predicting what lies on the other side of the mountain range or what *should be* built there. It would be presumptuous to say that these changes describe "that's the way it is," as Walter Cronkite assured us. The intent here is to leave it to others to decide what the changes and issues mean for them.

The remainder of this chapter provides a context for each of the chapters.

TECHNOLOGY

This book is not about information technology *per se*, but with topics that were relevant for study because of some direct or indirect connection to the changing technology. These include, for example, broadcast regulation in Chapter 4, literacy concepts in Chapter 5, or privacy issues discussed in Chapter 7. The significance of each chapter, as explained below, lies in one or more political, social, cultural, and economic issues.

Technology continues to promote change in the alignment of the media, creating new winners as well as losers. In the 15th century, the scriptoria were the losers, as new print shops took over. In the 19th century, the development of photography was a boon to magazines. Newspapers rose to the challenge with telephotographs and rotogravure sections. These were in turn killed by movie newsreels, which in turn died as the result of television. There is no apparent end in sight to the possibilities for information storage, transmission, and retrieval being created by new technologies or less-expensive applications of older technologies. The watchwords for information technology today are smaller, faster, cheaper, and better. At the same time, we are witnessing the blurring of the boundaries among heretofore distinct media forms.

This century has not only brought us broadcasting from earth based towers but broadcasting from satellites – essentially 22,300-mile-high towers. Newspapers have become electronic media in all but their final stage, as reporters and artists prepare text and graphics on computer terminals and the computers typeset the completed pages. In the case of the national newspapers, facsimiles of those pages are digitized and sent via satellite to far-off plants in a form that makes the signals indistinguishable from bits of television programs or telephone conversations traversing the skies.

Many of us are bypassing some paper altogether. *Compunications,* the product of the meshing of computers with telecommunications, is allowing us to use our computers and terminals to access the information we think we want directly from other computers. We read the results on a video screen, perhaps printing a few things out on our private "dot matrix" printing presses. Our personal computers and laser printers are indeed turning the office into a print shop, as nearly typeset quality newsletters are turned out by secretaries rather than by the highly skilled linotype operators of yore.

In Chapter 2, Richard Hooper engages in a somewhat metaphysical analysis of Prestel, the British granddaddy of consumer electronic information services. Technology was the easy piece of the venture. In "Prestel, Escher, Bach: Changes Within Changes," Hooper notes that sorting out the economic, marketing, and regulatory variables was still not complete 4 years after the service started – and is being fine tuned to this day.

ECONOMIC AND STRUCTURAL IMPACTS

Chapter 3, "New Media and New Competition," explores the dimensions of media competition given the evolving technology and its related consequences. The changing economic picture of information and the media is in large measure tied to a host of technological forces. Electronics have created new competition for the print media while at the same time providing the wherewithal to improve the printed product and reduce its costs. With newer technologies blurring the boundaries of traditional media formats and content, media companies are struggling to adjust to the need for new configurations. At the same time, media users – both advertisers and consumers – are assessing their options for using media.

Figure 1 highlights the entries in the corners of the information business

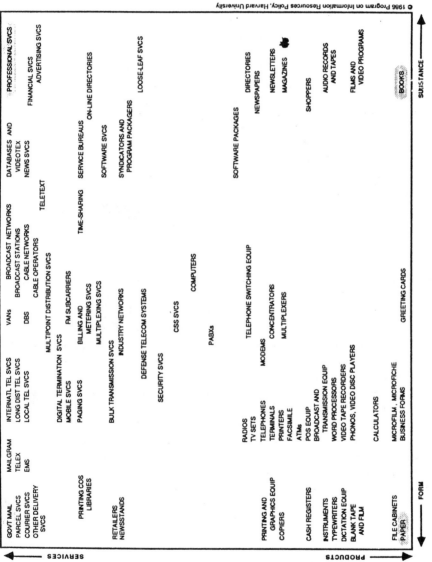

Figure 1A.   Corner Entries

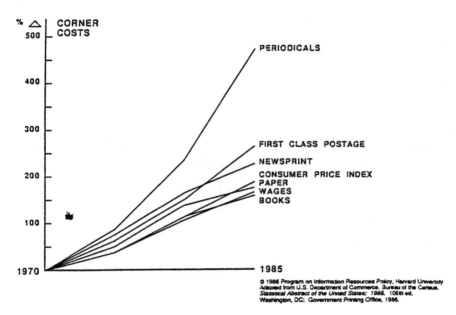

Figure 1B.   Costs in the Corners

map.[2] These products and services are labor and energy intensive – and are most closely associated with print. Figure 2 traces the growth in unit costs for several of these entities from 1970 through 1985. During those years cost have exceeded or approximated the consumer price index (CPI). The situation is just the reverse for those entries occupying the center of the map in Figure 3. Figure 4 traces a dramatic decrease in unit costs of several representative products.

Geopolitical developments in the form of the energy crisis in the 1970s brought on by Middle Eastern politics resulted in rapid and sharp rises in the cost of the two basic raw materials of print: paper and ink. The cost of physical distribution, via trucks, is also energy intensive. These factors combine to make electronic distribution of information, centered around computers and various terrestrial and satellite transmission methods, an attractive alternative to the old way of mechanically distributing information. Such developments are only one component of the forces that have changed the rules of media structure.

REGULATORY QUANDARIES

What we are seeing today in both the competitive and regulatory arenas of the media business is a continuation of this centuries-old process of

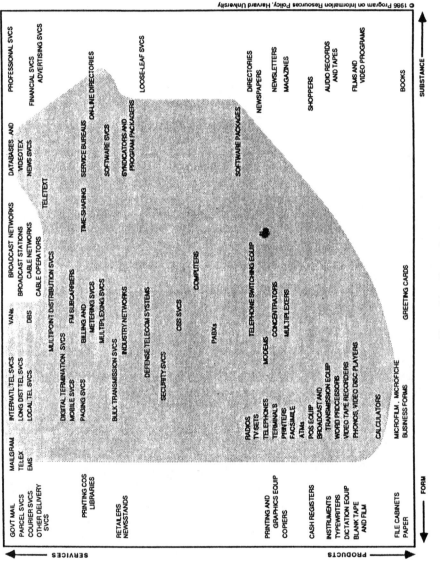

Figure 2A. Center Entries

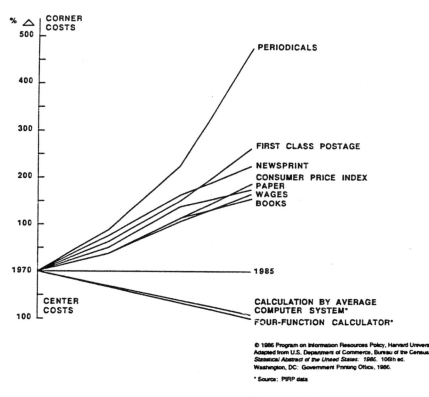

Figure 2B.   Costs in the Center

constant realignment as the technology changes. Thus it is timely to evaluate those changes and ask what it means for what Erwin Krasnow and Jill Stern call in Chapter 4 "The New Video Marketplace."

Technology may have undercut the need for some of the regulatory apparatus that was established around broadcasting 50 to 60 years ago. At that time, the new broadcasting media were separated from print media for government restrictions on ownership and content, largely on the basis of "spectrum scarcity." That is, unlike the printing press, which had only an economic price, getting a broadcasting frequency ran into the limitations of the laws of nature as well. The debate these days is over *how much* and *what parts* of the regulatory regime is outdated and what, if anything, needs to be modified or preserved. Today, spectrum scarcity alone is less of justification. We have become much more proficient at dividing up the spectrum, so that there are few shortages. Outside of the 10 or 15 largest markets, many cities and towns have radio or television channels that are available but unclaimed. There is an overcapacity of satellite channels. Cable in particular has unleashed an avalanche of programming services, some of which have proven nonviable only from an economic standpoint. But cable has helped strengthen independent (nonnetwork) television stations and the programmers along with them. Videocassettes have lowered the costs of getting distribution for video programming even further.

Producers find themselves in much the same position as magazine and book publishers have been for a century: competing to get the attention of a highly fragmented audience. Now, rather than hearing talk of scarcity, the pundits warn about *too much* information or the ability of people to pay for all it (as if anyone would want more than a tiny fraction of what's out there).

CULTURAL FORCES

The work on New Literacy, represented in this volume in Chapter 5 by "Information Technology and Cultural Change," was initiated in 1984 with the observation that each generation is a product of the media dominant at the time. This generalization reaches back into antiquity. Every time someone complains that today's kids are being ruined by television or video games, think back to the 7th century B.C. to the fear expressed by Thamus, King of Egypt, as described in Plato's *Phaedrus*. In his day, the burning issue was the impact that the new-fangled written alphabet would have on the contemporary form of literacy, memory, and oral recounting of events. In 11th and 12th century England, the oral record was still considered the superior form of documentation. The word of honest knights was accepted with greater credulity than a written parchment. All sorts of conventions had to be invented, such as the indenture, to bring the written word into dominance. It is relatively recently in man's history that reading and writing took over from memory and rhetoric as the cornerstone of literacy.

The need for reading and writing skills was directly related to the needs of the Industrial Revolution. In the agrarian society prior to the 19th century, such skills were not widely needed. Subsequently the Industrial Revolution made possible—and more necessary—the spread of reading and writing skills. The technology of the steam engine and knowledge of making paper from pulp rather than rags made inexpensive mass printing feasible. The railroads increased the geographical market for print products, creating new economies of scale. Improvements in optics made inexpensive mass printing feasible. The railroads increased the geographical market for print products, creating new economies of scale. Improvements in optics made eyeglasses available to adults who otherwise would be physically unable to read in their middle age.

Today, we may be in an early stage of yet another step in the evolution of literacy. Technology has made it easier to present information graphically. Video has become cheap and easy to use with minimal training. A new generation, brought up with video all around it, is comfortable with that presence, whether in the form of a fast paced television program or a text-filled computer screen.

Important as broadcast television has been since the 1950s, the implementation of cable and, perhaps even more crucially, videocassettes and optical disks, may be the beginning of the technologies that make video a serious tool for more forms of information transfer. The decline in the cost and size of video cameras might help expand the visual creation of art and literature. Thus, some of those artists who in the past had to channel their creative expressions into the written word—because that was the dominant technology—are increasingly finding it feasible and acceptable to engage in different visual forms of expression, using new tools.

More consequentially, by reducing the skill needed to be literate, more people are able to participate in literate society. The few people in 700 B.C. who were able to take the time to memorize were replaced over 1200 years later by a society that has the resources to be almost universally literate. Today, one need not even know how to read to be far better informed about the state of the world and to have access to more culture in the form of music and drama than even the most literate person could using the media of only 100 years ago.

SOCIAL EQUITY: INFORMATION POVERTY?

Although much attention has been focused on information technology getting smaller, faster, cheaper, and better, we also hear about database services that charge $100 for an hour of "connect" time. Cable television is no longer free television. And computers and software cost more than books. Is the technology creating an information gap between those who can afford the technology and those who have the skills to use the technology and those who cannot or will not learn how to use it? Or does it refer to some gap between entire information-rich societies and information-poor ones?

Chapter 6, "Information Gaps: Myth or Reality," started life as a major study for the Harvard Program. However, exploratory research indicated that there seemed to be more smoke than fire to the issue. A quick trip through history pointed to repeated instances where technologies have been crucial factors in the spread of both information and the skills to use information. The first alphabets must have seemed terribly confusing to a society immersed in the technology of oral literacy. But eventually writing did spread and make communication easier. The original printing press, though a relatively expensive piece of technology itself, was the first link is making information widely available at far lower costs than manual copying. Then came the harnessing of the steam engine to the rotary press in the 1830s, improvements in making paper from pulp, and the ability—via the railways—to reach wider audiences with the printed product. Film and broadcasting have further broadened access to all types of information.

We have also developed innovative techniques for keeping the price low for the user of information. Advertising shifts the direct costs for many products to third parties. Postal subsidies helped keep the price of shipping printed matter below cost. Libraries have become ubiquitous institutions.

Moreover, compared to 100 years ago, a far greater proportion of the population has the skills needed to make use of the information and to know how to seek it out (which may be as simple as pushing a button on a television set's remote control device). Thus, the chapter concludes that raising the specter of widening gaps appears to assume a discontinuity in of historical trends.

PRIVACY ISSUES

Among the more salient political issues related to the changing information technology landscape are copyright and privacy. Copyright is of most direct relevance to a fairly small group of players: the creators and distributors of created material. It is to a great extent an economic issue. Certainly, how copyright is treated has significance for everyone else, for the greater or lesser economic incentive to create words, pictures, and sounds determines what we have to watch, read, or listen to.

Privacy—or the other side of the coin, the right to know—cuts even deeper and tends to be more emotional. Images of Big Brother can be drawn on to make privacy quite personal and visceral. In Chapter 7, "Privacy and Computer-Based Information Systems," Meredith Mendes delimits within the broad concept of privacy the smaller zone of *information* privacy. Because of changes in the way information is being gathered, stored, and transmitted, the notion of privacy may require different legal or other forms of protection than in the past.

Many of the assumptions about the distinctiveness of various media and the legal categorizations that regulate these media may no longer be applicable. Yet Mendes is not an alarmist and believes that much of the existing law is quite robust. Changes may need only be at the margin, as opposed to massive rewrites. Although the focus of analyses of the impact of technology on access to computer-stored personal data is often on the potential for *misuse* of the data bases, the same technology can be used to create more formidable electronic "locks" than was possible by mechanical locks.

THE POLITICAL ARENA

Politics pervades far more of the information business than is generally perceived. It is reflected in the regulatory decisions in the new video marketplace and the antitrust assumptions involved in determining whether new media mean new competition. Like the technology, it permeates the fabric of the information society. And this society is becoming more, not less political. *Political* means here the governmental rationale for policy decisions. For example, the decision of the French government to allow private television channels or the decision of a judge to prohibit a telephone company from offering an "information service" are made with at least as much of an eye to political compromise or effects as on pure economic, marketplace, or social rationales.

Technology itself sometimes has political fallout. The printing press was much feared by monarchs, and the English and French crowns responded by creating a government-controlled monopoly. More recently, the ability of computers and telephone lines to turn the staid Yellow Pages directory into an electronic classified system so frightened the newspaper publishers in the United States that they rallied to convince Congress and a federal judge that local telephone companies should be barred from providing such services (at least for a time). In the days when print ruled the roost, no such confrontation ever occurred.

The forces for open information and controlled information have been in a battle around the world since the written record came into existence. In recent decades, radio and then television were the technologies of contention, with most nations strictly limiting who could broadcast and what material could be on the air. Then along came the videocassette player: small, relatively inexpensive. And the cassettes they played were highly portable and readily duplicated. Television was no longer synonymous with the technology of broadcasting. "Spectrum scarcity" could no longer be used as a rationale for control. As the Ganleys discovered in "The Political Implications of the Global Spread of Videocassette Recorders and Videocassette Programming," Chapter 8, VCRs are quickly changing the rules of video. The chapter in this volume is only a brief abstract of their complete study.

NOTES

1. Anthony Lewis, "At Home Abroad. Why Reagan Blinked," *New York Times,* October 2, 1986, p. A-23.

2. For a detailed explanation of the Business Information Map, see John F. McLaughlin with Anne E. Birinyi, "Mapping the Information Business," in Benjamin M. Compaine, ed., *Understanding New Media* (Cambridge, MA: Ballinger Publishing Co., 1984), pp. 19–67.

Chapter 2

PRESTEL, ESCHER, BACH: Changes Within Changes — Lessons of a Videotex Pioneer

Richard Hooper

The title of this paper is a play on the title of Hofstadter's book *Gödel, Escher, Bach.*[1] Many of the themes in Hofstadter's book illuminate recent events in British telecommunications policy and practice. Indeed, Hofstadter's notion of the "prototype principle" led directly to the structure of this paper. Hofstadter: "The most specific event can serve as a general example of a class of events."[2]

For the purposes of this paper, Prestel, British Telecom's first in the world videotex service, constitutes the "specific event," and recent changes in British telecommunications constitute the "class of events." I hope to show that changes within Prestel have been mirrored in changes within the British telecommunications landscape.

PRESTEL AFTER 4 YEARS

Prestel is the trademark of British Telecom's videotex service, which opened in September 1979. It is the largest videotex service in the world. In October 1983* the statistics show:

---

*Compatible figures for end of 1986 in brackets, provided by Prestel in telephone conversation, April 23, 1987 — B.C..

- 33,000 [74,000] sets connected to the service – the majority in the U.K., the rest in 32 countries around the world; of subscribers, 70% were business customers, 30 residential;
- more than 1,000 [1,200] information providers (IPs) had filled 270,000 pages on Prestel;
- fourteen gateways connected to Prestel (a gateway is an external computer connection);
- monthly frame accesses totaled 11 million [39.4 million];
- 120,000 + messages (e.g., mailbox, teleshopping orders, etc.) were carried on the system monthly.

Although these specific figures are now dated, getting to these from 1979 is a case study in change and adaptation.

PRESTEL – CHANGES

The initial launch of Prestel in 1979/1980 did not achieve a sufficiently fast growth of subscribers. The launch was highly successful in building product awareness, far less successful in generating actual sales.

To improve sales performance, a large number of changes were made to the initial strategy:

- a marketing strategy that focused on selling the services that the technology could deliver, not selling the technology itself;
- a redefinition of the business Prestel was in; Prestel, from being a one-way information retrieval business, is today deeply into transaction processing and electronic mail, which are two-way interactive services;
- the price of the service initially was too high, and, more significant, the pricing structure was too complicated to understand;
- jack socket* policy; Prestel sets are increasingly connected to the telephone network via telephone/universal jack sockets and not through special videotex jack sockets;
- the dumb Prestel set of the late '70s is gradually being overtaken by the intelligent Prestel set, composed of a micro plus screen plus
- Prestel adaptor/modem;
- the Prestel computer system is being changed to match the redefinition of the business.

---

* Analogous to modular plugs in the U.S. and Canada.

But the biggest change of all was the move away from the so-called "common carrier" policy. This is the change on which I will focus.

PRESTEL'S COMMON CARRIER POLICY

To many Americans' surprise, the term *common carrier* has no standing in British telecommunications law and is not used in any of the telecom munications laws enacted (e.g., 1969, 1981). The term *common carrier* has, however, great importance in British freight history. In medieval times, certain road hauliers working between key cities were formally designated as common carriers. This meant that rates were regulated and that all and any freight had to be carried without discrimination.[3]

Prestel in 1977/1978 adopted a common carrier policy, inspired by the use of that term, not in medieval road haulage, but by U.S. telecommunications regulation. For Prestel, it came to have a specific meaning. Prestel, acting as an arm's length business within British Telecom, would own and operate the videotex computer system. Any information provider could take space on the computer system on a first-come, first-served principle, with the sole constraint being the law of the land. Prestel would provide that space, index the information supplied, and provide billing services to enable IPs to receive revenue from page charges. Prestel would not get involved in information provision, except indexing. In addition to Prestel and the IPs, there was one other major player—the television set supply industry. Any company could manufacture and market videotex sets and adapters with integral modems as long as the receiving equipment had the necessary attachment approval. Prestel decided not to get involved with set supply (except editing terminals for IPs). Thus, the common carrier policy was born—a loose federation of three interested parties, Prestel, IPs, and set suppliers, often referred to as a "three-ring circus."

The common carrier policy was justified by British Telecom on three main grounds. It was politically wise for the telephone company to avoid getting involved in editorial content, even through an arm's length business. It was administratively wise, since the supervision of hundreds of thousands of different pages would be difficult. It was commercially wise, because market forces and competition would ensure that low-priced Prestel sets would be produced, and that good pages on the database would drive out bad.

However, the common carrier policy did not work in practice, for a number of reasons. It did not solve the fundamental marketing dilemma. It did not solve the problem of building new subscribers from a zero base. It would probably be an excellent policy when Prestel has 200,000 subscribers, but it did not help Prestel get from 0 to 200,000! In other words, common carrier policy did not solve the chicken/egg problem at the heart of the marketing requirement. Subscribers will only subscribe when there are good information and transaction services. But IPs cannot afford to invest in good services until there is a good population of subscribers. Common carrier policy seemed to offer no mechanisms for breaking into the vicious circle and transforming it into a virtuous circle of growth.

Common carrier also did not seem to satisfy the customer. It led to a poor quality database where, instead of the good driving out the bad, the bad dragged down the good. The problem of indexing for the system operator was horrendous because of the incomplete and variable nature of the services on offer. The service was also difficult for the customer to understand, since he or she had to deal with three separate entities (in fact four, if you add the jack socket and telephone transmission aspects provided by the "telco" end of British Telecom).

Common carrier had another basic defect. In a competitive industry such as UK videotex where "private" videotex systems jostle increasingly with Prestel to provide services to business customers, there is no clear evidence that the system operator can make sufficient revenues from "pure bit transport." The system operator can end up being squeezed out of the chain of communication as an unnecessary and expensive middle-man.

Finally, common carrier did not resolve the publisher/printer dilemma — what to do about sex, politics, and religion. In theory, British Telecom could stand back and allow legal but distasteful pages to be displayed on Prestel, quoting common carrier policy. In practice, the service is seen by the receiving customer and by politicians as Prestel, belonging to and being endorsed by British Telecom. In practice, it is not analogous to the telephone service with its single-point to single-point communications axis. It is more like broadcasting, with single-point to many homes being the model. Thus, in practice, Prestel and British Telecom found it could not stand back and remain indifferent to the carriage of content which was controversial. Even in traditional paper publishing, printers, wholesale distribution agencies and retail outlets have to make commercial, moral, and legal decisions about which publications to handle.

COMMON CARRIER POLICY DISCARDED

The old common carrier policy led to the development of many "incremental" services, services which people would use if they had Prestel but which would not trigger people to get Prestel. News is a classic example of an incremental service. As a result, the common carrier policy has increasingly been dismantled. It has largely been replaced by a growing range of vertically integrated services produced for targeted market sectors, with joint ventures between Prestel and selected IPs/set suppliers. Examples would be Prestel Citiservice, serving the business community with fast updated information on stocks, foreign exchange and commodity prices, and Micronet 800, a service aimed at home computer users. These services, which marry conduit, content, and receiving equipment, are designed to trigger new subscribers—hence the term *trigger* services.

BRITISH TELECOM AND BRITISH TELECOMMUNICATIONS

Let me now, in Godel, Escher, Bach style, move up (down?) one level to examine British Telecom, of which Prestel is a small corner.

British Telecom is the fourth largest telecommunications operator in the world, with 245,000 employees and a turnover of £6-1/2 billion ($9.1 billion at January 1984 exchange rates). Telecommunications was nationalized in 1912 and became part of the Post Office. In 1969, the Post Office ceased being a Government department and became a public corporation. In 1981, Post Office Telecommunications was split off and became British Telecommunications. In late 1984 British Telecom's status changed to that of a PLS (public limited company) through a public offering of 51of the shares of BT, thus returning telecommunications to the private sector.

Since the arrival of Mrs. Thatcher's Conservative Government, there have been major changes to the telecommunications landscape, much influenced by U.S. experience of deregulation. Mercury has been granted a licence to become a second "public telecommunication operator," thus opening up BT's trunk (interexchange) network to competition. Licenses have been awarded to the first group of cable TV operators, which brings potential competition into the local loop. Cable TV operators will be able to carry data traffic in certain parts of the country. If they team up with Mercury or BT, they can carry local voice traffic as well. BT is itself involved in consortia for 10 of the initial cable TV franchises—unlike the USA, where AT&T has not been involved in cable TV. Customer equipment has been liberalized, with attachment approval functions passing from BT to other agencies. Value-added network services (VANs), defined as "applicable systems," have also been liberalized, with licences being awarded by the Government but not by BT. Two competing cellular radio operators have been licensed, of which BT is only a part shareholder in one. Finally, the Government is examining the possibility of allowing resale of BT private circuits—the final liberalization.

The turbulence in the British telecommunications airspace is caused by the political desire to deregulate a monopolistic industry. But the turbulence is constantly increased by the difficulties of defining and managing the telecommunications business. Although it is technically possible to separate out the conduit—content components of the telecommuni cation business—network (transmission and switching), enhanced or value- added services (data processing, protocol conversion, customer equipment (PABXs, telephones)—there are stronger forces at work which are driving the components together and blurring boundaries between content and conduit. It is this which continues to generate turbulence.

The effects of this turbulence are many and varied. Because the boundaries between the different parts of telecommunications tend to coalesce, for reasons that will be identified in the final section of this chapter, deregulation has a cascading effect throughout the business. In the words of Michael Beesley, who wrote an influential paper for the British Government on VANs and resale: "Once competition is introduced, unforeseeable forces build up which accumulate to further competition and entry to the network and transmissions, the lowest three layers of [the seven-layer ISO (International Standards Organization) model]."[4] There are many examples of this in recent British telecommunications history. For example, the liberalization of simple telephones began by excluding the prime instrument, which was to remain a monopoly of BT. The prime instrument monopoly could not be sustained and is already being phased out.

A second effect of this turbulence is organizational difficulty within British Telecom. If network, equipment, and value-added services could be kept apart, then this would be a good framework within which the organizational decisions could be made. BT could create different business units operating in complementary business areas. In reality, British Telecom is creating business units which operate in complementary and competitive business areas, thus raising the headaches of internal competition management and control.

A third effect of the turbulence is the growth of definitional disputes. Is the jack-socket customer equipment? Is AT&T's local area data transport (LADT) service an enhanced service because it includes protocol conversion? These may look like technical questions; they are in fact political/commercial questions. Part IV of the Telecommunications Bill has been a definitional battlefield. Part IC is concerned with defining "cable program services" as distinct from telecommunications services, since cable program services are to be regulated through a new Cable Authority whereas telecommunications services are to be regulated through a new Office of Telecommunications. In the first wording of Part IV, Prestel ended up as a cable program service. Under the latest version, Prestel is not a cable program service, but recorded information services on the public switched telephone network are! Recorded information services and radio broadcasting are difficult to segregate in legal terms.

A final effect of turbulence is, of course, intense regulatory difficulties. For example, the same advertisement could be carried over broadcast teletext, in print, over Prestel, and over teletext on cable (cabletext) and could theoretically be regulated by four different agencies.

THE POWERS BEHIND VERTICAL INTEGRATION

There are two power sources which are driving content-conduit and network-customer equipment-services together, despite regulatory desires to keep them apart.

The first is commercial—the needs of the supplier. All telecommunications forecasters seem to agree on one thing: over the next 20 years, you cannot live by bit transport alone. Revenues and profits from pure bit transport will tend to flatten out (at the top of the familiar S-shaped curve of innovation adoption) as a result of the declining costs of microelectronics allied to increasing competition. Thus a network business is forced by commercial logic to extend into businesses beyond pure bit transport if revenues and profits are to show consistent growth. Those businesses are enhanced or value-added services, customer equipment manufacturing-/marketing, and systems provision.

The notion of bit transport is a slippery one. Gödel, Escher, Bach: "Levels are not cleanly separated...."[5] Looked at from Prestel's point of view, the public-switched network and private circuits constitute the bit transport level. Looked at from the point of view of an organization using Prestel Gateway, Prestel is the bit transport level. The commercial imperative is to move up a level to avoid being squeezed on the current level. Thus, packet-switching networks move up into electronic mail and protocol conversion spawning new services such as IBM's Advanced Information Service and AT&T's Net 1000 [since abandoned], which attempted to do a lot more than transport bits. A few years ago, it was of course voice telephony/traditional circuit switching moving up into packet switching. Similar commercial logic has been hitting the computer bureau business. Originally, bureaus made their money out of selling raw time and power to users. Today, they have been forced to integrate vertically into premises equipment and software product marketing, to survive. Raw time, like bit transport, has become cheap and plentiful, with little value added. Moving up levels equates with increasing value added. For the same reasons, computer manufacturers are being forced to extend their territories beyond hardware (the base level), beyond systems software (level 2), into applications software (level 3). Hardware, like raw time and pure bit transport, is declining fast in price.

The second power which drives content and conduit together is commercial in the other sense – the needs of the customer. While it is difficult to generalize, there is certainly a large group of customers who want simple systems solutions from one supplier, and who do not want to deal with lots of different entities to get a service. The biggest customers may be able to afford the staff time and expertise to shop around in the market and buy disaggregated products to their own specification. But smaller customers would be confused by this. The family expects the cable-TV company to provide them one interface for all aspects of the service from the technology to the programming. Prestel is expected to provide one coherent service from jack sockets, through what appears on the screen, to the bill. Consumers do not necessarily make the conduit-content distinction that can look obvious from inside the suppliers' operation. Television is just television, a unitary service, not separable functions such as program production (16 mm film) to program storage (VCR) to program transmission (broadcast network) to program reception (TV receiver).

STRANGE LOOPS

The "needs of the customer" takes us straight back via a Gödel, Escher, Bach Strange Loop to the organizational difficulties for the telecommuni cations operator/supplier. How does he organize himself to meet the needs of the customer? There are really only two choices, and neither will ever resolve the problem perfectly. The business can be sliced, first of all, by market sector. Market sector can mean three rather different things: *either* "all those customers and potential customers living in Birmingham," which is the dominant organizational structure both for old Ma Bell and the new regional Bell operating companies, and for British Telecom; *or* all those in the freight industry (one of my BT businesses, the National Data Processing Service, is organized in this way, serving air, maritime, and roadfreight interests across the U.K.); *or,* biggest potential organizational headache of all, all big customers billed more than £-x million a year. Secondly, the business can be sliced by product/service line, as with British Telecom Prestel and British Telecom's packet-switching service.

The difficulties embedded in all this can be summarized in one example. How do you organize, produce, market, and account for the sale of Prestel service to a large airline in the freight business which is based in London? There is only ever an imperfect answer – despite what Government proponents of "purist" competition policy and fair trading requirements might think. "What was once a nice clean hierarchical set-up has become a Strange Loop, or Tangled Hierarchy. The moves change the rules, the rules determine the moves, round and round the mulberry bush.... There are still different levels, but the distinction between 'lower' and 'higher' has been wiped out."[6]

SUMMARY

Prestel, the world's first and largest videotex service, was 4 years old in 1983. Major changes had been made to all aspects of the business to bring it into commercial viability; for example, the initial common carrier policy has had to be severely modified. These major changes to Prestel have been happening within the British telecommunications landscape, which itself is undergoing radical change. Experience with Prestel and with British Telecom suggests that conduit-content separation remains as elusive, in practice, as ever, despite its theoretical attractiveness.

ENDNOTES

1. Douglas G. Hofstadter, *Gödel, Escher, Bach* (London: Penguin Books, 1980).
2. *Ibid.*, p. 352.
3. Gerald L. Turnbull, *Traffic and Transport, an Economic History of Pickfords* (London: George Allen & Unwin, 1979), pp. 8-9.
4. Michael E. Beesley, *Liberalisation of the Use of the British Telecommunications Network* (London: Her Majesty's Stationery Office, 1981), p. 29.
5. Hofstadter, *op. cit.*, p. 458.
6. *Ibid.*, p. 688.

Chapter 3

EVOLVING TECHNOLOGY AND BLURRING BOUNDARIES: NEW PERSPECTIVES FOR EVALUATING MEDIA COMPETITION

Benjamin M. Compaine

Since the first drawings on the walls of caves, there has been a regular infusion of "new" competition in the realm of the media. Often, some new technology or technologies applied to the task have fostered this new competition. The development of an alphabet in Greece in the 7th century B.C., improvements in the implements of writing over succeeding centuries, and the familiar litany of printing press, steam engine, and electronics quickly bring us to contemporary media processes.

Each development in some way expanded competition, in that new media processes generally have added to rather than replaced older media processes. Whereas the laboriously handwritten manuscript was once the only form for text—and therefore the scriptorium maintained control over its reproduction, price, and distribution—today we have mass-printed books and even electronically transmitted text for viewing on a video tube.

This latter is therefore simply the latest in the historical linage of new technology creating new competition for the old. With perhaps the exception of cave drawings, just about all previous technologies have survived in parallel as means for mass communication.

Still, life has become more complicated for anyone interested in the subject of competition in media. In part, this is because competition in media has at least one dimension more than does competition in, say, toothpaste or virtually any other commodity. The mass media—newspapers, magazines, books, television, radio, records, films, electronically accessible data bases—have a special place in virtually all literate societies, as they are charged with conveying messages. In democratic societies, we are usually interested in maximizing a diversity of ideas, opinions, and information of all sorts. In closed societies, the media are as important, but usually with the goal of providing a uniform "party line," and hence with limited diversity. This paper focuses on competition in pluralistic societies that hold dearly diversity of information sources.

QUANTIFYING THE MEDIA INDUSTRY

Economists who specialize in measuring the extent of competition – or its obverse, concentration – tend to treat each of the media the same as any other industry, counting up who owns what, calculating percentages, devising indices of pricing power.

Problem One: What is the Relevant Market?

Although this may seem rather straightforward, the first problem is that the technology of recent years has made the definition of the appropriate divisor for concentration indices debatable. That is, what is the appropriate market? The right side of Figure 2 includes the boundaries of the traditional media business.[1] But to study media competition, should one look at the market for newspapers isolated from that for magazines? To what extent are broadcast television and even radio fungible for the substance of the print media? Traditionally, economists have looked at a specific medium, such as newspapers. It can be legitimately argued that that approach, if it ever was valid, is becoming less so as the technologies of the alternative media forms merge into one another.[2]

Also relevant to the problem of market definition, is the question of defining the user of the medium. Some media such as newspapers and magazines, and in the United States to a degree more than almost anywhere else broadcast television and radio, are paid for in total or large measure by advertisers. Thus, an appropriate measure of economic concentration for these media may lie, not in how much consumers pay to receive them, but in the extent to which there is market power in the pricing of advertisements. On the other hand, media forms such as books, records, and theatrical films are funded mostly or totally by their users, in which case the economic consideration is the ability of suppliers to charge nonmarket prices to consumers.

In addition to competition within a particular media segment and competition among media industries, geographical competition is a factor. Newspapers in the United States and Canada, and to lesser degrees elsewhere, are largely local media. Although the United States has about 1700 daily papers, and no more than about 7% of total daily circulation is controlled by any one firm, only about 30 central cities have fully competitive newspapers and only one, New York, has three alternatives.[3] By comparison, according to the 1985 *Broadcasting Cablecasting Yearbook*, the New York metropolitan area had 39 radio stations in 1984 and, depending on where one lived, 12 to 14 over-the-air television channels. Even the 50th ranked market, Dayton has four over-the-air TV channels and 12 radio stations. Thus most people have more choice in the number of television signals they receive, even though there are fewer television stations nationally than there are newspapers. Book and magazine publishers, relying as they do on large regional and national markets, compete in a larger geographical context. Cable operators, while providing a dizzying array of channels, for the most part are monopoly providers within their highly restricted franchise territories and are subject to a decreasing amount of government control over their pricing. Finally, there is a new factor of potential global competition, as video cassette player/recorders proliferate and as direct broadcast satellite systems, perhaps out of the control of the nation to which their programming is receivable, start beaming signals in competition with land-based—and often government-controlled—television. In effect, the traditional market boundaries with which so many were so comfortable are receding toward the horizon.

Problem Two: How Much is Enough?

The second problem for a discussion of competition is anchored to the lessening of the distinction among what had been well-understood media formats. Today, "television" can be delivered not only over-the-air, but via cable, cassettes, discs, or directly from a satellite. The picture on the screen can be the type of text and graphics typically associated with magazines, books, and newspapers. Thus, the conventional labels are less useful than ever. "Print" or "video" are essentially examples of *formats* in which some content or substance can be displayed or otherwise manipulated by users. Words can come as speech or as writing. And that writing can be gouges carved in rock, toe marks in the sand, ink on paper, or glowing phosphors on a screen.

These are among a multitude of ways in which we can express information *substance*. Substance may be data, knowledge, news, intelligence, or any number of other colloquial and specialized denotations and connotations that can be lumped under the general rubric of "information."

Process is the application of instruments, such as typewriters, computers, printing presses, the human brain, telephone wires, or delivery trucks to the creation, manipulation, storage, and transmission/ distribution of substance in some intermediate or final format. For example, a traditional newspaper, an ink-on-newsprint format, relies on processes including entering thoughts of a reporter into a computer by manipulating a keyboard of a video display terminal with storage in the computer, and the eventual creation of a printing plate and distribution to consumers via trucks. Part of that process may be different should the same article be distributed to some consumers via a telephone link to a video display terminal. In that case, some of the process is the same (the entering and storing of information), the formats are different for the end user (text on screen vs. ink on paper), but the substance may remain constant.

How then does one measure how much diversity of sources is "enough?" If 20 firms account for 50% of newspaper circulation in the U.S., is that too few, enough, or can this be a sign of too many firms creating too much fragmentation in society? If not this number, then what? An even stickier question is, what are the adequate ground rules for assuring that any person's or institution's ideas—political, social, commercial, or whatever—have some opportunity for access to the media? And more difficult still, how does one measure which formats should have what conditions for access? That is, it may be relatively easy to provide access to a print newspaper for messages, as these have the most space flexibility. And as authoritarian societies know, the photocopying machine has become Everyman's printing press.

On the other hand, what about access to prime time broadcast television? We know that, up to now, there has been limited spectrum available, particularly in the major metropolitan areas, and that prime time cannot be expanded by more minutes than nature has provided for us. Cable television, a newer process for a familiar format, alleviates the spectrum problem, but it can never eliminate the fact that a handful of channels will likely get the bulk of the viewing audience at any given time. Thus, even as technology provides us with more conduits for distributing information, there is no guarantee that the mass audience will want to receive much more than what has traditionally been mass entertainment. Indeed, in the United States, dozens of cable networks have been struggling to achieve even a 1% or 2% market share, as the bulk of the audience with access to dozens of stations persists in viewing the four traditional broadcast networks, plus three or four of the newer offerings, the most successful of which—the pay television networks—are showing other forms of mass audience fare.

The extent of competition in the media, as in other industrial sectors, is in large measure a function of the national policies that encourage or limit market forces. Societal norms set the boundaries for these policies, and politics then establishes the rules. In England, the spread of the printing press in the 16th century led to the establishment of the Royal Stationer, created by the Crown, through which all printing was controlled in the 17th and 18th centuries. In France, a government edict in 1686 fixed the allowable number of printing masters. Backed by government, an oligopoly gained control of the printing business. Thus, in 1644, Paris had 75 print shops with 180 presses. By 1701, the number of presses had grown to 195, but these had consolidated into 51 shops.[4] This early tradition of government's involvement in the structure of the information business was in large measure the motivation for the strong prohibition against such intervention written into the U.S. Constitution. Thus, whereas European governments have to varying degrees extended such early intervention into newer media processes, such as telephone and broadcasting, the U.S. has maintained a relative hands-off attitude.

NEWSPAPERS IN CONTEXT

Newspapers and books are the oldest formats and continue to be one focus of the media concentration issue. Thus they warrant an extended discussion to illustrate the complexity of looking for simplistic answers to trends in that segment of the information industry.

There are fewer directly competitive newspapers today than there were 50 years ago. In part, this involves the essential role of the newspaper combined with demographic trends. The daily newspaper in this country has always been an intensely local medium. It has specialized in covering local events and in providing an advertising base for local advertisers. National advertising provides only about 15% of advertising revenue. However, it is well documented and readily observable that, since 1946, the population of the cities has been moving out to the suburbs and beyond. They were not as well served by the big city dailies, with their focus on the core city, as they are by local newspapers that sprang up or expanded to meet the expanded local market. Newspapers in older cities, such as Philadelphia, New York, and Boston, found themselves competing for circulation with thriving newspapers in nearby Doylestown, Long Island, and Quincy. Retailers, following the population to the suburbs, found that their budgets were being stretched thin and increasingly concentrated their center city advertising in the paper with the larger circulation so that they might also advertise in the suburban papers. Herein lies reason one for the demise of competing city newspapers.

Second, newspapers, especially evening newspapers in the cities, have had to compete for readers' time with other and newer media. Since the heyday of daily newspaper penetration in the 1920s, we have seen first radio and then television introduced into the daily media mix. With television, in particular, newspapers have been competing, not directly for consumer or advertising dollars, but for audience attention.

Newspapers, after all, are not just news. They are filled with entertainment items, human interest articles, and commercial information. Television is not just entertainment. Although media elitists disparage local television news in particular, the fact remains that the evening hour of news, weather, sports, and fluff is not all that different than the content of most daily newspapers. It is also time that takes away from the newspaper. At the very least, it helped speed the end of the two-newspaper family.

These are two compelling forces, among others, that have conspired to change the structure of the newspaper industry. They are not insidious forces. Instead, they suggest something of a zero sum game: competing center city newspapers being replaced by a single city paper competing with numerous suburban papers and electronic media. For the residents of the suburbs, there continues to be a real choice of newspapers. For everyone, there is a net gain in the number of media alternatives. Individuals can get news, information, and entertainment from the daily paper, a variety of weekly newspapers, and three or more similar (although not identical) television stations, and national news from at least three major magazines—another factor that was not much of a factor 60 years ago. For much of the population, all-news radio stations are another alternative. The development of locally based cable and the as yet unknown potential creative uses of computer-based services may also serve to enhance this diversity. The variety and number of outlets in many markets today, representing almost as many separate owners in each market, contrasts sharply with the fewer total number of outlets—virtually all newspapers—in any comparable list of cities in 1920.

A related issue is that of newspaper chain ownership. No one really worries about chains of supermarkets or retail stores around the country. Newspaper chains are supposedly an issue because newspapers—and the rest of the media, for that matter—are concerned with ideas and information rather than commodities. Therefore, this argument goes, they must be judged by a different standard than is other commerce. Chain ownership means that control is in the hands of a publisher and editor who might have no ties to the community. It could mean that a single individual can dictate the editorial policy of many newspapers. The implication associated with this line of reasoning is that chain ownership is bad for society.

Among the pertinent facts are that two-thirds of all daily newspapers are owned by about 160 groups. They are concentrated in the larger newspapers, as these chain-owned papers account for about 75% of daily circulation. As recently as 1960, there were 109 groups owning fewer than a third of the daily papers, although they still accounted for close to 50% of daily circulation. Almost one-third of these chains actually consist of six or fewer newspapers.[5] The chain trend, though slowed considerably in the 1980s by a reduced number of newspapers available for sale, is indisputable. What are the reasons for this trend? What are its implications?

There are at least two reasons. First, the introduction of new technology into the production of newspapers in the 1970s resulted in substantial cost reductions and an increase in profit, which had been sagging terribly before then. Some family-owned newspapers could not afford the investment in the technology, however. Thus, their newspapers were more valuable to other firms that could introduce new technology and quickly boost profits to a level greater than under the owning family. Hence, the price offered for newspapers escalated dramatically. In fact, the restoration of reasonable profit margins to newspapers made them an attractive investment for the first time in years. And although newspapers that were fighting head to head with a local competitor had problems, those papers that did not have direct competition at least had greater room to adjust their price and expenditures to earn an attractive return on investment. (Despite the term, *monopoly newspaper*, these papers could not derive what economists recognize as true monopoly profits. They did face competition from other media, including weekly and all-advertising "shopper" papers, as well as suburban papers in the case of central- city papers).

A second reason for the growth of chains was federal tax policy. In a Rand Corporation study, public policy, in the form of tax regulations, was shown to explain most of the reason for independent publishers selling out, most often to chains.[6] On the death of the owner of the family-owned newspaper, the estate tax laws required setting the value of the newspaper at its market value—that is, what it was worth if sold. This might be many times its book value and frequently created a tax liability well in excess of the heirs' ability to pay the tax. Thus, the property was sold—at an appropriate market value—either after the owner's death or in anticipation of the problem. On the acquirer's side, another tax law requires a very high tax on corporate retained earnings, unless they are being held for necessary business purposes, such as expansion. Thus, profits had to be spent. Acquisitions were one outlet.

Has all this been bad or good for society? Here, of course, facts take a back sent to evaluation. In general, one argument holds that society is probably no worse off, and perhaps better off, than it was 30 or 50 years ago. There is nothing inherent in either the one-newspaper city nor the chain trends that is cause for alarm for media diversity or for concern for the role of newspapers in the practice of democracy.

In the first place, the demise of direct competition is a function of economics, technology, and social patterns. Not much that is practical can be done about it. Corporations cannot be forced to start businesses. They cannot be forced to stay in business if they don't want to. Except for zoning-type regulations, business can't be told where to operate or what markets to serve. Perhaps some might argue that society could provide tax breaks to corporations that start newspapers in places that already have them. That alone is not likely to compensate for the risk. Any direct subsidy runs into First Amendment barriers.

The chain ownership question is more complex. Given that, in traditional economic terms, there is nothing approaching a national newspaper monopoly in this country, the only restriction to date has been in preventing common ownership of newspapers that had been competing in adjacent communities. For that reason, the Times Mirror Co., owner of *The Los Angeles Times*, had to sell the newspapers it bought in nearby San Bernardino. But it was permissible for Gannett, another chain, to purchase them. The alternative to chain ownership would require establishment of a different standard for unacceptable concentration of ownership of newspapers than for other private-sector business. Both the justification and standard would have to be quite subjective. And here too, the First Amendment would come into play. The result might be more long-term damage than leaving things alone.

Indeed, there is no compelling evidence that newspaper readers have been ill-served by the trend toward groups. There are at least as many documented cases where a paper purchased by a group was substantially improved as there are cases where a paper was weakened.[7]

One dramatic example of improvement is in Philadelphia. There, the locally-owned *Bulletin* long had a commanding presence compared to the *Inquirer*, which was also independently owned by Walter Annenberg. But the *Inquirer* had a reputation for being politically biased in its treatment of the news. By almost any standard it had substanial deficiencies. In about 1970 the paper was sold to what is now Knight-Ridder, Inc,. the country's second largest chain in circulation. Since then, the *Inquirer* has been built into one of the most respected newspapers in the country, regularly winning Pulitzer Prizes for both national and local coverage. It has outlasted the now defunct *Bulletin* and opened a string of foreign bureaus with some of the funds it could divert from its days of competitive battling.

There are many other less spectacular but substantial examples. There are also cases where a new chain owner has come in and cut the staff and raised ad rates. As in any other business, owners have different styles and priorities. The good ones or poorer ones are not necessarily determined by the chain ownership.

The matter of local versus absentee ownership is another issue in which the pluses and minuses probably get canceled out. On the negative side of absentee ownership, the publisher and top editors put in by the major chain owner hope to distinguish themselves and get promoted to a larger newspaper. Their long-term ties to the community may be minimal: each time a new person gets sent to town, he or she must spend time learning about its idiosyncrasies—or perhaps they never do. But this can be balanced by the negative aspect of the family-owned small city newspaper, where the owning family has long been part of the local establishment. The publisher may have been a childhood buddy of the president of the bank and the head of the local department store. Local owners plan on staying in town, as did their parents and, they hope, their children. A cynic could ask how much of a crusader such publishers can allow their papers to be. To what extent will they question the bank's practices or criticize friends on the school board? Excessive local boosterism may prevail. None of this is inevitable, but, just as with chain ownership, there is nothing that automatically makes local ownership more beneficial.

Finally, an evaluation of the quality of chain-owned newspapers risks falling into the trap hereby dubbed the *New York Times* Syndrome. This is the tendency of journalists and media critics to judge all newspapers by the *Times*. The fact is, small town newspapers were never very good. If we fault them today for their front page news capsules and reliance on wire service copy, we should also go back and analyze what they were like in the supposed good old days. Did they have a reporter in Washington doing occasional local pieces, as the chain papers can order up from the chain's own bureau? How many column inches was the newshole, compared to total inches today? How large was the full-time staff? How well were they trained? How objective was the reporting by today's standards? How much did the paper cost in constant dollars, compared to today? An unscientific eyeballing of newspapers around the U.S. today, and some understanding of newspapers in history, suggests that the typical chain-owned paper today is probably much better than the locally owned paper of 50 years ago.

A BRIEF LOOK AT THE BOOK PUBLISHING BUSINESS

Journalists and authors have frequently fostered the impression that the business side of their industry was a rather messy subject and would either disparage the commercial considerations or just avoid them. One measurement of this tendency is in the large number of books written about the personalities, history, or role of journalism compared to the almost total absence of works discussing the structure and economics of the press. Perhaps that is one reason why newspapers and magazines disappear so regularly, and book publishers come and go or merge with such regularity. Many writers who start publishing operations know the content side, but neglect the business end. In 1973, the only solid material available on the commercial side of the newspaper business was in a few unpublished doctoral dissertations. For magazine publishing, there was not even that. There were only two books on the book publishing business, one of whose findings, written in 1931, could have been reprinted almost verbatim because there had been so little change in the conduct of this "gentleman's" business.

Slowly, the term *business* is being applied to book publishing, and most signs indicate that this has been an overall positive development for the universe of potential book purchasers. In the book publishing industry, there were 635 publishing companies in 1947. Today, there are about two and a half times that number. Between 1970 and 1980, an average of 50 new publishers emerged annually, each bringing out a minimum of three titles a year.[8] They replaced some of the firms that failed or merged. Between 45,000 and 55,000 new book titles and editions, are published annually, adding to the more than 550,000 in print faster than old titles are taken out of print,[9] a rate of growth greater than that of the U.S. population.

Most of the publishers and books are not aimed at the market for literature or trade nonfiction. Many publishers specialize in textbooks, professional books, reference works, and so on. Still, 5470 new fiction titles were published in 1983, well over twice the number of 1960. There was an even greater increase in literature, and an 85% increase in juvenile titles.[10]

The number of bookstores also has shown a sharp increase. For years, bookselling was primarily a trade dominated by mom and pop stores in big cities. Book clubs grew because of the notoriously poor distribution of books.[11] Outside the Northeast, bookstores were hard to find, and a well-stocked one even rarer. Booksellers, like many publishers, were often in business because they enjoyed books themselves. They stocked what they liked, not what would necessarily sell well to the nonliterati.

Into this void came two multibillion-dollar retail chains, Dayton Hudson Corp. and Carter Hawley Hale Stores. In the 1970s, they started opening up B. Dalton and Waldenbooks outlets, respectively. Most of these went in suburban shopping malls outside the Northeast. For the first time, they brought books to where the people were. Both groups now have hundreds of stores, including downtown locations. They have been criticized by the media elitists for stocking only the most popular books and for having undue influence on what gets published due to their sizable orders for publishers.

Such criticisms are reminiscent the 19th century English literati who were critical of the growth of mass literacy among the working class. They too were concerned about the masses "reading the wrong things, for the wrong reason, in the wrong way."[12] That is, they were reading fiction when the literati thought they should be reading self-help books. Recently a respected trade book editor complained, paradoxically, that people are reading too many how-to and similar "light" books at the expense of literature.[13] She might find ironic the British librarian who told a meeting in 1879 that "schoolboys or students who took to novel reading to any great extent never made much progress in after life."[14]

In 1958, the retail trade census counted only 1675 bookstore large enough to have a payroll (and only 2885 including the real mom and pop stores). In the 1982 tally, the number had grown to 9300 with a payroll.[15]

Book publishing is a unique business that lends itself to boom and bust. Every book published has to be sold as a separate product. It is almost as if Pillsbury had to introduce a new cake mix every week, pay for the research and development, promote it, get distribution on crowded supermarket shelves, and then move on to develop and promote the next cake mix. Meanwhile, the competition is doing the same thing. The economics of publishing are such that most of the cost is a fixed first-copy cost. That means that on a best seller there is a very high marginal profit. But such successes must be balanced with the many others which never even recover the advance paid the author.

Book publishing, like its magazine cousin, is a business that has a very low entry cost (except for a few segments, such as mass market paperback and school textbooks), but a fairly high failure ratio. Combined with the nonbusinesslike approach that typified much of the industry until the past decade, one begins to understand the forces that led to the mergers of the Harpers with the Rows. It was for survival. But there is a constant stream of new entries, like Workman Press or David Godine, constantly looking for publishing niches and hoping to grow with them. Perhaps they too will be acquired, only to open up new opportunities for others.

FORCES OPPOSING CENTRALIZED CONTROL

With the dispersion of substance available via common carrier satellite and telephone, access *by* more sources *to* more sources is likely to increase further, not diminish. Some commentators are in fact concerned now about fragmentation of society and information overload as the result of the overwhelming variety of formats for substance.

The proliferation of new communication processes over the years has made it increasingly difficult for any single entity or small cabal, even governments that have the will and power, to have total control over the mass media. The Shah of Iran learned that lesson the hard way. Although his government controlled the broadcast and major press spigot, it was not able to stop the inflow of messages from the Khomeini forces in Paris, which used small, cheap audio cassettes to smuggle in instructions and inspiration for low-tech duplication and distribution. By putting in a sophisticated telephone system, the Shah gave his enemies direct dial international phone calls, much harder to monitor than those going through an old-fashioned switchboard. And the Xerox machine became the printing press of choice—cheap and harder to control than a large roll-fed offset press.[16]

One of the most dramatic pieces of evidence that technology is moving faster than the ability of governments or business to control the media is the competition that video cassette recordings are providing for broadcasters and movie house operators. As might be expected, the penetration of VCRs has been greatest in those countries that already had the largest number of television sets. But, as Table 1 indicates, in the early years of VCR sales, the United States and Canada lagged well behind Western Europe in their use. Moreover, these figures likely understated penetration in Europe at the time, in that they counted only machines exported by Japan. Although Japanese- made machines account for almost all sales in the U.S. and Canada, the tabulation did not count the sizable number of the machines manufactured and sold in Europe. But even with those counted, leading the world in VCR ownership are the oil-rich Middle Eastern nations. It has been reported that bootlegged copies of the controversial movie "Death of a Princess" were being shown in living rooms in Saudia Arabia at the same time it was being broadcast—over that government's protests—in Great Britain and the United States.[17] What determines the penetration of VCRs? It appears that where there are not significant government-imposed barri-

TABLE 1
Videocassette Recorder
Penetration in Selected Regions, 1983[a]

	TV sets in Use (000)	VCRs Exported to (000)	VCRs as % of TV sets	Medium # of Broadcast Nets
W. Europe[b]	119,222	16,844	14.1%	2
U.S. & Canada	189,280	14,426	7.6	5
Middle East[c]	2,470	1,938	78.5	2
Australia & New Zealand	6,422	1,561	24.3	2

[a]Videocassette recorders exported from Japan to indicated destination, 1976–1983. Does not take into account transhipments once in destination country ornon-Japanese-made VCRs, primarily those made by Thomson in Europe.

[b]Belgium, Denmark, Finland, France, Greece, Iceland, Ireland, Italy, Luxembourg, Malta, Monaco, Netherlands, Norway, Portugal, Spain, Sweden, Switzerland, United Kingdom, W. Germany.

[c]Major oil producing or supported countries' Bahrain, Iran, Kuwait, Qatar, Saudi Arabia, United Arab Emirates.

Source: Calculated from compilation by CBS Inc. from Table & Television Factbook, 1984; Japan Tariff Association, Japan Exports & Imports, 1976–1983 editions.

ers, a substantial factor is competition from other forms of television. In Western European nations, where there are typically two government-controlled or highly regulated television networks, VCRs gave viewers their first opportunity to become their own programmers, through renting or buying tapes. In England, where the tradition of renting televisions has carried over to VCRs, there is a booming tape rental market, with prices as low as 50p per night. A cynic might conclude that, when it has the chance, the mass audience demonstrates that it is not being fulfilled by the fare that the broadcasters are providing – at least not enough of the time. (The other side of this coin is that viewers may find the quality of programming so compelling that they find it desirable to record one for later viewing while watching the other in real time.) In the United States, which has four over-the- air-networks and a growing number of cable-supplied networks, VCRs have seen healthy growth only since 1982, and overall penetration is still relatively low.

Substitutability Among Video Options

If the need to foster diversity is a policy objective in democracies, then the degree to which various media processes are fungible is of import. The manufacturers of steel cans learned quite a while ago that their ability to set prices and gain market share was determined not only by their relatively few steel can competitors, but by others who made aluminum, glass, and even cardboard containers. Similarly, broadcasters, whether private or government controlled, must recognize that they are not the only rooster in the video barnyard anymore, and that it will likely get more competitive rather than less so.

A statistical study by two economists at the Federal Communications Commission (FCC) has found "strong support [for] the proposition that VCRs and cable [television] are substitutes."[18] It also reported "some support to the conclusion that VCRs and broadcast television are complements."[19] While noting some paradoxes and data problems, the authors believe that their statistical evidence "tends to support the proposition that the video product market should be broadly defined – to include (at least) broadcast television, cable and VCRs."[20]

It is much too early to make any judgments about the impact of DBS. For all pratical purposes, it does not exist as a mass market service anywhere in the world, although bits and pieces are starting to become available. Hundreds of thousands of rural households in the United States are the largest identifiable market for DBS to date, having purchased large antenna dishes to capture the signals intended as raw feeds to cable headends and broadcasters. For this constituency, DBS is a substitute for a lack of broadcast television.

Substitutability Among Print Options

Print publishers have felt the heat of competition longer than their newer electronic brethren. Before radio made its way into the mass media mix in the 1930s, the newspaper industry in the U.S. held 45% of media advertising, and consumer magazines about 8% (see Figure 1). While magazines held their share through the 1950s, radio and, to a lesser extent, television, eroded newspaper share to 31% by 1960. Newspapers have lost a small amount of market share to television in the past 25 years, with newspapers' share now down to about 27% and magazines' near 6%. In large measure, this erosion accounts for the inability of cities to support the competing newspapers that existed before there was electronic media competition for consumer attention and advertiser expenditures.

Newspaper publishing companies in the U.S. did not sit around idly while their franchises deteriorated. In 1983, one third of the 447 television stations in the 100 largest markets were owned by firms that also published newspapers. However, as the result of an FCC policy discouraging newspaper-television affiliations in the same market, by 1983 only 8% of the stations in the 100 largest markets were owned by the local newspaper.[21] They also owned about 600 out of about 9500 radio stations. Companies that own newspapers have been a diversified group, as the holdings of seven companies on Figure 2 indicate.

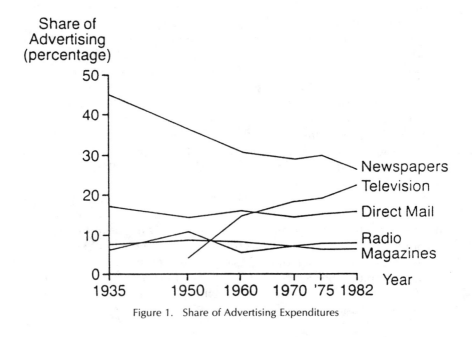

Figure 1.   Share of Advertising Expenditures

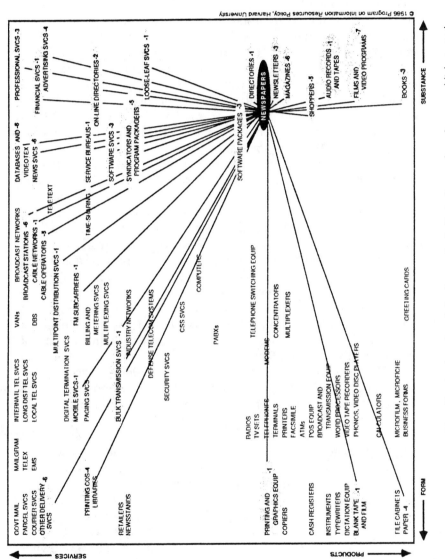

Figure 2.   Newspaper Diversification (numbers following entries indicate the number of seven publicly owned newspaper groups have holding in the indicated business)

Today, publishers of newspapers face two forms of real and potential competition. As far as most publishers are concerned, the real competition they face is from the U.S. Postal Service and the highly computerized firms that have grown to take advantage of postal rates for mailing printed circulars that the publishers themselves compete to deliver as part of the newspaper. The direct mail business has thrived through the years. Before television, direct mail accounted for about 14% of advertising expenditures. With no dramatic shifts over the years, it now has about a 16% share. The ability of direct mailers to compete with newspapers is purely a function of price, which in turn is determined by several layers of postal agencies. The mailing companies, as have publishers themselves, have taken full advantage of computer technology to improve their product, but still depend on physical handling and delivery for reaching the consumer.

The potential competitor for newspapers goes under the name of videotex or electronic publishing. It is much too soon to know when, if at all, these computer and telecommunications-based services will have an effect on local newspapers. This is because such services still require hardware in the home that costs hundreds of dollars at a minimum and ongoing telecommunications costs that alone could be greater than the current price of a printed newspaper. Advertisers, who provide about 80% of the revenue for daily newspapers in the U.S., are far from certain as to how they could use the videotex systems.

One of the most feared potential entrants into the media business in the U.S. is AT&T, now about one-third its December 1983 size in revenue, but still a major player. The court overseeing the AT&T break-up mandated that AT&T be excluded from providing substance over its own lines at least until 1990. This action was the direct result of political intervention by the newspaper industry, which feared that AT&T could have gotten into the electronic classified business, thereby threatening the most profitable piece of the print newspaper.

In the meantime, an industrial power, IBM, has teamed up with CBS,* with its broadcast and publishing interests, and Sears, the merchandiser and lately financial services provider, to put together a videotex system a few years hence. Other players in videotex have included Knight-Ridder, one of the largest newspaper publishers and owner of broadcaster properties; Times Mirror Co., with similar holdings; Dow Jones, a publisher with an expanding electronic financial and general information service; Compu-Serve, originally a computer time-sharing company; Readers Digest, owner of The Source electronic information database; Citibank, Chase Manhattan, Bank of America, E.F. Hutton, Merrill, Lynch & Co., and several other

---

*CBS withdrew from the venture in 1987.

financial concerns interested in providing customers value-added services and at the same time cutting down on the paper flow for financial transactions. Some of these firms have already withdrawn from efforts in this arena. But it is expected that other firms will be getting involved, despite the uncertainties.

IMPLICATIONS

What does all this say about concentration or competition? Where does it leave the small player who wants to get a piece of the action, including those who want to make sure they have access to be "speakers" or providers of substance? And what, if anything, are the implications of the U.S. experience for Europe and the rest of the world?

Clearly, many of the players involved with the newer media services are the same ones we know in the traditional media. But many of the newer players are from territory that seemed light-years from the media. In that sense, the number of competitors is increasing as the interests of the players blur and merge. This may add to the already growing confusion over the appropriate boundaries for identifying the relevant industry to investigate or regulate.

We might look to the old print business for some hint of the future of the electronic one. One reason that the print business has had more freedom to operate is that it was not constrained by the limits of the technology, as was broadcasting. Printing presses might be expensive, but there was no technological limit to the number that could be made available, unlike 6 MH frequencies, for example. Moreover, publishers rarely had to depend on owning their network for distribution. The existence of a government-supported, common carrier postal system that reached every household and business, from the top of the Cascades to the bottom of the Grand Canyon, assured publishers access to customers.

The parallel institutions in electronics have been the telegraph and telephone networks. Until recently, however, these were largely restricted to point-to-point carriage of voice or low-volume analog signals. Today, the harnassing of computers to the telecommunications networks makes possible the economic transmission of a vast volume of data. The twisted copper wire pair goes nearly every place the postman goes. So long as the telephone system is a common carrier, virtually anyone will be able to become an electronic publisher with a far lower capital investment than was necessary when one also had to own – or pay for the use of – a printing press.

CONCLUSION

The empirical evidence indicates that the media structure in the United States is by far the most open, diverse, and responsive to public needs and wants than at any time in history, notwithstandsing the contrary sense that is suggested by the headlines created when media companies merge. There are no headlines proclaiming arrival of a new journal and the growth of phenomena such as a Cable News Network. Independent television ad hoc networks are another subtle but substantial change in the balance of media competitiveness.

Ownership in the aggregate is constantly shifting, but is far from concentrated except in a very few specific geographic locations. Since the days of the old media barons like Greeley, Pulitzer, and Hearst, few owners of media groups have sought to manipulate the editorial thrust of their properties. At best, their objectives have been to produce quality editorial publications and programs. At worst, it has simply been to make a profit. But this motive can be consistent with acceptable, if not always great, substance.

In general, however, as time goes on, any entity or small group of entities will likely have more difficulty attempting to control the substance or process of delivery of that substance, short of implementing a totalitarian regime. And even totalitarian societies will find their job of control more challenging. Over the centuries, technology has helped expand competition for the creation and distribution of ideas, information, and entertainment. We are not at the beginning of an era, but in the midst of that long-term trend.

NOTES

1. For a complete discussion of the construction and application of the information business map, see John F. McLaughlin, "Mapping the Information Business," in Benjamin M. Compaine, ed., *Understanding New Media* (Cambridge, Mass.: Ballinger Publishing Co., 1984).
2. Similar technology is being used to produce media that are called by different names. National newspapers such as *USA Today* and *The Wall Street Journal* are sending facsimiles of their composed pages to remote printing sites using data transmission and satellites similar to the way that programmers send their materials to cable operators. Internally, the electronic newspaper is for real, as computers and video displays have replaced typewriters and copy paper. Videotex and teletext use broadcast, cable, or telephone transmission to video displays for text and graphics that otherwise would look at home printed on paper.

3. This tendency to one-newspaper cities is not quite as bleak as it may sound. Accompanying the demise of competition in central cities has been the development of newspapers in suburban areas that have grown up around the central city in the past 35 years. Thus, many people and advertisers still do have a choice of newspapers—the metropolitan daily or the local daily.

4. Robert Darnton, *The Great Cat Massacre and Other Episodes of French Cultural History* (New York: Basic Books, Inc., Publishers, 1984), p. 79.

5. Benjamin M. Compaine Christopher H. Sterling, Thomas Guback, and J. Kendrick Noble, Jr. *Who Owns the Media? Concentration of Ownership in the Mass Communications Industry*, 2nd ed., (White Plains, NY: Knowledge Industry Publications, Inc., 1982, p. 41, Table 2.15. Hereafter cited as *Who Owns the Media?*

6. James M. Dertouzos and Kenneth E. Thorpe, "Newspaper Groups: Economies of Scale, Tax Laws and Merger Incentives" (Santa Monica, California: Rand Corp., 1982), pp. 4-8.

7. Compaine et al., *Who Owns the Media?* pp. 42-46.

8. *Ibid.*, pp. 452-453, Table 8-1.

9. *Statistical Abstract of the United States, 1985.* U.S. Bureau of the Census, p. 225. Table 379. Hereafter cited as *Statistical Abstract.*

10. *Ibid.* See *Statistical Abstract, 1979,* p. 593, Table 997 for 1960 figures.

11. O.H. Cheney, *Economic Survey of the Book Industry 1930-1931.* (New York: R.R. Bowker Co., 1931).

12. Richard D. Altick, *The English Common Reader: A Social History of the Mass Reading Public, 1800-1900.* (Chicago: University of Chicago Press, 1974), p. 368.

13. At a meeting convened on "Reading and the Book" at the American Academy of Arts and Science, June 25, 1982.

14. Altick, p. 233.

15. *Statistical Abstract,* p. 786, Table 1406.

16. Majid Tehranian, "Iran: Communication, Alienation, Revolution," *InterMedia,* March 1979, pp. 6-12.

17. Thomas White and Gladys Ganley, *The "Death of a Princess" Controversy* (Cambridge, Mass: Program on Information Resources Policy, Harvard University, 1983), P-83-9, p. 39.

18. Jonathan D. Levy and Peter K. Pitsch, "Statistical Evidence of Substitutability Among Video Delivery Systems," Federal Communications Commission, Washington, D.C., April 1984, p. 27.

19. *Ibid.*

20. *Ibid.*, p. 31.

21. Herbert H. Howard, "Group and Cross-Media Ownership of Television Stations, 1984," National Association of Broadcasters, June 1984, p. 3.

Chapter 4

THE NEW VIDEO MARKETPLACE: A REGULATORY IDENTITY CRISIS

Erwin G. Krasnow
Jill Abehouse Stern

Justice Holmes' observation that "it cannot be helped . . . the law is behind the times"[1] has particular relevance to the communications industry which, since its inception, has been characterized by the "rapid pace of its unfolding."[2] Today, the Federal Communications Commission (FCC) finds itself in the midst of a regulatory identity crisis precipitated by technological change and by its stated policy of promoting competition in the video marketplace.

As a result of technological and regulatory developments, an increasing number and diversity of video services compete with traditional broadcast television to deliver information and entertainment to the home. At present, cable television, multipoint distribution service (MDS), subscription television (STV), satellite master antenna television (SMATV), videocassette recorders (VCR), and videodisc players (VDP), or some combination of these video services, are available to consumers. Direct broadcast satellites (DBS), low power television (LPTV), electronic publishing services (teletext and videotex), and private operational-fixed microwave (OFS) stations offer additional potential video programming outlets. Fiber optic technology could further expand the delivery of video, voice, and data signals to the home. Increased spectrum efficiency, through analog compression, digital transmission, spectrum sharing, and multiplexing techniques, could provide even more delivery system opportunities.

The changing competitive nature of the video marketplace can be attributed in large part to the proliferation and continual refinement of communications satellites as vehicles of video programming distribution. By making possible an economical, efficient, national means of program transmission, satellite technology has contributed to the growth of independent television stations, cable television, SMATV, and MDS. The impact of satellites may become even more apparent over the next decade with the attempts of various providers to sell home satellite broadcasting on a mass scale. As a result of recent developments in spectrum efficiency, such as reduced spacing between satellites and greater spectrum reuse, domestic satellites promise continuing growth in video delivery services.

This abundance of video delivery systems, many of which do not utilize broadcast spectrum, and the introduction of new firms seeking to employ these systems in the video marketplace, have led the FCC, the courts, and Congress to reevaluate the fundamental tenets of broadcast regulation. The growth in number and diversity of broadcast outlets, and in nontraditional program sources, has called into question the notion that spectrum scarcity justifies the imposition of public interest obligations upon broadcasters.[3] Moreover, with technological developments blurring the distinctions between broadcasting, common carriage, and private radio, stakeholders in these video technologies have forced the FCC to reevaluate traditional regulatory classifications based upon those distinctions.[4] Reflecting an increased recognition that there may be little difference to the consumer whether a movie is provided by broadcast television, MDS, cable, or VCR, the Commission appears to be moving toward a regulatory approach under which the function of the service and the manner in which it is offered to consumers, rather than the spectrum allocation, determines the regulatory treatment. In the wake of a 1984 federal court decision[5] expressing concern with the FCC's exemption of certain video delivery systems from broadcast regulation, the current FCC is likely to strive for a more consistent approach to regulation of the new technologies.

The emergence of a more diversified and flexible video marketplace — as well as a shift in regulatory philosophy—has been accompanied by a "marketplace" approach to regulation. Under that approach, the FCC seeks to promote competition by eliminating governmental interference with market forces and by easing regulatory burdens. That approach also reflects a belief that the marketplace is workably competitive and will achieve the desired public interest objectives without government regulation.

Objectives

In an effort to assist policymakers, both in and out of government, this chapter attempts to provide a framework for the analysis of the video marketplace, leading to a more consistent and uniform approach. To this end, the video technologies that are presently, or will shortly be, available are described in an appendix entitled "A Primer on the Video Marketplace." This chapter begins with a discussion of the FCC's efforts to develop a coherent regulatory approach which accommodates the rapidly changing technology. It also traces the efforts of the Commission and the Congress to replace the traditional "public trustee" model of regulation with a marketplace approach. The chapter concludes with a discussion of the issues that are likely to occupy telecommuni cations policymakers over the rest of the decade and perhaps beyond, and an assessment of how various stakeholders will fare as a result of changes in technology and regulation.

I. AN IMPENDING REGULATORY IDENTITY CRISIS LOSS OF SCARCITY AS A REGULATORY RATIONALE

A fundamental tenet of broadcast regulation is the scarcity of broadcast frequencies. Because one person's transmission is another's interference, Congress concluded in the Radio Act of 1927 and the Communications Act of 1934 that the federal government has the duty both to select who may and who may not broadcast and to regulate the use of the electromagnetic spectrum to serve the public interest. Justice Frankfurter observed in 1943: "The radio spectrum simply is not large enough to accommodate everybody."[6] Government regulation, therefore, has been deemed essential to prevent "etheric bedlam."[7] In addition, the "inherent physical limitation"[8] of spectrum has justified the imposition of certain public service or program-related obligations upon broadcasters in return for the "free and exclusive use of a limited and valuable part of the public domain . . . ."[9]

Apart from natural limitations, the Commission's television allocation scheme has perpetuated spectrum scarcity.[10] The table of assignments adopted in 1952[11] confined television to the VHF and lower UHF spectrum,[12] even though other portions of the spectrum could have been reserved for home video and audio programming. Moreover, due to limitations in television receiver performance and the nature of the spectrum, not all of the commercial television channels allocated in 1952 are available for assignment in each community. As a result, only three VHF commercial outlets prevail in most markets.[13]

In the years since the scarcity rationale for broadcast regulation was first articulated, there have been dramatic changes in technology and in the broadcasting marketplace. In 1934, for example, there were 583 AM stations and no FM or television stations on the air.[14] As of December 31, 1984, there were 4,754 AM stations, 3,716 commercial FM stations, 1,172 noncommercial FM stations, 904 commercial television stations (539 VHF, 365

UHF) 290 noncommercial educational television stations (114 VHF, 176 UHF), and 316 low power television stations (204 VHF, 112 UHF).[15] The increase in television outlets, moreover, has not been confined to the major markets but has occurred in markets of varying size and in every region of the country.[16]

The increased number of broadcast outlets can be attributed, in part, to passage of the All Channel Receiver Act in 1962, which required manufacturers to equip most television sets to receive UHF signals.[17] The implementation of that legislation through various proceedings at the FCC has had a considerable impact on the growth and viability of the UHF service.[18] Improvements in receiver technology may further improve receivability of UHF stations. A 1983 report by the FCC's Office of Science and Technology describes the results of laboratory testing of an advanced UHF television receiver and other options for UHF receiver improvement.[19] Widespread interest in the development of better television pictures led to the formation of the Advanced Television Systems Committee, an industry-wide group dedicated to the investigation and standardization of new television systems and techniques.[20]

As a result of the growth in television outlets, broadcast service is now widely available. The average television household can receive 9.8 signals. And 97% of all television households can receive four or more signals.[21] The Commission's television allocation goal – to provide a choice of at least two television services to all parts of the United States[22] – has thus largely been met. The authorization of LPTV and DBS may further expand the availability of free over-the-air television nationwide.[23] Moreover, outside the larger markets, channels in the VHF and UHF bands are still available.[24]

The growth in number of broadcast outlets has been accompanied by an increase in the number of video programming offerings. The use of satellites for program distribution has been largely responsible for this development, by providing a new source of programming for network affiliates as well as independent stations and alternative distribution networks.[25] Satellite technology has been perhaps the most significant reason why independent stations are more competitive.[26] For example, there are currently 86 different TV markets, with independent stations accounting for 78% of all TV households.[27] The networks' combined share of the television audience dropped 10% in one year when it fell in 1982 from 90% to approximately 80%, while independents and other over-the-air TV stations achieved a 17% share.[28]

Alternatives to conventional television further undermine the scarcity rationale. Although additional VHF outlets may be foreclosed in the larger markets, cable, MDS, LPTV, DBS, and videocassettes are increasingly available to American households.[29] Many of these delivery modes do not utilize broadcast spectrum, and thus are not subject to the natural limitations upon the use of those frequencies. Moreover, ownership of the newer video technologies is not highly concentrated.[30]

There has been an increase in the number of subscribers to these alternatives to standard television service. The number of cable subscribers almost tripled between 1976 and 1983.[31] The A. C. Nielsen Co. estimates that in 1983, cable television households increased 18%, to 39.3% of all television homes.[32] It has been predicted that up to 58% of television households will subscribe to cable channels by 1990 when cable will be available to an anticipated 84% of television households.[33]

In addition, there were about 500,000 MDS subscribers in 1983, with as many as 3 million subscribers predicted by 1990.[34] VCRs were present in more than 3.5 million homes in 1983, about 4.2% of all television households.[35] By early 1985, more that 17 million VCRs were in use, or nearly one television household in five.[36] Video disc players were in 300,000 TV households.[37] It has been predicted that by 1990 more than 40 million television households – almost 50% – will own VCRs.[38] SMATV (satellite master antenna television – found mostly in apartment complexes) has shown rapid growth and passed approximately 500,000 households in 1983, of which 150,000 subscribe.[39] It could reach an estimated 800,000 subscribers by 1990.[40] DBS and LPTV are other alternatives which have been described as having considerable audience potential in the future.[41] Except for cable and VCRs, these projections are for nascent industries and may not develop in the manner envisioned by industry prognosticators.[42]

The media environment is thus substantially different from that of 1927 when Congress, fearing that a small number of stations and equipment manufacturers were about to monopolize the limited frequencies available, passed the Radio Act of 1927.[43] In contrast to the early history of broadcasting, a 1982 FCC study suggests that the supply of video programming exceeds demand, since only 43.9% of homes with access to cable, STV, and MDS services actually subscribe.[44] The same conclusion can be drawn from the fact that television channels outside the larger markets remain unused.[45] Moreover, even greater abundance has been predicted over the next decade as the result of growth in non traditional programming sources and more efficient use of spectrum.[46]

Recognizing that changing competitive conditions in the video marketplace may have invalidated regulatory approaches based upon notions of spectrum scarcity,[47] the Commission, in several rulemaking proceedings, pointed to the growth in the number and diversity[48] of broadcast outlets and nontraditional programming sources as reason for reevaluating certain program-related rules. As more fully discussed below, these proceedings include the decisions not to impose mandatory programming quotas for children's programming and to eliminate ascertainment requirements, nonentertainment programming guidelines, and commercial time standards for commercial television stations. In a July 1984 decision in *League of Women Voters of California v. FCC*, the Supreme Court indicated, in a footnote, its awareness that "the prevailing rationale for broadcast regulation based on spectrum scarcity has come under increasing criticism in recent years" and stated that it might be prepared to reconsider its long-standing approach to the notion of broadcast spectrum scarcity upon receiving "some signal from Congress or the FCC that technological developments have advanced so far that some revision of the system of broadcast regulation may be required."[49]

EMERGENCE OF NEW TECHNOLOGIES AND NEW REGULATORY CLASSIFICATIONS

Traditional Regulatory Classifications.

Technological developments have blurred the distinction between broadcasting and other services, leading to what one commentator has called a "convergence of modes."[50] To illustrate the extent to which the traditional classifications have been strained, the basic features of broadcast, cable, common carrier and private radio regulation are outlined below.

Broadcasting.   The Communications Act of 1934 defines broadcasting as the "dissemination of radio communications intended to be received by the public, directly or by the intermediary of relay stations."[51] The meaning of the term derives mainly from a comparison with common carrier services, since, as the Act provides, "a person engaged in radio broadcasting shall not . . . be deemed a common carrier."[52] Broadcasting is also distinguished from "point-to-point" communications addressed to one or more specified reception points.[53]

Broadcasters are regulated under Title III of the Communications Act.[54] Under Title III, broadcasters are given broad discretion to determine the content of the programming they transmit and, with limited exceptions, are not required to provide access to their stations by others.[55] Detailed technical regulations are imposed upon licensees to prevent interference with other stations, and to insure maximum service to the community and the nation.[56] The main objectives are spectrum management, compatibility of receiving and transmitting equipment, and assurance of a high-quality signal.

Broadcast licensees are considered to be public trustees with a responsibility to provide public service to their communities. For example, the Communications Act requires broadcasters to provide equal opportunities, reasonable access to their facilities, and the lowest rates to candidates for political office.[57] FCC rules prohibit broadcasting lottery information,[58] running rigged contests,[59] and failing to disclose the source of consideration for material broadcast.[60] Broadcasters have specific obligations concerning coverage of political events and issues,[61] and they must provide adequate coverage of public affairs.[62] Broadcast regulation is also concerned with ensuring a diversity of voices. To this end, the Commission restricts ownership of multiple broadcast stations[63] and cross-ownership of broadcast stations by owners of other communications media.[64]

The FCC has also allocated spectrum exclusively for noncommercial broadcasters—public radio and television.[65] Stations using these reserved frequencies are licensed by the FCC and, with a few exceptions, are subject to the same regulations as commercial licensees.

Underlying the regulation of noncommercial broadcasters is the belief that freedom from profit-oriented commercial pressures will produce distinctive programs appealing to small, highly differentiated markets. Thus, licensees of public television stations are required to be nonprofit institutions with a cultural or educational orientation.[66] To maintain their non-commercial character, public broadcasters are not permitted to accept compensation for on-air promotion of the goods and services of "for-profit" organizations.[67]

Unlike their commercial counterparts, many public broadcasters receive federal funding. A primary means of distributing such funds is through the Corporation for Public Broadcasting (CPB), a nonprofit entity created by the Public Broadcasting Act of 1967.[68] Between 1975 and 1980, the Public Broadcasting Act authorized $634 million in matching grants to be distributed to public stations through CPB.[69]

Cable Television. The FCC was initially reluctant to regulate cable television, believing that it lacked jurisdiction under the Communications Act. In the mid-1960s, however, the Commission resolved these doubts and embarked upon a period of active regulation in order to promote nationwide television service.[70] The Commission's jurisdiction over cable television was upheld in *United States v. Southwestern Cable Co.*[71] insofar as this jurisdiction is "reasonably ancillary . . . for the regulation of television broadcasting."[72] The Supreme Court subsequently applied the "reasonably ancillary" standard in *United States v. Midwest Video Corp. (Midwest Video I)*[73] to uphold FCC rules requiring cable systems to originate programming and to make available facilities for local production of programs.

The Supreme Court later limited the FCC's jurisdiction over cable television in the second *Midwest Video* case (*Midwest Video II*).[74] It interpreted section 3(h) of the Communications Act as preventing imposition of common carrier-type obligations upon cable operators. In so holding, it struck down Commission rules requiring systems with more than 3,500 subscribers to provide access channels, to increase capacity to 20 channels, and to provide two-way nonvoice communications.[75]

Since *Midwest Video II*, the Commission has retreated from further regulation of cable systems, and has, in fact, repealed the core of the cable regulatory structure which was based on an interindustry consensus reached in 1972.[76] In particular, the Commission rescinded distant signal carriage and syndicated program exclusivity restrictions on cable retransmissions.[77] Presently, the FCC ensures nonduplication protection for network and sports programs[78] and requires carriage of local broadcast signals by cable systems.[79] To the extent that a cable system engages in origination cable-casting, it must comply with equal time, fairness, lottery, and sponsorship identification requirements.[80]

Cable television systems, unlike broadcasters, are also subject to extensive local and, in some cases, state regulation. However, in the 1984 *Capital Cities Cable* decision the Supreme Court appears to have recognized the Commission's authority to regulate cable directly and not only as "reasonably ancillary" to its jurisdiction over broadcasting.[81] Shortly thereafter, the Commission clarified its claim of exclusive jurisdiction over the regulation of cable content and of rates charged for other than basic service, pre-empting state and local regulation in this field.[82]

Subsequent to the *Capital Cities* decision, Congress enacted the Cable Communications Policy Act, and it is unclear whether the Supreme Court's apparent affirmation of the FCC's plenary or direct jurisdiction over cable remains viable.[83] The Cable Act, signed into law on October 30, 1984, establishes a national policy to encourage the growth and development of cable television services and to assure that cable systems are responsive to the needs and interests of the local communities they serve.[84] The Act, which reflects a compromise between the National Cable Television Association and the National League of Cities, limits franchise fees to 5% of a system's gross revenues, prohibits rate regulation except in areas with fewer than three over-the-air television signals, largely guarantees renewal of franchises, restricts the number of access channels required by local governments, and allows cable operators unilaterally to abrogate certain franchise terms.

Common Carrier.   The Communications Act defines a common carrier as "any person engaged as a common carrier for hire."[85] In wrestling with this circuitous definition, the courts have concluded that a common carrier holds out, as available to the entire public for hire, facilities whereby all members of the same class of users who choose to employ such facilities may transmit intelligence of their own design.[86] Although AT&T still dominates the interexchange domestic common carrier industry, diverse new entities have entered the market.

Although common carriers and common carrier service offerings are regulated, in general, under Title II of the Communications Act, the FCC forbears from imposing some of these requirements where the carrier is nondominant. As a general matter, Sections 20l and 202 of the Communications Act outlaw unjust, unreasonable, and discriminatory practices by common carriers furnishing interstate and foreign communications.[87] The Act also requires the common carrier to file with the FCC "schedules showing all charges for itself and its connecting carriers for interstate or foreign wire or radio communications . . . and showing the classification, practices, and regulations affecting such charges."[88] The Commission is empowered to determine the lawfulness of any new or existing charge, classification, regulation, or practice of a common carrier, and to prescribe just and reasonable ones.[89]

A common carrier must obtain a certificate of public convenience and necessity before constructing, expanding, or terminating lines of communication.[90] It must also establish terms and conditions of the service offering pursuant to a tariff. Common carriers are subject to rate of return and rate base regulation and may not discriminate unreasonably against users.[91] Unlike broadcasters, common carriers are subject to overlapping state and local as well as federal regulation of their rates and services. The states maintain their own regulatory agencies to exercise jurisdiction over common carriers operating within their borders.

Private Radio.   Private radio services "include nationwide and international uses of radio by persons, businesses, state and local governments, and other organizations licensed to operate their own communications systems for their own use as an adjunct of their primary business or other activity."[92] Such services, which range from taxicab radios to police radios and radios used by persons in the motion picture, petroleum, and forestry industries, include almost all users of the spectrum that fit neither the broadcast nor the common carrier model. The regulations are primarily technical and procedural, because the primary functions of private radio regulation are to allocate spectrum and to ensure its efficient and orderly use.[93]

Unlike broadcast and common carrier regulation, eligibility is usually restricted to those engaged in a specific activity. These special eligibility requirements are used as a means of allocating spectrum among classes of users and controlling the number of users. Technical regulation beyond allocation and frequency assignment is limited to interference control.[94]

The FCC's Attempts To Forge A New Regulatory Approach

The traditional, and discrete, regulatory classifications have been strained by the new technologies and older technologies used in new ways. DBS, MDS and STV, for example, resemble traditional, over-the-air broadcasting in that the programming may be similar to conventional television fare and they use a portion of the spectrum. When they transmit in scrambled form to subscribers, however, these services are akin to point-to-point communications which are directed to specific reception points. Entertainment programming, traditionally provided by broadcasters, can now be delivered by MDS, a common carrier service, and OFS, a private radio service. Regulatory dilemmas are also created by electronic publishing (e.g., teletext), which combines features of the print media, broadcasting, and computers.

The FCC's efforts to adapt the existing regulatory scheme to these new technologies have not always been consistent. Nonetheless, three distinct trends can be perceived. First, the Commission has, in an effort to encourage greater autonomy, permitted the licensee essentially to self-select the manner in which it will be regulated. This approach appears in the Commission's treatment of DBS, teletext, and subsidiary communications services, and in its decisions authorizing licensees to share excess spectrum capacity in the ITFS and broadcast auxiliary service. Second, the Commission has professed a goal of "regulatory parity," which seeks to place providers of comparable services on the same regulatory footing. Third, the Commission has declined to apply the traditional regulatory classifications to services it has characterized as "hybrid" (such as STV, teletext, DBS, and LPTV) on the grounds that it may forbear from imposing particular regulations where the public interest warrants.[95]

Although the Commission has, in some instances, eliminated artificial regulatory distinctions between services delivering comparable programming, it has in other proceedings, most notably in MDS, perpetuated these distinctions. Following the 1984 NAB v. FCC decision, however, the Commission has expressed its intention to initiate a new proceeding for the purpose of reexamining the regulatory classifications of such pay video services as DBS, MDS, STV, and teletext.[96] And, at least in the case of multichannel MDS, the FCC has reversed its prior treatment of that service and decided, for the purpose of lottery selection, to classify it as a "medium of mass communication."[97] In addition, the Commission's reorganization of the Cable Television and Broadcast Bureaus into the Mass Media Bureau, including branches for cable, TV, LPTV, DBS, and other technologies, indicates an interest in establishing a structure for a more uniform approach.[98]

Subscription Television.   Ever since STV was introduced, the Commission has been troubled by the appropriate classification for the service and has attempted to reconcile the subscriber relationship with the definition of broadcasting as a service intended for general public reception.[99] Although the Commission concluded that the subscription operations of radio stations were point-to-point communications, not broadcasting,[100] it reached the opposite conclusion about subscription television.[101] The FCC based its decision on the STV industry's "intent to provide a radio or television program service without discrimination to as many members of the general public as can be interested in the programs."[102]

The Commission more recently acknowledged that subscription television may be a hybrid, possessing qualities of both broadcasting and point-to-point services. In discussing subscription television operations, the Commission observed:

> While a service authorization by the Commission cannot at the same time be classified as both broadcasting and common carrier, it does not follow that all services which may be authorized by the Commission must be classifiable by the Commission as either one or the other. There is no question as to the Commission's authority to authorize the use of radiofrequencies [sic] for numerous kinds of services which are neither broadcast services nor common carrier services. The safety and special radio services abound in examples.[103]

Consistent with this approach, the Commission concluded that it had authority to exempt subscription broadcast services from regulatory provisions that apply to conventional broadcasting.[104] It so held in the *Third Report and Order*,[105] which, among other things, relieved STV operators of ascertainment and conventional programming requirements. In eliminating these "behavioral" rules, the Commission compared STV to other pay services, such as cable, which are not hampered by traditional broadcast regulations.[106]

Direct Broadcast Satellite Service.   The Commission opted for a flexible regulatory approach in its interim rules for DBS.[107] It declined to specify a particular service classification, emphasizing the need to gather experimental data as to whether, for example, "satellite operators find it most feasible to operate as broadcasters, common carriers, private radio operators, or some combination or variant of these classifications."[108] In the meantime, the appropriate regulatory approach will be determined on an ad hoc basis. The Commission stated:

> The appropriate statutory provisions will depend on the specific characteristics of the service each applicant proposes, including the proposed method of

financing, whether the service would be offered to the general public, and the degree of control the applicant would exercise over program content. If the proposal falls within any of the conventional regulatory classifi cations for radio services, i.e., broadcast, common carrier or private radio, we will impose the statutory requirements of that service.[109]

Departing from the traditional approach whereby utilization of spectrum allocated to a particular service defines the appropriate regulatory approach, the Commission indicated that a DBS applicant could choose the manner in which it would be regulated. Direct-to-home subscription services, over which the applicant retains control of the transmission content, would generally be classified as broadcast services.[110] On the other hand, if a DBS applicant chose to operate as a common carrier, it would have been required to offer its satellite transmission facilities indiscriminately to the public pursuant to tariff, under Title II of the Communications Act.[111] Under this approach, a DBS operator could "function as a broadcaster with respect to some channels and a common carrier with respect to others."[112]

The DBS proceeding also raised the question of how to regulate programmers who provide service directly to the public through facilities and frequencies licensed to a common carrier. The existing regulatory scheme, which clearly distinguishes broadcasters from common carriers, does not address this problem. The Commission concluded that Congress did not intend that customers of common carrier operators be licensed and regulated as broadcasters. It cited the fact that similar systems, such as MDS, which provide subscription programming services to individual residences, were not subject to traditional broadcast regulation.[113] In so concluding, the Commission essentially permitted DBS channel programmers to avoid the same basic responsibilities and limitations as their counterpart terrestrial broadcasters, including the broadcast multiple ownership rules.

In 1984, the U.S. Court of Appeals for the District of Columbia Circuit vacated the portion of the FCC's interim DBS regulations exempting DBS programmers from the statutory requirements imposed upon broadcasters. The court held that "nothing in the statutory definition [of broadcasting] allows the Commission to elevate form over function in this way nor suggests that the definition of broadcasting turns on whether the provider of the service leases satellite facilities from a common carrier or owns the satellite outright."[114] Noting the FCC's "strained statutory construction,"[115], the court expressed concern that the FCC's exemption of common carrier DBS lessees from broadcast restrictions—particularly the political broadcasting provisions— could lead to "consequences at odds with the basic objectives of the Communications Act."[116] The court held that "DBS, at least when directed to individual homes, *is* radiocommunication intended to be received by the general public – despite the fact that it can be received by only those with appropriate reception equipment."[117]

The court's decision creates uncertainty about the Commission's finding of "no inherent inconsistency" between the DBS rules and the proposal of the now-defunct United Satellite Communications, Inc. (USCI), a video programmer, to use a fixed-satellite system for a DBS-type service.[118] In so concluding, the Commission relied on the technical differences between the fixed and DBS services, such as power, satellite spacing, and antenna size.[119] As a result, however, two separate regulatory schemes govern the provision of essentially the same services. While home video programming is permitted under the fixed-satellite service rules, the satellite licensee leases or sells transponder capacity to a program distributor and is usually treated as a common carrier[120] in contrast to the DBS licensee who may, under certain circumstances, be regulated as a broadcaster. Like the DBS programmer, however, entities such as USCI are exempt from broadcast regulation.

Teletext.   Teletext, which combines characteristics of publishing and broadcasting, has also posed a regulatory dilemma for the FCC.[121] On the one hand, teletext resembles the print media, which are free from government regulation of programming content. On the other hand, broadcasters who lease transmission time to teletext operators may have little meaningful control over the programming transmitted, and, therefore, resemble common carriers. Teletext could also be considered broadcasting in that broadcast frequencies are often leased and the teletext transmission is frequently linked to the broadcast material, consisting, for example, of program schedules or subtitles. In authorizing the service, the Commission addressed the regulatory implications of teletext's hybrid nature, characterizing the service as representing a "unique blend of the print medium with radio technology."[122]

From all appearances, the Commission intends to perpetuate the traditional common carrier and broadcast distinctions in regulating teletext. The novel aspect of the Commission's approach is that broadcasters may, in certain circumstances, be subjected to common carrier or private radio regulation. The broadcast licensee who uses the VBI for teletext would be responsible for all transmissions of a broadcast nature. Nonbroadcast teletext activities, such as data trans mission and paging, will be subject to the private radio and common carrier rules.[123] The licensee bears the responsibility for determining which regulatory classification applies.

The decision is significant in acknowledging that teletext's "unique blending of the print medium with radio technology fundamentally distinguishes it from traditional broadcast programming," and for exempting the service from political broadcasting and fairness requirements on those grounds.[124] The Commission did not, however, eliminate the fundamental discrepancy in regulatory treatment based upon the delivery system utilized. If teletext is delivered by a common carrier service, for example, it would be free from content regulation. In contrast, the television licensee who uses the VBI for teletext would be required to retain control over all material transmitted in a broadcast mode, with the right to reject any material that it deems inappropriate or undesirable.[125]

Multipoint Distribution Service.   Licensees in the Multipoint Distribution Service have traditionally been subject to the full panoply of Title II common carrier regulation. In reallocating an additional eight channels for MDS use in 1983, the Commission initially declined to alter the service's traditional regulatory status. Under that scheme, MDS licensees are treated as common carriers, while MDS programmers are essentially unregulated even though those programmers are, in many respects, functionally similar to broadcast licensees. In a partial retreat from this traditional view, the FCC decided that, for some purposes, an MDS facility may be a medium of mass communication.[126] In so holding, the FCC moved closer to Commissioner Rivera's previously minority view that, "while MDS is nominally regulated as a common carrier service . . . to the viewer, the wireless cable transmission is indistinguishable from other home video mediums [sic], no matter what their regulatory classification."[127] As he further pointed out, "MDS transmissions can influence social, cultural, political and moral values to the same extent as conventional broadcast television."[128] In Commissioner Rivera's view, the similarity between MDS and conventional television calls for the imposition of broadcast structural and behavioral regulation upon MDS licensees. Among the regulatory options proposed by Commissioner Rivera were various tariff prescriptions (e.g., preventing MDS licensees from leasing channels to entities already owning other media interests in the same market), a dual licensing scheme for MDS carriers and their programmer-customers, or reclassification of MDS as a broadcast service.

Following the 1984 decision in *NAB v. FCC,* and the court's suggestion that the FCC's exemption of MDS programmer-customers from broadcast regulation may not withstand judicial scrutiny, the FCC indicated its intention to reevaluate its regulatory scheme for multichannel MDS and to resolve the question of whether any Title III broadcast responsibilities apply to MDS licensees.[129] That reevaluation could ultimately mean that MMDS operators would be permitted to fully program their facilities and to be classified as noncommon carriers.[130]

Instructional Television Fixed Service.   The Commission has authorized licensees in the Instructional Television Fixed Service (ITFS) – reserved for the transmission of instructional and cultural materials[131] – to share or lease excess spectrum capacity to other entities.[132] As a result of that decision, ITFS frequencies can now be used by pay TV entrepreneurs and others to offer MDS-type services.

Even though ITFS licensees who engage in leasing will functionally resemble MDS carriers, the Commission decided that common carrier regulation would be inappropriate. It reasoned that such treatment might discourage or inhibit ITFS licensees from making spare capacity available. The Commission concluded that ITFS licensees were unlikely to deal with the public indiscriminately, since the primary purpose of the service, and the individual licensee's growth requirements, would require lessees to be selected on an individualized long-term basis. As the Commission explained: "We find nothing inherent in the potential leasing activities of ITFS licensees that would lead them to make indifferent offerings of excess capacity on the main channel."[133] In so holding, the Commission essentially adopted the approach it had utilized with respect to the sharing of broadcast auxiliary facilities.[134]

As in the teletext and FM subcarrier proceedings, however, the Commission indicated that, to the extent that the ITFS licensee uses its subcarrier or VBI to provide services of a common carrier or private radio nature, it will be treated in the same manner and with the same benefits, obligations and responsibilities as the providers of similar services.

Private Operational-Fixed Service.   The Commission had an opportunity, in authorizing the use of OFS systems for video entertainment distribution, to clarify the regulatory status of the service. It had deferred a decision on that issue at an earlier stage of the proceeding, pending the outcome of the DBS rulemaking.[135]

Initially, the Commission concluded that, due to the more limited, point-to-multipoint nature of the signals to be transmitted, the licensing of program distributors in the OFS does not prompt the same regulatory concerns as does nationwide DBS. It further held that OFS services are not broadcasting, even though the programming content may be similar. The key difference, in the Commission's view, was the fact that "OFS services are 'addressed' communications intended for, and directed to, specific points of reception—the licensee's paying customers."[136] For this reason, the Commission characterized OFS entertainment transmissions as "hybrid" and exempted them from broadcast regulation. Such services will be exempted from common carrier regulation as well, since, under Commission rules, OFS licensees are required to have an ownership or contractual interest in the information or services they distribute.[137] However, the Commission has proposed to liberalize the scope of permissible sharing arrangements in the OFS by allowing eligible licensees to sell their excess capacity on a for-profit, private carrier basis.[138]

Noncommercial Broadcasting. Another distinction that has been blurred, in recent Commission decisions, is the one between commercial and noncommercial broadcasters. Reflecting a decrease in federal financial support of public broadcasting and a Congressional interest in encouraging alternative sources of funding,[139] the Commission has eliminated some of the distinctions between commercial and noncommercial broadcasters.[140] In authorizing noncommercial television broadcasters to share their auxiliary facilities on the same basis as commercial stations, the Commission expressly acknowledged its desire to insure the viability of public stations:

> Several factors lead us to this conclusion. First, it clearly reflects the intent of Congress in its recent decision to permit noncommercial broadcast stations to offer their facilities to others for remuneration. The noncommercial broadcasters commenting on this issue indicate that the additional revenues gained through offering their auxiliary stations to others may prove crucial in their efforts to overcome reduced federal funding. By allowing profitmaking, we are continuing our efforts to develop a regulatory environment that permits public broadcasters to make the most efficient use of their facilities and thereby supplement their revenues in the face of dwindling federal financial support.[141]

The FCC has also amended its rules to permit public broadcasters to broadcast logos and to identify product lines of program underwriters, thus relaxing the prohibition against promotional announcements of any kind.[142] It has also authorized public television stations to offer teletext services on a profit-making basis.[143] ITFS licensees, many of whom are public broadcasters, have been authorized to lease excess spectrum capacity for profit.[144] The FCC decided against allowing noncommercial television stations to offer STV services, but indicated that it would consider waiver requests for such operations.[145] Thus, noncommercial broadcasting has become more like commercial broadcasting as the Commission has sought to create profitmaking opportunities for those licensees to offset decreases in funding.[146]

II. THE INTERPLAY BETWEEN INDUSTRY CHANGES AND REGULATORY PHILOSOPHY

As growth in the video marketplace has undermined the traditional rationale for, and regulatory distinctions of, mass media law, the FCC has increasingly relied upon market forces to effectuate the policy objectives underlying its regulatory scheme. After describing the role that Congress has played in establishing national policies favoring the encouragement of new technologies and the elimination of burdensome regulatory requirements, this section discusses the FCC's efforts to implement a marketplace approach.

CONGRESSIONAL ACTION

Rewriting The Communications Act

Congressional actions have influenced the Commission's regulatory philosophy and have reflected changes in industry characteristics. From 1976 to 1980, Representative Lionel Van Deerlin, Chairman of the House Communications Subcommittee, proposed in the 94th, 95th, and 96th Congresses a "basement to attic" rewrite of the Communications Act.[147] Although Van Deerlin's rewrite bill was not adopted, the introduction of other rewrite bills and the debate they elicited has had a significant impact on communications policy. For example, congressional oversight of the FCC's actions improved. Former FCC Commissioner Glen Robinson observed:

> As part of a studied effort over the last two years [1976-1977] to review and revise the entire legislative mandate of the FCC, the Subcommittee on Communications and its staff have shown greater attentiveness to, and more understanding of, important policy issues than has been evident for at least twenty years .[148]

Robert Bruce, former FCC General Counsel, said he regards the "rewrite process" as having "an enormous impact" on the development of substantive policies by the Commission.[149]

The rewrite proposals, by threatening the FCC's survival, spurred the agency to action. The Commission adopted major decisions deregulating radio,[150] cable television,[151] and earth station licensing.[152] The FCC also took several bold initiatives providing open entry and federal deregulation in the common carrier industry.[153] With respect to the provision of new broadcasting outlets, the FCC "dropped in" four VHF television channels,[154] created a new low power television service,[155] and authorized a direct-to-home satellite broadcast service.[156] Van Deerlin and many other Washington, D.C., observers concluded that the FCC's bold actions "would have been impossible without the thunder and lightning sparked by those first two comprehensive bills."[157] The Commission implemented administratively many of the rewrite's legislative goals of deregulation and increased marketplace competition, thus taking some of the steam out of the drive for legislation and establishing the agency in a leadership role.

Federal Paperwork And Regulatory Flexibility Policies

The Commission has been influenced by recent Congressional policies placing a greater obligation upon federal agencies to reduce and/or minimize the scope of the regulations they generate. For example, the Regulatory Flexibility Act of 1980 is specifically designed to relieve small businesses and other entities from pervasive government regulation.[158] That Act requires the Commission and other administrative agencies to limit the potential impact of new regulations, and to reassess the continued necessity of existing regulations. Of particular significance, the Act requires the Commission to reassess existing rules periodically so as to determine "the degree to which . . . economic conditions or other factors have changed in the area affected by the rule."[159]

The Congressionally mandated goal of federal paperwork reduction has also spurred the FCC's deregulatory efforts. In recognition of mounting and unprecedented paperwork burdens, Congress in 1974 determined that a renewed effort was necessary to control federal information requests, and created a Commission on Federal Paperwork to study the federal government's information-gathering activities.[160] In 1980, incorporating many of the Paperwork Commission's recommendations, Congress enacted the Paperwork Reduction Act to minimize the federal paperwork burden. That Act set a statutory goal of reducing the burden of existing information demands upon the public 15% by October 1, 1982, and an additional 10% the following year through the elimination of regulatory burdens that are found to be unnecessary and thus wasteful.[161] Heeding this Congressional mandate, the Commission has taken a number of actions designed to reduce paperwork burdens, including simplifying the license renewal application for broadcast stations.[162]

National Policy Favoring The Encouragement Of New Technologies

In enacting the "Federal Communications Commission Authorization Act of 1983,"[163] Congress added language expressing a national policy "to encourage the provision of new technologies and services to the public."[164] Not only has a statutory presumption been created that any new technology or service is in the public interest—placing the burden on those opposing introduction—but the Commission is now obligated to make a public interest determination as to any new technology or service within 1 year after a petition or application is filed, or 12 months after the date of enactment of the statutory provision, if later.[165] This statutory amendment thus makes more ex plicit the Commission's obligation under Section 303(g) of the Communications Act to "study new uses for radio, provide for experimental uses of frequencies and generally encourage the larger and more effective use of radio in the public interest."[166] It reflects an intention to provide for a more competitive telecommunications market place by easing entry: "The development of new technologies and the efforts of competitors seeking to respond to consumer demands will bring more service to the public than will administrative regulations."[167]

National Policy Promoting Competition In Cable Communications

The Cable Communications Policy Act of 1984 amends the Communications Act to establish a comprehensive national cable television policy.[168] The Act reflects a wide variety of political tradeoffs and policy decisions, many of which resulted from last-minute negotiating sessions between the National Cable Television Association, the National League of Cities, and the U.S. Conference of Mayors.[169] The Act's ambivalent nature (namely, a mixture of regulatory and deregulatory provisions) is underscored by the statements of purpose scattered throughout its legislative history. The Senate bill (S.66) contained "findings" that "competition is a more efficient regulator than government," and that "the deregulation of telecommunications services should occur."[170] A stated "purpose" of S.66 was to "eliminate government regulation in order to prevent the imposition of an unnecessary economic burden on cable systems."[171] As passed by the Senate in June 1983, S.66 was largely deregulatory by limiting the powers of state and local governments. On the other hand, the House bill (H.R. 4103) restricted local authorities less and imposed new federal regulations on cable operators.[172] Its legislative purposes included, not deregulation, but rather the growth of the cable industry, its responsiveness to local needs, and the provision of a diversity of information sources and services to the public.[173]

The final compromise measure retained the "purposes" of the House bill, to which the Senate added one further goal: "promot[ing] competition in cable communications and minimiz[ing] unnecessary regulation that would impose an undue economic burden on cable systems."[174] This weakened version of the original Senate declaration is in keeping with the Act's reduced emphasis on deregulation. Perhaps the most noteworthy achievement of the Act is its assurance of stability of franchise renewal. One of the Act's stated purposes is to "establish an orderly process for franchise renewal which protects cable operators against unfair denials of renewal where the operator's past performance and proposal for future performance meets the standards established by [the Act]."[175]

FCC IMPLEMENTATION OF A MARKETPLACE APPROACH TO BROADCAST REGULATION

Changes In FCC Regulatory Philosophy

The FCC's conception of a wide-open video marketplace and the resulting structural changes within the agency (such as the creation of a Mass Media Bureau) are rooted in actions taken by President Carter's FCC chairman, Charles Ferris. Ferris in effect transformed the Office of Plans and Policy into an office of "Chief Economist." He introduced a substantial number of economists into the highest levels of FCC decision making and created an atmosphere in which past legal structures for broadcast regulation were challenged by economic models favoring open entry for new technologies.[176] His legacy includes the Network Inquiry Special Staff Report, which has served as the basis for many of the recent deregulatory initiatives.

The succeeding chairman, Mark Fowler, appointed by President Reagan, has also endorsed an open entry philosophy, whereby "new players [are] encouraged to come into the field."[177] Calling the FCC the "last of the New Deal dinosaurs,"[178] Fowler advocates a marketplace approach under which broadcasters are viewed, not as fiduciaries of the public, but as marketplace competitors.[179] Instead of defining public demand and specifying categories of programming to serve this demand, Fowler believes that the Commission should rely on "the broadcasters' ability to determine the wants of their audience through the normal mechanisms of the marketplace."[180]

Reflecting these new regulatory philosophies and changing competitive conditions in the video marketplace, the Commission has consolidated all video services under one Mass Media Bureau, including branches for cable, broadcast television, LPTV, DBS, and other new technologies.[181] In the Commission's view, "this reorganization creates an integrated organizational structure for the administration of Commission policies regarding traditional broadcasting, cable television and the emerging television delivery systems by combining these essentially similar consumer services into a single Bureau."[182] This consolidation, the Commission believes, will lead to faster and more efficient authorization of service, reduction of duplicate record keeping, less confusion about FCC services among consumers, greater flexibility of staff utilization and more orderly development of emerging television delivery technologies.

Specific FCC Actions

Radio Deregulation. The analysis employed in the FCC's radio deregulation decision has served as a basis for the "marketplace approach" employed in later deregulatory actions. In that proceeding,[183] the Commission eliminated its internal processing guidelines, which required fullCommission consideration of any renewal application proposing less than 8% (AM stations) or 6% (FM stations) nonentertainment programming, or proposing to broadcast more than 18 minutes of commercial matter per hour. Formalistic requirements for ascertainment of community leaders and for a general public survey were also eliminated for commercial radio licensees, as was the Commission's program log requirement.

These Commission actions were upheld by the U.S. Court of Appeals for the D.C. Circuit.[184] The court decision made clear that none of the Commission requirements under consideration is mandated by the Communi cations Act or judicial intepretation of that statute, but, rather, that they are regulatory devices created by the Commission and can be changed in light of experience.[185] While the court held that nothing in the Communications Act compelled the FCC to retain program logs, it directed the Commission to give further consideration to that issue, particularly the alternatives that might be employed to permit the public to assess individual station performance and to permit the agency to monitor the success of its deregulatory regime.[186]

The Commission, with court approval, relied upon present market conditions in the radio industry as the basis for deregulation. In particular, the agency noted the dramatic growth of the radio industry, of FM radio service, and of alternative sources of informational programming.[187] It stressed that the increased number of outlets has led, in turn, to increased specialization and competition in the radio marketplace.[188] Radio, the Commission concluded, has been largely transformed into a specialized medium, offering programming geared to narrower audiences.[189]

The Commission concluded that its public interest mandate compelled it to review and modify its regulations in light of changes in the radio industry. Indeed, it observed, "failure to so do could constitute less than adequate performance of our regulatory mission."[190] The Commission stated:

> It is well settled that [the public interest] standard was deliberately placed into the Act by Congress so as to provide the Commission with the maximum flexibility in dealing with the ever changing conditions in the field of broad casting. Moreover, a wide latitude has been provided the Commission to modify its regulations in the face of such changes. We believe that it is entirely consistent with our authority, and our mandate, to consider the changes in broadcasting that have occurred, at an ever accelerating pace, over the past half century, and to adapt our rules and policies to those changes.[191]

In addition to establishing the Commission's authority to adapt its regulations to changing characteristics of the industry, the decision also evidences a belief that marketplace forces, rather than government regulation, can act as an incentive for licensees to provide program diversity.

In this regard, the radio program format case, *FCC v. WNCN Listeners Guild*,[192] is also significant. The Supreme Court there upheld the Commission's decision to no longer review format changes in radio license renewal or transfer cases, but instead to rely upon market forces rather than government supervision to promote diversity in entertainment programming.[193] Calling the market the "allocation mechanism of preference," the Commission found that competition had already produced a "bewildering array of diversity" in entertainment formats.[194] In the Commission's view, the market is more flexible than government regulation and responds more quickly to changing public tastes.[195] The Supreme Court agreed with the FCC's conclusion that, for these reasons, "its statutory duties are best fulfilled by not attempt ing to oversee format changes."[196]

Television Deregulation.   In authorizing a low power television service, the FCC relied upon "marketplace forces" to fulfill many of the policy objectives underlying conventional broadcast regulation.[197] This decision, therefore, established a framework for further deregulation.

The Commission adopted minimal programming requirements for the new service. As a result, LPTV stations need not comply with the formal ascertainment, minimum hours of operation, commercial time, program log, and programming requirements applicable until June of 1984 to full service television stations except where compelled by statute.[198] The Commission reasoned that "government surveillance" of LPTV stations would interfere with marketplace conditions.[199] Given the limited coverage areas of LPTV stations, the FCC concluded that responsiveness to local needs would be a condition of economic survival. The technical nature of the new service, the Commission observed, also warranted departure from the general principle of broadcast regulation that all elements of the community be provided with program service.[200] For these reasons, the agency left programming decisions to the discretion of licensees, and to the demands of the marketplace:

> In many instances, particularly in rural or remote areas, low power stations will be set up specifically to fill local needs. In areas where the marketplace demands coverage of local events of common interest, licensees can be expected to provide it. In some urban markets, unserved ethnic enclaves may be targeted for low power service. But in a major market that already receives adequate local coverage from several full service stations, a low power licensee may discover and attempt to fill a need for additional national news, sports or entertainment programming. Such judgments properly are left to licensees; it is in their interest, and the public's, to garner audience by attempting to serve unmet needs.[201]

The Commission also adopted flexible ownership policies for the new service, dispensing with limits on the maximum number of stations per mitted in common ownership, and with the restrictions on ownership by existing broadcast licensees in their markets. Due to the uncertain viability of the new service, it concluded that the possible loss of new entrants would be outweighed by the benefit of permitting experienced broadcasters to develop the service initially.[202]

Children's programming has been a long-running issue. Concluding a 13-year inquiry into television programming and advertising addressed to children, the Commission, in December 1983, declined to impose a national mandatory quota for children's programming.[203] Instead, the Commission stressed each licensee's continuing duty, under the statutory public interest standard, to respond to the needs of the child audience.[204] In so holding, the Commission disagreed with the 1979 conclusions of the Children's Television Task Force that the economic incentives of the advertiser-supported broadcasting system do not encourage the provision of specialized programming for children. In particular, the Commission found that the Task Force had erroneously failed to consider (a) the growth in the number of commercial stations and their increased receivability, (b) programming on noncommercial stations, (c) cable program service, and (d) child viewing of "family"-oriented television.[205] The growth of alternative video outlets, the Commission noted, tended to result in market segmentation and a resultant greater attention to specific subgroups such as the child audience.[206]

On another front, in 1984, the Commission eliminated the minimum program percentages, ascertainment requirements, commercial time standards, and program log rules for commercial television stations,[207] paralleling the rule changes previously adopted for radio. In instituting the proceeding a year earlier, the Commission had announced an intention "to evaluate the marketplace to determine whether the public interest can be furthered by competitive forces rather than by the Commission's existing rules and policies."[208] While inviting comment on several options, ranging, from substantial deregulation to no deregulation at all, the Commission's decision ultimately opted for the most extreme revisions, reflecting its view that the marketplace will achieve the underlying regulatory objectives without government intervention.

As justification for regulatory review, the Commission noted several factors. First, it pointed to the increasingly competitive nature of the video marketplace.[209] Second, it raised a question of whether these changing competitive conditions could inhibit the ability of television licensees to compete with other unregulated or less- regulated technologies.[210] Third, the Commission noted the Congressional expression of a strong national policy against government regulation, reflected in the Paperwork Reduction and Regulatory Flexibility Acts.[211] Fourth, the Commission noted that its programming guidelines and commercialization policies relate to the sensitive area of program content and could impinge upon the broadcaster's editorial discretion, presenting an even more compelling case for reassessment.[212] Finally, the Commission acknowledged that broadcasters appear to be presenting more informational, local, and nonentertainment programming than called for under the programming guidelines, and less commercial material than permitted.[213]

The Commission has also instituted a proceeding in 1984 to reexamine the fairness doctrine obligations of broadcast licensees.[214] The fairness doctrine imposes upon broadcasters the obligation to cover controversial issues of public importance and to provide reasonable opportunities for the presentation of contrasting viewpoints on such issues.[215] In initiating reexamination of the 30-year-old policy, the Commission noted that "significant new developments and changes in the electronic and print media over the past decade have contributed to an extremely dynamic, robust, and diverse marketplace of ideas that may call into question the continued necessity of the doctrine as a means of insuring the attainment of First Amendment objectives."[216]

Cable Television Deregulation.   In June 1981, the United States Court of Appeals for the Second Circuit affirmed the Commission's decision to deregulate cable television by rescinding the distant-signal and syndicated-program exclusivity rules.[217] The distant-signal rules limited the number of signals from distant commercial stations (beyond 35 miles of the cable system) that the system could retransmit to its subscribers, in order to protect local stations.[218] The syndicated-program exclusivity rules authorized local television stations, which had purchased exclusive exhibition rights to a program, to demand that local cable systems delete that program from distant commercial signals.[219] The extent of this protection varied according to market size, program type, and time of showing.[220]

The Commission based cable deregulation upon several econometric and case studies concerning the impact of cable television on local station audiences and future cable penetration rates.[221] It found that deregulation would have a negligible impact on local broadcast stations, and would, in fact, increase viewing options for consumers due to the greater availability of expanded cable services.

The Commission also cited the imposition by Congress of copyright liability upon cable television systems as a justification for deregulation.[222] In 1976, Congress established a compulsory licensing system, under which cable operators would be permitted to retransmit programs without the consent of the copyright owners, in return for payment of a prescribed royalty fee based upon the system's gross revenues and its carriage of distant signals.[223] The Commission believed that enactment of this statutory scheme eliminated the need for regulations that had served to protect broadcast property rights in the absence of copyright liability.[224]

Since deletion of those rules, it appears that copyright royalties may, in fact, operate to limit carriage of distant signals and syndicated programming. The Copyright Royalty Tribunal substantially increased the rates that cable operators must pay for broadcasting such signals.[225] This economic factor initially caused many cable systems to drop the programming they picked up after the Malrite decision and substitute other, made-for-cable program services for some distant television signals.[226] However, during 1984, the distant carriage of television stations WTBS, WOR, and WGN increased, with two additional "superstations" (WPIX, New York, and KTVT, Dallas-Ft. Worth) being offered to cable systems.

Subscription Television Deregulation.   The Commission has deregulated subscription television in significant respects in an effort to give free reign to marketplace forces: (a) It eliminated the "complement-of-four" rule that restricted STV operation to communities primarily served by at least five commercial television stations including the STV operator; (b) it deleted the requirement that STV stations broadcast at least 28 hours of conventional (free) programming per week; (c) it decided to permit operators to sell, as well as lease, decoders; and (d) it relieved STV licensees from ascertainment obligations with respect to STV programming.[227] More recently, the Commission has exempted STV stations from the conventional television signal quality standards.[228]

The "complement-of-four" rule was originally adopted to assure that pay TV would not replace an existing free service or utilize a vacant channel that would otherwise be available for a conventional station. The Commission later concluded, however, that current market conditions ensure that conventional programming would not be significantly impaired by eliminating the rule. Moreover, the Commission observed that the rule placed STV licensees at a competitive disadvantage compared to pay cable operators.[229]

The "28 hour" rule, also designed to ensure the availability of conventional programming, mandated that a minimum amount of such programming be broadcast by STV stations. In deleting this requirement, the Commission noted that the "mix of conventional and pay programming might better be determined by the judgment of the individual entrepreneur and the demands of the marketplace,"[230] than by "an arbitrary government rule."[231] The rule, in the Commission's view, served no public interest function, and its elimination would result in greater programming diversity by enabling the licensee to make pro gramming determinations in response to audience demands.

Other elements of STV deregulation were also motivated by the FCC's analysis of the video marketplace. The decision to permit the sale of decoders by STV licensees and other entities, over the objections of system operators concerned about piracy, was influenced by the fact that "other pay technologies, such as cable, are offered on a lease or pur chase basis."[232] Elimination of ascertainment obligations for STV licensees also reflected a marketplace approach. The Commission stated:

> We believe that ascertaining the community's STV interests can be more than adequately accomplished by the operation of the marketplace. It seems evident that consumers subscribe only to those pay television systems offering programs meeting their STV interests. It is clearly in the operator's best interest to fashion station offerings to meet those needs.[233]

In sum, this recent deregulatory decision is significant in its assumption that STV competes with alternative forms of home video entertainment such as cable, pay cable, and MDS, and that the STV licensee should be placed on an equal footing with its competitors.

Common Carrier Deregulation. The FCC has decreased its regulation in the common carrier field in ways that parallel its marketplace approach in the broadcast area. While a detailed discussion of this issue is beyond the scope of this paper, some of the more noteworthy FCC decisions in this area are briefly mentioned.

In its *Second Computer Inquiry (Computer II)*, the Commission provided the conditions under which AT&T could engage in the competitive data processing business.[234] The FCC there decided to limit common carrier regulation to "basic transmission services," defined as the provision of pure transmission facilities indifferent to the information transmitted.[235] Any offering that is more than a basic transmission service is considered an "enhanced service" not subject to common carrier regulation.[236] The Commission also decided that all new customer premises equipment (CPE) would be offered on an unregulated basis after January 1, 1983.

The decision reflects the Commission's recognition that any new attempt to formulate regulatory distinctions between communications and data processing would be quickly outdated by technological advances, further blurring the already elusive boundary. The Commission identified several advantages in forbearing from regulation of enhanced services. First, it would be able to focus its regulatory efforts on the underlying basic services clearly covered by the Communications Act, and would be relieved of the time-consuming chore of ad hoc determinations to distinguish enhanced services which may arise from future techno logical advances. Second, it would provide maximum flexibility to service vendors in structuring their enhanced offerings to meet individualized customer needs without fear of overstepping some arbitrary boundary delineating the regulated from the unregulated. Third, consumers would benefit from the additional economies of scale that would be likely to result from the greater use of the basic telecommunications network.[237]

Other than almost complete deregulation of customer premises equipment, the basic interexchange telecommunications business is still regulated, especially as it applies to AT&T. Moreover, the FCC has to contend with the effect of the ruling of Federal District Judge Harold Greene, under whose auspices the restructuring of AT&T is proceeding, Congress also continues to make waves in this area. The 50 state utility regulatory commissions continue to hold a tight rein over the local exchange telephone companies. It may take years, if it happens at all, to evaluate the ultimate ability of AT&T, the local telephone companies, and other common carriers such as MCI and Western Union, to compete in the video and data-carriage markets with cable and Title III regulated entities.[238]

In another decision, the FCC concluded that it has the authority to forbear from regulating common carrier services under appropriate circumstances.[239] In particular, Title II regulatory requirements may be waived "where [the FCC] determine[s] that the cost of such regulation outweigh[s] any perceivable benefits."[240] Initially, this authority will be exercised to eliminate section 214[241] and tariff requirements with respect to certain "pure resellers" (i.e., carriers that do not own any transmission facilities). This action represents a limited first step toward deregulation that is probably intended to serve as a court test for the FCC's newly asserted discretion to forbear from regulating common carriers under the Communications Act.

Technical Standards.   The FCC's actions with respect to technical standards reflect a belief that the marketplace, not the government, should determine which technical system will prevail. With respect to new communications services, the Commission has opted merely to establish minimum performance standards. In the case of existing services, the FCC has undertaken to examine the continued validity of various technical standards, proposing in some cases to retain these standards only as voluntary guidelines.[242]

After a half-decade of deliberations, the FCC decided to allow the marketplace to determine the AM stereo system or systems best suited for United States broadcasting.[243] Faced with five competing systems proposed by five different manufacturers, the Commission elected simply to set minimum performance standards that all five systems would be capable of meeting.[244]

In pursuing its "marketplace" approach, the FCC wrote that its failure to select a system could mean that no system would be adopted widely enough to sustain AM stereo in the market.[245] The Commission, however, viewed this outcome as preferable to one in which the government, by endorsing a particular technical system, guarantees its success.[246] Governmental interference with normal market development, in the Commission's view, could only be justified by extraordinary circumstances. The Commission observed:

> A very strong case would have to be made in order to over ride the inherent benefits of consumers making their own choices rather than having their decisions made by government . . . . Our society generally has not seen fit to supplant the free decisions of consumers with those imposed by government, and there is no convincing reason why AM radio represents a special case.[247]

The Commission employed a similar "open marketplace" approach in the DBS proceeding. It declined to impose technical standards upon DBS systems since, in its view, such standards could stifle development of the new service.[248] A flexible approach was perceived as the best way to permit DBS operators to respond to advances in technology, and to encourage the introduction of new services.[249]

In authorizing broadcast teletext, the Commission similarly concluded that the choice of a technical system should be left to the discretion of individual licensees.[250] The Commission pointed out that an open market approach would allow licensees the freedom of choice necessary to operate teletext services tailored to their own specific situations and to respond to changes in demand and technical options.[251] The open market approach, in its view, would best provide a mechanism for resolving the trade-offs among system features and prices that are extremely difficult for regulatory decision makers to resolve. Additionally, the Commission believed that its approach would hasten introduction of the service, by avoiding years of delay while the agency attempted to specify standards for a single system.[252]

A marketplace approach was also adopted in the Commission's pro ceeding to authorize multichannel television sound (popularly referred to as "TV stereo").[253] Consistent with its AM stereo, DBS, and teletext decisions, the Commission declined to select a single technical system, opting instead to "allow the processes of change and development associated with both user preference and technology to evolve unen cumbered by the costs and delays associated with changing government regulations."[254] In addition, the Commission proposed to govern TV aural subcarrier use only by the technical rules necessary to ensure integrity of service and to preclude interference to other licensees.

Unlike AM stereo, the TV stereo proceeding was marked by general industry agreement. Industry representatives, through the Multichannel Sound Subcommittee of the Electronic Industries Association, presented the FCC with a specific proposal for adoption of a single technical system, known as the Broadcast Television Systems Committee (BTSC) system. The Commission sought to reconcile the investments of television receiver owners who purchase units designed for BTSC reception with the opportunity for marketplace advances in technology. It did so by insuring that receivers designed for the BTSC system will not respond to non-BTSC signals.[255]

In another development affecting technical standards, the Commission instituted a proceeding in April 1983 with the view to eliminating many of its technical rules and policies.[256] The FCC proposed the deletion of all transmission system requirements for AM, FM, and television stations and began an inquiry into the continued useful ness of minimum quality or performance standards for equipment and services, equipment interoperability requirements, interference control regulations, and spectrum efficiency rules.

Section 624(e) of the 1984 Cable Communications Policy Act confirms the jurisdiction of the FCC to establish technical standards relating to the facilities and equipment of cable systems that are required by a franchising authority. While the FCC has proposed to delete regulation of the technical quality standards for carriage of broadcast signals by cable systems, it intends to retain those standards as simply unenforce able guidelines in order to preempt state regulation.

Ownership Rules And Policies.   The Commission's ownership rules and policies have been directed toward insuring diversification of control over local mass communications media as a means of promoting ideological and economic diversity.[257] By 1985 the Commission had undertaken at least seven significant revisions of its ownership rules and policies under the marketplace rationale.

For one, the Commission deleted the "trafficking" rule in 1982, which, in effect, required that broadcast licenses be held for at least 3 years before an assignment or transfer of stock control could be consummated.[258] The Commission concluded that, in the present competitive environment, the public interest would be best served by allowing marketplace forces to regulate station sales.[259] Under the new approach, broadcast licensees who obtain their licenses through means other than the comparative hearing process are no longer required to hold their licenses for a particular period before those licenses can be sold for a profit.[260]

The FCC's decision, characterized by Chairman Fowler as "a true blockbuster in the unregulation process,"[261] marks a significant step forward in the Commission's overall policy of increased reliance on marketplace forces rather than restrictive regulation to achieve its public interest objectives.[262] Consistent with Chairman Fowler's view, the Commission's "trafficking" decision finds profit and public service to be compatible.

Responding to the concern that "a licensee who acquired a station with a primary interest in imminent resale would work to increase the station's resale value rather than making a meaningful effort to provide programming in the public interest,"[263] the Commission observed that marketplace forces would mitigate against such a result. "In broadcasting, like any other business, important services can be performed by people who trade broadcast properties, rehabilitate ailing stations with new capital and ideas or relieve unwilling licensees of the responsibility of running a station they no longer want."[264]

A second change, adapted by the FCC effective in June 1984, was comprehensive revisions to its rules specifying the ownership interests in broadcast, cable television, and newspaper properties that will be considered in determining whether particular media transactions are consistent with its multiple and cross-ownership rules and policies.[265] The rule revisions greatly expand the opportunities for ownership by entities with existing media interests and thus narrow the scope of the Commission's multiple and cross-ownership rules and policies. Prompting the revisions was the Commission's recognition that "the industry and the investment community have evolved dramatically" and its belief that a relaxation of the benchmark "might serve the public interest by increasing investment in the industry and by promoting the entry of new participants, particularly minorities, by increasing the availability of start-up capital."[266]

A third change was the Commission's "Top-50" policy, which required those seeking to acquire a fourth TV station (either UHF or VHF) or third VHF station in the top 50 television markets to make a compelling public interest showing that the benefits of such ownership would "overcome the detriment with respect to the policy of diversifying the sources of mass media communications to the public."[267] In abolishing this policy, the Commission relied largely upon changes in the video marketplace that had lessened concentration levels.[268]

The Commission noted that the creation of new, competitive video outlets such as LPTV, and the existence of other multiple ownership rules, tend to foster diversity of program voices on the local and national levels.[269] Based on an analysis of economic concentration in the top-50 markets since 1968, the Commission found no trend toward increasing concentration.[270] To the contrary, the Commission determined that "the top fifty markets are the very markets with the greatest number of competing voices, so that each owner's expected share of that potential audience will be much less."[271]

Fourth, the Commission has carved out a limited exemption from the ban on cable telephone cross-ownership, for rural areas.[272] Now telephone companies may operate cable television systems in rural areas, defined as places with fewer than 2,500 inhabitants, a definition encompassing roughly 26.3% of the United States population.[273] Waivers of the rule are still required where a competing cable system is under construction or in existence.

In authorizing this limited entry by telephone companies, the Commission noted that competition would facilitate service to under served rural areas. This benefit, in the FCC's view, outweighed the need to protect the cable television service from competition.[274]

Congress, in enacting the Cable Communications Policy Act of 1984, codified the thrust of the FCC's rules governing cable/telephone company cross-ownership. The Act makes it unlawful for a telephone company to provide video programming to cable subscribers in its service area, but exempts telephone companies in "rural areas."[275] Unlike the FCC's rules described above, the Act provides that a telephone company need not apply for waiver.

A fifth substantive FCC policy revision, also in 1984, modified the so-called seven-station rule which prohibited a single person or entity from owning more than seven AM stations, seven FM stations, or seven TV stations, only five of which may be VHF.[276] The FCC opted for a gradual phase-out of these broadcast ownership restrictions, adopting a 6-year transitional limitation of 12 AM, 12 FM, and 12 TV (whether VHF or UHF) stations. As initially proposed by the FCC, the transitional limitation would expire at the end of 6 years, permitting unrestricted national ownership of broadcast stations, unless experience should show that continued FCC involvement is warranted to prevent undue concentration.

Following the FCC's action, several members of Congress requested that implementation of the rule changes, with respect to television stations, be suspended to permit review and reconsideration of the issues raised. Responding to this expression of strong Congressional interest, the FCC first stayed the effect of the decision insofar as it relates to television station ownership,[277] and then modified the rule to provide an ownership cap for television stations of a 25% aggregate national audience reach. The FCC also eliminated the 6-year phase-out, and provided for ownership of up to 14 broadcast stations in the same service, with an ownership ceiling of 30% national audience reach for television stations for minority group-controlled organizations.

In relaxing the national limits on the ownership of radio and television stations, the FCC emphasized that it was retaining its local "one-to-a-market" and duopoly restrictions, and that it would defer to the Department of Justice and/or the Federal Trade Commission for challenges to particular acquisitions.[278] The group ownership restrictions, in their final form, incorporate limits on the ownership of radio and/or television stations based upon a national economic concentration index measured in terms of various audience standards, (an approach strongly favored by Commissioner Mimi Dawson but initially opposed by the majority).[279] The FCC did reject two other options outlined in its 1983 Notice of Proposed Rulemaking, namely, proposals (a) to abolish all limits but adopt a limitation which would be applicable to local markets which are noncompetitive,[280] or (b) to allow a single entity to own the number of radio and television stations which are equivalent (in relation to present radio and television stations) to the 7-7-7 limits when adopted in 1953-1954.[281]

In modifying the seven-station rule, the Commission relied upon changes in the video marketplace since 1953, when the 7-7-7 rules were adopted. These marketplace changes, including growth in the broad casting industry and the emergence of new technologies, render the rules "obsolete," in the FCC's view.[282] Underlying the FCC's decision was the belief that media cross-ownership at the national level would not reduce the number of independently owned radio, TV, and cable outlets available to the consumer and could, in fact, foster viewpoint diversity by facilitating group ownership with the resultant economies of scale.[283]

Sixth, acting upon a Notice of Proposed Rulemaking and Inquiry adopted more than 10 years earlier, the Commission, in a 1982 decision, refused to adopt any rule limiting, nationally, the ownership of cable television systems.[284] The Commission there concluded that, "while the amount of concentration in the cable television industry is increasing, it is still not a concentrated industry."[285] It pointed to numerous studies and analyses which reached this conclusion, including the Network Inquiry Special Staff Report and a comprehensive study of cable ownership prepared by the Office of Plans and Policy.[286] The Commission also noted that it had reviewed a series of merger proposals involving firms in the cable television industry and ruled, in each instance, that the merger was in the public interest.[287]

The Commission also noted that national ownership limits could prevent certain efficiencies of scale. In this regard, it pointed to the conclusion of the OPP study that "substantial benefits may be derived from multiple system ownership and that, given the absence of a real threat from over-concentration, cable owners and subscribers should be permitted to realize these organizational benefits."[288]

Consistent with these studies and with the growth in the cable television and video markets, the Commission concluded that no national limitations on the ownership of cable television systems were warranted.

Finally, in April 1984, the FCC repealed the regional concentration-of-control rules,[289] which prohibited the acquisition of a broadcast facility where the result would be common ownership of three stations where any two are within 100 miles of the third and any of the three has primary service contour overlap with another.[290]

In proposing to eliminate the rules, the FCC again cited the significant changes in the telecommunications marketplace that have occurred, namely, the growth of both broadcast and nonbroadcast outlets.[291] As a result of these changes, the Commission stated, "the potential influence of any given combination of commonly owned outlets is diluted and our concern with the impact of such combinations on diversity and levels of competition declines accordingly."[292] The Commission ultimately concluded that marketplace developments and the continued applicability of local market (i.e., duopoly and one-to- a-market) rules have obviated the need for regional ownership restric tions as a means of ensuring diversity and economic competition. As further reason for repeal, the FCC also noted the administrative and opportunity costs of the regional ownership rules.

ANTITRUST LAW AS A REMEDY FOR MARKET FAILURE

The FCC's increasing reliance upon marketplace forces has been accompanied by a renewed emphasis upon antitrust law[293] as a means of ensuring that those forces remain unrestricted. Civil actions brought by the federal government and private parties[294] are perceived as a remedy for market failure. In addition, the Commission has shown a heightened interest in antitrust law, and in economic measures of concentration, as a source of guidance for its public interest determinations.

AT&T-Department Of Justice Consent Decree

On August 24, 1982, the United States District Court for the District of Columbia approved a settlement agreement in the Department of Justice's antitrust suit against AT&T and Western Electric Company.[295] In exchange for divestiture of the 22 Bell Operating Companies which provide local telephone services, AT&T was allowed to retain its manufacturing and research subsidiaries (Western Electric and Bell Laboratories) and to engage in certain business activities prohibited by the 1956 Consent Decree.

The 1956 Consent Decree restricted AT&T to the provision of regulated common carrier services. The settlement agreement, as originally proposed by AT&T and Justice, would have eliminated any line-of-business restraints on AT&T following divestiture of its operating companies. In approving the settlement, however, Judge Harold Greene imposed a number of restrictions on AT&T, including one with respect to provision of "electronic publishing services" transmitted over facilities owned by AT&T.

Based upon First Amendment concerns, the nascent nature of the industry, and AT&T's ability to delay time-sensitive transmissions of its competitors, Greene required a modification of the decree, barring AT&T from the provision of "electronic publishing over its own trans mission facilities" for at least 7 years.[296] Judge Greene defined electronic publishing as "the provision of any information which AT&T or its affiliates has, or has caused to be, originated, authorized, compiled, collected, or edited, or in which it has a direct or indirect financial or proprietary interest, and which is disseminated to an unaffiliated person through some electronic means."[297]

The modifications, however, would not preclude AT&T from offering electronic directory services that list general product and business categories, the service or product providers under these categories, and their names, telephone numbers, and addresses. Nor is AT&T prevented from providing the time, weather, and such other audio services, already offered as of the date of the entry of the decree, to the geographic areas of the country receiving those services as of that date.

National Association of Broadcasters-Department Of Justice Consent Decree

In 1982, the United States District Court for the District of Columbia ruled that the commercial advertising format restrictions in the Television Code of the National Association of Broadcasters (NAB) violated the antitrust laws by artificially enhancing the demand for commercial time.[298] The legality of the other code advertising restrictions was reserved for trial. An underlying issue in the litigation was the appropriate role to be played by broadcast industry self-regulation, government regulation, and the free play of market forces.

The Justice Department argued that the competition resulting from elimination of the Code provisions would operate to prevent excessive commercialization, as would the "emergence of new technologies (e.g., satellites) and the proliferation of new entertainment sources (e.g., cable, video tape)."[299] The court did not speculate on the accuracy of this prediction, but said the commercial restrictions were inconsis- tent with the basic Sherman Act policy favoring "free and fair competition."[300]

Judge Harold Greene approved a proposed consent decree between the NAB and Justice on November 23, 1982.[301] In exchange for the government's promise not to object to the dismissal of Judge Greene's March 3, 1982 order, the NAB agreed to stop disseminating or enforcing any rule governing the quantity, placement, or format of nonprogram material.

Networks-Department Of Justice Consent Decree

The three national commercial television networks — ABC, CBS and NBC — are subject to consent decrees terminating the government antitrust suits that were first instituted in 1972.[302] The Department of Justice alleged in the suits that the networks, by refusing to exhibit programs they did not produce, or in which they did not have a monetary interest, had abused their power to control the access of program producers and advertisers to commercial television audiences.

Each of the decrees provides for restrictions on the networks that generally parallel (but sometimes exceed) those imposed by the syndication and financial interest rule.[303] The consent judgments limit the exhibition rights and interests in a program that each network may obtain from independent program suppliers. The judgments also limit each network's program production to 2½ hours per week in prime time hours, 8 hours per week in daytime hours, and 11 hours in fringe time. Although the FCC has instituted a proceeding which looks toward elimination of the financial interest and syndication rules,[304] FCC repeal of the rules would have little practical effect unless relevant provisions of the decrees are vacated or modified.[305]

Economic Models For Measuring Competition In the Marketplace

While the Commission technically does not enforce the antitrust laws, it takes cognizance of antitrust policies as an important part of its public interest calculus. The Commission has acknowledged its duty, for example, "to refuse licenses or renewals to any person who engages or proposes to engage in practices which will prevent either himself or other licensees or both from making the fullest use of radio facilities."[306] Although the Commission has the responsibility to reach its own conclusions as a matter of communications policy, it has increasingly turned to antitrust law models for guidance. Illustrative of this trend is the renewed interest in economic concentration indices as a means of measuring competition in the marketplace.

The interest in concentration indices is most apparent in recent Commission proceedings involving ownership restrictions. Commencing with the 1980 Network Inquiry Special Staff Report, the FCC has employed tools of antitrust policy and economic analysis in order to distinguish "patterns of ownership integration that threaten competition and diversity from those that will not harm these vital interests but, instead, may encourage a more efficient system of television net working."[307] In seeking to identify harmful conduct, the Network Inquiry Report used a traditional antitrust framework classifying ownership patterns as horizontal, vertical or conglomerate.[308] Using this approach, the staff recommended the elimination or substantial modification of several ownership rules, including the prohibition against network cable cross-ownership and the restriction on group ownership (the so-called seven station rules).

The theoretical approach recommended by the Network Inquiry Special Staff was utilized in the Commission's proceeding to delete the network-cable cross-ownership rule, which prohibits ownership by the three national broadcast networks of any cable television system.[309] In a 1982 Notice of Proposed Rulemaking, the Commission requested comments on a methodology for defining the product and geographic boundaries of the relevant market and specific techniques for measuring concentration in that market. The Commission indicated that "we do not expect to arrive at a simple 'magic' number but may wish to employ several measures and/or a zone within which proposed combinations may be scrutinized rather than a strict 'cutoff' point."[310]

Commissioner Mimi Weyforth Dawson suggested that the public and the Commission focus on the larger question of the need for a sophisticated measure of concentration in the expanding video marketplace as a whole, with particular attention paid to the extent of concentration in communications properties that any one entity, or group of entities, may accumulate before public interest concerns are raised. In her view, "such an approach of adopting a 'safety net' is essential to ensure a procompetitive transition to a deregulatory marketplace."[311]

In response to the request of FCC Commissioners for an analysis of appropriate measures of concentration in the relevant markets, the Office of Plans and Policy (OPP) prepared a staff report entitled *Measurement of Concentration in Home Video Markets*.[312] The report examines techniques for measuring concentration and market definition issues and recommends procedures the Commission could follow to develop a "media concentration index" as part of a program for monitoring ownership. Although the staff report recommends an expansive definition of product and geographic markets, including video discs and cassettes as well as the audio and print media, it makes sample calculations based on four "core" media in a video delivery market—broadcast television, STV, MDS, and cable.[313]

The OPP Study found that the video market, even if limited in definition to the four core media, is extraordinarily unconcentrated.[314] It concluded, therefore, that no rigid national ownership rules are appropriate.[315] The OPP Study recommends, however, that mergers and acquisitions in non-competitive local markets be scrutinized, by means of the Justice Department's Herfindahl-Hirschman Index, to determine the effect upon concentration.[316]

In proposing to abolish the 7-7-7 rules, the Commission again called for a definition of the relevant marketplace and for a uniform measure of concentration in that marketplace.[317] The Commission used the Herfindahl-Hirschman Index and the market share approach—two measures of market concentration applied by the Justice Department to ensure that mergers do not violate the Clayton Act—in order to demonstrate that the broadcast industry is extremely unconcentrated.[318]

On reconsideration of its decision to adopt a transitional ownership cap of 12 AM, 12 FM, and 12 television broadcast stations per owner, the FCC stated that it had become increasingly aware of the limitations of proceeding solely with a numerical multiple ownership limit in the event that there was a rapid expansion of group ownership in the wake of its decision to relax the 7-7-7 rule.[319] The Commission also acknowledged that a numerical approach may not give appropriate consideration to wide discrepancies in population coverage, because a station in the largest market is deemed equivalent to a station in the smallest market for purposes of ownership regulation.[320] While recognizing that the concept of audience reach is an untested regulatory mechanism as applied to multiple ownership regulation, the FCC concluded that retaining the numerical limit would provide the Commission with an opportunity to gain experience with this type of regulation without risking an entire regulatory system should it find that the audience reach approach proves unworkable.[321]

As the OPP Study and the 7-7-7 proceeding reflect, the Commission has relied increasingly on the Herfindahl-Hirschman Index to identify anticompetitive behavior. In seeking to redefine the interests taken into account under the multiple ownership rules, for example, the Commission indicated that the rule should be tailored to avoid inhibition of "the most efficient combination of video distribution resources by erecting ownership standards which proscribe combinations that would not be suspect under the Justice Department's recently revised antitrust and merger guidelines."[322] Similarly, the Commission's proposal to delete the network cable cross-ownership rule was based largely on the desire to eliminate restrictions that could interfere with the formation of more efficient business arrangements. As the Commission noted in proposing to modify the Syndication and Financial Interest Rule, the Communications Act requires that the Commission's regulations "not impose undue costs or unreasonably interfere with the efficient conduct of business."[323]

COPYRIGHT LAW

A fundamental problem of copyright law, like communications law, has been to keep pace with technological change. Each new use for broadcast programs—cable transmission, distribution by DBS, MDS, STV, or video-taping—raises new problems of defining property rights. While the complex area of copyright law cannot be fully discussed in the context of this paper, it must be noted as an additional factor which influences the video marketplace and the course of FCC regulation.[324]

Of particular importance, both the FCC and the courts have been reluctant to make the choice between two communications policies grounded in the Constitution—encouraging the free flow of information and protecting intellectual property rights— without express Congressional direction. Reflecting this reluctance, the FCC and the courts have declined to impose onerous and potentially crippling copyright restrictions upon the emerging cable television and videotaping industries.

With respect to cable television, the Supreme Court held in the *Fortnightly*[325] and the *Teleprompter*[326] cases that transmission of distant signals by cable systems has no copyright significance since, in the Court's view, a cable system is a passive intermediary that "simply carr[ies], without editing whatever programs [it] receive[s]."[327] As a result, cable systems were free to retransmit broadcast programming without any copyright liability. While the Commission had, at various times during the late 1960s and early 1970s, considered action directed to protection of property rights in broadcast programming, it also deferred to Congress.[328] To resolve the conflict between traditional copyright law principles and the emergence of a viable cable industry, Congress amended the Copyright Act in 1976 to create a compulsory license scheme under which cable television systems are permitted to retransmit broadcast programs in return for payment of royalty fees based upon the number of distant television broadcast signals transmitted.[329] The 1976 Act also created the Copyright Royalty Tribunal to adjust the rates cable systems pay and to determine how the royalty fees should be distributed.[330]

Reflecting a similarly narrow construction of the Copyright Act, the Second Circuit held, in October 1982, that retransmission of the New York Mets baseball games by Eastern Microwave, Inc., a resale carrier which distributes the signal of television station WOR-TV, New York, New York, to more than 600 cable systems via microwave and satellite net works, was exempt from the copyright laws under the "passive carrier" exemption.[331] That exemption applies to those carriers which have "no direct or indirect control over the content or selection of the primary transmission or over the particular recipients of the secondary trans mission, and whose activities with respect to the secondary transmission consist solely of providing wires, cables, or other communications channels for the use of others."[332]

The Seventh Circuit has shown a reluctance, however, to apply the passive carrier exemption to inhibit the growth of a new technology. In 1982, it held that teletext services transmitted over the television vertical blanking interval are entitled to copyright protection as part of the station's main signal.[333] Chicago superstation WGN had brought suit for copyright infringement against United Video, a telecommuni cations common carrier, based upon United Video's deletion of WGN's teletext service and substitution of Dow Jones' teletext service in its place. In the court's view, United Video was not entitled to exemption from copyright liability as a passive carrier since it altered the copyrighted work by deleting the teletext service. Although the court held that WGN's copyright for its news program included the teletext transmission, it suggested that a contrary conclusion might be reached where the teletext was unrelated to the main program and was not intended to be viewed with, and as an integral part of, that program.[334]

In another copyright case involving the new technologies, *Sony Corporation of America v. Universal City Studios*, the Supreme Court held that off-the-air taping of audio visual materials by owners of VCRs, in their homes, for private, noncommercial use does not constitute copy right infringement and, therefore, that the sale of VCRs to the general public is consistent with the Copyright Act.[335] Emphasizing that "sound policy, as well as history, supports our consistent deference to Congress" and that "Congress has the constitutional authority and the institutional ability to accommodate fully the varied permutations of competing interests that are inevitably implicated by such new technology,"[336] the Court was clearly reluctant to expand the protections afforded by the Copyright Act without explicit legislative guidance.

Reversing the Ninth Circuit and affirming the district court, the Supreme Court held that home "time-shifting" (recording a broadcast for later playback) is a fair use under the Copyright Act. It concluded that time-shifting for private home use is a noncommercial, nonprofit activity,[337] and that time-shifting merely enables viewers to see a televised work which they had been invited to witness in its entirety free of charge.[338] The Court also pointed out that substantial numbers of copyright holders who license their works for broadcast on free television would not object to having their broadcasts time-shifted by private viewers.[339] The copyright holders, in the Court's view, failed to demonstrate that time-shifting would cause any likelihood of non- minimal harm to the potential market for, or the value of, their copyrighted works.[340]

As the foregoing cases illustrate, the courts and the FCC hesitate to impose copyright burdens upon new technologies such as cable, tele text, and home videotaping. Not only does that hesitation reflect the practical difficulty of finding activities that have become widespread (as in the case of private satellite dishes[341] and videotaping) to be illegal, but it also reflects the fact that the courts and the FCC lack the tools to fashion compensatory schemes. As Justice Stevens commented in the *Sony* case, "It may well be that Congress will take a fresh look at this technology, just as it so often has examined other innovations in the past. But it is not our job to apply laws that have not yet been written."[342] That task lies with Congress, which could decide, for example, to impose a surcharge on the sale of blank tapes to compensate copyright holders, just as it adopted a compulsory license scheme for cable systems. In enacting the Cable Communications Policy Act of 1984, Congress included a provision which makes clear that unauthorized interception and use of encrypted or "scrambled" satellite signals is illegal, whether by individuals in their homes or by commercial enterprises.[343] A specific limited exemption was adopted under which individual satellite dish owners are authorized to receive *unscrambled* satellite-delivered services. Such reception of cable programming delivered by satellite is legal as long as no marketing mechanism has been established by the programmer to make a program service available to backyard dish owners and that the signal is not used for commercial resale.[344]

FEDERAL PREEMPTION

The FCC's Mass Media Bureau Chief James McKinney has warned: "As we move to deregulate at the federal level, we cannot ignore what is happening at the local and state levels. Mini-FCCs, disguised as public utility commissions, cable franchising authorities and public health and radiation authorities are now ready and willing, and some are even able, to fill any vacuum created by FCC unregulation."[345] Congress and the Commission recently have acted to insure that state or local regulators do not interfere with the implementation of national telecommunications policies.

One observer characterized the most important accomplishment of the Cable Communications Act of 1984 as ending an era where conflicting state and local laws in many areas could jeopardize the growth of cable and its ability to compete against other video technologies.[346] The Act reflects the use of preemption as a means of achieving deregulation, a strategy which is particularly effective with a locally regulated medium such as cable.[347] The Act eliminates local rate regulation except in areas where cable is found by the FCC to be "subject to effective competition."[348] Significant restrictions are placed on the ability of local governments to exercise editorial control over the content of programming on cable channels.[349] In some respects, however, the Act confirms and even expands the powers of local authorities. Most significant in this regard is the requirement that every cable operator obtain an authorization to operate from a local or state government;[350] states and cities also retain authority to regulate cable consistent with the Act.[351]

Paralleling these Congressional efforts, the FCC has also sought to prevent state and local governments from imposing burdensome require ments upon the new technologies. For example, the Commission pre-empted an order of the Nevada Public Service Commission which would have instituted rate regulation for "all cable television service provided other than pay channel services."[352] Community Cable TV, Inc., operator of a cable television system serving Las Vegas, Nevada, had filed a "Petition for Special Relief Requesting Declaratory Ruling" as to this state action. In its ruling, the Commission made clear that the proposed Nevada Order would be inconsistent with the federal objective of unregulated availability and pricing of nonbroadcast services.[353] Indeed, the Commission expressed concern that the Nevada Order would inhibit the flexibility of system operators and nonbroadcast programming entrepreneurs to experiment with types of program offerings and methods to pay for such programs.[354] Federal preemption, in the Commission's view, is necessary to prevent artificial and unnecessary skewing of the market by nonfederal regulation of price and entry. "It is in the public interest for entrepreneurs and firms engaged in dynamic industries, such as video programming for cable television, to enjoy maximum flexibility in their responses to innovations and developments within the industry."[355]

The Commission sent a similar message to the State of New Jersey, which had sought to exercise jurisdiction under its Cable Television Act over SMATV systems by enjoining operation of an SMATV facility until it obtained a certificate of approval from the State.[356] The Commission upheld its authority to preempt state regulation which interferes with the reception of satellite-transmitted signals. Emphasizing the federal interest in the interstate transmission of satellite signals, the Commission made clear that "State or local government regulatory control over, or interference with, a federally licensed or authorized interstate communications service, intentionally or incidentally resulting in the suppression of that service in order to advance a service favored by the state, is neither consistent with the Commission's goal of developing a nationwide scheme of telecommuni cations nor with the Supremacy Clause of the Constitution."[357] The Com-mission held that the interposition of prior approval requirements at the state or local level interferes with the development of a more rapid and efficient telecommunications marketplace.[358]

The Commission had before it in 1984 a "Petition for Declaratory Ruling," filed by Cox Cable Communications, Inc. ("CCCI"), which also illustrates the type of issue that pits federal preemption against local or state government jurisdictional claims in the introduction of new communications services.[359] CCCI, a multiple cable system operator, developed two inter-active cable services: "Commline," an institutional cable service which provides a high-capacity business and institutional communications service for dedicated private line data, nonswitched voice, and video communications; and INDAX, a residential subscriber service which permits a variety of transactional and information retrieval services to be conducted from the home. The Nebraska Public Service Commission invoked jurisdiction over Commline and Index, ordering the cable operator to cease and desist until the state commission issued a certificate of public convenience and necessity. CCCI has now asked the FCC for a declaratory ruling that "state regulation which impedes the development and use of institutional cable for interactive services on a noncommon carrier basis frustrates and interferes with Federal policies as enunciated and administered under the Act by this Commission, and is federally preempted."[360]

Under the standards laid down by the courts, the potential scope of FCC preemptive action seems boundless in light of the interrelationship of virtually all matters affecting the furnishing of interstate and intrastate communications service.[361] While the FCC has not attempted to preempt the full range of regulation, it has opportunities to expand its preemptive jurisdiction as long as it carefully establishes a plausible case that preemptive action is necessary for the implemen tation of Congressional objectives.[362]

III. FINDINGS: WINNERS AND LOSERS IN MARKETPLACE REGULATION

The video marketplace is currently undergoing a period of rapid change and expansion. Due to technological developments and regulatory change, new media technologies supplement, complement, or compete with conventional broadcast television to offer entertainment and information to the home. Some stakeholders will benefit, and others will not fare as well, as a result of changes in technology and regulation.

The FCC finds itself at a transition point where, as Justice Holmes said, "the law is behind the times." In seeking to respond to these marketplace changes, the FCC has faced a variety of new questions of control and access, of regulation and classification. While a new, coherent regulatory structure has not yet emerged to replace the FCC's traditional regulatory policies, a number of distinct trends are emerging, with implications for new and old players.

EROSION OF TRADITIONAL REGULATORY CLASSIFICATIONS

Substantial inroads have been made, for example, in the traditional regulatory classifications. Utilizing a hybrid approach, the Commission has exempted new video services such as teletext, and DBS, from many of the broadcast ownership and content regulations. With respect to video services such as LPTV and STV, the FCC has adopted a policy of forbearance whereby these services are exempted from complying with various Commission program restrictions. To a great extent, however, the FCC has shown a reluctance to depart from the traditional regulatory classifications and seems to be motivated largely by a reluctance to encumber new technologies with onerous broadcast regulation. Thus, MDS continues to be regulated as a common carrier service despite its functional equivalence to STV. Similarly, DBS and satellite programmers are unencumbered by broadcast regulation, despite the resemblance to their terrestrial counterparts. The Commission has indicated, however, that it intends to initiate a rulemaking for the purpose of adopting a more uniform regulatory approach to such "hybrid" services.[363] The outcome of such a proceeding would directly impact on the competition among players in the video marketplace since the classification of a service determines the level of regulatory restrictions.

In *NAB v. FCC*, the DBS appeal, the D. C. Circuit suggested that there may be limits on the FCC's exemption of the new technologies from broadcast regulation when it classifies those technologies as hybrid. The decision thus raises questions, which the FCC must answer, about the classification of MDS, OFS, ITFS, DBS, and teletext. The court's decision represents the first judicial test of the FCC's classification of the new video technologies. That decision, at the least, makes clear that the FCC must define the new technologies as broadcasting to the extent that radio communications are disseminated with the intent that they be received by the public, rather than by a narrow class of sub scribers.[364] While the court's holding appears to presage a more coherent approach to regulatory classification by the FCC,[365] it also introduces a new "wild card." The decision is the first time that a customer of a common carrier has been deemed subject to contact regulation.

SPECTRUM ALLOCATION UNDER A MARKETABLE APPROACH

The erosion of the traditional regulatory classifications has been accompanied by changes in spectrum allocation policies. Whereas spectrum allocation had been achieved by defining the permissible uses and users of particular frequencies, the disintegration of a one-to-one relationship between the medium and the use has rendered that approach unworkable. Over the next decade, using this spectrum allocation approach, the Commission appears set on a course to open up spectrum to new types of services and classes of users, by permitting licensees to determine the best use of their authorized channels.

The trend toward greater licensee autonomy is apparent in the FCC's increased willingness to permit licensees to select the method by which they will be regulated. In authorizing nonbroadcast uses of the tele vision VBI and FM subcarriers, for example, the FCC has moved away from the traditional service distinctions based upon spectrum allocation. In those instances, the broadcast licensee may be regulated as a common carrier or private radio licensee if it offers services in competition with those entities, enabling it essentially to self-select the manner in which it will be regulated. By permitting licensees to share their excess spectrum capacity—in the ITFS and broadcast auxiliary service — the Commission has also shown a willingness to let individual licensees determine the best use of spectrum.

The FCC appears to be moving toward a greater emphasis on electro magnetic compatibility, rather than the type of regulatory use, as the basis for allocation. Illustrating this approach, the Commission has, for example, proposed to reallocate frequencies for shared use by private fixed service users, common carriers, and cable systems, enabling electronically compatible but diverse spectrum users to coexist.[366] Another illustration is the decentralized radio service, proposed in an FCC staff report, in which entities would be allowed to decide on their own initiative, and in response to their own best judgments, the types of communications offered on their authorized channels.[367]

This approach is premised on the view stated in an FCC staff report that decisions rooted in private perceptions of market value will achieve a more economically efficient and socially desirable use of frequency spectrum than government decisions.[368] If carried to its logical extreme, this approach would allow natural economic forces to perform the Commission's current allocation and interference control functions, replacing regulatory or service distinctions. Licensees would be able to use their channels for whatever purpose they want consistent with their frequency rights and international and United States laws.[369]

LICENSING OF THE NEW TECHNOLOGIES

Not only has the Commission increasingly permitted the marketplace to determine *how* frequencies are used, but it has also begun to implement a marketplace solution for determining who uses frequencies. It has, for example, moved away from its comparative licensing policies which seek to find the best qualified licensee, relying instead on lotteries for selecting among applicants in such services as LPTV and MDS.[370] While relying heavily on the premise that lottery procedures will permit the prompt establishment of new and valuable communications services, the Commission has invoked its new Congressional authorization to abandon the comparative criteria (for example, minority ownership, diversification of media ownership, technical superiority) that have developed over the last 50 years.[371] Although lottery procedures may expedite the introduction of service, as well as encourage new entities to enter the field, that approach also results in the filing of skeletal applications and, as evidenced by multi-channel MDS and LPTV, vast numbers of applications.

Other possible methods of deciding who uses the spectrum under a free market approach include auctions and spectrum fees.[372] Proponents of auctions contend that, by making spectrum available to the highest bidder, auctions would substitute decisions of the market for those of a regulatory agency, with the market determining the price for a given channel and its highest use.[373] Spectrum fees could duplicate the results of a competitive market, but would require Congress (or the FCC) to take into account all relevant information, such as class of license, location, bandwidth, and area of coverage, in order to set a "fair market value" for the spectrum.[374] To date, however, the Commission's legal authority to utilize auctions or spectrum fees remains in doubt.[375]

BROADCAST REGULATION

While the Commission has exempted the new technologies from strict broadcast regulation, it has also taken steps to ease the restrictions on conventional broadcast stations under the rationale that the marketplace will achieve the regulatory objectives underlying those restrictions without government intervention. Reflecting its view that the radio-television market is workably competitive, the Commission has eliminated formal ascertainment requirements, minimum program percent ages, commercialization guidelines, and program logs for radio and commercial television stations.[376] In the ownership area, the regional concentration rules have been repealed and the group ownership restrictions have been significantly relaxed. Steps have also been taken to lift cross-ownership restrictions.[377] While Chairman Fowler has stated that he will not propose further ownership rule revisions, other Commissioners believe that there is still room for more sweeping deregulation of television consistent with the Communications Act.

FIRST AMENDMENT RIGHTS OF BROADCASTERS

The telecommunications changes spawned by cable and other technologies have also spurred a reexamination of the merits of content regulation of programming carried by broadcast stations. Content regulation in the broadcast area has traditionally focused upon nonentertainment and public affairs programming, and upon the licensee's responsiveness to community needs and interests.[378] Under a marketplace approach, market forces, not government prescriptions, determine the appropriate mix of programming. Consistent with this approach, the Commission has shown renewed sensitivity to program-related regulations that touch upon First Amendment concerns by limiting the licensee's editorial discretion.[379]

There have also been efforts to repeal portions of the Communi cations Act which are perceived as interfering with the First Amendment rights of broadcasters to make editorial judgments.[380] These statutory provisions include sections 312 and 315, which impose "reasonable access" obligations and "equal opportunities" requirements upon broad casters in their dealings with political candidates.[381] Also targeted by the Commission are those sections of the Criminal Code prohibiting the broadcast of obscenity and lottery information.[382] In calling for First Amendment parity for the electronic media by eliminating the fairness doctrine, which requires licensees to present contrasting viewpoints on controversial issues of public importance,[383] the Commission stated:

> The "Fairness Doctrine" is a significant government intrusion on the First Amendment rights of broadcasters. The traditional spectrum scarcity argument which has provided the basis of the Doctrine has become increasingly less valid as new technologies proliferate and the number of broadcast facilities increases, particularly as compared with the print media. Consequently, there is no longer any justification for imposing these obligations on broadcasters when it would be unconstitutional to do so on the print media.[384]

Consistent with this view, Senator Robert Packwood has proposed statutory reform for the electronic media to bring their First Amendment rights more in line with those accorded print and speech communication.[385] While the fate of such legislation is uncertain, the Supreme Court's July 1984 *League of Women Voters* decision has given the FCC added impetus to repeal or modify of the Fairness Doctrine.[386]

ENDING THE FCC'S "TRAFFIC COP" ROLE

In the area of technical standards, the Commission is also moving toward greater reliance on the marketplace. Marketplace forces may in some instances be substituted for technical regulations, effectively ending the

Commission's "traffic cop" function. Such technical deregulation could potentially eliminate transmission performance standards, allow any type of innovative transmission system to begin broadcasting without prior Commission approval, and allow for the existence of multiple, incompatible transmission systems.[387] The Commission took a novel step in this direction in August 1982 when it established a "spectrum bubble" for certain land mobile radio licensees.[388] The licensees are permitted to follow any technical standard they want within their assigned frequencies so long as they do not interfere with reception on other channels. By decontrolling technical standards in this way, the FCC expressed a desire to give manufacturers of transmission equipment a greater incentive to innovate.

ECONOMIC, SOCIAL, REGULATORY CONSEQUENCES

Among the consequences of a marketplace approach is increased competition. Some of the rules and policies deleted by the FCC under Chairman Fowler have resulted, either directly or indirectly, in protecting existing services from competition. For example, while the FCC's cable policies in the 1960s were based on a desire to protect conventional television from destructive competition, the FCC today is less likely to restrict a new service on the grounds of harm to existing broadcasters. The Commission has said, in this regard, that it will consider the economic effect of a new service only if there is "strong evidence that a *significant* net reduction in service will result."[389] This means that broadcasters, and existing services such as cable television, are less able to obtain regulatory protection from competition from the new technologies. Alternatively, some of the new technologies may not survive in this competitive environment, making the heralded abundance of video outlets just so much hype.[390]

Another likelihood of a marketplace approach is that authorization of new services will interfere with other publicly beneficial services, as in the case of the existing terrestrial users of the 12 GHz band who will be displaced by DBS service, forcing the FCC to make difficult choices about future spectrum needs.[391]

A marketplace approach can entail a certain degree of uncertainty, as the area of technical standards illustrates. Widespread use of AM stereo, for example, has been indefinitely delayed because of market place uncertainties and manufacturers and broadcasters' difficulties in reaching a consensus due to antitrust law concerns.[392] It now appears that consumers may not get the opportunity the FCC has in mind for them, namely, of "voting" with their dollars for the best system. Similar problems have delayed implementation of teletext.[393] The Commission's accommodation of an industry-recommended standard for multichannel television sound, however, signals a partial retreat from the pure marketplace approach espoused in the AM stereo proceeding, and reflects a recognition that the market may require FCC-selected standards to protect customers.[394]

Carried to its logical extreme, a marketplace approach could lead to the withdrawal of regulatory involvement or termination of regulatory programs designed to fulfill social objectives.[395] One result might be the elimination of Commission policies requiring broadcasters to air children's and public affairs programs which would not otherwise be justified by the marketplace.[396] Other Commission policies designed to implement social objectives, such as equal employment opportunity, could fall by the wayside under the pure marketplace approach. Also, if the FCC were to embrace Chairman Fowler's characterization of television as "just another appliance – it's a toaster with pictures,"[397] it would make little sense for the Commission to be concerned about the qualifi cations or character of licensees.[398]

Implementation of a marketplace approach could potentially expand the role of the states in telecommunications matters. For example, to the extent that broadcasters are permitted to use their frequencies for common carrier purposes, regulation by state regulatory commissions may become a factor.[399] However, the FCC has been careful to indicate to the states that deregulation at the federal level does not constitute an invitation for state regulations, and that the decision not to regulate can establish a preemptive national policy as well as can a detailed regulatory scheme.

While the FCC has been unwilling to abdicate authority over communications matters to the states, it has increasingly deferred these questions to the expertise of other federal agencies, particularly those charged with enforcement of the antitrust laws[400] and deceptive trade practice regulations. Indeed, to the extent that other agencies, such as the FTC and the Justice Department, are empowered to scrutinize the business practices of communications entities, the FCC has found a justification for eliminating duplicative FCC review.

On the one hand, as the FCC strips away regulatory accretions, seeking to impose only those requirements mandated by the Communications Act, pressure from some stakeholders will mount on Congress to pursue further deregulation through statutory reform. As the Court of Appeals suggested in the radio deregulation decision, Congress and not the "unrepresentative bureaucracy and judiciary" may be the ultimate source of deregulation over the next decade.[401] On the other hand, other players may find they were better off in a stable regulated environment and seek Congressional relief.

Moreover, a shift in the political philosophy of the Executive Branch could relatively quickly lead to a slowdown or even reversal in FCC policy.

CONCLUSION

The regulatory issues posed by classification of new video services, similar to other questions involving structure and technical standards for players in the new video marketplace, are not abstractions of interest primarily to a small coterie of communications lawyers, consulting engineers, and FCC staff members. Underlying these issues are battles between the holders of vested interests who wish to preserve (and, indeed, expand) their turf and the new players who see technology as opening up new avenues for their own entry into telecommunications businesses. Battles over spectrum have important economic results for the stakeholders, and there will be as yet unpredictable winners and losers.

One observer described the battle over spectrum allocation as "beginning to look less like a regulatory process and more like the range wars a century ago between cattlemen and sheep ranchers"− "already, the competition for the ungrazed piece of electronic pasture has become a multi-million dollar business for Washington consultants and lobbyists who want to persuade the FCC or Congress to open new frequencies or oust other users from old ones."[402] The turf battles are being fought in a variety of forums, from the FCC to Congress, from courts to state legislatures.

While the FCC has been recognized as "one of the foremost advocates of across-the-board deregulation for the entire broadcast industry,"[403] it has not, to date, successfully formulated a coherent regulatory framework that responds to the significant technical and industry changes that have occurred. As the House Subcommittee on Telecommuni cations, Consumer Protection and Finance suggested in a 1981 Report, "Deregulation is not an end in or of itself."[404] The challenge of policymakers over the rest of the decade is to minimize regulatory "jet lag" by developing a regulatory structure that accommodates the new and emerging technologies and the interests of conflicting stakeholders, consistent with the Communications Act and marketplace principles. Policymakers must not only weigh the needs of different spectrum users, but also accommodate the desire of players with existing markets for stability and restrictive rules on entry. Commenting on the random and incoherent national policy governing the new communications media, one observer has asserted that the resulting unsettled state of affairs, and the tensions to which it gives rise, are bound to affect adversely the long-term financial and market prospects of the various posttelephone, postbroadcasting technologies of information distribution.[405] Of course, one person's adverse effects are others' opportunities.

APPENDIX: A PRIMER ON THE VIDEO MARKETPLACE
OVER-THE-AIR VIDEO SERVICES TO THE HOME

Low Power Television (LPTV)

In 1982, the FCC established the first new broadcast service in 20 years. The service, known as low power television (LPTV), utilizes vacant ultra-high frequency (UHF) and very-high frequency (VHF) channels, and operates at power levels of 10 to 1,000 watts, significantly below those of full-service television stations. When fully developed, low power television could provide up to 4,000 additional video outlets across the country. Indicating interest in the new service, some 23,000 applications were pending at the FCC as of December 1984.

The limited coverage area of low power television stations (typically no more than 25–30 miles), and the relatively low start-up cost (in comparison to conventional television stations), was expected to encourage programming directed to specialized audiences. A sampling of the pending applications for low power television licenses reveals a wide diversity of proposals for religious, public affairs, sports, news, and educational programming in addition to programming for Blacks, Hispanics, other minority groups, and women. (It remains to be seen, however, if such programming will be financially viable.) [By 1987, relatively little of LPTV's potential had been developed – ed.] Other specialized programming proposals include a consumer-oriented network backed by Ralph Nader; a system of low power stations featuring programming with country-western and rural American themes proposed by Neighborhood Television, a Sears Roebuck affiliate; and a children's programming network.

Television translators, the forerunners of LPTV, were first authorized by the Commission in 1956 as a means of receiving and rebroadcasting television signals into regions that otherwise would have been bypassed. Licensees of television broadcast stations have also used translators to reach unserved areas within their Grade B contours and, in some instances, to carry their signals beyond the Grade B contour. Translator operators were forbidden, however, to originate their own programming.

Under the new LPTV rules, stations can originate live programming from a local studio, broadcast prerecorded video tapes or movies, and broadcast programs received from a distant source, such as a satellite. The rules allow

low power stations to carry advertising or to "scramble" transmissions so that viewers must lease a decoder and pay a subscription fee to view the scrambled programming. Existing translators may commence program origination merely by filing a notification with the Commission.

As of October 1983, the FCC had licensed some 245 low power television stations and granted construction permits for hundreds more. Implementation of computer processing and a lottery procedure for selecting applicants is expected to increase greatly the pace at which authorizations are granted.

Direct Broadcast Satellites (DBS)

In June 1982, the Commission authorized a Direct Broadcast Satellite (DBS) Service, a regulatory development that could make available as many as 40 additional channels of video programming nationwide. DBS is a radiocommunication service in which signals from earth are retransmitted by satellites located in the geostationary orbit for direct reception by small, relatively inexpensive receiving antennas. (See Figure 1.) Direct broadcast satellites, which were allocated spectrum in the 12 GHz band for downlinks and in the 17 GHz band for uplinks, are capable of transmitting a signal up to 40 times more powerful than those of current communications satellites. As a result, they send a television signal which can be picked up by a two-foot dish antenna, typically mounted on the rooftops of subscribers homes. Since the satellite's antenna beamwidth is narrower than conventional ones, up to four DBS satellites would be required to reach the entire country.

After establishing interim rules for the DBS service, the FCC granted conditional construction permits to eight applicants with diverse service proposals. However, the Commission also imposed a due diligence test on the eight applicants, requiring them to enter into contracts for the construction of suitable communications satellites by July 17, 1984. Of the original applicants, only the Satellite Television Corporation (STC, a subsidiary of Communications Satellite Corporation) and United States Satellite Broadcasting Company (USSB) had satisfied the Commission that it met the due diligence test by that date. Subsequently, STC, after 5½ years of planning and some $140 million in expenditures, announced that it would not move ahead with its plans for what would have been ultimately a six-channel national service.[1] By mid-1985, of the original eight applicants, only three—United States Broadcasting, Direct Broadcast Satellite Corp., and Dominion Satellite Corp.—were still committed to building and launching high-powered DBS systems. The FCC granted the additional applications of Satellite Syndicated Systems, Inc., National Christian Network, Advanced

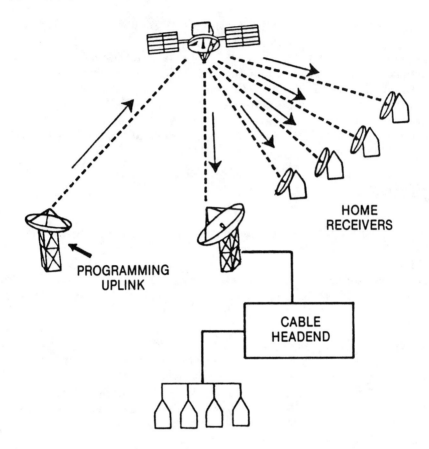

PROGRAMMING
UPLINK

HOME
RECEIVERS

CABLE
HEADEND

Figure 1.   Direct Broadcast Satellite System (DBS)

Communications Corp., and Hughes Communications Galaxy, Inc.[2] The grants were conditioned on the applicants' demonstrating due diligence by contracting for satellites within a period of 1 year.

The proposals submitted by the original applicants reflected a wide variety of approaches to DBS service. For example, the Direct Broadcast Satellite Corporation proposed to provide transmission capability as a common carrier, while STC said it would provide programming funded in whole or in part by audience subscriptions and USSB proposed some advertiser-supported programming.

When or if any of the applicants become fully operational, DBS systems could provide as many as 10 channels of programming. While most of this programming is expected to be similar to conventional television and pay-cable fare, the proposals include some technically innovative services, such as high definition television (HDTV), teletext, stereophonic sound, and dual-language sound tracks. Other potential benefits of DBS include the provision of service to remote areas that receive no over-the-air television, the availability of additional channels of service throughout the country, and the development of more specialized programming.

The FCC conditioned the construction permits on the outcome of the 1983 Region 2 Administrative Radio Conference (RARC), which determined the assignment of frequencies and orbital positions. The applicants thus risked the possibility that insufficient spectrum or orbital positions would ultimately be available to accommodate all the systems. The Commission believed, however, that authorization of interim DBS systems would permit earlier implementation of the service due to the long lead times required for satellite construction. At the 1983 RARC, the United States received eight orbital slots, which are sufficient to accomodate all the pending applications.[3]

Although most attention had been focused on STC's announcement of plans to launch its service by late 1984, "back door" or quasi-DBS programming services—using other frequency bands—were the first to offer direct-to-the-home satellite service. For example, United Satellite Communications, Inc., backed by General Instrument and Prudential Insurance Co., launched a five-channel home video programming service in November 1983 using fixed service satellites in the Ku-Band (11.7–12.2 GHz) instead of the high-power direct broadcast satellites.[4] The service was initially offered to households throughout central Indiana, with plans to add 30 additional markets within 1 year, but USCI abandoned the operation because of its inability to attract sufficient customers or raise sufficient capital while waiting for business to build. Recent technological developments have made possible the use of small home receiving dishes (2½ to 4 feet) in connection with satellites operating in the fixed satellite bands. [By 1987 there were no DBS services in operation. Several million satellite receiving antenna were in use, however, used for picking up the same programming being transmitted to cable systems and the broadcast network's affiliate—ed.]

Satellite Master Antenna Television (SMATV)

With satellite-fed master antenna television (SMATV), an operator puts an earth station (satellite dish antenna) beside or on top of an apartment building or complex of buildings to obtain satellite programming. The programming is delivered from the earth station to individual homes through coaxial cable. (See Figure 2.)

SMATV, also referred to as "mini-cable" or "private cable," is economically practical today only in high density dwellings, where installation costs can be absorbed by a large number of apartment units.

Technological, regulatory, and marketplace developments have spurred

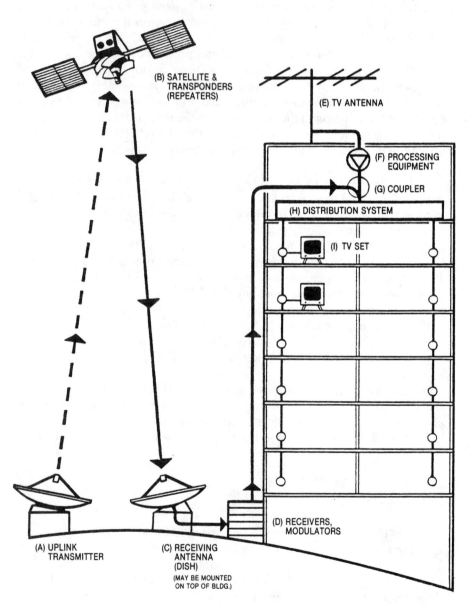

Figure 2.   Satellite Master Antenna Television (SMATV)

the growth of SMATV. Technical advancements led to a precipitous drop in the cost of earth station receivers, making such facilities practical for a wider range of users and purposes. In 1979, the FCC deregulated receive-only domestic earth stations, and dispensed with licensing requirements for these facilities. Commencing with the launching in 1975 of Time, Inc.'s Home Box Office (HBO), numerous satellite-delivered program networks have materialized, including "superstations," such as WTBS in Atlanta, as well as specialized news, cultural, sports, and religious programming services, which, in turn, have stimulated consumer demand for cable and SMATV. There is a technological breakthrough in the offing which is designed to remedy one of SMATV's limitations—limited channel capacity; Cablecom, Inc., a Chicago SMATV system, is developing a 60-channel addressable system to overcome that limitation.

Several developments could spur further growth of SMATV. HBO is offering its programming to SMATV systems, reversing its previous position. In another development, reflecting the increased "legitimization" of SMATV systems, the FCC held that, when an SMATV operator seeks to offer its programming service to residents of apartment buildings not under common ownership, the operator is eligible for microwave licenses, effectively treating SMATV operations under those circumstances as cable television systems. The use of microwave stations to transmit programming between buildings could facilitate program transmission and lower costs by eliminating the need for expensive wiring. SMATV systems received another favorable ruling from the FCC when it held that SMATV systems which do not use public streets and rights of way are exempt from local and state "entry" regulation (i.e., franchise) under the doctrine of preemption. The Commission struck down a New Jersey ordinance requiring SMATV operators to obtain prior approval from the state cable regulatory commission.

Multipoint Distribution Service (MDS)

In 1974, the FCC allocated two channels to MDS for the purpose of providing a common carrier microwave service for closed circuit television or nonvideo transmissions from a central location to multiple fixed receivers. MDS transmissions are receivable on the conventional television set with a special antenna and a "down converter" which converts the signal from a microwave frequency to a selected VHF television frequency. (See Figure 3.) Although the FCC originally contemplated that MDS would satisfy educational, business, and governmental needs, entertainment programming emerged as its primary use.

Since the MDS licensee is a common carrier, it cannot produce, write or influence the content of any information transmitted over its facilities, and may lease only 50% percent of the total transmission time to an affiliated entity. Typically, the licensee leases transmission time to a pay TV service, such as HBO or Showtime/The Movie Channel, which obtains the rights to distribute programming in an area and solicits customers. As a common carrier, the MDS operator sets rates pursuant to a tariff, and must offer its services to programmers on a first-come, first-served basis.

MDS primarily serves high-rise, multiunit structures such as apartment buildings and hotels, because of the limited distribution range of the transmitter (25 miles), the need for line-of-sight transmission to reception antennas, and the cost of installing the special receiving antenna. It is used increasingly, however, in private homes and to distribute entertainment programming to cable television systems. Through MDS, subscribers are able to receive programming similar to that carried on pay cable channels without the need for cable wiring. In urban areas particularly, MDS provides a faster and, in many cases, cheaper method of providing broadband channels than cable, which has franchising requirements and extended construction periods. MDS has an advantage over distribution modes such as STV and LPTV, in that it can increase the availability of video programming without utilizing broadcast frequencies.

Several developments could potentially expand the availability of MDS. In May 1983, the Commission adopted a proposal to increase the number of channels available for MDS by giving the service access to eight channels in the 2500-to-2690 MHz band previously allocated to the Instructional Television Fixed Service (ITFS).[5] In a related proceeding, the Commission adopted new MDS technical standards, which could facilitate, among other things, closer spacing of stations using the same frequency.[6]

The spectrum reallocation effectively authorizes two four-channel systems in each market nationwide. By making possible the transmission of multiple channels of video programming – with associated efficiencies of scale and expansion of consumer choice – the Commission enhanced the attractiveness of MDS as a delivery system. Indeed, multichannel MDS could become a viable competitor of cable television since, as the Commission noted in adopting the rule changes, the growth of MDS has been limited by the lack of multichannel capacity. The rule changes could also facilitate use of MDS frequencies for electronic publishing, home banking and shopping, and high speed data transmission.

Reflecting interest in the new service, close to 17,000 applications for the new multichannel MDS frequencies were filed with the Commission in September 1983. The Commission has proposed to select among these applicants by means of rather than through the time-consuming comparative hearings employed for single channel MDS systems. [In 1987, MDS was still in the realm of "potential." Few MDS systems were in operation and fewer if any, were profitable – ed.]

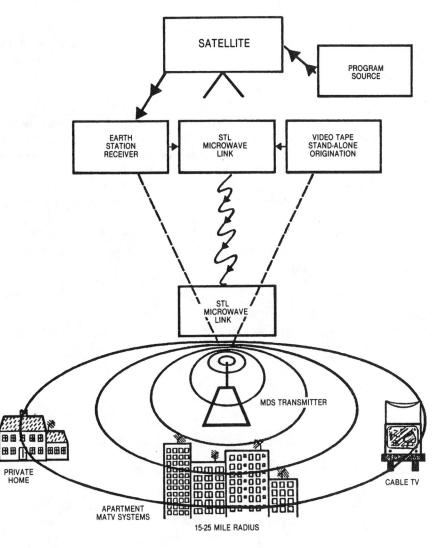

Figure 3.   Multipoint Distribution Service (MDS)

Instructional Television Fixed Service (ITFS)

The Instructional Television Fixed Service (ITFS), which uses the same portion of the microwave spectrum as MDS, was established in 1963 for the primary purpose of transmitting instructional material to educational institutions. Also authorized, as an incidental use, was the transmission of cultural and entertainment programming to schools, and the transmission of training, instructional, and professional materials to other locations. Eligibility was limited to accredited educational institutions and to those eligible to hold a noncommercial educational TV license. Twenty channels are presently allocated to the ITFS.

A number of new and innovative uses of ITFS were announced in 1983. The Commission granted 82 applications of the Public Broadcasting Service (PBS) for authority to construct ITFS stations. PBS announced that it will use the facilities to establish a "National Narrowcast Service" with its member stations. PBS intends to form a nationwide system of ITFS stations through its satellite distribution network, to provide instructional, educational, cultural, professional training, and informational video materials throughout the country.

Other uses of ITFS frequencies may result from the Commission's decision to permit ITFS licensees to lease their excess channel capacity to third parties. By negotiating directly with ITFS licensees, anyone will be able to provide an MDS-type service without the delays and costs inherent in the FCC selection process. Indeed, in 1983 Microband Corp. of America, one of the nation's largest MDS providers, announced plans to offer a multiple-channel television service, to be called MCTV, by leasing ITFS frequencies from National Instructional Television, Inc. (formerly National University of the Air, Inc.) and other ITFS operators.[7]

Private Operational-Fixed Microwave Service (OFS)

Through a rule change which became effective in 1983, the FCC created new video opportunities by expanding the use of the Private Operational-Fixed Service (OFS).[8] This private radio service was previously restricted, as a result of FCC regulations, to aural transmissions by business entities among different parts of the same company. The rule changes open up a distribution path between the licensee and its customers for the transmission of the licensee's own products, including video programming. This places OFS on a comparable footing with MDS as a video entertainment delivery outlet. The FCC foresaw a variety of potential uses for OFS systems including video material distribution, voice, and, in the future, high-speed data services distribution.

As a result of the Commission's rulemaking, OFS frequencies can also be used for the first time to transmit video programming to the home. OFS licensees may use frequencies above 21.2 GHz for the delivery of their own products or services to any receiving location, including hotels, other commercial establishments, apartment house master antenna systems, and private residences.

Subscription Television (STV)

Subscription or over-the-air pay television is not, technically, a new entrant in the video marketplace. The technology dates back to 1950, when the first STV test was conducted in New York. STV is simply pay television transmitted over the air by local television stations that have chosen to offer subscription, rather than conventional advertiser-supported programming. To limit reception to subscribers, STV stations, most of them in the UHF band, broadcast a scrambled signal which must be "decoded" by a device attached to the subscriber's television set. (See Figure 4.) Because subscription television operates over-the-air on a specific allocated frequency, STV

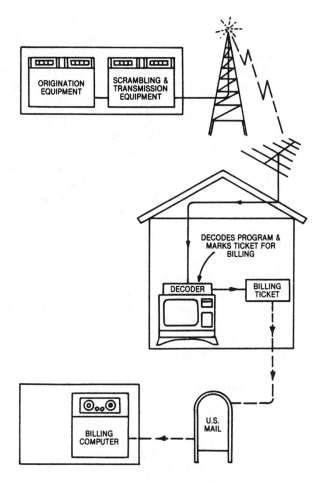

Figure 4. Subscription Television (STV)

stations have only one channel to program. The program fare is typically movies, entertainment specials, and sporting events.

Although nonexperimental STV stations were permitted by 1961, none commenced operation until almost a decade later. Between 1980 and 1983, the number of STV operations have more than tripled as a result of increased public interest in pay television programming and the relaxation of FCC regulations. Growth in the number of subscribers has been slow, however. As of September 1983, 19 STV stations were on the air, serving some 985,560 subscribers. Although the STV industry is currently experiencing economic difficulties, it remains a video alternative, at least in certain markets, particularly those without large cable television penetration.

The elimination of virtually all regulatory restrictions upon STV activity has not done much to stimulate growth of this video service. In a 1982 rulemaking proceeding, for example, the FCC deleted the so-called "complement-of-four" rule. This rule restricted STV operation to those markets with at least four commercial television stations on the air, and allowed only one station in a community to engage in STV operations. This regulatory change made vacant UHF and VHF allocations eligible for STV in 74 markets, encompassing more than 70% of television households. In 1983, the Commission exempted STV stations from compliance with virtually all of its television technical standards.

Increasing judicial protection against unauthorized distribution of decoding devices is another factor which could encourage the growth of STV. The United States Courts of Appeals for the Sixth and Ninth Circuits have both held that STV transmissions are protected by Section 705 of the Communications Act, which prohibits interception of certain radio communications not intended for use by the general public.[9] Those cases establish an implied right of action by STV licensees against unauthorized distributors of decoders. In addition, improvements have been made in securing STV systems against signal theft, especially in the area of "addressable" systems which use a central computer to "address" or activate individual decoders.

Teletext

Teletext is a generic term for systems which transmit textual and graphic information on a one-way basis to the home viewer. (See Figure 5.) Teletext may be "narrowband," often utilizing the vertical blanking interval (VBI) of the television signal, or "broadband," using an entire television channel. Broadband service would be delivered primarily by cable and MDS, while narrowband may be carried by cable, MDS, television stations (including low power), DBS and the subcarriers of FM stations.

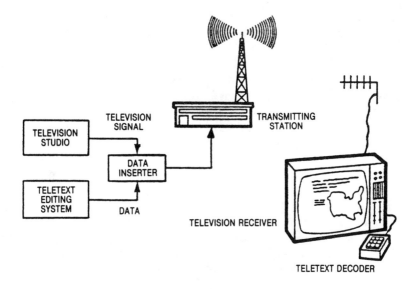

Figure 5.   A Broadcast Teletext System

Teletext offers substantial opportunities for diversifying television service into new areas and for improving the efficiency of spectrum usage. It has the potential to be used for a wide variety of services, including closed-captioning for the deaf, weather reports, news, comparative shopping prices, community bulletins, stock prices, movie listings, telephone directories, advertisements, and airline schedules. It also offers interesting possibilities to enhance television viewing, such as permitting a viewer watching a baseball game the option of seeing a page of statistics about the batter. Such information could be transmitted as an advertiser-supported or subscription service.

In March 1983, the Commission amended its rules to permit teletext transmissions by television stations. Favoring an "open environment" for teletext systems, the FCC declined to adopt technical standards for a single, nationwide system with compatibility for all teletext operations. Instead, television licensees can choose any technical system for transmitting data signals, subject to minimum standards designed to prevent interference with the broadcast service of the originating station, signals of other broadcast stations, or those of nonbroadcast radio stations. This means that the two principal systems currently vying for acceptance—the World System Teletext Standard (based on the British Ceefax system) and the compromise North American Broadcast Teletext Standard (adapted from the French Antiope and Canadian Telidon teletext systems)—could be represented in a single television market, with viewers required to invest in multiple decoders to receive all services. (Or, more likely, viewers would hesitate to purchase *any* decoder so long as confusion on standards prevailed.)

Consistent with its current marketplace approach, the Commission authorized transmission of broadcast and nonbroadcast material. Licensees can also choose to operate services on a lease, franchise, or common carrier basis. In addition, the Commission declined to require mandatory carriage of teletext transmissions by cable systems, thus enabling cable operators to delete the teletext service provided by television stations and provide their own competing teletext or videotex services.

The first commercial broadcast teletext service made available in the United States was Taft Broadcasting's 100-"page" teletext service called "Electra," which began broadcasting over WKRC-TV, Cincinnati in mid-1983. Since the Commission's rules were amended, superstation WTBS, carried on many cable systems, launched a cable teletext service in 1984 provided by Keycom Electronic Publishing, a joint venture of Honeywell and Centel. In addition, several other companies announced plans to offer on-screen teletext magazines. CBS, for example, planned, then cancelled "Extravision" as a national teletext service. The service would have had 100 pages of text, including airline schedules, movie and theater listings, weather, and stock market reports, and was expected to be supported by national and local advertising. At one point NBC also planned to offer a 100-page nationwide advertiser-supported magazine to its affiliates. NBC, however, began transmitting a 100-page nationwide advertiser-supported magazine to its affilitates in May 1983, but decided to end the service in late 1984 because of the high cost of decoders.[10] Satellite Network Delivery Corp., together with the Tribune Co., proposed a satellite-delivered teletext system, Business Teletext Network.

CLOSED TRANSMISSION VIDEO SERVICES TO THE HOME

Cable Television

Cable television, as distinguished from over-the-air services, relies upon a wired network. The wire or coaxial cable is strung along utility poles or through underground conduits and is connected to the subscriber's residence. (See Figure 6.) About 39% of American television households subscribed to cable television by the start of 1984.

From a technical standpoint, there is virtually no limit on the number of cable channels that can be provided. While older cable systems typically provided 12 channels, the development of converters in the 1960s in-

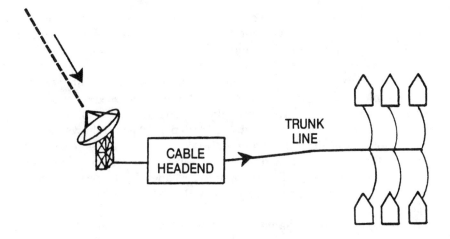

Figure 6.   Cable Television System

creased the capacity of CATV systems to 20 channels. Refinements in line amplifiers have made possible the provision of 52 channels on a single cable line; by using two cables, systems can offer 104 channels of programming. Other advances, such as General Electric's Comband technique, whereby two video program services can be transmitted over a single cable television channel through the use of analog compression, promise to expand further cable's already abundant channel capacity.

The increases in channel capacity have, in turn, had an impact on programming, spawning new satellite-interconnected cable networks, such as the Entertainment and Sports Programming Network (ESPN), Cable News Network (CNN), MTV (music video), and Nickelodeon (children's programming). In addition, the excess channel capacity of local cable television systems has been utilized by third parties, such as newpapers and broadcasters, on a leased or joint venture basis, to deliver program or information services to subscribers. By the end of 1981, 69 newspapers had arranged to provide video, audio, or text services on local cable systems.

These technological and marketplace developments have been accompanied by the relaxation of federal regulation. The deregulatory trend began with the Supreme Court's 1979 Midwest Video decision, which circumscribed the Commission's jurisdiction over cable television.

Interactive Cable Television

While cable systems normally connect the home to the programming source with one coaxial cable, many of the newer systems possess interactive capacity, using two cables so that information can flow in both directions simultaneously. Warner-Amex Cable pioneered interactive cable with its "Qube" system in 1977, and other operators have since developed their own versions.

Two-way capability offers the potential for new and innovative services. For example, it permits the cable operator to poll its viewers on such matters as the expected winner of the next college football game, or a presidential press conference. Viewers have played game shows, "gonged" local talent off the air, ordered library books, and indicated their solutions to moral dilemmas dramatized by actors. Subscribers have also been asked to offer their opinions (via limited options provided by the programmer) on President Carter's 1979 energy speech and Ralph Nader's petition to change children's advertising.

A two-way shopping channel is available in markets served by the Times Mirror Cable systems. Cox Cable experimented in San Diego with a system called "Indax" that provides textual information, electronic mail, home banking, and shopping services to subscribers. In addition, interactive technology simplifies "pay-per-view" programming by eliminating the need for the installation of special decoders to unscramble the signal. With interactive cable, the viewer registers a preference on the console, the computer supplies the signal, and the viewer is automatically billed. [In general, interactive cable has not proved viable except for the growing use of pay-per-view programming – ed.]

Cable Interconnect Systems

Another significant development in the cable area is the use of "interconnects" to transform numerous, discrete cable systems into a mini-network. Interconnects may be of the "hard" or "soft" variety. Hard or physical interconnects link neighboring systems together by a microwave network or coaxial cable. The soft or simulated interconnects do not actually establish electrical connection among the participating systems. Instead, they involve agreements allowing a common entity to sell advertising time on participating cable systems as a single network.

Hard interconnect systems have attracted more interest, since they allow the appearance of commercials on multiple systems simultaneously. The first hard interconnect was the Bay Area Interconnect, linking 475,000 subscribers in the San Francisco area. Gill Cable, the San Jose cable operator that conceived the idea, receives satellite programming, inserts commercials supplied by national and regional advertisers, and sends the mixture over a microwave network to 31 other systems. Other hard cable interconnects, based upon the Bay Area model, include Harron Cable, which is building a four-channel microwave network in the Philadelphia market; Cox Cable, which distributes KCOX, a programming service, via a one-channel microwave to two other systems in San Diego County; and Heritage Communications, a one-channel network interconnecting 21 systems in Iowa.

Soft interconnect systems, although not as numerous, permit advertisers to choose the markets they want to reach, require no capital investment, and provide more flexibility to insert local advertising. Existing soft interconnects include New England Cable Rep, which represents 20 systems with 500,000 subscribers in an area stretching from Maine to Connecticut, and Eastman Cable Rep, which operates on a national level. Most recently, Group W and Viacom launched a soft interconnect, offering advertisers the opportunity to make a single buy for 245,000 cable subscribers in the Seattle area. The system's four common services—ESPN, CNN, MTV and USA—will screen the same commercials through the use of "bicycled" (or physically delivered) tapes.

Common Carrier Wireline Or Fiber Optics Services

Fiber optic technology is a relatively recent development. Unlike conventional wire, fiber optics transmit pulses of light from a tiny laser through flexible strands of glass. Since light waves are higher in the spectrum than radio waves and have a greater bandwidth, a much greater amount of information can be transmitted through an optical fiber than through a conventional wire. Fiber optics are also free from signal interference. It is technically feasible for optical fiber to provide telephone and video service to homes, as well as providing the delivery path for many additional services not previously available on terrestrial telecommunications systems.

In the view of some, improvements in fiber optics communications technology will ultimately make an integrated wideband delivery system using fiber "loops" to the home the most efficient means of delivering voice, data, and video services. Other countries have experimented successfully with optical fiber home connections. In 1978, for example, Japan completed a fiber optic system which offers 158 subscribers a number of video signals, still pictures, and textual material. In the same year, Bell Canada installed fiber optic cables at 36 of its subscribers' residences in Toronto, offering telephone, FM, and video services.

Domestic cable and telephone companies have also demonstrated interest in applying fiber technology. For example, a system supplied by the telephone company for the Los Angeles Olympics made extensive use of fiber optics. In 1983, AT&T began carrying some telephone calls between New York City and Washington, D.C. by means of a 372-mile fiber optic link said to be the largest transmission system in the world using optical fibers. MCI Communications Corp. plans to install fiber optic data and communications lines along railroad tracks in the Washington–New York corridor and elsewhere around the United States. The Port Authority of New York and New Jersey has proposed a "teleport" on Staten Island, with 12 to 17 earth stations linked by fiber optic cable to the World Trade Center and other points in New York and New Jersey. Southern New England Telephone Co. and the CSX Corporation, a major railroad company, plan to install a 5,000-mile fiber optic system to provide essentially a closed loop over railroad rights-of-way between the Boston, Detroit, New Orleans, and Miami areas. In the cable field, Fisher Communications has announced plans to build a 120-mile fiber optic cable system for United Cable Television in Alameda, California. According to one report, a dozen companies planned to spend approximately $6 billion by 1990 to build new long-distance telephone networks that could be the backbone of the U.S. communications system in the next decade.[11]

Although FCC rules prohibit the cross-ownership of cable and telephone companies, inhibiting the use of fiber optics for video transmission, the replacement of conventional telephone lines with fiber optics could facilitate telephone companies' entry into the video marketplace if those restrictions are lifted. Under the Cable Communications Policy Act of 1984, a telephone company is not prohibited from constructing or leasing a local distribution system capable of delivering video programming and other communications services to multiple subscribers in a community.

Videotex

A variety of interactive systems, called videotex, utilize telephone or two-way cable lines to disseminate text and sometimes graphic information for display on television screens or video display terminals. (See Figure 7.) In addition to information retrieval, videotex offers the possibility of conducting transactions, such as shopping and banking, from the home. Electronic mail is also a potential use.

Several videotex services are now offered, including The Source, CompuServe, and Dow Jones News Retrieval [current text-only services – ed.], which make available national data bases to personal computers via telephone lines. The Source offers programs that include text editing, income tax preparation packages, games, airline ticketing services, the UPI News Wire Service, and electronic mail. CompuServe, operating from Columbus, Ohio, offers similar services. CompuServe enlisted 11 newspapers for an experiment with electronic news and classified advertising, among other services. Dow Jones provides sports, movie reviews, and

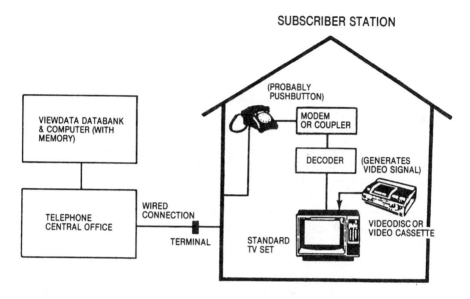

Figure 7.   Electronic Publishing Services or Videotex

shopping in addition to its mainstay, financial data. Among them, they count several hundred thousand subscribers, although many are not regular users.

Viewtron, provided by a subsidiary of Knight-Ridder Newspapers, Inc., was an interactive system that began operating on a commercial basis in Coral Gables, Florida, in late 1983 [and shut down in 1986—ed.]. It transmitted over telephone lines, using a special data network. Subscribers can retrieve news, weather, sports, product ratings, and classified ads, as well as order airline and theater tickets over the system. Unlike Dow Jones, The Source, and CompuServe, Viewtron offered color graphics in addition to the text provided by others. However, Viewtron was designed as a purely local service and has reportedly found little mass appeal at its initial price of about $30 monthly; the other three are available nationally.

Other electronic publishing ventures include Newsnet, which uses telephone lines to transmit the contents of l00 newsletters to the personal computers of subscribers. Two major consumer-oriented videotex systems—Times Mirror's Gateway videotex service in Orange County, California, and Keycom Electronic Publishing Company, to be broadcast over Station WTBS, Atlanta—began operations in late 1984. [and were subsequently shut down—ed.] In 1982, CBS and AT&T conducted a joint videotex experiment which offered l00 households in Ridgewood, New Jersey, a broad range of local and national consumer information and transaction services.

PROGRAMMED VIDEO SERVICES FOR HOME USE

Videocassette Recorders and Videodisc Players

Videocassette recorders (VCRs) and videodisc players (VDPs) have altered the traditional pattern of television viewing. Fundamentally the same as audio recording devices, VCRs are capable of playing prerecorded tape cassettes and of recording and playing back material from television or other video sources, including an attached video camera. (See Figure 8.) VDPs use phonograph-type "records" rather than tape to store video information. They are still restricted to playback of prerecorded material only, however.

Videocassettes have had a twofold impact on the video marketplace. First, the "time-shift" cabability of VCRs permits viewers to tape television or cable shows for viewing at home at more convenient times. Time-shift viewing liberates viewers from the programmer's rigid schedules, and, for this reason, conceivably expands the audience for television and cable programming. Second, VCRs make available a wide range of specialized, nonbroadcast programming. Many users purchase or rent video material for personal use to supplement the video information that is otherwise available through broadcast or cable services.

Videodisc players also allow the release of video information to the home market. The advantage of the VDP is its ability to provide high quality stop action, slow motion, and random access to individually addressed frames, thus providing a capability to display text and still photographs. Despite these advances, decreasing prices and increasing popularity of VCRs prompted RCA's announcement in April 1984 that it would stop manufacturing VDPs and abandon a 3-year attempt to gain "mass market" acceptance for the product.

Video Game Cartridges and Systems

Video games are not directly competitive with broadcast and cable television as are VCRs and VDPs which offer similar entertainment. They are significant, however, in that they use the television screen as a display device, permitting viewers to control the images on the screen. Video games were present in 25% of the nation's television homes in 1982. The video game business suffered a slowdown in 1983, however, as home computers began to take over as a game player from the more specialized video game-only units.

Video games are also melding with other new technologies. Plans have come and gone to distribute video games over subcarrier channels on FM stations, via telephone and cable lines. The Nabu Network, for example,

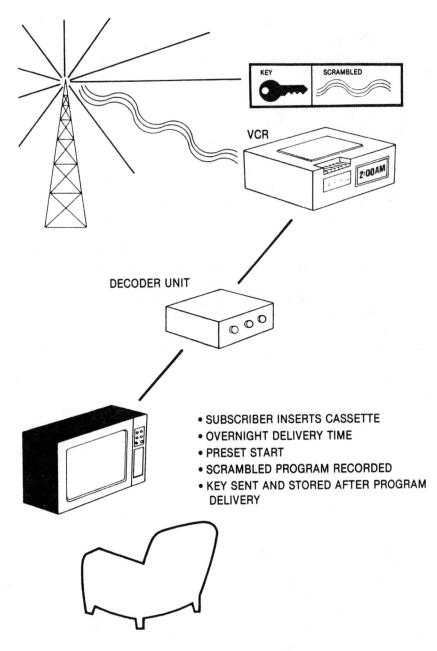

Figure 8.   VCR Applications

which wanted to download home computers over satellite and through cable affiliates for monthly subscription fees, planned to offer cable subscribers new video games software each month in the same way HBO offers new movies. However, the principal backer of Nabu abandoned the operation in late 1984 in the wake of heavy financial losses.

Telesoftware Applications

By combining VCR and broadcast technologies, entrepreneurs hoped to distribute programming electronically for over-the-air taping. Music, movies, video games, and other forms of entertainment or information can be electronically transmitted to homes and recorded by machines automatically activated to receive the transmission. A new word, "telesoftware," has been coined to describe any form of electronically downloaded software. ABC launched a telesoftware venture, known as "TeleFirst," in January 1984 over its owned-station WLS-TV in Chicago. The service, which broadcast satellite-distributed broadcast pay programming in scrambled form over ABC's owned and affiliated stations during the early morning hours for taping by subscribers, was discontinued after 5 months, due to the rapidly dropping costs of VCRs and videocasette rentals. ECO, Inc., an electronics company in Santa Ana, California, announced plans to broadcast magazines, newspapers, or catalogues over the air or by cable for taping on a VCR.

DEVELOPMENTS THAT COULD PERMIT MORE VIDEO DELIVERY SYSTEM OPPORTUNITIES

General Electric Company's Two-for-One Comband System

The General Electric Company Television Division, in November 1982, announced the development of Comband, an analog compression system intended to allow transmission of two video program services over a single cable television channel. As reported in the trade press, "by installing a Comband encoder at the headend and Comband converters in subscribers' homes . . . the cable operator can quickly and relatively inexpensively double the capacity of his own system."[12]

Comband will be marketed initially for the cable television industry, but GE indicates that the system will have future applications to over-the-air services such as television, STV, LPTV, MDS, and satellite and microwave links. If successful, this system could permit an inexpensive doubling of services provided over broadband (6-MHz) allocations to broadcast, STV, LPTV, and MDS licensees.

Conversion From Analog To Digital Transmission Techniques

Television signals are normally transmitted in analog "wave" forms moving across the 6 MHz frequency range. AT&T, ITT, and others are developing digital transmission techniques that convert audio and video signals into "on and off" impulses, thereby permitting a number of different services to be transmitted over the same 6 MHz allocation. The principal disadvantages of digital systems are the current high cost of conversion equipment and the transition costs of moving from an analog to a digital approach for existing broadcast communications services. Nonetheless, if sufficient demand for new transmission delivery systems exists, such digital multiplexing techniques will provide another method of "squeezing" more uses out of the same frequency allocations.

To cite one example, domestic satellites are relying increasingly upon digital modulation to increase capacity. Also, digital television makes it possible to display multiple images—for example, Matsushita Corp., which placed on the market the first digital television sets in June 1984, designed the set so that it will display two images at once, thereby allowing the viewer to watch one show while monitoring a second channel or a VCR or videodisc playback in a corner of the screen. NEC of Japan has developed a digital set that can freeze up to four frames in memory and print out the images on a thermal printer. Digital technology, in addition to enabling such innovations, has the potential of eventually cutting the cost of television assembly by putting much of the circuitry on a few silicon chips.

Shared Use Of Broadcast Auxiliary Stations

In April 1983, the FCC amended its rules to permit licensees of television auxiliary stations (studio-transmitter links, intercity relays, and TV pickup stations) to use those facilities to transmit, on a profit-making basis, broadcast or nonbroadcast material to other entities. The only restriction is that the use must be secondary to the primary purpose of the spectrum allocation, which is transmission of live program feeds to the associated television station.

The Commission's decision enables licensees to use excess capacity for nonbroadcast purposes, as well as to transmit program material to cable television systems and to other broadcast stations. The licensee may also, through multiplex techniques, transmit simultaneously two video channels, with one feeding the licensee's associated broadcast station while the second is being used for alternative purposes.

The Commission's decision facilitates a number of new business arrangements. For example, a broadcaster could relay signals received from a satellite over TV relay stations or transmitter studio links to the broadcaster's studio or another location. Interconnection of broadcast auxiliary stations with nonbroadcast microwave stations would also be a possibility, enabling linkage to police or other governmental systems. TV pickup or electronic news-gathering facilities could also be made available to nonbroadcast users.

In giving broadcasters wide latitude to use excess capacity on their broadcast auxiliary facilities, the Commission intended to foster more efficient use of the spectrum and to encourage the development of spectrum-efficient technologies such as channel compression. It stated, "forcing auxiliary stations to remain idle when legitimate demands for frequencies exist is precisely the situation that we are attempting to avoid."[13]

Subsidiary Communications Services

In 1983, the FCC amended its rules to eliminate most restrictions on the use of FM subcarriers, greatly facilitating the provision of subsidiary communications services. FM subcarriers—the unused portion of the broadcast signal adjacent to the main channel frequency — have, for many years, been used for the provision of broadcast-related services, such as background music, ethnic and foreign language programming, medical and business information, and reading services for the blind. The Commission's action, however, enables broadcasters to use their subcarriers to transmit material of either a broadcast or nonbroadcast nature (for example, paging by means of "beepers"), for a full 24 hours per day, irrespective of main channel operation.

Besides eliminating content restrictions, the new rules facilitate more efficient use of broadcast spectrum by expanding the technical parameters of FM subcarriers. As a result, broadcasters will now have available two or more audio subcarriers or several data channels. In authorizing the use of modulation methods other than frequency modulation (FM), the Commission also encouraged the use of FM subchannels for new and emerging technologies.

The potential uses of FM subcarriers include nonaural services (such as slow-scan video, display data, telemetry, facsimile services, electronic mail delivery); enhancement of main channel service (such as paging services); and control signals (such as utility load management, municipal traffic light and sign control). Since the rule changes were adopted, a number of new ventures have been announced. Mutual Broadcasting System, for example, plans to launch a series of specialized voice and data networks to be transmitted over its satellite system to the subcarriers of participating FM stations. A Montpelier, Vermont, FM station (WNCS-FM) has joined with a local company, Mad River Video, to deliver ski slope information and maps to video displays at condominiums and hotels in the Vermont resort area by means of the station's subcarrier.

Paralleling the Commission's actions with respect to FM subcarriers, the Commission has similarly expanded the use of television subcarriers and AM subcarriers.

MAPPING VIDEO REGULATION

As recently as 1978 the regulatory jurisdiction of the Federal Communications Commission was relatively straightforward. As seen in Figure 9, the main area of fuzziness was in the degree of regulation of certain types of telecommunications equipment. Title II (common carriage) and title III (broadcasting) areas were clearly delineated.

By 1985, however, an attempt to draw neat boundaries had become a frustrating exercise as Figure 9 suggests. Some services, such as MDS and DBS, could be regulated under Title II or Title III strictures, depending on individual circumstances. In the case of cable operators, Congress and the courts had become definitive in what could be regulated by the FCC and the states. States and local governments have some jurisdiction over cable operators, and there has been some question over state authority for MDS under some conditions. In teletext, the FCC elected to forebear from regulation.

The map summarizes the regulatory identity crisis. For those players— including users—who preferred a stable, known business environment, life has perhaps become less enjoyable. For those previously on the outside or others who thrive on the challenge to find new niches, the current regime presents opportunities for success and failure.

NOTES

1. Oliver Wendell Holmes, *Collected Legal Papers* (Boston: Little, Brown, 1921), at 231.
2. *National Broadcasting Co. v. United States*, 319 U.S. 190, 219 (1943).
3. *See, e.g.*, S. Rep. No. 562, 86th Cong., 1st Sess. 8 (1959), where Congress said in amending the Communications Act: "Broadcast frequencies are limited and,

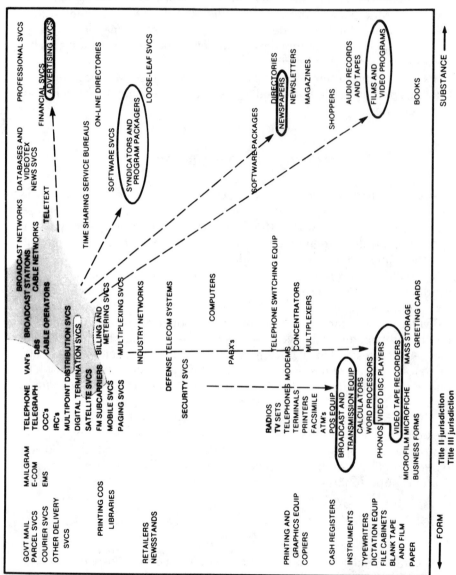

Figure 9.   A Map of the New Video Marketplace

therefore, they have been necessarily considered a public trust. Every licensee who is fortunate in obtaining a license is mandated to operate in the public interest." FCC Chairman Mark Fowler has questioned the continuing vitality of scarcity as a justification for regulation. Fowler, "The Public's Interest," *Communications and the Law* 4 (1983): 51.

4. "The way a [television] service is classified may have substantial bearing on how it is regulated. And how it is regulated has profound consequences not only for the service providers but, ultimately, the public. Until recently, the FCC's service classifications were straightforward – services were either broadcasting, common carrier or private, and the lines between these categories were distinctly drawn. The lines of demarcation between classifications are no longer so sharp, and new classifications are emerging." Remarks of Henry M. Rivera, FCC Commissioner, Before the American Law Institute-American Bar Association, March 29, 1984, at 1 [hereinafter cited as *Rivera Remarks*].

5. *National Association of Broadcasters v. FCC,* 740 F.2d 1190 (D.C. Cir. 1984). *See* discussion *infra* at text notes 113–117 and accompanying text, and text note 364.

6. *National Broadcasting Co. v. United States,* 319 U.S. 190, 213 (1943). *See also id.* at 226 ("Unlike other modes of expression, radio inherently is not available to all . . . . That is why, unlike other modes of expression, it is subject to governmental regulation").

7. *Id.* at 212–13.

8. *CBS v. Democratic Nat'l Comm.,* 412 U.S. 94, 101 (1973).

9. *Office of Communication of United Church of Christ v. FCC,* 359 F.2d 994, 1003 (D.C. Cir. 1966). *See also Red Lion Broadcasting Co. v. FCC,* 395 U.S. 367 (1969) ("It does not violate the First Amendment to treat licensees given the privilege of using scarce radio frequencies as proxies for the entire community, obligated to give suitable time and attention to matters of great public concern."); *National Broadcasting Co.,* 319 U.S. at 215–16. One commentator has expressed a contrary viewpoint: "Spectrum scarcity justifies, if anything, diversity of speech in the broadcast medium, not government censorship." Thomas G. Krattenmaker and Marjorie L. Esterow, "Censoring Indecent Cable Programs: The New Morality Meets the New Media," *Fordham L. Rev.* 51 (1983): 606, 621. Another commentator asserts that scarcity is primarily the product of rather than the justification for, regulation. Bruce M. Owen, *Economics and Freedom of Expression: Media Structure and the First Amendment* (Cambridge, Mass.: Ballinger, 1975).

10. *See* Network Inquiry Special Staff, Federal Communications Commission, *New Television Networks: Entry, Jurisdiction, Ownership and Regulation* 14–30 (Oct. 1980) [hereinafter cited as *Network Inquiry*].

11. *Sixth Report and Order on Television Allocation,* 41 F.C.C. 148 (1952).

12. Very high frequency (VHF) and ultra high frequency (UHF) are in the 30-3,000 MHz band. *See* Head and Sterling, *infra* appendix note 178, at 31.

13. Co-channel and adjacent-channel stations must be separated geographically to avoid interference. *See* 47 C.F.R. secs. 73.610(b)(1) and (c)(1) (1982). UHF operation results in interference problems, known as "UHF taboos," which may preclude the use of up to 16 channels in a particular area. *See* Michael

Wilhelm, "UHF and the FCC: The Search for a Television Allocations Policy," *U. Fla. L. Rev.* 28 (1976): 399, 402.

Based on an analysis of the A.C. Nielsen Company's *Directory 1984–1985,* there are fewer than three commercial VHF stations in 108 out of the 205 DMAs.

14. *See Deregulation of Radio,* 73 F.C.C.2d 457, 484 (1979).
15. "Broadcast Station Totals for December 1984," FCC News Release, No. 1810 (Jan. 9, 1985). A proposal is pending to increase the number of VHF stations by means of short-spaced television "drop-in" assignments. *See Notice of Proposed Rulemaking* (Gen. Docket No. 80-499), 45 Fed. Reg. 72902 (Nov. 30, 1980). Under the FCC proposal, as many as 139 new VHF stations would be allocated at less than the full traditional mileage separation from stations operating on the same channel.
16. National Telecommunications and Information Administration, *Print and Electronic Media: The Case for First Amendment Parity* (May 1, 1983): 98-109 *reprinted in* Staff Report to the Chairman, Senate Comm. on Commerce, Science & Transportation, 98th Cong., 1st Sess. (Comm. Print 1983) [cited as "*NTIA Report*"]. Some of the statistics concerning the number of operating television stations are somewhat misleading. A substantial number of television stations—mainly UHF stations—are "not reportable" by either Nielsen or Arbitron because their viewing levels are too small to be measured in any day-part. For example, as of May 1984, 36 television stations assigned to the "top 10" markets were "not reportable" with respect to viewing in those markets.
17. Pub.L. 87–529, 76 Stat. 150, 47 U.S.C. sec. 303(s)(1962).
18. *See* Philip B. Gieseler, "UHF Television: A Review and Update," *Proceedings of the IEEE* (Nov. 1982): 1254.
19. "Advanced Technology UHF Receiver Study, Part 1, Receiver Performance Measurements," FCC/OST R83-1 (March, 1983).
20. "Perspective 1984," *Broadcasting,* Jan. 2, 1984, at 68.
21. Jonathan D. Levy and Florence O. Setzer, *Measurement of Concentration in Home Video Markets* 81 (Office of Plans and Policy, Dec. 23, 1982) [hereinafter cited as "*OPP Report*"]. For a summary of the report, *see* 48 Fed. Reg. 41 (Jan. 3, 1983).
22. *See Sixth Report and Order on Television Allocation,* 41 F.C.C. 148, 160 (1952).
23. At least one DBS applicant (Hubbard Broadcasting's United States Satellite Broadcasting) proposed offering advertiser-supported programming services. *See infra* appendix note 31 and accompanying text.
24. *See* FCC Public Notice, *Television Channel Utilization* (Apr. 27, 1983).
25. *See OPP Report, supra* note 21, at 101.
26. *See* "After 10 Years of Satellites, the Sky's No Limit," *Broadcasting,* Apr. 9, 1984, at 43.
27. *See Tentative Decision and Request for Further Comment* (BC Docket No. 82-345), 48 Fed. Reg. 38020, 38035 (Aug. 22, 1983) [hereinafter "*Tentative Decision*"].
28. *Id.*
29. The Commission's Office of Plans and Policy has broadly defined the home

video market to encompass all services that deliver information and entertainment into the home. *OPP Report, supra* note 21, at 101. It concluded that "[a] narrow market definition, excluding the alternative media, will result in a severe underestimate of actual competition." *Id.*

30. The deconcentrated nature of the cable market, for example, has been acknowledged by the Commission. *See Network Inquiry, supra* note 10, at III-157-59; *FCC Policy on Cable Ownership, infra* appendix note 141, at 4.

31. *Notice of Proposed Rulemaking* (MM Docket No. 83-670), 48 Fed. Reg. 37239 (Aug. 17, 1983), Appendix A, Table III [hereinafter "TV Deregulation"]; *Tentative Decision, supra* note 26, at 38035.

32. "Nielsen Says Cable Penetration Nears 40%, Up 18% from 1982," *Broadcasting,* Sept 5, 1983, at 90.

33. *TV Deregulation, supra* note 30, at para. 28; *Tentative Decision, supra* note 26, at 38036-37, and Table 9 (58 million basic cable subscribers and 45 million pay cable subscribers by 1990).

34. *Tentative Decision, supra* note 26, at 38036, 38037 and Table 9.

35. *Id.,* at 38036, para. 116; *TV Deregulation, supra* note 31, at para. 31.

36. Robert Lindsey, "VCR's Bring Big Changes in Use of Leisure," *N.Y. Times,* March 3, 1985, at A1.

37. *See* note 35 *supra.*

38. *NTIA Report, supra* note 16, at 81.

39. *Tentative Decision, supra* note 26, at para. 115.

40. *Id.* at 38037, Table 9.

41. *Id.*

42. The danger of relying on such projections was recently noted by Les Brown, editor-in-chief, *Channels* magazine: "People with a stake in the media are understandably on edge these days because fotunes are at risk, and they will seek out almost any educated theory on what's to come. The danger is that they may give too much credence to transitory indicators. The present is a notoriously poor guide to the future. It tends to by myopic and always on the edge of change. Anyone who had used the present as a road map in 1982 would have seen Atari as the future. A much better guide is the past, which affords some perspective and reminds us that we have lived through this, or something like it, before." *1984 Field Guide, infra* appendix note 21, at 5.

43. For a further discussion of the early history of broadcast regulation, *see Deregulation of Radio,* 73 F.C.C.2d at 497–98.

44. *OPP Report, supra* note 21, at 84, table 2.

45. FCC Public Notice, Release No. 4772 (June 16, 1983). *See* Mark Fowler and Daniel Brenner, "A Marketplace Approach to Broadcast Regulation," *Tex. L. Rev.* 60 (1982): 207, 225 n.81.

46. As one commentator notes, "technology is an independent variable that makes scarcity a relative concept." Fowler and Brenner, *supra* note 45, at 222.

47. Some commentators urge that in any discussion of scarcity, a distinction be drawn between *availability* and *accessibility.* "First-class airline tickets are *available* to everyone, but they are only *accessible* to those who can afford the fare. Similarly, cable, MDS, STV and DBS may (or may not) add up to meaningful diversity; yet is is doubtful whether more than one of these will be

accessible to the average consumer. (Indeed, all may not be available in many geographic areas)." Geoffrey A. Berkin, "Hit or Myth?: The Cable TV Marketplace, Diversity and Regulation," *Fed. Comm. L.J.* 35 (1983): 41, 49.

48. The term *diversity*, in the context of television programming, is difficult to define. Economists Robert Crandall, Roger G. Noll, and Bruce M. Owen assert that the concept has to do with whether the programs offered on television span a sufficiently wide spectrum of qualitative attributes. They state that, in this sense, diversity has two somewhat different but equally useful meanings. One is the range of social, cultural, and political points of view, values, and information that is presented. The second meaning focuses on whether the kinds of programs that are offered serve the broadest possible range of viewers. A premise of this meaning of diversity is that viewers differ widely in their tastes for programming, that differing combinations of the qualitative attributes of a program will consistently and systematically appeal to distinctly different groups of viewers. Crandall, Noll, and Owen, "Economic Effects of the Financial Interest and Syndication Rule: Comments on the ICF Report," Reply Comments of CBS Inc., BC Docket No. 82-345 (April 26, 1984), at Vol. II, App. A, 10-11.

49. *FCC v. League of Women Voters of California*, 104 S.Ct. 3106, 3116 n. 11 (1984).

50. Ithiel de Sola Pool, *Technologies of Freedom* 23 (Cambridge, Mass.: Harvard University Press, 1983).

51. 47 U.S.C. sec. 153(o) (1976). *See also National Subscription Television v. S&H TV*, 644 F.2d 820 (9th Cir. 1981); *Functional Music, Inc. v. FCC*, 274 F.2d 543, 548 (D.C. Cir. 1958), *cert. denied*, 361 U.S. 813 (1959); *Subscription Television*, 15 F.C.C.2d 466, 472 (1968).

52. 47 U.S.C. sec. 153(h) (1976).

53. *See H.R. Rep. No. 1850, 73d Cong., 2d Sess. 2 (1934); S. Rep. No. 781, 73d Cong., 2d Sess. 3 (1934). See also Subscription Television Service*, 3 F.C.C.2d 1, 9 (1966) ("The primary touchstone of a broadcast service is the intent of the broadcaster to provide radio or television program service without discrimination to as many members of the general public as can be interested in the particular program as distinguished from a point-to-point message service to specified individuals").

54. 47 U.S.C. secs. 301-386 (1976).

55. *See, e.g., FCC v. WNCN Listeners Guild*, 450 U.S. 582 (1981); *CBS v. Democratic Nat'l Comm.*, 412 U.S. 94 (1973).

56. 47 C.F.R. secs. 73.603-73.615 (1982). The Commission has the authority to impose less than the full complement of technical, behavioral, and structural rules. It recently eliminated ascertainment requirements, nonentertainment programming guidelines, and commercial limits for licensees of commercial radio stations. *Deregulation of Radio*, 84 F.C.C.2d 968, 971 (1981), *aff'd in part, remanded in part sub nom. Office of Communication of the United Church of Christ v. FCC*, 707 F. 2d 1413 (D.C. Cir. 1983), *reh. denied*, Dec. 12, 1983, *cert. denied*, 104 S.Ct. 3545 (1984). The commission also declined to impose many of the traditional broadcast regulations on LPTV. *Report and Order* (BC Docket No. 78-253), 47 Fed. Reg. 21468 (May 18, 1982).

57. 47 U.S.C. secs. 311, 315.
58. 47 C.F.R. at sec. 73.1211 (1982).
59. *Id.* at sec. 73.1216.
60. *Id.* at sec. 73.1212.
61. *New Primer on Political Broadcasting and Cablecasting,* 69 F.C.C.2d 2209 (1978).
62. *Fairness Report,* 48 F.C.C.2d 1 (1974).
63. *See* 47 C.F.R. sec. 73.636 (1982).
64. *See* 47 C.F.R. secs. 73.636, 76.501(a) (1982).
65. *See Sixth Report and Order on Television Allocation,* 41 F.C.C. at 158-67, 227-563.
66. *See* 47 C.F.R. sec. 73.621(a) (1982).
67. *Id.* Noncommercial stations receiving public funds have also been prohibited by law from editorializing. 47 U.S.C. sec. 399 (1976) (as amended by Pub. L. No. 97-35, 95 Stat. 357, 730 (1981)). The Supreme Court, however, held that the editorializing prohibition is an impermissible burden on the First Amendment rights of noncommercial stations. *FCC v. League of Women Voters of California, supra* note 49.
68. Public Broadcasting Act, Pub. L. No. 90-129, 81 Stat. 365 (1967), 47 U.S.C. secs. 390–399 (1976 and Supp. III 1979) (as amended by the Public Telecommunications Financing Act, 92 Stat. 2405 (1982)). In addition, grants for construction of broadcasting facilities are provided through the Department of Commerce. 47 U.S.C. secs. 390-394 (1976). The Department of Education funds the production of television programs for use by public television stations. 20 U.S.C. secs. 3201(a)(2) (1976).
69. *See* 47 U.S.C. sec. 396(k) (1976). Between 1981 and 1986, $1.061 billion in matching grants has been authorized. *See* Federal Communications Commission Authorization Act of 1983, Pub. L. No. 98-214, 97 Stat. 1467 (1983) (*codified at* 47 U.S.C. sec. 396(k) (1) (c)).
70. *See, e.g., CATV,* 2 F.C.C.2d 725 (1966), *aff'd sub nom. Black Hills Video Corp. v. FCC,* 399 F.,2d 65 (8th Cir. 1968).
71. 392 U.S. 157 (1968).
72. *Id.* at 178.
73. 406 U.S. 649 (1972).
74. *FCC v. Midwest Video Corp.,* 440 U.S. 689 (1979).
75. *Id.* Some cable systems, however, do provide these services pursuant to franchising agreements, negotiated with municipalities.
76. *See CATV Syndicated Program Exclusivity Rules,* 79 F.C.C.2d 663 (1980), *aff'd sub nom. Malrite TV of New York v. FCC,* 652 F.2d 1140 (2d Cir. 1981), *cert. denied, sub nom. National Ass'n of Broadcasters v. FCC,* (1982). 454 U.S. 1143 (1982). The FCC's cable policy, in the view of one commentator, "has been characterized by frequent reversals of protectionism of broadcasting at the expense of cable television and misguided efforts to shape cable television into preconceived molds." George H. Shapiro, Philip B. Kurland, and James P. Mercurio, "Cable Speech," *The Case for First Amendment Protection* (1984), at 15.
77. *CATV Syndicated Program Exclusivity Rules,* 79 F.C.C.2d at 813-15.

78. 47 C.F.R. secs. 76.67, 76.92 (1982).

79. *Id.* at secs. 76.57, 76.59, 76.61.

80. *Id.* at secs. 76.206, 76.209, 76.213, 76.215, 76.221. In 1972, in connection with the passage of legislation making the lowest unit advertising rate available to candidates for public office, Congress amended Section 315 of the Communications Act to provide that for the purposes of the Section, "the term 'broadcasting station' includes a community antenna system." 47 USC sec. 315(c). Section 315(a) specifies equal opportunities and fairness doctrine obligations. *See also Notice of Proposed Rulemaking* (MM Docket No. 83-331), 48 Fed. Reg. 26472 (1983), in which the FCC proposed to revise the fairness doctrine and political telecasting rules applicable to cable systems.

81. *Capital Cities Cable, Inc., v. Crisp,* 104 S.Ct. 2694 (1984), *infra* appendix note 120.

82. *See* "FCC Affirms Cities Can Regulate Only Basic Cable Rates," *Communications Daily,* July 13, 1984, at 1.

83. *See* Joseph R. Fogarty and Marcia Spielholz, "FCC Cable Jurisdiction: From Zero to Plenary in Twenty-Five Years," *Fed. Comm. L.J.* 37 (1985): 113, 123.

84. Cable Communications Policy Act, Pub.L. No. 98-549, sec. 1 *et seq.,* 98 Stat 2779, (1984). *See also* H.R. Rep. No. 934, 98th Cong., 2nd Sess. (1984).

85. 47 U.S.C. sec. 153(h) (1976).

86. *See National Ass'n of Regulatory Utility Comm'rs v. FCC,* 525 F.2d 630, 640-42 (D.C. Cir. 1976) (*NARUC I*); *National Ass'n of Regulatory Utility Comm'rs v. FCC,* 553 F.2d 601 (D.C. Cir. 1976) (*NARUC II*). The Commission adopted the NARUC I test for determining common carrier status in *Domestic Fixed Satellite Transponder Sales,* 52 Rad. Reg. 2d (P&F) 78, 87 (1982). It identified two criteria of common carrier status: "(1) whether there will be any legal compulsion to serve the public indifferently; and (2) if not, whether there are reasons implicit in the nature of the service to expect an indifferent holding out to the eligible user public." *Id.* The key features of common carrier regulation are that services must be provided on a "first come, first served" basis, without discrimination, and that common carriers cannot influence the content of the messages transmitted, but must act merely as conduits. The Commission has discretion to forbear from imposing the full panoply of Title II regulations where the entity lacks market dominance. *See Competitive Common Carrier Serv.,* 52 Rad. Reg. 2d (P&F) 187, 189 (1982). *See also ACLU v. FCC,* 523 F.2d 1344 (9th Cir. 1975).

87. 47 U.S.C. secs. 201, 202 (1976)

88. 47 U.S.C. sec. 203(A) (1976).

89. *Id.* at secs. 204, 205 (1976).

90. *Id.* at sec. 214 (1976).

91. *Id.* at secs. 203, 205 (1976).

92. 47 C.F.R. sec. 0.131 (1976).

93. *See generally* Federal Communications Commission, Office of Plans and Policy, Policies for Regulation of Direct Broadcast Satellites (Sept. 1980) at 53-56 [hereinafter cited as "DBS Report"].

94. *See generally* 47 C.F.R. Part 90 (1982). The Commission limits the ways in which various private radio users can share frequencies and equipment, and

also restricts the types of communications which may be made in the private services.

95. In this regard, the Commission's actions in the broadcast area have paralleled those in the common carrier field. *See*, e.g., *Competitive Common Carrier Serv.*, 91 F.C.C. 2d 59 (1982). The Commission there concluded that Title II (common carrier) requirements may be waived "where [the FCC] determine[s] that the cost of such regulation outweighs any perceivable benefits." *Id*. at 61. For a discussion of the forbearance and experimental authorization approaches in the DBS context, *see* John Lyons and Mike Hammer, "Deregulatory Options for a Direct Broadcast Satellite System", *Fed. Comm. L.J.* 33 (1981): 185.

96. *See Fourth Report and Order* (Docket No. 21502), FCC 83-485, released Nov. 16, 1983, at para. 32.

97. *See Second Report and Order* (Docket No, 80-112), FCC 84-568, released Feb. 1, 1985.

98. See *infra* text notes 181-182, and accompanying text. The proceeding would also include reexamination of the FCC's classification approach in light of the Court of Appeals decision in *NAB v. FCC*. Commissioner Henry Rivera has stated that such a reexamination should include the Commission's decisions concerning multichannel MDS, home delivery in the OFS, "private" DBS, and recent suggestions that pay television is not broadcasting. Remarks of Commissioner Henry M. Rivera before the Advance Program IEEE Broadcast Symposium, Sept. 21, 1984, at 12-13.

99. Adding to the confusion have been a number of court cases interpreting sec. 605 of the Communications Act, 47 U.S.C. sec. 605 (1976). That section, which prohibits unauthorized reception of radio signals, does not apply if the service is classified as broadcasting. *Compare National Subscription Television v. S&H TV*, 644 F.2d 820 (9th Cir. 1981) and *Chartwell Communications Group v. Westbrook*, 637 F.2d 459 (6th Cir. 1980) (holding that STV transmissions are not broadcasting and therefore entitled to protection under sec. 605) *with Orth-O-Vision, Inc. v. Home Box Office*, 474 F. Sup. 672 (S.D.N.Y. 1979) holding that HBO's MDS transmissions are broadcasting for purposes of sec. 605). For a discussion of the provisions of the Cable Communications Policy Act of 1984 governing the unauthorized reception of satellite signals, *see infra* text notes 343 and 344 and accompanying text.

100. *Report and Order* (Docket No. 10832), 11 Rad. Reg. (P&F) 1590, 1591 (1956). *See also Functional Music, Inc., v. FCC*, 274 F.2d 543 (D.C. Cir. 1958), *cert. denied*, 361 U.S. 813 (1959).

101. *Subscription Television Serv.*, 3 F.C.C.2d 1, 9 (1966). *See also Subscription Television*, 15 F.C.C.2d 466, 472 (1968), *aff'd sub nom. National Ass'n of Theater Owners v.FCC*, 420 F.2d 194 (D.C. Cir. 1969), *cert. denied*, 397 U.S. 922 (1970).

102. *Subscription Television*, 15 F.C.C.2d at 472.

103. *Amendment of Part 3 — SubscriptionTelevision*, 23 F.C.C. 532, 541 (1957).

104. *See Greater Washington Educ. Telecommunications Ass'n*, 49 F.C.C.2d 948 (1974) (fairness doctrine, personal attack, and political broadcast rules not applicable); *Subscription TV Serv.*, 90 F.C.C.2d 341 (1982). *See generally DBS*

Report, supra note 93, at App. C.

105. 90 F.C.C.2d 341 (1982).

106. *See also Subscription Television Movie Restrictions,* 41 Rad. Reg. 2d (P&F) 1491 (1977) (restrictions of feature films); *Subscription Television Rules,* 42 Rad. Reg. 2d (P&F) 1207 (1978) (restrictions on sports events); *Enforcing Section 312(a) (7),* 68 F.C.C.2d 1078, 1093 (1978) (exempting STV operators from sec. 312 requirements).

107. *Direct Broadcast Satellites,* 90 F.C.C.2d 676, 708 (1982), *aff'd in part, rev'd in part, sub nom. National Ass'n of Broadcasters v. FCC,* 740 F.2d 1190 (D.C. Cir. 1984).

108. *Direct Broadcast Satellites,* 90 F.C.C.2d at 708-09.

109. *Direct Broadcast Satellite Servs.,* 86 F.C.C.2d 719, 750-51 n. 64 (1981). *See also Direct Broadcast Satellites,* 90 F.C.C.2d at 708. At the oral argument in the *NAB v. FCC* appeal, Judge Abner Mikvah "rapped [the] FCC's non-regulatory view of DBS," and "expressed incredulity that neither authorized DBS companies nor satellite programmer United Satellite Communications (USCI) was being subjected to laws governing broadcasters." He chided the attorney for the FCC: "You have something that looks like broadcasting, smells like broadcasting, tastes like broadcasting and has all of the benefits of broadcasting, but we're not going to treat it as braodcasting because Congress didn't know about it [when it passed the Communications Act]?" "Court Hits FCC View of DBS," *Television Digest,* March 5, 1984, at 8.

110. *Direct Broadcast Satellites,* 90 F.C.C.2d at 709.

111. *Id.* The Commission, however, begged the question of how "common carrier" will be defined. *See, e.g., Domestic Fixed Transponder Satellite Sales,* 52 Rad. Reg. 2d (P&F) 78 (1982), where the Commission concluded that transponder sales are not common carrier offerings.

112. *Direct Broadcast Satellites,* 90 F.C.C.2d at 709.

113. *Id.* at 710. *See* the discussion of *National Assn. of Broadcasters v. FCC,* 740 F.2d 1190 (D.C. Cir. 1984), *rehearing en banc denied,* _____ F.2d. _____ (1984). The FCC chose not to seek Supreme Court review.

114. *NAB v. FCC, id.* at 1202.

115. *Id.*

116. Id. at 1202-1203.

117. *Id.* at 1204.

118. *GTE Satellite Corporation,* 90 F.C.C.2d 1009, 1011, n.5 (1982), *reconsideration,* 94, F.C.C.2d 1184 (1983). *See also WARC Implementation,* 54 Rad. Reg. 2d (P&F) 101 (1983), *aff'd sub. nom. United States Satellite Broadcasting Co., Inc. v. FCC,* 740 F. 2d 1177 (1984) (remand to the FCC to consider which of the two entities, the common carrier or the customer-programmer, should bear the braodcast restrictions imposed by the Communications Act).

119. *GTE Satellite Corporation,* 94 F.C.C.2d 1184, 1195-96 (1983).

120. *See Domestic Fixed Transponder Satellite Sales,* 52 Rad. Reg. 2d (P&F) 78 (1982). By classifying domestic satellites ad nondominant carriers, the FCC has significantly deregulated the satellite field by exempting domestic satellite operators from the burdensome tariff and Section 214 certification requirements. *See Fourth Report and Order* (CC Docket No. 79-252), FCC 83-481,

released Nov. 2, 1983.

121. *Teletext Transmission,* 53 Rad. Reg. 2d (P&F) 1309, 1333 (1983). Former FCC Commissioner Anne Jones proposed "a single regulatory treatment" for broadcast and print media using the print model. She predicted that "[new] services like teletext and videotex . . . may provide the catalyst for change from the present regulatory scheme." Remarks of Commissioner Anne P. Jones Before the American Newspaper Publishers Ass'n, FCC News Release, Rep. No. 07762 (Mar. 5, 1981).

122. *See Teletext Transmission,* 53 Rad. Reg. 2d (P&F) 1309 (1983).

123. *Id.* at 1324-27. The Commission indicated that common carriage treatment will depend upon the manner in which the licensee conducts its business (*i.e.,* whether the broadcaster holds out its transmission facilities to all people indifferently or whether it establishes stable, long-term contractual relationships with customers who are selected on a highly individualized basis). An analogous approach was utilized in the FM subcarrier proceeding (53 Rad. Reg. 2d (P&F) 1519 (1983)), and in the Commission's decision authorizing sale of excess capacity by television auxiliary stations (*Broadcast Auxiliary Facility Sharing,* 53 Rad. Reg. 2d (P&F) 1101 (1983)).

124. 53 Rad. Reg. 2d (P&F) at 1322-24. Implicit in the FCC's decision is that broadcasters will fulfill fairness doctrine and political broadcasting obligations on their main channel. *See also Memorandum Opinion and Order* (BC Docket No. 81-741), released Jan. 24, 1985. Telecommunications Research and Action Center and Media Access Project have asked the U.S. Court of Appeals to review these portions of the FCC's decisions holding that teletext transmissions are not subject to the fairness doctrine and the equal opportunities and lowest unit rate provisions of the Act.

125. *Id.* at 1321.

126. *See* note 97 *supra.*

127. Statement of Comissioner Henry M. Rivera, Concurring in Part, Dissenting in Part, CC Docket Nos. 80-112 and 80-116.

128. *Id.*

129. Second Report and Order (Gen. Docket No. 80-112) released Feb. 1, 1985, at n. 17.

130. *See* 47 C.F.R. secs. 21.903(b) (1)-(2) (1982), which prohibit MDS licensees from exercising control over the program content of their transmissions.

131. 47 C.F.R. sec. 74.931.

132. *Instructional Television Fixed Service (MDS Reallocation),* 54 Rad. Reg. 2d (P&F) 107, 138-142 (1983).

133. *Id.* at 140.

134. *Broadcast Auxiliary Facility Sharing,* 53 Rad. Reg. 2d (P&F) 1101 (1983).

135. *Use of Private Microwave Frequencies,* 86 F.C.C.2d 299, 311 (1981).

136. *Operational-Fixed Microwave Service,* 54 Rad. Reg. 2d 439, 448, n.29 (1983).

137. *See* 47 C.F.R. sec. 94.9(a) (1) (1982). *See also Use of Private Microwave Frequencies,* 86 F.C.C.2d at 304, 309.

138. *Notice of Proposed Rulemaking* (PR Docket No. 83-426), 48 Fed. Reg. 24950 (June 3, 1983).

139. *See* Public Broadcasting Amendments Act of 1981, secs. 1231-1233 of the

Omnibus Budget Reconcillation Act of 1981, Pub. L. No. 97-35, 97th Cong., 1st Sess., which created the Temporary Commission on Alternative Financing for Public Telecommunications to explore alternative sources of funding. The Act also authorized public stations "to engage in the offering of services, facilities, or products in exchange for remuneration" provided that "any such offering by a public broadcast station shall not interfere with the provision of public telecommunications services by such stations." *Id.* at sec. 1231, 47 C.F.R. sec. 399B(b) (1).

140. *See* Craig A. Dunagan, "Commercialization of Public Broadcasting," *Comm./Ent. L.J.* 5 (Winter 1982-83): 241.

141. *Broadcast Auxiliary Facility Sharing,* 53 RAd. Reg. 2d (P&F) 1101, 1107 (1983)

142. *Public Broadcasting Service,* 86 FCC 2d 141 (1981).

143. *Teletext Transmission,* 53 Rad. Reg. 2d (P&F) 1309, 1322 (1983); *see also, Memorandum Opinion and Order* (BC Docket No. 81-741), released Jan. 24, 1985 (public broadcasters allowed to use their teletext facilities on a remunerative basis as an alternate source of financing).

144. *Instructional Television Fixed Service (MDS Reallocation),* 54 Rad. Reg. 2d (P&F) 107, 138-42 (1983). The Commission, however, has declined to permit noncommercial TV stations to engage in subscription operations. *See* FCC News Release, Report No. 17919, released March 30, 1984.

145. *Report and Order* (BC Docket No. 82-441), 49 Fed. Reg. 15581 (April 19, 1984). The Commission adopted its proposal to allow noncommercial FM stations to use their subcarrier channels for commercial purposes. *See Report and Order* (BC Docket No. 82-1), 48 Fed. Reg. 26608 (June 9, 1983).

146. The FCC initiated a rulemaking proceeding in 1985 on whether the licensee of a commercial UHF station could swap its facilities for a VHF station licensed in the same community to a public broadcaster without opening up the affected channels to application by third parties. *Notice of Proposed Rulemaking* (MM Docket No. 85-41), FCC 85-73, released March 8, 1985.

147. For a detailed discussion of this effort, *see* Erwin Krasnow, Lawrence Longley, and Herbert Terry, *The Politics of Broadcast Regulation* (3d ed., 1982), at 240-69.

148. Glen O. Robinson, "The Federal Communications Commission: An Essay on Regulatory Watchdogs," *Va. L. Rev.* 64 (1978): 169, 182.

149. Interview with Robert Bruce, Wash., D.C. (July 8, 1981).

150. *Deregulation of Radio,* 84 F.C.C.2d 968, *aff'd in part, remanded in part, Office of Communication of the United Church of Christ v. FCC,* 707 F. 2d 1413 (D.C. Cir. 1983).

151. *See Malrite T.V. v. FCC,* 652 F.2d 1140 (2d Cir. 1981).

152. *Reregulation of Receive-Only Domestic Earth Stations,* 74 F.C.C.2d 205 (1979).

153. For a discussion of these common carrier decisions, *see* Daniel Brenner, "Communications Regulation in the Eighties: The Vanishing Drawbridge," *Ad. L. Rev.* 33 (1981): 255.

154. *VHF TV Top 100 Markets,* 81 F.C.C.2d 233 (1980).

155. *Low Power Television Serv.,* 51 Rad. Reg. 2d (P&F) 476 (1982).

156. *Direct Broadcast Satellites,* 90 F.C.C.2d 676 (1982).

157. Lionel Van Deerlin, "Progress Made Via 'Rewrite' Dialog," *Variety,* Jan. 9, 1980,

at 213.

158. Regulatory Flexibility Act of 1980, Pub. L. No. 96-354, 94 Stat. 1164 (1980) (*codified at* 5 U.S.C. secs. 601 et seq.). The Act requires federal administrative agencies such as the FCC to prepare an "initial regulatory flexibility analysis" before issuing a notice of proposed rulemaking. The analysis must identify the burden the proposed rule might place on small businesses, show how the proposed rule might overlap or conflict with other rules, and describe significant alternatives that might accomplish the same objectives. If an agency issues a final rule adopting its original proposals, it must show why it did not adopt one of the less burdensome alternatives. Agencies are also required to review and identify existing rules that place especially heavy burdens on small businesses.

159. 5 U.S.C. sec 610 (b) (5) (1980).

160. Commission on Federal Paperwork, Publ. L. No. 93-556 sec. 1(a), (c), 88 Stat. 1789 (1974), *reprinted in* 1974 *U.S. Code Cong. and Ad. News,* 93rd Cong., 2nd Sess. at 2057, 2058.

161. Pub. L. No. 96-511, sec. 2(a), 94 Stat. 2818 (44 U.S.C.A. sec. 3505, West Supp. Dec. 1981). Between fiscal years 1981 and 1982, the FCC reduced by nearly 65% the paperwork burdens it places on the public, making it the single most successful agency in the federal government in eliminating unnecessary paperwork. Council of Independent Regulatory Agencies, *Regulation Relief at the Independent Regulatory Agencies* (Nov. 1982) at 19.

162. *Radio Broadcast Services: Revision of Applications for Renewal of License of Commercial and Noncommercial AM, FM, and Television Licensees,* 49 Rad. Reg. 2d (P&F) 740 (1981), *aff'd sub nom. Black Citizens for a Fair Media v. FCC,* 719 F. 2d 407 (D.C. Cir. 1983).

163. In 1981, Congress changed the FCC from a permanently authorized agency to one with a two year authorization. The short-term authorization is designed to provide "regular and systematic oversight" and to "increase Commission accountability for the implementation of Congressional policy." H. Rep. No. 208, *Omnibus Budget Reconciliation Act of 1981, Conference Report,* 97th Cong., 1st Sess. 899 (1981).

164. Federal Communications Commission Authorization Act of 1983, Pub. L. No. 98-214, 97 Stat. 1467 (1983).

165. *Id.*

166. 47 U.S.C. sec. 303(g) (1982).

167. S. Rep. No. 67, 98th Cong., 1st Sess. 31 (1983).

168. Pub.L. 98-549, 98th Cong., 2d Sess. (1984); *see* discussion *supra* at text note 84 and accompanying text.

169. *See* David M. Rice and Michael Botein, "The Ambivalent Nature of the Cable Communications Policy Act of 1984: An Analysis," *N.Y.L.J.,* March 22, at 5-6. The courts, in questioning the constitutionality of certain provisions of the Act, may provide for greater deregulation than Congress. In *Preferred Communications, Inc. v. City of Los Angeles,* No. 84-5541, slip op. (9th Cir. March 1, 1985), the court held that when the public rights-of-way are physically capable of accommodating more than one cable system, First Amendment principles bar a local government from using a competitive franchising process to limit

access to a single cable television company. The court observed that "the mandatory access and leased access requirements in the City's franchising scheme and called for by secs. 611-612 of the Cable Communications Policy Act . . . pose particularly troublesome questions." *Id.* at 37-38, n.4.

170. S. 55, 98th Cong., 1st Sess. sec. 601(4) (1983).

171. *Id.* at sec. 601(2).

172. H.R. 103, 98th Cong., 1st Sess. (1983).

173. *Id.* at sec. 601(2), 4.

174. *Id.* at sec. 601(6).

175. *Id.* at sec. 601(5). One commentator notes that while the objectives stated in the "purposes" section of the Act are laudable, the following goals were not stated: the promotion of universal cable service, the provision of cable at reasonable rates, the encouragement of a nationwide system of cable television, and the need for protection of the interstate, satellite, and distant signal aspects of cable from conflicting local regulations. Remarks of Daniel L. Brenner, Special Adviser to the Chairman, FCC, NCTA State Leadership Conference, Washington, D.C., Nov. 15, 1984, at 4.

176. *See* Krasnow, Longley, and Terry, *supra* note 147, at 46.

177. *Id.* at 26; *see also* Fowler and Brenner, *supra* note 45, at 246-48. Chairman Fowler told a group of broadcasters in 1982: "I pledge to take deregulation to the limits of existing law." Martha Middleton, *National Law Journal,* Jan. 21, 1985, at 1.

178. Mark Fowler, "Broadcast Unregulation in the 1980's," *Television Quarterly* 8-9 (Spring 1982). *See also* Fowler and Brenner, *supra* note 45, at 256.

179. Fowler and Brenner, *supra* note 45, at 210. *See also* Statement of Mark S. Fowler Before the Subcomm. on Telecommunications, Consumer Protection and Finance Oversight Hearing on the Broadcast-Mass Media Activities of the Federal Communications Commission (Dec. 1, 1982).

180. Fowler and Brenner, *supra* note 45, at 209-10.

181. *Order,* 47 Fed. Reg. 47828 (Oct. 28, 1982).

182. *Id.* at 47829.

183. *Deregulation of Radio,* 84 F.C.C.2d 968 (1981), *aff'd in part, remanded in part, Office of Communication of the United Church of Christ v. FCC,* 707 F. 2d 1413 (D.C. Cir. 1983). The Court remanded that aspect of the decision eliminating program logs and instructed the FCC to conduct a further proceeding to determine what records should be retained to demonstrate service to the community.

184. *Office of Communication of the United Church of Christ v. FCC,* 707 F. 2d 1413 (D.C. Cir. 1983).

185. *Id.*

186. *Id.* The Commission subsequently adopted a requirement that licensees compile local public inspection files, on a quarterly basis, a list of the significant issues facing their communities and examples of responsive programming. *Second Report and Order* (BC Docket No. 79-219), FCC 84-67, released Apr. 27, 1984.

187. 84 F.C.C.2d at 969.

188. *See Deregulation of Radio,* 73 F.C.C.2d 457, 486 (1979):

The dramatic growth in the number of radio stations, particularly FM, has not simply represented an increase in the number of fringe or marginal stations in urban areas, but rather has increased the number of strong, viable competitors in these markets. This kind of competition tends to force stations, in their own self interest, to be responsive to shifts in consumer tastes or else lose their audience to more responsive stations.

189. *See id.* at 487-91; *Deregulation of Radio,* 84 F.C.C.2d at 969, 1065-66 ("the economic theory that holds that an increase in the number of stations promotes service to narrower and narrower segments of the community is correct"). *See also* Staff of House Subcomm. on Telecommunications, Consumer Protection and Finance, *Telecommunications in Transition: The Status of Competition in the Telecommunications Industry,* 97th Cong., 1st Sess. 340 (1981); *FCC v. WNCN Listeners Guild,* 450 U.S. 582, 590 (1981) ("competition among broadcasters had already produced 'an almost bewildering array of diversity' in entertainment formats").

190. *Deregulation of Radio,* 84 F.C.C.2d at 969.

191. *Id.*

192. 450 U.S. 582 (1981).

193. *Entertainment Formats,* 60 F.C.C.2d 858 (1976), *reconsideration denied,* 66 F.C.C.2d 78 (197).

194. 450 U.S. at 590.

195. *Id.*

196. Id. at 595.

197. *Low Power Television Serv.,* 51 Rad. Reg. 2d (P&F) 476, 484-85 (1982).

198. *Id.* at 518-20.

199. *Id.* at 518-19.

200. *Id.* at 513-17.

201. *Id.* at 518-19.

202. *Id.* at 515, para. 89.

203. *Children's Television Programming and Advertising Practices, Report and Order* (Docket No. 19142), FCC 83-609, released Jan. 4, 1984 [cited as "Children's Television"], *aff'd sub nom. Action for Children's Television v. FCC,* No. 84-1052, slip op. (D.C. Cir. March 27, 1985). In 1971, Action for Children's Television, a consumer group based in Massachusetts, filed a petition with the FCC to require television stations to carry 14 hours of children's programming each week and to prohibit the broadcasting of commercials on such programs. *See Children's Television Report and Policy Statement,* 50 F.C.C.2d 1 (1974), *recon. denied* 55 F.C.C.2d 1 (1974), *recon. denied* 55 F.C.C.2d 691 (1975), *aff'd sub nom. Action for Children's Television v. FCC,* 564 F.2d 458 (D.C. Cir. 1977).

204. *Children's Television,* at para. 43.

205. *Id.* at para. 26.

206. *Id.* at para. 32.

207. *Report and Order* (MM Docket No. 83-670) FCC 84-293, released Aug. 21, 1984; *see also Report and Order* (BC Docket No. 81-496), FCC 84-924, released Aug. 22, 1984 (deregulation of noncommercial television ascertain-

ment and programming requirements). FCC News Release, Report No. 18040 (June 28, 1984); "FCC Deregulates Commercial TV," *Communications Daily* (June 28, 1984), at 1-3.

208. *Notice of Proposed Rulemaking* (MM Docket No. 83-670), 48 Fed. Reg. 37239 (Aug. 17, 1983), at para. 5.
209. *Id.* at para. 34.
210. *Id.* at para. 35.
211. *Id.* at para. 36.
212. *Id.* at para. 37.
213. *Id.* at paras. 45-46.
214. *Notice of Inquiry* (Gen. Docket No. 84-282), 49 Fed. Reg. 20317 (may 14, 1984). The Commission, in June 1983, instituted a rulemaking proceeding which looks toward the repeal or modification of the personal attack and political editorializing rules. *Notice of Proposed Rulemaking* (Gen. Docket No. 83-484), 48 Fed. Reg. 28295 (June 21, 1983).
215. *See* 47 C.F.R. sec. 73.1910.
216. *Notice of Inquiry, supra* note 214, at para. 1. In August 1987 the FCC voted to eliminate the fairness doctrine. Some congressional leaders responded by announcing an intent to codify its provisions in legislation.
217. *Malrite T.V. v FCC* 652 F.2d 1140 (2d Cir. 1981), *cert. denied*, 454 U.S. 1143 (1982).
218. 47 C.F.R. secs 76.59(b)-(e), 76.61(b)-(f), 76.63 (1980).
219. *Id.* at secs. 76.151-76.161.
220. For a summary of the history of FCC regulation of cable television, *see* Stanley M. Besen and Robert Crandall, "The Deregulation of Cable Television," *Law and Contemp. Probs.* 44 (1981): 77, 81-107.
221. *See, e.g., Economic Relationship Between TV Broadcasting and CATV, 71 F.C.C.2d 632 (1979).* The Report concluded that cable penetration might, at most, reach 48% of all households, *id.* at 672; that the presence of cable television would reduce local station audiences by less than 10%; and that the incremental audience diversion caused by eliminating the signal carriage rule would be less than 10%, *id.* at 674. It should be noted that the study dealt with retransmission of over-the-air signals, not pay cable, and was conducted before most cities were wired for cable.
222. *CATV Syndicated Program Exclusivity Rules,* 79 F.C.C.2d 663, 763-64 (1980).
223. 17 U.S.C. sec. 111 (1976 and Supp. V 1981).
224. *See CATV Syndicated Program Exclusivity Rules,* 79 F.C.C.2d at 763-64.
225. *Federal Communications Commission's Deregulation of the Cable Industry,* 47 Fed. Reg. 52146 (Nov. 19, 19872), *aff'd Christian Broadcasting v. Copyright Royalty Tribunal,* 720 F. 2d 1295 (D.C. Cir. 1983).
226. The "superstations" such as WTBS, Atlanta; WOR-TV, New York; and WGN-TV, Chicago, which have grown 50% since *Malrite,* could be the hardest hit. *See* "Cox's San Diego System to Drop Superstation," *Communications Daily,* Dec. 23, 1982, at 4; "Feeling the Weight of the CRT Signal Fee Increases," *Broadcasting,* Jan. 10, 1983, at 31-32. In June 1984, the House Copyright Subcommittee reported out H.R. 5879, a bill designed to modify the Copyright Royalty Tribunal's cable rate-setting procedures, and to modify the existing

royalty structure for distant signals. As approved by the Subcommittee, H.R. 5879 would allow cable operators to import two distant non-network-affiliated signals without paying the new royalty rate (3.75% of gross revenues for each distant signal) imposed by the CRT in 1982. H.R. 5879 would also provide the CRT with a full-time economist and general counsel, and it would reduce the body from five to three commissioners. *See* "New Copyright Bill goes to House Panel," *CableVision,* July 2, 1984, at 24.

227. *Subscription TV Serv.,* 90 F.C.C.2d 341 (1982).

228. *Fourth Report and Order* (Docket No. 21502), 95 F.C.C. 2d 457 (1984).

229. "The growth of pay cable and other pay services provides a compelling reason for removing restrictions to the introduction of STV. In facing the competition offered by pay cable, STV stations are at a potential disadvantage because they operate on a single channel, whereas cable offers multiple channels. It has been found that pay services which enter a market first have an advantage over similar types of services which follow. We do not believe that the public interest is served by a regulation which restricts market entry by one pay service but leaves those markets open to others. Rather, the public is best served by allowing interested parties to establish STV stations wherever they believe a market exists and a channel is available." 90 F.C.C. 2d at 350 (citations omitted).

230. *Id.* at 351.

231. *Id.* at 353.

232. *Subscription Television Serv.,* 88 F.C.C.2d 213, 231-32 (1981).

233. *Id.* at 231-32.

234. *Second Computer Inquiry,* 77 F.C.C.2d 384 (1980), *reconsideration,* 84 F.C.C.2d 50 (1980); *further reconsideration,* 88 F.C.C.2d 512 (1981), *aff'd sub nom. Computer and Communications Indus. Ass'n v. FCC,* 693 F.2d 198 (D.C. Cir. 1982), *cert. denied sub nom. Louisiana Pub. Services Commission v. FCC,* 103 S. Ct. 2109 (1983).

235. 77 F.C.C.2d at 419-20.

236. *Id.* at 420.

237. *Id.* at 425-30.

238. *See Illinois Bell Tel. Co. v. FCC,* 740 F.2d 465 (67th Cir. 1984) (FCC affirmed in continuing to apply the *Second Computer Inquiry* restrictions to the divested Bell operating companies).

239. *Common Carrier Services,* 91 F.C.C.2d 59 (1982).

240. *Id.* at 61. *See also Domestic Fixed Satellite Transponder Sales,* 52 Rad. Reg. 2d (P&F) 79 (1982).

241. 47 U.S.C. sec. 214 (1976) and Sup. V 1981) (requiring common carriers to obtain a certificate of convenience and necessity).

242. *See Report and Order* (BC Docket No. 79-145), FCC 85-123, released March 22, 1985 (designating current maximum blanking interval standards as recommended limits for broadcasters, production houses and manufacturers).

243. *AM Stereophonic Broadcasting,* 51 Rad. Reg. 2d (P&F) 1 (1982).

244. *Id.* The Commission adopted a similar "open environment" for teletext. *Teletext Transmission,* 53 Rad. Reg. 2d (P&F) at 12.

245. *AM Stereophonic Broadcasting,* 51 Rad. Reg. 2d (P&F) at 12.

246. *Id.*

247. *Id. See generally* Christopher Sterling, "The FCC and Changing Technological Standards," *J. of Comm.* 137 (Autumn 1982). *See also "The Odd Couple," Broadcasting,* Nov. 29, 1982, at 40; "Technology: Waiting for the Marketplace," *Broadcasting,* Jan. 3, 1983, at 80.

248. *Direct Broadcast Satellites,* 90 F.C.C.2d at 716-17.

249. *Id.*

250. See Teletext Transmission, 53 Rad. Reg. 2d (P&F) 1309, 1327-28 (1983).

251. *Id.*

252. *Id.*

253. *Second Report and Order* (Docket No. 21323), FCC 84-116, released Apr. 23, 1984. *See also Further Notice of Inquiry* (Docket No. 21323), 48 Fed. Reg. 37475 (Aug. 18, 1983); *Notice of Inquiry (Docket No. 21323), 42 Fed. Reg. 38606 (July 29, 1977); Notice of Proposed Rulemaking* (Docket No. 21323), 44 Fed. Reg. 70201 (Dec. 6, 1979); and *First Report and Order* (Docket No. 21223), 46 Fed. Reg. 39145 (July 31, 1981). On July 27, 1984, the FCC denied petitions for reconsideration of its decision authorizing multichannel sound transmission on television. FCC New Release, Report No. 5652 (July 27, 1984).

254. *Further Notice of Inquiry* (Docket No. 21323), 48 Fed. Reg. 37475, 37478 para. 22 (Aug. 18, 1983).

255. The Zenith/dbx standard approved by the FCC provides three audio channels for each video channel—two for stereo sound and a third for separate audio programs, which broadcasters are expected to use for simultaneous foreign-language broadcasts. "TV Sets of the Future," *Newsweek,* Aug. 6, 1984, at 56. In Japan, where stereo TV has been available since 1978, the extra audio channel is used by television stations to give baseball viewers a choice of listening to announcers who root either for or against the hometown team. *Id.*

256. *Notice of Inquiry and Proposed Rulemaking* (Gen. Docket No. 83-114), 48 Fed. Reg. 14399 (April 4, 1983).

257. *See, e.g., FCC v. National Citizens Committee for Broadcasting,* 436 U.S. 775, 780 (1978); *Policy Statement on Comparative Broadcast Hearings,* 1 F.C.C. 2d 393, 394-95 (1965); *Multiple Ownership of Standard AM, FM and Television Broadcast Stations,* 45 F.C.C. 1476, 1476-77 (1964).

258. *Transfer of Broadcast Facilities,* 52 Rad. Reg. 2d (P&F) 1081 (1982). The Commission defined "trafficking" in broadcast licenses and permits as the licensee's acquisition of a station "for the purpose of reselling it at a profit rather than for the purpose of rendering a public service." *Powel Crosley, Jr.,* 11 F.C.C. 3, 23 (1945).

259. 52 Rad. Reg. 2d (P&F) at 1087, para. 23.

260. *Id.* at 1089, para. 34. Licenses obtained as a result of a comparative hearing must be held for at least 1 year before they can be sold for a profit. The Commission concluded that this restriction was necessary to maintain the integrity of its hearing processes.

261. 47 Fed. Reg. at 55930.

262. The decision also acknowledges that "artificial mechanisms" such as the trafficking rule may, by disturbing marketplace forces, inflate station prices. *Id.* at 55927.

263. *Transfer of Broadcast Facilities,* 52 Rad. Reg. 2d (P&F) at 1088.
264. *Id.*
265. Report and Order (MM Docket No, 83-46), FCC 84-115, released Apr. 30, 1984.
266. *Id.* at para. 6.
267. *Multiple Ownership of TV Broadcast Stations,* 22 F.C.C.2d 686, 700 (1968).
268. *Top 50 Ownership Policy,* 75 F.C.C.2d 585, 590 (1979), *aff'd sub nom. NAACP v. FCC,* 682 F. 2d 993 (D.C. cir. 1982).
269. *Id.* at 592-93.
270. *Id.* at 593-96.
271. *Id.* at 595.
272. *Telephone Co. CATV Cross-Ownership,* 88 F.C.C.2d 564 (1981).
273. *Id.* at 574-75.
274. *Id.* at 572.
275. 47 U.S.C. sec. 613(b) (1) (1984). *See also Notice of Proposed Rulemaking* (MM Docket No. 84-1296), released Dec. 11, 1984.
276. *Report and Order* (Gen. Docket No, 83-1009), FCC 84-350, released Aug. 3, 1984, *appeal pending sub nom. Black Citizens for a Fair Media, v. FCC,* No. 84-1503 (D.C. Cir., 1984). *See also Notice of Proposed Rulemaking* (Gen. Docket No, 83-1009), 48 Fed. Reg. 49438 (Oct. 25, 1983).
277. *Order* (Gen. Docket No. 83-1009), FCC 84-400 (Aug. 9, 1984).
278. *Id.* at 49446-47 para. 41.
279. *Id.* at 49447, para. 42.
280. *Id.* at 49450, para. 56.
281. *Id.* at 49451, paras. 64-65.
282. *Id.* at 49445-46, para. 37.
283. *Id.* at 49451, para. 61. The FCC's Report and Order states that, while "the record contains no evidence of potential harm from the ownership changes that would be made possible by immediate repeal of the rule," the decision to establish a transitional limitation for a period of 6 years was made "out of an abundance of caution." *Report and Order* (Docket No. 83-1009), 49 Fed. Rg. 31877, 31891 (Aug. 8, 1984). *See also* "FCC Considers 12-12-12 'Cautious' Action," *Broadcasting,* Aug. 6, 1984, at 28.
284. *Diversification of Control of Community Antenna Television Systems,* 52 Rad. Reg. 2d (P&F) 277 (1982).
285. *Id.* at 280, para. 6.
286. *Id.* at para. 8.
287. *Id.* at 279, para. 7.
288. *Id.* at 280, para. 8.
289. *Report and Order* (MM Docket No, 84-19), FCC 84-15, released May 1, 1984, *appeal pending sub nom. National Association of Better Broadcasting v. FCC,* No. 84-1274 (D.C. Cir. Filed June 29, 1984).
290. *See First Report and Order* (Docket No. 20548), 63 F.C.C. 2d 824 (1977) and *Notice of Proposed Rulemaking* (Docket No. 20548), 54 F.C.C. 2d 331 (1975).
291. *Notice of Proposed Rulemaking,* (MM Docket No. 84-19), FCC 84-10, released Jan. 17, 1984, at paras. 2, 21-23.
292. *Id.* at para. 20.

293. *See* Michael Botein, "New Communications Technology: The Emerging Anti-trust Agenda," *Comm./Ent. L.J.* 4 (1981): 685, 686; *see also* Michael Botein, "Jurisdictional and Antitrust Considerations in the Regulation of the New Communications Technologies," *N.Y. Law School L. Rev.* 25 (1980): 905-23.

294. Alberto-Culver Co., for example, filed a class-action suit in the U.S. District Court for the District of Columbia against CBS, NAB, and 10 group owners over restrictions against television commercials that promote two or more unrelated products in a 30-second spot. *Alberto-Culver v. National Assoc. of Broadcasters,* Case No. 83-3427 (D.D.C. filed Nov. 17, 1983). *See* "Alberto-Culver Sues Over TV Commercial Guidelines," *Broadcasting,* Nov. 21, 1983, at 25. The suit was subsequently settled.

295. *United States v. American Telephone & Telegraph Co.,* 552 F. Supp. 131 (D.D.C. 1982), *aff'd* 103 S. Ct. 1240 (1983).

296. *Id.* at 225. The modified consent decree, in recognition of the rapidly changing nature of the market, provides that "this restriction shall be removed after seven years from the date of entry of the decree, unless the Court finds that competitive conditions clearly require its extension." *Id.* at 231. This means that, in 1989, AT&T could petition the court for permission to enter the electronic publishing market and, unless another party could show that competitive conditions clearly require maintenance of the ban, the prohibition would be lifted.

297. *Id.* at 225.

298. *United States v. National Assn. of Broadcasters,* 536 F. Sup. 149 (D.D.C. 1982). The Code restricted the number of products or services an advertiser could promote in a single commercial announcement.

299. *Id.* at 166-67.

300. *Id.* at 167.

301. *Memorandum, United States v. National Assoc. of Broadcasters,* Civil Action No. 79-1549 (D.D.C. 1982). For a discussion of the implications of Judge Greene's decision and the consent decree, *see* Patricia Brosterhous, "United States v. National Association of Broadcasters," *Fed. Comm. L.J.* 35 (Fall 1983): 313.

302. *United States v. National Broadcasting Co.,* 449 F. Supp. 1127 (C.D. Cal. 1978), *aff'd mem.* No. 77-3381 (9th Cir. April 12, 1978), *cert. denied sub nom. CBA v. U.S. District Court for Central Division of Calif.,* 48 U.S. L.W. 3188 (1979); *United States v. CBS Inc.,* Civ. No. 74- 3599-RJK (C.D. Cal. July 31, 1980), *reprinted in* 45 Fed. Reg. 34463, 34466 (1980); *United States v. ABC, Inc.,* Civil No. 74-3600 RJK (C.D. Cal.), *reprinted in* 45 Fed. Reg. 58441 (1980).

303. 47 C.F.R. sec. 73.658(j). *See* Network Inquiry Special Staff, Federal Communications Commission Leading to the Adoption of the Prime Time Access Rule, the Financial Interest Rule, and the Syndication Rule (Oct. 1979).

304. *Notice of Proposed Rulemaking* (BC Docket No. 82-345), 47 Fed. Reg. 32959 (July 30, 1982).

305. In light of President Reagan's support of a 2-year moratorium on any FCC action on repeal or relaxation of the financial interest and network syndication rules, the Department of Justice is unlikely to counter the President's expressed desires. "Fin-Syn Repeal Doubtful," *Broadcasting,* Apr. 2, 1984, at 70.

306. *Report on Chain Broadcasting,* Commission Order No. 37, Docket No. 5060 (May 1941), at 83, *aff'd NBC v. U.S.,* 319 U.S. 190 (1943).

307. *Network Inquiry,* supra note 10, at 165.

308. *Id.* at III-23, III-157-63.

309. *Notice of Proposed Rulemaking* (CT Docket No. 82-434), 47 Fed. Reg. 39212 (Sept. 7, 1982).

310. *Id.*

311. Id. (Separate Statement of Commissioner Mimi Weyforth Dawson).

312. *OPP Report,* supra note 21.

313. *Id.*

314. *Id.*

315. *Id.* at Executive Summary.

316. *Id.* The Herfindahl-Hirschman Index is used by the Department of Justice as a measure of relative market concentration. The index is designed to quantify the threat of anticompetitive practices and undue economic power based upon the structure of the industry.

317. *Notice of Proposed Rulemaking* (Docket No. 83-1009), 48 Fed. Reg. 49438 (Oct. 25, 1983).

318. *Id.* at paras. 44-45.

319. *Memorandum Opinion and Order* (Gen. Docket No. 83-1009), FCC 84-638, released Feb. 1, 1985, at para 36.

320. *Id.*

321. *Id.*

322. Notice of Proposed Rulemaking (Docket No. 20221), 48 Fed. Reg. 10082, 10084 (Mar. 10, 1983).

323. *Tentative Decision, supra* note 26, 48 Fed. Reg. at 38034.

324. In a statement dissenting to the FCC's rejection of a petition for rulemaking which would provide television stations with full syndicated program exclusivity in all markets for carriage of distant television signals, Commissioner James Quello observed: "The broadcast industry does not operate in a vacuum. Copyright issues are a crucial element of the broadcast marketplace, and the Commission cannot fulfill its responsibilities it it ignores the effects of its actions on the very market place forces on which it has placed such heavy reliance. *Memorandum Opinion and Order,* FCC 84-336, released July 17, 1984 (Dissenting Statement of Commissioner James H. Quello).

325. *Fortnightly Corp. v. United Artists Television, Inc.,* 392 U.S. 390 (1968) (holding that the reception and distribution of television broadcasts by cable television systems does not constitute a performance within the meaning of the Copyright Act).

326. *Teleprompter Corp. v. CBS, Inc.,* 415 U.S. 394 (1974) (holding that program origination, sale of commercials and interconnection by cable systems are extraneous functions with respect to copyright infringement).

327. 392 U.S. at 400.

328. *Report and Order* (docket Nos. 20988 ane 21284), 74 FCC 2d 663 (1980), *aff'd Malrite TV of N.Y. v. FCC,* 652 F. 2d 1140 (2d Cir. 1981), *cert. denied,* 454 U.S. 1143 (1982).

329. Pub. L. No. 94-553, 90 Stat. 2541 (1976) (*codified at* 17 U.S.C. sec. 111 (Supp.

III 1979)).

330. *Id.* at sec. 801. *See National Cable Television Association v. CRT,* 689 F. 2d 1077 (D.C. Cir. 1982). Almost as soon as the Copyright Royal Tribunal began setting cable royalty rates, broadcasters and program producers contended that the rates were much too low. As noted earlier, in 1982, the CRT responded by approving higher rates for the carriage of distant signals by cable, and Congress in turn responded to that change in policy by considering legislation that would again allow cable operators to carry two distant independent television stations without any copyright royalty liability at all.

331. *Eastern Microwave, Inc. v. Doubleday Sports, Inc.* 691 F. 2d 125 (2d Cir. 1982), *cert. denied,* 103 S.Ct. 1232 (1983).

332. 17 U.S.C. sec. 111(a) (3).

333. *WGN Continental Broadcasting Co. v. United Video, Inc.,* 693 F. 2d 622 (7th Cir. 1982).

334. *Id.* at 628.

335. *Sony Corporation of America v. Universal City Studios, Inc.,* 104 S.Ct. 774 (1984).

336. *Id.* at 783.

337. *Id.* at 789.

338. *Id.* at 792-93.

339. *Id.*

340. *Id.*

341. Satellite dishes (also referred to as TVROs, television receive-only private earth stations) are "one of the most rapidly expanding segments of the American economy." "Satellite Dishes Vie With Cable," *N.Y. Times,* Aug. 9, 1984, at C 18. As of August 1984, approximately 400,000 private or "backyard" satellite dishes were in use in the United States—sales are growing at an annual rate of 300%. *Id.*

342. *Sony Corporation of America, supra,* 104 S. Ct. at 789. The narrow grounds upon which the Supreme Court acted left open the legal consequences for home tapers of programming transmitted on cable and other new technologies. Edward Samuels, "'Betamax' The Cable Issues Remain Open," *Cable T.V. Law & Finance,* March 1984, at 3.

343. 47 U.S.C. sec. 705 (1984).

344. *Id. See also* Timothy Wirth, "No Free Lunch in the New Satellite-Dish Law," *N.Y. Times,* Dec. 10, 1984, at A30.

345. "McKinney Warns of Deregulation Roadblocks at State, Local Levels," *Broadcasting,* Oct. 24, 1983, at 58.

346. Remarks of Daniel L. Brenner, Special Advisor to the Chairman, FCC, NCTA State Leadership Conference, Washington, D.C., Nov. 15, 1984, at 10.

347. *See* David M. Rice and Michael Botein, "The Ambivalent Nature of the Cable Communications Policy Act of 1974: An Analysis," *N.Y.L.J.,* March 22, 1985, at 5.

348. 47 U.S.C. sec. 541(b). *See also* "3 Signals Chosen as Cable Competition Standard," *Television Digest,* April 15, 1985, at 5.

349. 47 U.S.C. sec. 531(e).

350. *Id.* at sec. 541(b).

351. *Id.* at sec. 556(a)(b).
352. *Community Cable TV, Inc.,* CSR-2269, FCC 83-525, released Nov. 15, 1983.
353. *Id.* at para. 13.
354. *Id.* at para. 20.
355. *Id.* at para. 21.
356. *Earth Satellite Communications, Inc.,* 55 R.R.2d (P&F) 1427 (1983), *aff'd sub. nom. New York State Commission on Cable TV v. FCC,* Nos. 83-2190, 83-2196 (D.C. Cir. Nov. 30, 1984).
357. *Id.* at para. 20.
358. The Commission has also preempted State regulation that has the effect of prohibiting or impeding entry of radio common carrier services operating on FM and television subcarriers. *See Memorandum Opinion and Order* (BC Docket No. 82-536), FCC 84-187, released May 2, 1984; *Second Report and Order* (Docket No. 21323), FCC 84-116, released Apr. 23, 1984, at paras. 28-30.
359. In the matter of Cox Cable Communications, Inc., Commline, Inc. and Cox DTS, Inc., Preemption of and Jurisdiction over Broadband Coaxial Cable's Local Distribution of Inter/Intrastate Communications and Interconnection with Digital Termination Systems, Petition for Declaratory Ruling, filed Apr. 22, 1983.
360. *Id.* at 12.
361. Richard McKenna, "Pre-Emption Under the Communications Act," *Fed. Comm. L.J.* 37 (1985): 1 at 5.
362. *Id.* at 62.
363. *See supra* note 96.
364. The court noted that, while the FCC's discretion is "particularly capacious when the Commission is dealing with new technologies unforeseen at the time the Communications Act was passed, that discretion is not boundless: the Commission has no authority to experiment with its Statutory obligations." *NAB v. FCC, supra* note 113 at 1200-1201.
365. *See* however, Separate Statement of Commissioner Henry M. Rivera, *Further Notice of Proposed Rulemaking* (MM Docket No. 83-523, FCC 84-363, released Aug. 10, 1984) characterizing as an "unfortunate head-in-the-sand approach," the FCC's failure to include in the *Notice,* which raised a broad array of issues pertaining to the ITFS service, questions as to the appropriate regulatory classification for ITFS.
366. *Notice of Proposed Rulemaking* (Gen. Docket No. 82-334), 48 Fed. Reg. 6730 (Feb. 15, 1983).
367. Alex Felker and Kenneth Gordon, *A Framework for a Decentralized Radio Service* (Office of Plans and Policy, FCC, Sept. 1983) at 11 n. 17.
368. *Id.*
369. Douglas W. Webbink, *Frequency Spectrum Deregulation Alternatives* 25 (Office of Plans and Policy, FCC, Sept. 1982). *See also Notice of Proposed Rulemaking* (MM Docket No. 85-523 48 Fed. Reg. 29553) (Comments were solicited as procedures for selecting among mutually exclusive applicants, including lotteries and "first-come-first-served.")
370. *See* 47 U.S.C. 309(i) (supp. v 1981). *See also* Conference Rep. No. 765, 97th

Cong., 2d Sess. 37 (1982), for a discussion of the public interest parameters which limit the Commission's discretion to use a lottery system.

371. *Report and Order* (Gen. Docket No. 81-768), 88 F.C.C.2d 476 (1981), *Second Report and Order* (Gen. Docket No, 81-768), 93 F.C.C.2d 952 (1983), *aff'd sub nom., National Latino Media Coalition v. FCC,* No. 83-1785) D.C. Cir. Aug. 17, 1984). *See also Memorandum Opinion and Order* (Gen. Docket No, 81-768), released Dec. 4, 1984, *appeal pending sub nom. Bahia Honda, Inc. v. FCC,* No. 85-1046 (D.C. Cir. Jan. 29, 1985). *See* Arthur Stambler, "Carrying Lotteries to Logical Extreme," *Broadcasting,* Nov. 28, 1983, at 21.

372. *See* Webbink, *supra* note 369. The FCC has conducted both "pure" (i.e., even chance) and weighted lotteries. The lottery preferences in weighted lotteries are an attempted substitute for the comparative criteria of diversification and minority ownership.

373. *Id.* at 25. *See also* Ira Barron, "There's No Such Thing as a Free Airwave: A Proposal to Institute a Market Allocation Scheme for Electromagnetic Frequencies," *J. of Leg.* 9 (1982): 205, and Nicholas Johnson, "Towers of Babel: The Chaos in Radio Spectrum Utilization and Allocation," *Law and Contemp. Prob.* 34 (1969): 505. Fowler is considering asking Congress for authority to auction off unassigned spectrum. "Up for Bids," *Broadcasting,* Jan. 7, 1985, at 10.

374. *See* David R. Siddall, *Legal Analysis of Radio Spectrum Use Charges,* Congressional Research Service, Library of Congress (Apr. 20, 1979) (concludes that there is no legally sure method to collect fees for the use of spectrum which guarantees returns that exceed the cost of administering the fee system).

375. *See, e.g., Notice of Inquiry and Proposed Rulemaking* (CC Docket No. 80-116), 45 Fed. Reg. 29335 (May 2, 1980), at paras. 77-80.

376. FCC News Release, Report No. 18040 (June 28, 1984). *See also Notice of Proposed Rulemaking* (MM Docket No, 83-670), 48 Fed. Reg. 37239 (Aug. 17, 1983).

377. *See supra* notes 276-292 and accompanying text. The FCC, however, will not be able to rescind its restrictions on ownership of cable systems by local television stations. Section 613(a) of the Cable Communications Policy Act of 1985 prohibits the ownership of a cable system by a television licensee whose station's predicted grade B contour covers any portion of the cable community. Pub.L.No. 98-549 (1984).

378. *See supra* notes 57-62 and accompanying text.

379. *See, e.g., Notice of Proposed Rulemaking* (MM Docket No, 83-670), *supra* note 376; *Report and Order* (Docket No.l 19142), *supra* note 203; *Notice of Inquiry* (Gen. Docket No. 84-282), 49 Fed. Reg. 20317 (May 14, 1984) (Fairness Doctrine obligations of broadcast licensees); *Notice of Proposed Rulemaking* (Gen. Docket No, 83-484), 48 Fed. Reg. 28295 (June 21, 1983) (repeal of the personal attack and political editorializing rules).

380. *See, e.g.,* H.R. 2382, 98th Cong., 1st Sess. (1983) (introduced by Reps. Tauzin and Tauke).

381. 47 U.S.C. secs. 312, 315 (1976).

382. 18 U.S.C. secs. 1304, 1464 (1976).

383. 47 U.S.C. sec. 315(a) (1976). *See also Fairness Doctrine,* 40 F.C.C. 598 (1964).

384. "FCC Sets First Proposal for Amending Communications Act," FCC Report No.

5068 (Sept. 17, 1981), at 34.

385. Senator Packwood had supported a constitutional amendment to guarantee broadcasters full First Amendment protection, but dropped the proposal because of the difficulty of adoption. He now favors legislation to repeal the fairness doctrine and political broadcasting rules. See "'Pragmatic' Sen. Packwood to Drop First Amendment Push for Broadcasters," *Communications Daily*, Apr. 12, 1983, at 1-2. On October 3, 1983, Senator Packwood introduced S.1917, the "Freedom of Expression Act of 1983," which would repeal the fairness doctrine and Sections 312(a) (7) and 315 of the Communications Act, and strengthen Section 326, the "no censorship" provision of the Act.

386. See *FCC v. League of Women Voters of California*, 104 S.Ct. 3106, 3117 n. 12 (1984).

387. *Notice of Inquiry and Proposed Rulemaking* (Gen. Docket No. 83-114), 48 Fed. Reg. 14399 (Apr. 4, 1983). *Report and Order* (Gen. Docket No. 83-114), released Dec. 4, 1984 (enunciation of general principles which the FCC will use in an incremental approach to deregulation).

388. See "And Now, a Spectrum Bubble," *AEI Journal on Government and Society*, May/June 1983, at 8.

389. *Satellite Television Corp.*, 91 F.C.C. 2d 953, 976 (1982).

390. "The alphabet soup of the new media has grown cold. STV, MDS, MMDS, DBS and LPTV, which along with teletext and videotex were the technologically hot new media of the late '70s and early '80s, have failed to gain a collective foothold that could dislodge conventional broadcasters and cablecasters from their established places in electronic communications. Moreover, it is unlikely any will." "The New Order Passeth," *Broadcasting*, Dec. 10, 1984, at 83.

391. See, e.g., *Notice of Proposed Rulemaking* (Gen. Docket No. 82-334), 48 Fed. Reg. 6730 (Feb. 15, 1983).

392. See Mark P. Schreiber, "Don't Make Waves: AM Stereophonic Broadcasting and the Marketplace Approach," *Comm.L.J.* 5 (1983): 821.

393. "Teletext has suffered from the lack of a standard. . . . As a result [of the FCC's decision not to select a standard], bickering between proponents of the incompatible World System Teletext system and the North American Broadcast Teletext System has nearly eliminated what little momentum the media had," "The New Order Passeth," *Broadcasting*, Dec. 10, 1984, at 66.

394. One commentator points out that it is difficult to avoid the chicken-and-egg situation that arises in approaching the issue of setting standards. If standards are developed and enforced at too early a stage in hardware development, technological innovation could be retarded and the competitive marketplace for the service could be artificially skewed. However, absent standards, the production of necessary software may be inhibited, as software producers wait to see which system will win consumer acceptance. Stuart N. Brotman, "The Conundrum of Setting Standards: FCC Policy Options for New Communications Technologies," *Communications Lawyer*, Spring 1984, at 5.

395. In *Telocator Network of America v. FCC*, 691 F.2d 525, 544-50 (D.C. Cir. 1982), the Court of Appeals took special care to warn the FCC against pursuing "competition for competition's sake."

396. Commissioner Henry Rivera has criticized "the FCC's recent practice . . . to

advance a restrictive interpretation of the term broadcating wherever possible." *Rivera Remarks, supra* note 4, at 10. He commented that "this Commission abhors the program content-related duties that go with classification as a broadcaster."

397. *See* Caroline Mayer, "FCC Chief's Fears, Fowler Sees Threat in Regulation," *Wash. Post,* Feb. 6, 1983, at K6, col. 4.

398. In 1981, the FCC instituted a proceeding into the proper use of an examination into an applicant's character in the licensing process. *Notice of Inquiry* (Gen. Docket No, 81-500), 87 F.C.C.2d 836 (1981).

399. *See* 47 U.S.C. secs. 152(b), 221(b).

400. *See Policy Statement and Order* (MM Docket No. 83-842), FCC 85-25, released Feb. 5, 1985.

401. *Office of Communication of United Church of Christ v. FCC,* 707 F. 2d 1413 (D.C. Cir. 1983).

402. Michael Wines, "FCC Discovers That Carving Up The Spectrum Isn't What It Used To Be," *National Journal,* May 19, 1984, at 983.

403. *Office of Communication of United Church of Christ v. FCC, supra* note 401, 707 F.2d at 1443.

404. Staff Report, House Subcomm. on Telecomunications, Consumer Protection and Finance, *Telecommunications in Transition: The Status of Competition in the Telecommunications Industry* XII (Comm. Print 97-V, Nov. 3, 1981).

405. Roland S. Homet, Jr., "'Getting the Message': Statutory Approaches to Electronic Information Delivery and the Duty of Carriage," *Fed. Comm. L.J.* 37 (1985): 217, 288.

APPENDIX NOTES

1. "Comsat on the Verge of Changes," *Washington Post,* July 16, 1984, Business Week at 1. "The New Order Passeth," *Broadcasting,* Dec. 10, 1984, at 50.

2. *Broadcasting,* July 16, 1984, at 30; "Where Things Stand," *Broadcasting,* Jan. 7, 1985, at 42.

3. *CBS, Inc.,* 52 Rad. Reg. 2d (P&F) at 1117-24. *See also* "After 10 Years of Satellites, The Sky's No Limit," *Broadcasting,* Apr. 9, 1984, at 50. DBSC, for example, has proposed to broadcast, through spot beams, six channels of service to the continental United States and four additional channels to three discrete regions within the primary service area.

4. Simon Applebaum, "DBS Launch Detailed," *CableVision,* Oct. 10, 1983 at 20; *see also* Laura Landro, "United Satellite Plans TV Service Directly to Homes," *Wall St. J.,* Feb. 26, 1982, at 18, col. 4; "DBS Set to Debut," *Broadcasting,* Nov. 7, 1983, at 74; "Prudential Places a Bet on DBS," *Broadcasting,* Feb. 7, 1983, at 31-32.

5. *Instructional Television Fixed Service (MDS Reallocation),* 94 F.C.C. 2d 1203 (1983). *See also Notice of Inquiry, Proposed Rulemaking and Order* (Gen. Docket No. 80-112), 45 Fed. Reg. 29323 (May 2, 1980).

6. *First Report and Order* (Gen. Docket No. 80-113), FCC, 84-175, released June

14, 1984; *see also Notice of Inquiry and Proposed Rulemaking* (Gen. Docket No, 80-113), 45 Fed. Reg. 29350 (May 2, 1980); *Further Notice of Proposed Rulemaking and Notice of Inquiry* (Gen. Docket No. 80-113), FCC 84-175, released June 14, 1984.

7. "Microband Plans Multichannel Service Through ITFS Band," *Broadcasting,* Nov. 7, 1983 at 74. *See also* "Movement Afoot on MCTV Front," *Broadcasting,* Jan. 2, 1984, at 40.

8. *See Transmitting Program Materials to Hotels,* 39 F.C.C.2d 527, 532-33 (1973).

9. 47 U.S.C. sec. 705 (1984). This section specifically exempts from its general prohibition "receiving, divulging, publishing or utilizing the contents of any radio communication which is *broadcast* . . . for the use of the general public. *Id.* (emphasis added).

10. *See e.g., Broadcasting,* Sept. 5, 1983, at 90.

11. William B. Johnston, "The Coming Glut of Phone Lines," *Fortune,* Jan. 7, 1985, at 97.

12. "GE's 2-for-1 Proposition," *Broadcasting,* Oct. 18, 1982, at 30.

13. 53 Rad. Reg. 2d (P&F) at 1105.

Chapter 5

INFORMATION TECHNOLOGY AND CULTURAL CHANGE: TOWARD A NEW LITERACY

Benjamin M. Compaine

The New Literacy is the bundle of information skills that may be required to function in society, skills that may evolve from the capabilities made possible by the increasingly widespread use of inexpensive compunications (computer and communications) technology. It is a literacy that builds on, rather than replaces, contemporary notions of literacy. Literacy itself has never been a static concept. Over centuries, the bundle of skills we call a literacy has evolved with technology, as well as with the political, economic, and social systems. The current notion of literacy has evolved from the technology of the quill pen, paper, movable type, and the mechanically powered rotary press.

The New Literacy is *not* about the need or ability to program computers or even to work devices labeled "computer." But increasingly, information is being digitally stored in some electronic medium and being delivered to users by telecommunications or via devices that can make the information readable, viewable, or audible. The continuation of these trends, enabled by technology, impeded or aided by government regulation, accepted or resisted by our culture, is likely to create the need for a new bundle of skills and processes that will define the New Literacy. Should the notion that a New Literacy is emerging prove accurate, it will not happen overnight. More likely, it will be an evolution that involves a transition period in which the tools of the New Literacy are used with the substance of the traditional literacy.

The foundation of a New Literacy is the social and cultural change that is likely to come about from the increased use of digital electronic processes. At this stage, it is little more than a notion; testing its validity may take years or decades. However, there is basis in history for it and there is circumstantial evidence in the present that the consequences of a possible change in the fundamentals of literacy need to be taken seriously.

Still, it is almost impossible to predict the nature of any change. For example, historian Elizabeth Eisenstein, in considering the impact of printing on Western civilization, noted that,while it is relatively easy to describe the development of printing in the 15th century, "It is another thing to decide how access to a greater abundance or variety of written records affected ways of learning, thinking, and perceiving among literate elites."[1] The key issues in the notion of a New Literacy are in seeking some understanding of the influence of modern information technologies on learning, behavior, and perception, not only by literate elites but principally by the general public.

The long-term implications could be substantial. Along with the technological alterations in how we are able to construct, store, and use information are likely to evolve parallel changes in how we approach the situations for which we seek out information.

As a hypothetical example, imagine society prior to the development of a cheap, reliable straight edge and the ball point pen. Although the concept of a straight line may have been well known, the skill to draw a straight line free-hand would have been restricted to a relatively few skilled craftsmen. They would have been futher encumbered by the technology of the stylus and waxed tablets or reeds and papyrus as their media. Therefore, any sort of geometric problem whose solution required use of straight lines for solving, such as for structural designs, would have been difficult. By contrast, the widespread application of the straight edge would have broadened the base of those technically able to draw lines. The improvement in drawing implements, to quill pens, fountain pens and ball point pens, further reduced the difficulty in drawing lines and made their application feasible for more people.

The result is that, as several technologies change, the skill level need to perform a task declines, but the need to master the skill becomes more important because it is expected that the ability to be able to perform the task is part of the bag of skills widely available. Moreover, and at least as important, we could assume that the widespread ability to draw accurate straight lines meant that tasks that may have been previously unthinkable— such as complex architectural renderings—became quite thinkable and doable, and for a larger group of people than before.

Translated into New Literacy terms, compunications makes possible the previously hardly thinkable or unthinkable. Thus, the ability to randomly access information from a vast database and manipulate it (whether as market research or a crossword puzzle) is not new. We can always go to a library and randomly access its stacks. But it has been highly labor intensive and has required considerable skill on the part of the searcher. The trend in computer and communications use has been to lower the labor involved as well as the skill required. (Compare, for example, the use of the complex search routines for the bibliographic databases such as Dialog and the much simpler ones for Nexis/Lexis).

The question behind the New Literacy notion, then, is whether the pervasive use of compunications will reduce the skill levels needed for certain types of problem solving and general information seeking behavior in society and at the same time make it necessary for this new level of skill to become an integral part of what it means to be "literate?"* And, if this comes about, what are the implications for how we decide what can be done with information that previously was unthinkable — or at least too expensive to do?

TRADITIONAL LITERACY

History provides a wealth of precedents for the changes we are experiencing today. Each generation seems to think its problems or opportunities are unique. History sometimes shows us quite the opposite. The development of low-cost computer power and its attendant implications for educational, industrial, social, and political structures all have antecedents. For example, the introduction of photography in the 19th century collided with the popular wisdom about the role of art and painting. Then, the questions were about the new technology of the photographic process and how it might affect human views on the reality of war or on creativity. Today, similar types of questions are being raised about the effect electronic publishing is having on print and on the impact of television and video games on children.

The development of current notions of literacy is closely tied to the technologies of the printing press and the steam engine. An understanding of the previous evolution in technology and literacy is context for today's changes.

---

*Personal experience with combined spreadsheet/graphics programs on personal computers (Lotus 1-2-3 being the best known but not the only one) suggests there is already some of this new information manipulating behavior at work. Use of full text data bases, such as Nexis, suggest another way in which compunications enables researchers to seek answers to questions that were often unfeasible to ask before. These may be seen some day as the modern equivalent of the straight edge.

What is Literacy?

Literacy frequently describes a range of skills. It is used to mean the ability to read and write in one's vernacular. Being "literate" may mean being familiar with the great works of literature and philosophy of a culture. Sometimes it is also applied to basic skills, such as the ability to fill out a bank check properly or to understand simple written instructions. We also see literacy modified by very specific skills. A person who can identify the works of composers might be referred to as being musically literate. The ability to understand calculus may qualify one as being mathematically literate. And today, the ability to write programs in computer languages that make the computers perform tasks is being called computer literacy. Indeed, the mastery of almost any skill can be called a literacy: mechanically literate, visually literate, and so on. The term literacy itself comes from the Latin *litteratus*, or marked with letters. In medieval usage, to be literate meant to be learned in Latin, not simply the ability to read and write in the vernacular.[2]

This variety of uses of the term literacy both reinforces and muddies the concept as used in this paper. It reinforces because, as it is used here, literacy is not a simple commodity, but a dynamic bundle of skills that may encompass visual, auditory, mechanical, and other abilities, with the mix varying over time and among cultures. The variety muddies the waters because it is hopeless to try to describe literacy if the term is extended to include proficiency in any particular skill.

Thus, this paper is *not* about a narrow meaning such as computer literacy, or the ability to program a computer or work a computer for its own intrinsic worth. As a starting point, this paper accepts a point of view that literacy in modern Western society is "a complex cultural phenomenon involving relations between attitudes towards language and mechanical skills."[3] The attitudes involve a consciousness of the uses and problems of language, this awareness being the foundation of literacy. But the pragmatic aspect of a literacy is the means by which this consciousness is expressed. Twentieth-century American culture holds that the skills of being able to read and write are at the foundation of literacy. This has not always been the case, however. Before the written record came into widespread use in 11th-century England, the oral tradition predominated. To be literate meant the ability to compose and recite orally—in Latin, of course. Into the 12th century, to make a record of something meant to bear oral witness, not to produce a document for others to read. Even where written records existed, "the spoken word was the legally valid record."[4]

Moreover, because of the difficulty of writing with a quill on parchment or with a stylus on wax, writing was considered a special skill that "was not automatically coupled with the ability to read."[5] The most common way of committing words to writing in 12th-century England was by dictating to a scribe, who was an auxillary to literates and not necessarily himself able to compose. Indeed, the scribe may have sometimes had to read back the composed work to the "literate" who had dictated the poem or memorandum. Thus, composing and dictating were typically paired, rather than reading and writing.

Today, reading and writing are the basic skills of literacy. In 19th-century England, the goal of bringing reading and writing skills to the common man was not an end in itself. According to the literati, it was not merely the ability to read, but the reading of the "right" material, that separated the truly literate from the great unwashed. The printed word was supposed to bring spiritual enrichment and intellectural enlightenment to the English nation. Novel reading was held in particularly low esteem by some elements of the literati, with much the same disdain held today for commercial television, video games, and even the multitude of self-help and how-to books in some sectors of society. In 1879, an English librarian told a meeting that "school-boys or students who took to novel reading to any great extent never made much progress in after life."[6] The irony of this should not be lost on those who are convinced that television and even newer electronic media are eroding literacy. What they really mean is that they menace the *traditional* concept of literacy.

WRITING, PRINTING AND BEHAVIOR

History provides the strongest argument at this time that, if a new literacy emerges from the expanding use of compunications, it will have a profound – if unpredictable – impact on society. The precedent goes back, not just to the development of the printing press, but to the development of phonetic alphabets as the basis for writing. The fundamental impact of written compared to oral literacy cultures on thought processes has been grist for philosophers, sociologists, anthropologists, psychologists, historians, and linguists for thousands of years. Socrates told the story of the reaction of Thamus, King of Egypt, to whom the god Theuth brought the art of writing: . . .This invention [writing], "said Thamus, will produce forgetfulness in the souls of those who have learned it. They will not need to exercise their memories, being able to rely on what is written, calling things to mind no longer from within themselves . . . but under the stimulus of external marks...."[7]

Thus, the notion that writing fosters behavior or even thought process different from a verbal literacy is an old one. In more recent times, the writings of Goody, Innis, McLuhan, and Ong, among others, address the relationship between thought processes and the technology of expression.[8] In general, this group of writers proposes that the development of alphabets consisting of a small number of symbols made possible "a stage of logical thinking that is not possible in cultures with only an oral tradition."[9]

The merging of written and oral culture happened over time, with elements of the old oral tradition being incorporated into the growing use of written texts in Western culture. For centuries after written texts appeared, they remained largely subsidiary to their oral presentation. Manuscripts before printing were bulky volumes. They were often meant to be read aloud to others. Authors such as Chaucer and Boccocio wrote their stories in the form of stories being recited orally, and probably most people who were exposed to their writings heard them read aloud.

Printing had a different impact from writing. Greater legibility of print lead to more silent reading and a changed relationship between the reader and author. This lead in turn to styles of writing other than those mimicking the oral style.[10] Among other changes in attitude or behavior that have been attributed to print are:

- a sense of private ownership of words;
- a resentment of plagarism;
- a rise of the notion of creativity and originality;
- a sense that the words of an author were in definitive or "final" form, compared to manuscripts, with their marginal comments and hence in something of a dialogue with the outside world.[11]

Walter Ong suggests that the telephone, radio, audio records, and television have brought us to a period of "secondary orality."[12] Although bearing some resemblence to the old orality, today's orality is different because the audience today is most often invisible and inaudiable to the speaker. Moreover, he sees secondary orality as being more deliberate and self-conscious — more like writing and print — because it is based permanently on the use of writing and printing.

Symbols, such as letters, words and numbers, are used to convey information. Education to a large extent is the process of teaching children to master the manipulation of the symbols used in a given culture. Writing appeared as a complete system in Greece by the 7th century, B.C., although its final standardization was not reached until the 4th century.[13] It made possible a permanently recorded version of history and thereby created the basis for critical historical inquiry. It also made easier the teaching of logic and specialized learning. The relationship between writing and symbol manipulation skills is central to the notion of the New Literacy, because the power of digital information processes today has the potential to restructure the way in which we use writing.

Writing, particularly analytic writing, increased the explicitness of language compared to the oral tradition. David Olson argues that analytic writing minimizes the number of possible interpretations of a statement. The oral tradition appeals more to shared experiences, interpretations, and intuition; and it is interpersonal and rhetorical. Written texts, on the other hand, appeal to rules of logic for implications and are formal, not intuitive.[14]

Such hypotheses find some empirical support in studies of cultures that use nonphonetic written forms, such as Chinese ideograms, and in surviving oral cultures. In one comparison of written and oral literacy groups, Patricia Greenfield found that the oral cultures rely more on context for communication because communication is more often face-to-face and shared by smaller groups. Writing, however, uses linguistic context independent of immediate reference. She concluded that context-dependent forms of communication and thought were more primitive than context-free ones.[15]

There is an abundance of indicators—only a smattering of which is presented here—that suggests that writing, and, by derivation, printing, has helped develop a logical, sequential, sense of relationships in modern literate societies. Ideas of cause and effect are in the form of things in sequence, a relationship which some anthropologists, linguists, and others believe is alien to predominantly oral cultures. Even Chinese writing invests each ideogram with total intuition that leaves little role to the visual sequence of what follows and precedes it. David Hume argued in the 18th century that there is no causality indicated in any sequence, yet in Western literate society we adhere to the notion that certain things must follow from others.

Such suggestions about the relationships of oral literate and written literate cultures to approaches to thinking or behavior must not be taken as absolute. Homeric poetry, for example, though a creation of an oral society, consists of rigid hexameters, while the prose of William Burroughs or the painting of early 20th century Cubists are anything but sequential or logical. Rather, there appears to be evidence that societies tend toward predominance of certain effects associated with the existence or absence of a written alphabet and the widespread use or lack of printing. The traditional literacy, with its roots in the oral mode, is today associated with writing and print.

OTHER CONSEQUENCES OF CHANGE TO WRITTEN LITERACY

The gradual shift to a literacy that emphasized reading and writing skills brought political, social, economic, and cultural changes, few, if any, of which could have been foreseen by contemporaries of the printing press.

Print did not burst upon Europe in the 15th century and suddenly change what had been a predominantly oral culture. Indeed, the oral tradition did not and has not died. Robert Pattison reminds us: "When men learn to write they do not forget how to speak. Even with writing, much information — probably most information necessary for fundamental human activity — continues to be passed along solely by speech and held in the mind without written record."[16] The gradual emergence of written texts and then printing in medieval England, and with them the rise of reading and writing skills, did of course have their consequences. They included new kinds of social structures, such as bureaucracy and business, that were encouraged by reading and writing skills. Nonetheless, and perhaps contrary to some modern myths, literacy has not led to uniform outcomes across cultures. Widespread literacy cannot be automatically associated with any particular form of government or economy. Literacy has not always widened the perspectives of those who attain its skills.

In both the economic and political arenas, widespread basic literacy is not a reliable indicator of structure. Rome in the first century A.D. had a large literate population but was a military autocracy. Iceland has had nearly universal basic literacy since the 18th century and is a pacific democracy with an economy based on fishing and agriculture. Sweden and Scotland each achieved mass literacy prior to the 19th century yet remained far poorer than less literate neighbors.[17] On the other hand, in Saudi Arabia, where only 40% of the population can read and write, thanks to oil the per capita gross national product is 60% higher than in Great Britain. The Soviet Union takes great pride in figures of almost 100% literacy. Whether they are accurate is secondary; more important is the lesson that literacy and authoritarian regimes are not antithetical. This would seem to cast doubt on the belief that a literate people will always demand personal freedoms. Or put cynically, "There is no guarantee that because people can read and write, they can also think."[18]

There is evidence that suggests that a literacy is closely intertwined with the culture in which it is introduced. The outcome is thus specific to each culture. The Shah of Iran learned this lesson the hard way. Although he was successful in expanding reading and writing skills among his people, he either did not recognize or was unable to overcome their traditional religious and cultural values. Thus, the Iranians were simply able to have access to more information of national or global events on which to project their traditional Islamic values.

FORCES AND TRENDS SHAPING NEW LITERACY

Print was not so much a break with the past as it was a technological force that contributed to an already well-established trend exemplified in England in the 11th century: growing use of written records instead of records stored in human memory. Similarly, the current premise is that the effects of recent electronic technological developments in computers and communications are a continuation of a long and well-documented historical process. Video games, personal computers, the increasing cost of paper and physical delivery, widespread use of automatic teller machines, electronic mail, growth in electronic data base publishing, and others are not isolated no mutually exclusive developments. They are pieces of a dynamic process in much the same tradition as were, for example, the development of the steam-driven rotary press, the spread of the railroads, innovation in manu-facturing of cheap paper, and improvement in optics for eyeglasses. These latter forces led to profound changes in the nature and breadth of written literacy, from the elite to the masses. Now, other forces are coming together with a potential for a new set of effects.

Computers have been purchased by the millions for homes and schools, with prices of useable systems now under $600 and continuing to drop. Video games, which peaked with sales of about $8 billion in 1982, are merging with home computers that can play the games as well as perform simple word processing, educational programs, household programs, and write-it-yourself programs.

In offices, the success of the IBM personal computer and other computer systems in the $1000-plus category is largely due to the functions these machines have succesfully performed, in particular the spreadsheet calcu-lations, word processing, data base management and information retrieval for small and medium business that previously could not afford computer-ized operations. Well over 2 million personal computers in the $1000-plus category were shipped in 1983 alone. Large businesses are using the personal computers to place direct computer power at the hands of more people. Travelers Insurance Co., as one example, had 2000 PCs in its offices by 1983 and had formal arrangements for 10,000 more by 1986.[19] Aetna Casualty and Life figured it had one video display terminal for each six employees in 1982 but expected to have one terminal per two workers by 1985. Manpower, Inc., a temporary help firm, has experienced such a surge in requests for temporary office workers for word processing and personal computer operators that it is traininng 700,000 of its workers to use these tools. And it is equipping all 1050 of its own offices with personal computers.[20]

According to figures compiled by Xerox, there are perhaps 15 million adults working with VDTs as part of their daily routines.[21] They include secretaries using word processors, order takers for catalog retailers, reser-vation clerks at airlines, car rental agencies, and travel agencies, stockbro-kers checking securities prices, newspaper reporters and editors creating tomorrow's edition, and lawyers researching court decisions. These are not necessarily the people being thought of when "computer" literacy is discussed.

It is difficult to estimate the pace at which cultural change will take place. But the notion that there is something special about "the book" or about print is culturally derived. As noted in the first portion of this paper, the written word was not always held in high esteem. That is, we have become used to and comfortable with print. We have developed conventions for its use. As previously described in Chapter 3, "print" or "video" are examples of *formats* in which some content or substance can be displayed or otherwise manipulated by users.

These are among a numerous of ways in which we can express information *substance*. Substance may be any number of colloquial and specialized denotations and connotations that can be lumped under the general rubric of "information."

Process is the application of instruments, such as typewriters, computers, printing presses, the human brain, telephone wire, or delivery trucks in the creation, manipulation, storage, and transmission/distribution of substance in some intermediate or final format. (See Chapter 3 for an expanded example of the combination of substance, process and format.)

The implication of the New Literacy notion is that changing processes and formats may have a long-term effect on how users deal with substance. A generation of children is being exposed to video games and computers at home and school. Unlike print or even radio and television, these devices change the relationship between users and the process by which they interact with information.

Unlike users of a printed book or conventional motion picture, users of digitally based substance find they can manipulate the image on the screen, change it and often store it, without necessarily leaving the footprints of penciled marginal notes or splices that have been the basis for modifying substance provided in traditional formats. The thousands of engineers and draftsmen who are using computer-aided design terminals are in the forefront of what could be a fundamental change.

Behind this vanguard may be a generation that is starting to discover that a computer is more than a number cruncher or text manipulator. Anyone who has had access to a computer such as Apple's Macintosh, with a graphics program, quickly discovers that one no longer need be an artist to "draw". What the straight edge was to straight lines, so MacPaint may be to modern graphics. With virtually no more skill than is necessary to connect two points with a ruler today, a user of these types of programs, combined with an appropriate printer, can create diagrams and pictures, for use in correspondence, for business, for engineering study, for charts, or for pure art.

If the New Literacy notion is correct, then over time those literate in newer (but increasingly more commonplace) compunications processes such as these are likely to internalize fresh approaches to using substance, in much the same way that increasing familiarity and comfort with written records changed how information was used when it was stored predominately in memory and conveyed primarily orally. As the straight edge opened up the world to common use of straight lines, so may the widespread use of computers open up opportunities for lowering and expanding the skills associated with its powers for manipulating information.

STAGES OF DEVELOPMENT OF A NEW LITERACY

There is reason to expect a New Literacy to develop in at least two stages, as illustrated in Figure 1. If the current literacy can be dubbed Literacy I, the first stage of change is Literacy II. This stage might be characterized as "old wine in new bottles." That is, we may be using newer processes and formats for substantive manipulation, retrieval and storage, but thinking about the substance in traditional ways. This is analogous to the early days of television, when the first programs were often televised versions of radio shows (i.e., Fred Allen) or films shown in 20-minute segments (the length of time to show 400 feet of 16 mm film with introduction and commercials). Only after some years did the video medium yield programs that took advantage of its strengths, such as the sight gags of Milton Berle and Ernie Kovacs. The 30-minute segment also became predominant.

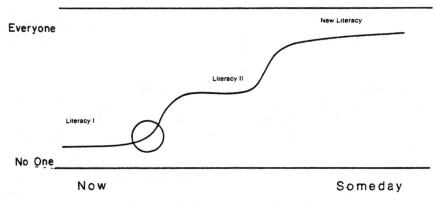

Figure 1   The Road to A New Literacy?

Parallel to the experiences of early television, today much information retrieval from computer data bases is handled as the automated equivalent of paper-based media. Videotex services present numbered "pages" of content. The concept of a logical sequence from first to last page remains. In the office, word processors are rapidly replacing typewriters, but they are still operated by secretaries who keyboard previously typed, handwritten, or dictated material. Spreadsheet programs replace pencil and calculator used for otherwise similar applications. In the schools, much of the use being made of personal computers is for drills and exercises that are little changed from the older printed versions. Such applications often do serve useful functions and may result in greater productivity or more timely information for decision making. They also create opportunities for experience with electronic information processes. But essentially the change is in using new products to perform conventional tasks using a recognizable work flow.

We may be at the threshold of a rapid take-off in Literacy II, the pre-New Literacy era. The merging of video games and home computers; the accelerating use of personal computers in the home, workplace, and school; the expanded use of intelligent devices as part of appliances and the ordinary telecommunications system, are among the indicators that the technology is finding its way into many aspects of life in the general population as opposed to only those in the computer priesthood.

Stage Three: The New Literacy

The New Literacy, however, is the stage in which there would be fundamental innovation in conceptualizing and processing information. This would involve a shift in perceptions about information formats and uses as fundamental as the shift from memory to written records was as the basis for traditional literacy. Is a learned essay the most effective way to make a point in an era of a multiplicity of audio and visual formats? Or, as one researcher has asked,

> How efficient is language of text in serially connected strings or sentences and paragraphs as a medium for communicating complex concepts and relationships? How can such a perfectly linear medium deal with multi-tiered parallelisms and connections of today's reality? With more words, longer sentences, fatter books?[22]

Paradoxically, New Literacy may see a return to the need for the older skills of oral composition. In the evolution to Literacy II managers and authors have discovered the increased efficiency of dictating messages and compositions onto audio tape for keyboarding into a word processor. Even with the rough edges of dictated composition, the ability to read the transcribed sentences and make pencilled corrections and then changes at the word processor is more productive than alternate means of getting thought into polished print. Although dictation has long been used, its combination with inexpensive and highly portable audio cassettes and word processing makes this technique viable for more people at lower labor costs than former methods of stenography and frequent retyping of imperfectly dictated thoughts.

The New Literacy application of such oral composition may arrive with reasonably reliable voice recognition capability of computers. This would permit bypassing the keyboarding of messages almost completely. Thus, skills of oral composition and even dictation (only now to a machine) may once again become essential components of literacy, as they were prior to the development of the printing press.[23]

One researcher, psychologist Howard Gardner, has recently introduced a reformulated theory of multiple intelligences in *Frames of Mind*. He argues that linguistic intelligence, the one most commonly measured by intelligence tests, is only one of six intelligences, the others being musical, logical-mathematical, spatial, bodily-kinesthetic, and personal. His theory is consistent with research that has provided evidence that different parts of the brain control different abilities or in Gardner's term, intelligences. For instance, to the extent that reading is a visual experience, it might be considered a form of spatial intelligence. Yet, linguistic skills have been shown to remain intact even when visual-spatial portions of the brain have suffered massive injury.[24]

Spatial intelligences, says Gardner, "are the capacities to perceive the visual world accurately, to perform transformations and modifications upon one's initial perceptions, and to be able to re-create aspects of one's visual experience...."[25] A spatial problem may be described in purely linguistic form. Figure 2 is a visual-spatial statement of a problem. It may also be described in linguistic form as follows: Take a square of paper, fold it in half, then fold it in half twice again. How many blocks would be created on the sheet after the final fold?

Different people will find the visual presentation more or less difficult than the linguistic description. It may be hypothesized that which one is easier for most people is largely dependent on the values a culture places on the development of these skills. Gardner points out, for example, that while traditional cultures place major emphasis on oral language, our culture places relatively greater emphasis on the written word.

Information is largely gained by reading and expressed in writing. He continues:

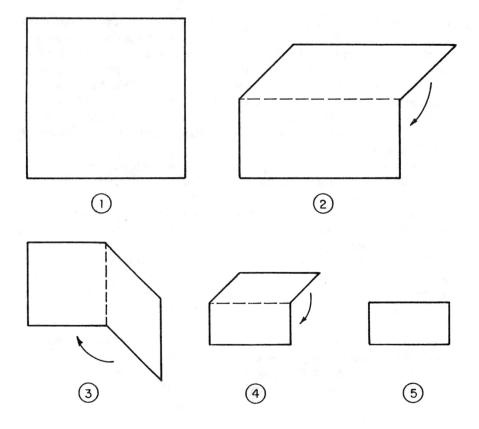

HOW MANY BLOCKS EXIST AFTER THE FINAL FOLD?

Figure 2   Spatial-Visual Presentation of a Problem

While oral and written forms of language doubtless draw on some of the same capacities, specific additional skills are needed to express oneself appropriately in writing. The individual must learn to supply that context that in spoken communication is evident from nonlinguistic sources [such as gestures].... *As an individual becomes more skilled in one means of expression, it may well become more difficult for him or her to excel in the other...*[26] [emphasis added]

If this somewhat controversial observation is valid, the New Literacy may involve a lessening of conventional print dominated behavior, accompanied by the development of intellectual and creative processes tied to the random access and "floating in space" nature of electronically stored information. Publishers of children's books in Great Britain, for example, are concerned about the 38% decline in retail sales between 1972 and 1981. They are placing much of the blame on television and video games. (They have apparently ignored the declining birth rate.) In their panic, they have cited Bettelheim and Pribram, who believe that books and reading are fundamental to the development of imaginative faculties.[27] Such beliefs, however, would seem to be precisely the trap of the cultural blinders imposed by the current concept of literacy. Print literacy may point minds toward a particular direction of creativity and imagination, but it may block out other forms. The interactive, manipulative, "real-time" processes fostered by computers (including video formats in conjunction with devices such as the video disk player) may therefore lead to entirely new or expanded forms of imagination for a greater proportion of society. While this may be unsettling to traditionalists, in itself it is likely (if it indeed comes about) to be neither good nor bad—just different. The types of seemingly random failures that sometimes plague automatic control systems, such as those that troubled the Oakland-San Francisco BART subway system, have been attributed to a weakness in holistic analysis. Eugene S. Ferguson, a historian and Curator of Technology at the Hagley Museum, reasons that such malfunctions are a product of the rationalistic numerical analysis that dominates over nonverbal thought. "Because perceptive processes are not assumed to entail hard thinking," says Ferguson, "it has been customary to consider nonverbal thought among the more primitive stages in the development of cognitive processes and inferior to verbal or mathematical thought."[28]

In fact, reasons Ferguson, just the opposite may be the case. He believes that the ability to think holistically and intuitively rather than sequentially and logically may be the skills more appropriate the tasks facing us in the coming decades. A less extreme—and more supportable—view would be that an increased proficiency at holistic/intuitive reasoning could be a helpful *supplement* to our traditional skills in logic.

Although we might think of intuitive behavior as opposite from logical behavior, the two concepts are not necessarily opposites. Watching kids work their way through screen after screen of a video game, avoiding apparently randomly appearing hazards while shooting moving targets, may seem to be intuitive. Yet perhaps there is some underlying logic these kids have internalized—and couldn't articulate if asked—that accounts for their seemingly intuitive moves. At the least, the argument could be made that some value system is behind the apparent intuition.

Sherry Turkle, a psychologist at the Massachusetts Institute of Technology, has studied and observed children and adults in various stages of their familiarity with computers, including video games. Among a particular subculture of computer users —hackers (computer fanatics whose lives revolve around programming computers)— she has reported that many describe their experience in terms of a "mind meld" concept popularized by the Mr. Spock character in the television series "Star Trek." What this extreme group of users describe is a situation where they feel their own minds become one with the computer (or with a person across space communicating in real time via electronic mail).[29]

Turkle has also identified stages computer users pass through that may apply to a more general population. First, she has observed a metaphysical stage. Users ask philosophical questions relating to artificial intelligence, such as "Can a machine really be made to think?" A second stage is that of mastery—winning over the computer. Hackers are obsessed with mastery. Other users finding themselves spending hours trying to get a "bug" out of a program or learning the functions and nuances of an applications program. The final stage is identity, wherein the benefit of the computer is internalized. It does more than perform a specific function but it "helps determine self." In the long term, speculates Turkle, the computer may result in a "new model of the mind," a somewhat controversial notion explored by linguist Noam Chomsky, among others. In analyzing the fascination of so many children (and adults) with computer-driven video games, Thomas Malone studied the components of the games. His conclusion is that they fulfill identifiable intrinsic needs, including the challenge of achieving a well-defined goal and stimulation of curiosity. Malone suggests that these intrinsic satisfactions can be built into educational applications of computer instruction.[30]

His work, as well as that of Turkle, suggest why interactive digital processes may have a more profound long term effect than television has had. Television, as it is generally used, is a far more passive medium — its severest critics would call the bulk of its programming mind deadening. Our intent here is not to become involved that debate. However, while at first brush we might see considerable similarity between the potential of television in 1950 and that of compunications today, the parallel is quite superficial. The three-dimensional, interactive nature of today's video games only begins to suggest the dimensions of the possibilities of changing processes. Creators of computer-controlled randomly accessible video disks are just starting to explore the nonlinear dimensions of that process. Consider a video "map" of the German city of Dusseldorf on a video disk created by Interactive Television, Inc., a Rossyln, Virgina firm. Using a keyboard, a user can type in the name of any street or landmark. It appears on the screen in full video. Manipulating a "joystick" allows the user to proceed down the street, looking straight ahead, as if driving a car. However, the user can request a view left, right, or rear. At any point, the user can switch to an aerial view of the street or an intersection. Another command allows zooming in or out to see details or surroundings. Or the user can change to a street map of either the immediate vicinity or, for context, of the entire city. A marker indicates the location of the user. On a second monitor, a computer-generated drawing constantly indicates where users are in relation to the sector of the street where they started and to nearby cross streets.

This application therefore combines full motion video, a printed map (on video), and a computer image. It allows users to alternate instantly between being amidst everyday reality (i.e., one's routine ground level view of the street) and levitating above it at will (the aerial shot). It mixes detail and context. It has neither an obvious beginning nor end. And it is controlled in infinite variations by individual users. In time it may turn out to be as primitive in technique and application as was D.W. Griffith's "Birth of a Nation" in the early days of motion pictures compared to George Lucas' high-tech "Star Wars." But it suggests the potential break with the basic literacy skills that has shaped much intellectual behavior for nearly 1000 years.

This digital map emphasizes the benefits that could accrue from combining holistic with sequential/logic skills. The written and spoken word, and much of the technology of these, have been useful for presenting discrete pieces of information. Man has had to pull these pieces together into some general principals. The skill needed to see a whole from the pieces varies widely in society. One consequence has been a tendency for us to lump things into discrete – and often polar – categories. We have good and bad, black and white, live or dead, high or low, and so on. The range of alternatives of the video map – and this is just a handy example – suggests the opportunity for organizing elements into a continuum of alternatives instead of the either/or we thought we were boxed into.[31] One strength of the computer is the ability to organize, to find commonalities, to switch from detail to overview. Instead of having to rely on a relatively small number of people who have the skills for high level synthesis, compunications technology may make synthesis available to a much larger number. This potential change has implications for modifying decision-making.

POPULAR CONCEPTIONS OF THE MEANING OF WIDESPREAD USE OF COMPUTERS

The mass media today are filled with articles about what is often characterized as computer literacy. Some of these representations are more thoughtful or accurate than others. But such articles do symbolize the rise in the popular consciousness of compunications in daily life. The following sampling is meant to suggest the range of understanding and perhaps the direction of at least the short term public agenda in this area.

Many of the subjects in these articles express the headlong dash of schools—or the need for the schools to get involved with—teaching students about the computer. Typical are articles such as "Educators See a New 'Must' for College Course: Computer Literacy"[32] and "At High-Tech High, Everyone Gets C's—in Computing."[33]

The pressure to put microcomputers in the classroom seems filled with the urgency of the Oklahoma Land Rush of the last century. A national survey from Johns Hopkins University indicates that, in Spring 1985, 86% of all elementary and high schools in the United States already had at least one microcomputer used for instruction. Between 1983 and 1985, three-quarters of the schools which had not previously used computers began to do so. More than 90% of the high schools had five or more microcomputers. During the 1984-1985 school year, nearly half of elementary and middle school pupils made some use of computers at school.[34]

At the college level, the scramble is as great. At Manhattan's New School, computer course registration accounted for almost 10% of the 25,000 enrollment in the Fall 1983 semester. A new course on "Computer Literacy" attracted two times the 1100 places that were available.[35] Colleges and universities including Drexel, Carnegie-Mellon, and Clarkson are requiring new students to purchase personal computers as standard equipment, along with textbooks and other routine supplies.

Summer seems to be no time to relax, either. One educator notes that computer camps "come into existence almost daily."[36] More than 100 of the traditional camps accredited by the American Camping Association offered computer instruction by 1983, and at least a similar number of camps have been established that specialize in computer instruction.

Contentiousness can be found in the variety of viewpoints of the role of computers in the workplace and in the home. One study, funded by the National Science Foundation, speculates that, by the end of this century, electronic information technology will have transformed American home, business, manufacturing, school, and political life.[37] Computer-based technology is being attributed with the beneficial ability to lead society to a new era of higher productivity and of improvements in the quality of work. But at the same time, there are warnings about implications for invasion of personal privacy by business and/or governments and so-called information gaps between information haves and have-nots.

A Congressional task force is assessing whether or not the information industry will be the "new engine of real economic growth" in coming decades.[38] Yet, rather than growth, some authorities worry about economic disarray and radical changes in the workforce. "Technological displacement is occurring everywhere, from the design shop to the supermarket checkout counter," observes an official of the AFL-CIO.[39] In response to either perceived opportunities or perceived threats to compunications-based technology, many public policymakers are looking to "high-tech" to bolster older manufacturing-based economies. Typical is Pennsylvania, which is allocating millions of dollars to buy computers for its public schools (more than $5 million in 1982-83), with substantial amounts being spent to train teachers to use this equipment in the classroom.[40]

Challenging Assumptions

These articles suggest that the link between the use of computers in schools and higher education and their long term role and impact in society and the economy appears to be based on the assumption that job opportunities in the industrialized world increasingly will be in professional and technical areas that require considerable education and training in computer-related skills. A corollary assumption is that high technology will require upgraded skills, because workers will be using computers and other technical equipment.

There are responsible studies that indicate that these are misleading assumptions. According to one analysis, the "expansion of the lowest skilled jobs...will vastly outstrip the growth of high-technology jobs."[41] Moreover, high technology industries and their products are "far more likely to reduce the skills requirements of jobs in the U.S. economy than to upgrade them."[42] Indeed, more than 20 years ago, Harvard Business School professor James Bright studied how automation affected job skill requirements in several traditional manufacturing industries. Contrary to the common assumption of a need for increased skills, Bright found that, after a short period of a need for increased skills, such requirements sharply declined as the degree of automation increased. He observed: "Many so-called key skill jobs, currently requiring long experience and training, will be reduced to easily learned, machine-tending jobs."[43]

Even at the professional level of management, there is today debate on the question of the need or even desirability of computers. One management consultant argues that "top managers must learn to cultivate ignorance. The higher you go, the less you should know about what is actually going on. Managers must rely on others to know."[44] Ray Moritz, a vice president of Computervision, a CAD/CAM manufacturer, claims that "even after 20 years in the computer business he wouldn't touch one of those things."[45]

This attitude has found at least some support, judging from the letters column of The Wall Street Journal. But it has also brought responses such as the newsletter editor's who wrote: "Realize that personal use of computers brings a new literacy to executives and managers by enabling them to exercise imagination and creativity."[46]

It is in this context that the notion of a New Literacy is worthy of study. Traditional literacy was not necessary for a worker to move from the farm to a factory although it became a requirement to move into supervisory and managerial positions. Perhaps the New Literacy may not be a requirement for a service or information-based economy. Still, the traditional literacy has been instrumental in creating an educated population, with attendant benefits for the personal quality of life and for growth of scientific and humanistic culture. What of a New Literacy?

PLAYERS AND STAKES

The notion of a New Literacy has implications that could permeate all aspects of society and institutions. Some constituencies are affected directly. Print media businesses are asking about the future of their ink-on-paper products. Should they take comfort in the current resistance of the mass consumer to switch to electronically delivered information services, or will the next generation of potential newspaper/magazine/book buyers be more responsive to electronic retrieval and manipulation? Banks and other financial institutions have already found a sizable segment of customers (initially their younger ones) ready to use automatic teller machines. Now, in Great Britain, a relatively small savings bank has made the strategic decision to channel capital funds into providing customers with video terminals for electronic home banking, instead of building branch offices.[47] Will similar decisions start to be made on a similar scale elsewhere in the industrialized world?

Educators are among the most concerned about immediate implications, in particular on issues of curriculum design and materials budgets. Questions are being raised about what schools and higher education should be teaching. Business institutions ranging from smokestack industries to high-tech research organizations are trying to predict their need for certain skills. They are looking for answers to concerns about productivity and product or service quality. Government policymakers are involved with direct questions, such as priorities for expenditures for education and job retraining, and indirect issues, as seen in international trade concerns and the desirability of an agenda for a national industrial policy. The breadth of the indirect effects of a potential New Literacy may be seen in recent evidence that a few bright, generally law-abiding middle class teenagers are using their new computers and skills to invade private computer facilities via telephone connections. The popular film "War Games," released in the summer of 1983, told the story of a teenager who first gained access to his school's computer and changed records in it, and then almost started a nuclear war, by tapping into a military computer, using his home computer and the public telephone network. Life mimicked art in 1983 when the FBI uncovered several groups and individual teenagers who had gained access to hospital, defense, and other private computer systems, for the most part apparently for the challenge rather than for sinister ends. The incidence of this new type of crime, much of it coming from adolescents who would never consider traditional burglary, is as much an indicator of a sociocultural change as are the more frequently cited positive indicators.

The stakes involved in the New Literacy are immense, although not all quantifiable. If the education community is slow to understand and respond to changes, the loss will not be in terms of jobs for teachers or in sales of textbooks, but in *long-term* effects on society and, in the case of a given state or locality, the ability of its industry to compete with others who were more responsive. The failure of a newspaper publishing company to recognize the coming of a New Literacy may result in an erosion of its traditional business and perhaps loss of market opportunity for new business. Nevertheless, neither type of change is likely to happen overnight. Change that is technologically inspired is difficult enough to track in real time. Change that is culturally derived, which is at the base of the New Literacy, tends to be incremental as well. For many years, there may be little hard evidence of fundamental shifts resulting from the skills incorporated into literacy. Then, the confluence of several needed technological developments and the maturing of cultural trends may result in relatively rapid effects.

For example, one frequently expressed technology-based reason given for why electronic display will not become a popular alternative to print is the relative crudeness of the resolution of video displays compared to printed text. Extended periods of reading text from a screen has been blamed for headaches and eye stress. Full-screen video displays also have not been portable and are thus considered at a disadvantage compared to print. Similarly, a typical culturally based apology for print is provided by a group that is funded by the book industry:

> In the public consciousness books lend permanence, respectability, and credibility to a venture. The popular image of the book—which some people had expected to be demolished by competition from the electronic and non-print media—remains unchallenged as a symbol of knowledge.[48]

However, recent experience with electronics in general and with semiconductor technology in particular suggests that portable, high-resolution flat screens are in the offing. Low resolution flat screen displays came on the market in substantial numbers in 1984, capable of showing as much text as a CRT monitor. Several manufacturers are already marketing portable television sets using liquid crystal flat screens. It is reasonable to assume that, within the foreseeable future, the argument of portability and resolution will cease to be an issue. Similarly, work is proceeding with downloading text (that is, sending text via telephone, cable, or even broadcast to an electronic storage medium such as a floppy disk or erasable read-only memory) or simply selling in retail stores complete works of print encoded in semiconductor modules. When, and at what cost, these developments will be ready for the mass market is less crucial for this discussion than is the point that technology is likely to provide the necessary infrastructure for a New Literacy.

TOWARD AN AGENDA FOR STUDYING THE NEW LITERACY

The agenda for research of the New Literacy clearly goes beyond such narrow questions of whether all children need access to a microcomputer and need to learn computer programming. Rather, the objective of this line of study is to understand better the forces that will determine when, or if, the model of Figure 1 will be played out and with what likely consequences. Thus, among the potential questions and issues — issues on which debate may not yet exist but on which the stakes may be high and the outcome therefore important— that may need to be addressed are:

- What are the underpinnings of traditional literacy, and what is their relationship to current forces that may impinge on literacy?
- What are the elements of newer information technologies that may shape future information processing?
- What is the correlation, if any, between available technology and the substance—or content—that is gathered, created, stored, and transmitted to seekers and users of information?
- What are the nontechnological factors that facilitate society's acceptance of elements of a literacy?
- What bundle of skills may make up a New literacy and how, if at all, will they complement/supplement the traditional bundle of literacy skills?

These and similar general questions and issues will form the basis for investigating areas of New Literacy as they may apply to institutions, organizations, and the individual. As such, it may affect policy in areas of education, labor, the workplace, law, and government.

Table 1 is suggestive of the areas in which the evolution of new tools and processes made possible by computers and computer-aided devices may have some affects that can start to be tracked today. The listings are not exhaustive, nor are they mutually exclusive. For example, in looking at institutions, one would also be concerned with organization. Or the study of skills overlaps with cognition and learning for individuals as well as with schools and universities as institutions. Table 1 does present the start of a framework for exploring areas that would be affected by a change that grew from the curve presented in Figure 2, from traditional to new literacy.

Literacy Skills

The ability to read and write is generally considered the entry point of literacy in most modern cultures. Reading, however, does not have to be from a printed page—it can be from light projected through film or glowing phosphors on a screen in the shape of words. Writing less often means a fine cursive hand than the ability to compose sentences to express ideas, independent of the technology (quill pen on parchment, keyboard to a VDT). We also assign degrees of literacy in relation to other skills that are considered either helpful or essential to function at some higher order of society, among them: the ability to speak well, to recall facts, to infer meaning, to analyze facts, to synthesize ideas.

Changing the array of tools available is not likely to affect the tools themselves, but may have an impact on the necessity to become more adept at one or more of these skills and the degree of ease or difficulty of doing so. As with the earlier example of the straight edge and the skill in drawing straight lines, there is antecdotal evidence that computers and certain applications programs may enhance the ability for more people to gain certain skills. Spreadsheet programs combined with an integrated graphics capability is one example. Relational data base programs for personal use may be another. The tortuous exercise that many students have to go through of creating an outline may be expedited by programs

TABLE 1
Framework for Research on the New Literacy

Skills	Organization	Institutions	Individual
Read	Hierarchies		
Write	Centralize/	Governments	
Infer	Decentralize	Corporations	
Synthesize	Power	Schools/Universities	Cognition &
Analyze	Authority	Workforce	Learning
Recall	Accountability	Organized Labor	Relationships
Speak	Responsibility	Professions	Home

that can create outlines from entered thoughts (whether the program can aid in the development of the thoughts themselves is still subject to debate). There is some evidence, from limited trials, that word processing programs have helped some school children become better writers—and readers.[49]

As an agenda item, research might include historical studies of forces that affected literacy skills in previous eras, such as writing, printing, and mechanization. This could be tied to an analysis of causes and effects (e.g., to what extent did cheaper printing techniques in the 19th century help push mass reading skills or did the need of industry pull mass literacy into society?) which policymakers today might find helpful in their need for crystal-ball gazing.

As another agenda item, developments in skills can be tracked as part of the socialization and education process—at home and in the schools, or as part of the work training process. One attempt at doing the latter is summarized in Table 2.

Are there any reliable measures that will enable some quantification of trends toward Literacy II and eventually the New Literacy? In one limited but ongoing published study of the Program on Information Resources Policy, the want ads in *The New York Times* have been analyzed annually for the same day since l977. It has tracked jobs for word processor operators and for secretaries required to have familiarity with word processing, for travel agents who must be familiar with online reservation systems, and for accountants with skills in using automated systems. Table 2 shows some of the results through 1985. Other indicies for which baseline and subsequent data might be useful include microcomputer sales to various user groups (e.g., home, school, workplace), sales of software, library expenditures on equipment and software, number of titles and sales volume of educational computer software, sales of interactive videodisk machines and programs, volume of use of online information services in both residences and the workplace, sales of modems, and volume of traffic over telephone local-area digital-transport networks.*

These and other measures might help to indicate the degree to which the infrastructure and operating components which would seem to be necessary for the evolution of the New Literacy are being put in place.

Productivity. The common wisdom holds that a well educated (therefore presumably literate) workforce, is a more productive one. What skills are associated with productivity in the growing service/information sector of the economy? Are they associated with a particular literacy? And can productivity be measured in qualitative terms as well as quantitative, e.g., a

---

*See Benjamin M. Compaine, *New Literacy Indicators* (Cambridge, MA: Program on Resources Policy, Harvard University, 1986).

TABLE 2
New Jobs/Skills in the Workplace as Measured by Want Ads*

A. Overall Demand for Communications Experience

	Total # Want Ads	# Requesting Experience	% Experience
1977	1234	72	5.8
1978	1531	103	6.9
1979	1402	122	8.7
1980	1476	127	8.6
1981	1449	133	9.1
1982	1160	120	10.3
1983	1094	155	14.2
1984	1529	257	16.8
1985	1667	323	19.4

B. New Jobs vs. New Skills

	# New Jobs	%	# Mentioning New Skills	%
1977	42	3.4	30	2.4
1978	67	4.3	39	2.5
1979	60	4.2	62	4.4
1980	66	4.0	67	4.5
1981	65	4.4	68	4.6
1982	50	4.3	70	6.0
1983	62	5.7	93	8.5
1984	60	3.9	197	12.9
1985	118	7.0	205	12.3

C. Automation in Selected Occupations

	% Travel Agents	% Bookkeepers	% Secretary/Typist
1977	0	12	0
1978	0	13	2
1979	11	14	3
1980	22	18	3
1981	50	15	8
1982	71	24	15
1983	79	31	16
1984	73	36	26
1985	75	36	33

*From The New York Times, fourth Thursday in June for each year. Counted were jobs or skills that mentioned communications skills. Examples of new jobs include: Vydec, Wang, CRT, mag card, NCR, keypunch, or computer operators; data entry clerks; word processors, systems analysts; programmers; telex operators, data processors. Examples of new skills include: "Experience with" or "Knowledge of" EDP, ADP, computerized systems, payrolls, etc.; "ability to use" word processing, mag card, SABRE, APOLLO (air reservations systems), Compugraphics, NCR, and IBM machines.

piece of market analysis that is more accurate because of the ability to access and manipulate more data?

Organization and New Literacy

If knowledge has anything to do with power, then the ability of more people to have more information (maybe knowledge, maybe not) may over time affect the relationships within and among organizations. Traditional concepts, such as current limits to managerial span of control, evolve new meaning. The ongoing debates over centralization vs. decentralization may be affected. And the traditional hierarchical relationship in most organization may come under new forms or pressure.

Implications for organizational structure.   At a design facility of a large Detroit manufacturer, seven draftsmen have replaced their "boards" with computer-aided-design (CAD) terminals. Although the objective of the change was to improve their productivity (it has—many jobs are done in half the time), some of the results were unexpected. The draftsmens' jobs had been to take a design from a product designer and make the drawings from which a product engineer could make molds to create the part. But using the CAD process, the draftsman is able to create a three-dimensional design that can drive the machines that cut the mold directly. The draftsmen are thus encroaching on the turf of the engineers. At the other end, their capacity for creating a three dimensional image and change its shape or other characteristics by a few instructions to the computer has made them into designers as well. This organization is now having to deal with the complications that arise when the boundaries among jobs blur as the result of technology.

Studies of information-intensive industries.   There are already several types of jobs and industries that are well along in a change to compunications-based structures. The securities trading business, for example, has always been an information-intensive one. Nathan Mayer Rothschild used his sophisticated news service to get word of the outcome of the Battle of Waterloo back to London hours before his rivals, providing him with a profitable trading advantage. Today, the trading rooms at investment and brokerage houses consist of more video display terminals and telephones than traders.

In the airline business, compunications has dramatically altered reservations handling, presumably giving airlines much greater control over load factors and scheduling. Pilots, who have long had to monitor dozens of instruments and make numerous calculations and judgments under pressure, are flying increasingly in cockpits where most of the monitoring is done by computers. As one report described the new planes: "130 microprocessors...control everything from flight paths to cabin temperatures." Six video displays in the Boeing 757 replace many gauges and dials. Two of the screens have replaced the flight engineer. Pilots, whom Boeing designers call "flight managers," are needed for less flying and "much more monitoring of sophisticated flight information."[50] This is already being translated into new designs for jets airplanes, taking advantage of the computer's superior ability to simultaneously control more surfaces than a human pilot.

In engineering and drafting facilities, T-squares and even calculators are giving way to computer-aided-design. Light pens are replacing ink pens, as designs can be drawn for representation on a video display screen and manipulated to reflect modifications, to simulate forces and stress on the element being designed, even to reveal a third dimension of a two dimensional drawing. In such cases, draftsmen are learning to use the system as more than an automated two-dimensional processor. They have started to think in three dimensions and as a result to add design and engineering features to their jobs.

Jobs such as securities trading, flying, scheduling, designing, and drafting may turn out to be unique exceptions to long term trends – or may indeed be in the forefront of changes that will permeate other jobs and industries. Either way, they are ripe for case studies, to better understand how these jobs differ from the precompunications era; what different demands they place on the people performing them; how, if at all, the technology has affected the skill mix and the skill levels of job holders; whether the newer way of performing the jobs has led to different ways of formulating solutions to problems or of creating opportunities that had not been considered previously.

Institutions and the New Literacy

There are implications in the New Literacy for government, business, schools and universities, professions, and the workforce. These include the relationship between these institutions and their constituent groups, and the role of the institutions themselves. As an example of the former, what may be the consequences for the workforce as many routine jobs are taken over by intelligent devices, such as the scanners at supermarkets check-out counters and robots in many phases of an increasing number of manufacturing jobs? What are the implications for organized labor and their employers? For the schools and universities which educate and train managers, lawyers, draftsmen, welders, and mechanics?

As for the role of institutions themselves, the challenge may be nowhere clearer than in the role of the education establishment, including schools and universities, public policymakers at boards of education, legislatures and Congress, publishers, and teachers organizations, among others.

In the near term, a salient question may be how to take advantage of the interests and cognitive skills that young children may be coming to school with as the result of experiences with computers in the home or learned in the first years of school. If the school children are at the threshold of New Literacy, while their teachers and the creators of learning materials stay planted in Literacy I, educational opportunities may be missed.

Indeed, the major crunch may be in this transition period. The issue will likely involve *what* should be taught. Electronic calculators are cheap, highly portable, and ubiquitous. Point-of-sale terminals, having replaced the cash drawer in stores, perform all calculations for clerks, including how much to charge for one bar of soap when its price is 3/$.85 and how much change to return to the customer. Word processing programs, quickly replacing typewriters, are incorporating dictionaries that check spelling and even aids that detect grammatical flaws. Thus, just as printing and typing undermined the need to teach fine cursive writing, perhaps the time will come when spending extensive classroom hours on memorizing multiplication tables, spelling lists, and the fine points of grammar will be as unnecessary as it has become ineffective, with the time devoted to other subjects.

If the technology permits breaking out of the print/film/audio sequential processes, how can it be – if indeed it should be – exploited to incorporate the new spatial, non-linear possibilities? In the longer term, this problem may disappear, as the snake gradually sheds its Linear Literacy skin. Eventually, today's 10 year-olds will become adults and assume their place in the curriculum-setting process. It will likely be at this point that we will have a more certain fix on whether there is the start of a change from the print model to an internalized use of digital/electronic processes.

In the meantime, will computers, video disks, or other pieces of hardware be incorporated into curricula with more fundamental impact than the film strip projectors purchased in the 1960s and now often gathering dust in a closet? Could the move toward New Literacy reduce the amount of time spent teaching spelling, grammar, and basic arithmetic skills in favor of time on history, language, or composition (this latter may be oral or graphic, as well as written), aided by programs that make use of spread sheet, data base, or word processing capabilities of intelligent devices?

The Workplace. Will fundamental changes be reflected in the workforce? Will these involve merely automating jobs to get higher productivity? Are there real implications for affecting those managerial tasks considered "brain" jobs? In the l950s and l960s, there were widespread predictions that automation—the replacement of manual labor by machines—would elimi-nate large numbers of jobs and extensively change the workforce. These predictions were largely correct, but without the massive structural unem-ployment that such a scenario implied. Instead, new technologies have established new industries to replace those that have declined, and created new types of jobs that more than made up the slack.

Among the institutions that are already having to rethink some practices as the result of technological change is the legal system. One area that is likely to be of ongoing concern is the nature and protection of intellectual property.

The notion of copyright has been closely allied with the development of the printing press. Initially, the control of printing under the British Crown and subsequently the high cost of presses themselves made protection of creative works relatively easy to control and monitor. The printing press made written words widely available, but they were still centrally pro-duced. Film and recorded audio disks have followed similar patterns.

Today, technology has had two consequences that underlie control over intellectual property. First came electrostatic copying, which made dupli-cation of the printed word cheap and highly decentralized. Audio and then video cassettes have made copying of sound and pictures readily available. Thus, not only production but distribution of created works has become democratized. Even more recently, software for microcomputers has be-come subject to regular unauthorized copying.

Closer to the concept of the New Literacy, however, is the second possible consequence. That is the determination of what really is the intellectual property that should be protected. If a computer manipulates data or other information entered into it, is the output copyrightable—and by whom? Should it belong to the creator of the algorithm of the object or source program the computer used? To whoever owns the computer? To whoever owned the original data? Thus, the very nature of what is the original creative work and what is a derivative work, often contentious and litigated points under normal circumstances, are likely to enter a new and less understood dimension.

Documentation and contracts.   In 11th-century England, the word of witnesses was given far greater weight in legal and commercial transactions than were written records.

> Witnesses were alive and credible because they could defend their state-ments; writing was dead marks on a dead surface, unable to clarify itself if it proved to be unclear or to defend itself against objections.[51]

That was one result of a society rooted in oral literacy. Not until the 13th century was the shift to written records complete. In the intervening years, conventions developed that helped make the written form more verifiable: dating documents, having witnesses sign them (so they could be used if the witness disappeared or died), and creating indentures (a jagged tear across a piece of parchment, each half of which had the agreement written in it, so that only the authentic versions would fit together), the use of seals and red tape (this latter running continuously from page to page of documents to insure no page has been removed) are other examples of verifying devices that helped promote acceptance of written records.

Today, we may be faced with a similar transition period. Videotapes are being used along with photographs for evidence. But to what extent are records on computer tapes legally binding? Would a will stored on a floppy disk carry the same weight in probate as a paper document? Can methods be devised to detect "erasures" or alterations of digitally stored records? How can digitally stored records be authenticated? What are the legal issues that may affect rules of evidence or contracts?

The Individual and New Literacy

Individuals are, of course, the central focus of the New Literacy. The development of, and indeed the existence at all, of a literacy depends ultimately on how individuals are affected by the forces around them, whether technological, political, social, economic, or otherwise. In roles as students, teachers, workers, parents, etc., people are the atomic units of any sociocultural change.

There is much speculation of how changing information technology will affect people in their homes and in their social relationships. One area that may be most helpful to explore further is that of how people learn and remember. As the tracking of the skills of a New Literacy needs to look at abilities such as inference or analysis, then it would be helpful to gain greater insight into relatively poorly understood areas such as learning and cognition.

Learning and cognition.   After years of study, researchers still do not have a firm grasp of how we learn or remember. What does the literature say about how learning takes place, especially as it relates to the types of formats used: reading, watching, listening? How does active involvement of students in learning (as in role playing) differ from passive involvement (as in listening to a lecture). What are the implications for the design of teaching materials incorporating the interactivity of computers, videodisks, etc.?

Effects of computer-mediated work.   To an extent never before possible, computers can control the speed, accuracy, and measurement of work, particularly office work. For example, it is possible for a computer to count the keystrokes of a sectretary or data input clerk, creating a degree of control that previously was restricted to factory work. Also, more layers of management can have access – if they choose to – to more information in a more timely fashion than ever before. The chief executive officer could check on daily sales directly, rather than wait for a report from a subordinate. In both these cases, the nature of jobs and reporting relationships might be shifted as the result of widespread use of computer systems. How do workers react when such systems are introduced? Are there long term effects on organizational structure? If so, what are they?

Education and the workforce.   Historically, mechanization and automation have lowered rather than raised the skills needed for many jobs. Where point-of-sale terminals and optical scanner readers reduce the need of clerks to read prices and calculate change, when programs that automatically check grammar and spelling can be used by a word processor, what will be the skills on which education should concentrate? According to U.S. Bureau of the Census projections, high-tech jobs will account for only 5% of employment growth during the 1980s, far behind the demand for secretaries, janitors, sales and office clerks, and waiters and waitresses. What are the implications for educators?

SUMMARY

Literacy is a learned skill, unlike real or nonverbal communicative processes. Western literacy is largely the product of the oral world in which it appeared. Although the direct causes and effects associated with literacy are controversial and unresolved, the ascendency of written over oral literacy in our society has had a profound impact on its development. The written record has enabled us to define concepts with greater precision, to maintain archives and refer back to them for facts and definitions, and to weigh more deliberately the local and persuasive elements of issues. "The capacity to employ various symbolized notations," writes Howard Gardner, "enables one to supplement one's memory, organize one's future activities, and communicate at one time with an indefinite number of individuals"[52]

Our interest in studying the potential confluence of forces which may be driving toward a fundamental change in the notion of literacy should not be confused with a prediction that it will indeed happen. Perhaps there is something inherent in print that will resist being upset by alternative way of information acquisition and processing. But, either way, the stakes are high, and the threats posed and opportunities presented are there facing players and stakeholders. Policy and strategy are going to be based on assumptions about the future held by those who make the decisions. By pursuing research on the subject of New Literacy, we hope to help policymakers sharpen these assumptions.

There is a body of evidence that supports the assertion that there are multiple components to a literacy and that these components have changed with technology and vary among cultures. Although we have much to learn about such areas as the functioning of cognitive skills, the weight of historical precedent would seem to come down in favor of being prepared for today's literate societies' acquiring an expanded set of skills, tools, and processes for literacy. The consequences of this will have to remain just speculation.

NOTES

1. Elizabeth L. Eisenstein, *The Printing Press as An Agent of Change* (Cambridge, England, and New York: Cambridge University Press, 1979), p. 8.
2. M. T. Clanchy, "Looking Backward from the Invention of Printing," in Daniel P. Resnick, ed., *Literacy in Historical Perspective* (Washington D.C.: The Library of Congress, 1983), p. 16. (Hereafter cited as *Literacy*).
3. Robert Pattison, *On Literacy* (New York: Oxford University Press, 1982), p. 118.
4. M. T. Clanchy, *From Memory to Written Record: England, 1066-1307* (Cambridge, Mass.: Harvard University Press, 1979), p. 56.
5. *Ibid.*, p. 88.
6. Richard D. Altick, *The English Common Reader: A Social History of the Mass Reading Public 1800-1900* (Chicago: University of Chicago Press, 1974), p. 233.
7. W. C. Helmbold and W. G. Rabinowitz, trans., *Plato's Phaedrus* (New York: The Liberal Arts Press, 1956), p. 68.
8. See for example: Jack Goody, *The Domestication of the Savage Mind* (Cambridge, England: Cambridge University Press, 1977); Harold A. Innis, *The Bias of Communication* (Toronto: University of Toronto Press, 1951); Marshall Mcluhan, *The Gutenberg Galaxy: The Making of Topographic Man* (Toronto: University of Toronto Press, 1962); Walter J. Ong, S.J., *Interfaces of the Word: Studies in the Evolution of Consciousness and Culture* (Ithaca, N.Y.: Cornell University Press, 1977).
9. Daniel P. Resnick, "Spreading the Word: An Introduction," *Literacy*, p. 3.
10. Walter J. Ong, *Orality and Literacy: The Technologies of the Word* (New York: Metheuan, 1982), p. 122.
11. *Ibid.*, pp. 130-133.
12. *Ibid.*, pp. 136-137.
13. Eric A. Hauelock, *The Literate Revolution in Greece and its Cultural Consequences* (Princeton, N.J.: Princeton University Press, 1982), p. 320.
14. David R. Olson, "From Utterance to Text: The Bias of Language in Speech and

Writing," *Harvard Education Review* 48 (1978), pp. 341-377.

15. Patricia Greenfield, "Oral and Written Language: The Consequences for Cognitive Development in Africa, The United States, and England," *Speech and Language 15* (1972), pp. 169-178.

16. Pattison, *On Literacy*, p. 96.

17. Harvey J. Graff, *Literacy and Social Development in the West: A Reader*. (New York: Cambridge University Press, 1981), p. 253.

18. Pattison, *On Literacy*, pp. 149-150.

19. "Personal Computers: And the Winner is IBM," *Business Week*, October 3, 1983, pp. 76-83.

20. "Agency to Train 700,000 Microcomputer, Word Processing Operators," *Computerworld*, July 30, 1984. p. 10.

21. Personal Conversation with Paul Strassmen, Vice President, Xerox, May 10, 1984.

22. Matthew Kuhn (Bell-Northen Research, Ottawa, Canada), "Will Electronic Information Technology Change Our Current View of Literacy in Communication?" Speech at Queen's College, Kingston, Ontario, February 9, 1983.

23. See Joshua Lederberg, "Digital Communications and the Conduct of Science: The New Literacy," *Proceedings of the IEEE* 66, (11) (November 1978): 1316-1317.

24. Howard Gardner, *Frames of Mind* (New York: Basic Books, Inc. Publishers, 1983), p. 98. Not all researchers support Gardner's theory and his being cited here should not be viewed as our endorsement of all his work. The notion of New Literacy and its possible implications were developed prior to the publication of Gardner's book. Still, he does bring considerable research and interpretation to bear on his theory and, if it does stand up under closer scrutiny, it would help explain why changing literacies can be affected by and have a broad effect on learning, thinking, and so on.

25. *Ibid.*, p. 173.

26. *Ibid.*, p. 95.

27. Bryan Appleyard, "The Struggle for Traditional Literacy," *The Times* (London), March 14, 1983.

28. Eugene Ferguson, "The Mind's Eye: Nonverbal Thought in Technology," *Science 97* (August 26, 1977), pp. 834-836.

29. Sherry Turkle, Seminar, Program on Information Resources Policy, Harvard University, December 14, 1983. See also "The Subjective Computer: A Study in the Psychology of Personal Computation," *Social Studies of Science* (Beverly Hills, California: Sage) 12 (1982) pp. 173-205, and *The Second Self: Computers and the Human Spirit* (New York: Simon & Schuster, 1984).

30. Thomas W. Malone, "What Makes Computer Games Fun?" *Byte*, December 1981, pp. 258-277. The research was conducted for his Ph.D. dissertation in psychology at Stanford University.

31. See John Nasbett, *Megatrends*,

32. Gene I. Maeroff, "New 'Must' In College Courses," *The New York Times*, April 5, 1983, p. C-1.

33. Jane Carroll, "At High-Tech High Everyone Gets C's—as in 'Computing'," *Boston Globe*, April 12, 1983, p. 39.

34. "Instructional Uses of Computers," Center for Social Organization of Schools,

The Johns Hopkins University, No. 1, June 1986.

35. "Call for Computer Classes Swamping Colleges," *The New York Times*, June 6, 1983, p. A1.

36. Ruth Bayard Smith, "Computer Camps Flourishing," *Boston Globe*, August 8, 1983, p. 39.

37. J. Tydeman, H. Lipinski, R. Adler, M. Nyhan, and L. Zwimpfer, *Teletext and Videotex in the United States* (New York, McGraw-Hill, 1982) pp. 272-273.

38. John Bowles, "The Economy in Transition," Public Policy, Inc., Somers, Conn., 1982.

39. "Worry Grows Over Upheaval as Technology Reshapes Jobs," *The New York Times*, July 12, 1982, p. A-1.

40. "Pennsylvania Plans Computer Training to Bolster Economy," *The New York Times*, September 23, 1983, p. A-1.

41. Henry Levin and Russell Rumberger, "The Low Skill Future of High Tech," *Technology Review*, Aug./Sept. 1983, pp. 18-21.

42. *Ibid.*

43. James Bright, "Does Automation Raise Skill Requirements?" *Harvard Business Review*, August 1981, pp. 42-55.

44. Jack Falvey, "Real Managers Don't Use Computer Terminals," *The Wall Street Journal*, February 7, 1983, p. 22.

45. *Ibid.*

46. Robert H. Long, "Computer Adds Up to a Useful Tool," Letter to the Editor, *The Wall Street Journal*, August 30, 1983, p. 29.

47. Richard Hooper, Chief Executive, Information Services, British Telecom, personal conversation, Oct. 18, 1983.

48. John P. Dessauer, "Trends Update," Book Industry Study Group, New York, August 1983. p. 2. Quote attributed to John Huenefeld.

49. Andee Rubin and Bartman Bruce, "Quill: Reading and Writing with a Microcomputer," *Reading Education Report* (Cambridge, Mass: Bret, Beranek and Newman, Inc. Sept 1983). See also Lawrence Feinberg, "Pupils Learn 2 R's with IBM," *Washington Post*, May 26, 1984, p.B1.

50. "Can We Keep the Skies Safe," *Newsweek*, January 30, 1984, p. 30.

51. W. J. Ong, review of M. T. Clanchy, *From Memory to Written Record*, in *Manuscripta* 23 (1979), p. 179.

52. Gardner, p. 359.

6

INFORMATION GAPS: MYTH OR REALITY?

Benjamin M. Compaine

A paper presented to a 1979 conference in the Netherlands warned:

> If information bases are centralized and distribution facilities are limited, *as they will inevitably be* [emphasis added], then the concept of freedom as we know it is seriously threatened.

If policy resolutions are neglected:

> then the information revolution may effectively enslave rather than serve people.... We must not end up with two classes, an information rich and an information poor; a small technological elite attempting to cope with a large, semi-skilled unemployed majority.[1]

Disraeli said that, "as a general rule the most successful man in life is he who has the best information."[2] The Bible[3], numerous pundits, self-proclaimed sages, scholars, and journalists have voiced similar truisms and expanded them to include groups, institutions, and entire societies. Ever since the ancient Greeks told us that "knowledge itself is power," that theme has created a mini-industry of those who today warn that the rise of an information society will promote widening gaps between those individuals and societies that are information rich and those that are information (and usually economically) poor.

Whether these warnings are sound or are merely good copy for the mass media, or are the creation of some academics with little tie to the real world, or are serving to further the political and social agenda of a cadre with a particular ideology, is the subject of this article. There is evidence that this "information gap" theme has struck a certain intuitive, popular chord and that it has been placed on the public policy agenda to some degree. Is this topic indeed a budding issue in which the political, if not the economic, stakes might be considerable?

Is There an Issue?

The concept of an information gap is ill-defined from the start. It may refer to the access individuals have to information or the ability of individuals to have the tools—intellectual or tangible—to manipulate, analyze, and synthesize information. In a sense, it is a moving target, because as society has evolved from an agrarian to an industrial and on to an information-intensive one, the importance of having access to and know-how for using information has increased.

To a large extent, the information or knowledge gap issue has been perceived by the academic community. Former NBC newsman and current Stanford University professor Elie Abel predicts there will probably be less common sharing of knowledge by the advantaged and disadvantaged within society, thus eroding the common database which makes the American system of democracy possible. Looking at the increase in user-supported information services (cable, electronic data bases, etc.), Abel sees

> a danger that sooner rather than later many Americans will be priced out of the market—debarred from the benefits promised by the new technologies because they cannot afford to pay for them.... The affluent would be even better informed than they are today; the lower orders could be even less well informed.[4]

Herbert Schiller, on the communications faculty of the University of California and perhaps the most cited writer on this subject, expresses his concern within a broader social context:

> The central questions concerning the character of, and prospects for, the new information technology are familiar criteria: for whose benefit and under whose control will it be implemented?[5]

This theme is picked up by others who differentiate between information and knowledge. While information technology may allow decentralization of information, they say, the real problem of knowledge monopoly is overlooked. What the modern computer enthusiasts monopolize, say professors James Carey and John Quirk,

> is not the data itself but the approved, certified, sanctioned, official mode of thought.... Rather than creating a "new future", modern technology invites the public to participate in a ritual of control where fascination with technology masks the underlying factors of politics and power.[6]

Yet another member of academe brings the information gap issue firmly into the "new literacy" arena.[7] Melvin Webber says that it was fairly easy to make the leap from preindustrial to industrial status in part because the necessary skills were not difficult to acquire. His contention is that the same may not be true today: the requisite skills take longer to learn; extensive education is necessary to become competent at the information-handling jobs, which tend to be cognitively difficult. Thus, there is the danger that "the spatial gap between lower-class districts and middle class ones may become too wide and thus too difficult for the typical person to bridge." He asks, "Can we be assured that the communications media of the next decades will accomplish for the underprivileged youth of the year 2000 what the free library and the free public school did for immigrant youth of 1900?"[8]

Wilson Dizard, a former career Foreign Service Officer now teaching in Washington, D.C. straddles the fence. On the one hand, he believes, that in democracies, every person can become his ro her own data collector and publisher for the price of the telephone and computer service bill. Like the Xerox machine previously, open electronic publishing allows any groups or individuals to offer their message on a new "universal information grid." Still, asks Dizard, is full information access one of our basic rights in postindustrial society, or is it simply a long range goal left to the play of economic and social forces? He adds that the degree to which "we extend our concept of education to include greater access to [computer and related] information resources" will shape the way our democracy evolves.[9]

Oliver Grey, an urban planner with the Urban Coalition, sees danger in that the "lure of maximum profits and the action of public officials, large corporations, and new interest groups, may prevent any significant minority inroads into CATV and result in the development of a new technological elite."[10] Although the information gap theme is often expressed as an issue within Western society, a related subject is gaps among societies. Much of the rhetoric has been related to a "New World Information Order" and such policy statements as UNESCO's 1978 Report of the International Commission for the Study of Communication Problems (the MacBride Commission). The problems caused by the export of films and television programs from the West, mostly from the U.S., is a topic frequently raised. Many of these critics have a political ax to grind. Kaarle Nordenstreng, who teaches mass communication courses in Finland, notes that "a critical approach to these popular theories reveals that they contain more ideological manipulation than social science."[11]

Most authors in the field have determined that the West has for too long tried to persuade those in the developing countries which technologies were appropriate to purchase, often at a disservice to those countries that did not have a suitable degree of technical sophistication. Herbert Schiller is skeptical of such persuasive efforts, even those encouraging these countries to use communications satellites. He feels that most benefits will accrue to "our own already privileged population." Schiller asks:

> Can the intolerable inequities that presently disfigure both domestic and international distribution be maintained?... Will the television programs, films and other entertainment produced in a small number of Western factories continue to preempt world screens and stages?.... Will U.S. data banks, plus a few more in Europe and Japan, provide the patterned information on which social, political, and technological decisions will be based in Latin America, Africa, and Asia?... In sum, will "interdependence" continue to be defined as binding relationships between unequals?[12]

If the information gap notion were simply the musings of a bunch of ivory tower noodlers, there would not be an issue. For the most part, the academic community has been the primary constituency of this idea. Nonetheless, other players have paid some attention, sometimes with far-reaching implications.

On the society-to-society level of discourse, UNESCO has gained high visibility. The MacBride Commission Report, debated at the General Conference of UNESCO in 1980, has become the primary document describing the need and blueprint for a new international information order. However, that report was viewed by the West in general and the United States and Great Britain in particular as a suspect document, produced by the so-called nonaligned movement that placed national sovereignty above the needs of the free flow of information—commercial and news. Moreover, with the actual or proposed withdrawal of U.S. and U.K. support of UNESCO, that body is not likely to be a significant player on the international scene for the immediate future.

On the domestic scene the perceived problem, in limited form, has surfaced in Congress. In his maiden speech to the Senate, New Jersey Sen. Frank Lautenberg warned that computers threatened to create a new class of poor people, those without access to computers for learning. In this 1983 speech, Lautenberg described the "potential for new and distressing divisions in our society," based on a gap between children in wealthy school districts, where there is money to provide computers, and children in poor districts.[13] To address this perceived gap, Lautenberg introduced legislation to provide $600 million in federal funds for computer education in public schools, with half the total going to the poorest districts. With much the same end in mind, Rep. Timothy Wirth proposed a bill that would have provided $3 billion over 10 years.

Concerns over local telephone rate increases after the breakup of AT&T have sometimes been couched in information-gap language. By July 1983, 7 months after the breakup, 13 bills had been introduced in Congress to protect the concept of universal telephone service. At one hearing, Rep. Edward Markey said that, if telephone service becomes a luxury, the U.S. could witness the creation of "an information aristocracy and underclass."[14]

This review of who has staked out what turf in the information gap arena, meant to be suggestive rather than exhaustive, has yielded elements of fears, speculation, and arm-waving. For the most part, it has found a lack of empirical analysis or any semblance of rigor in looking at historical developments in information technology or political responses. The "gap" proponents have said little on how they have measured or propose to measure the assumed gaps or even to provide a baseline from which to track prospective trends.

Diffusion of Technologies

Up to this point in history, all evidence indicates that technologies have been crucial factors in the spread of both access to information and the skills to use information. The original printing press was the first step in making information more widely available at lower prices. The big change came with the harnessing of the steam engine to the rotary press in the 1830s, combined with improvements in paper-making technology and the ability—via the railroads—to reach wider audiences with the printed product. In more recent history, film and broadcasting have further broadened access to all types of information. Moreover, compared to 100 years ago, a far greater proportion of the population has the skill to make sense of the information and to learn how to seek it out. Those who raise the specter of widening gaps therefore appear to assume a discontinuity in the historical trend, a burden which they have not overcome in their arguments.

Joseph Schumpeter was fond of noting that the achievement of technology was that it brought the price of silk stockings within the reach of every shopgirl, as well as of a queen. Sociologist Daniel Bell adds, more to the point, that technology has not only raised the standard of living but "it has been the chief mechanism of reducing inequality within Western Society." In *The Coming of Post-Industrial Society*, Bell quotes Jean Fourtastie, who calculated that by 1948 the Chief Justice of the Court of Accounts in France earned about four and a half times as much as an office boy on an hourly basis. In 1800, this disparity was 50 to 1.

Historically, innovations do indeed start with a small vanguard of adopters who tend to be better off economically than the population at large. Commercial interests are often among the leaders. But the market created by this vanguard often starts a process that leads to greater interest, higher volume, thus lower cost, reduced skill levels needed, and ultimately mass utilization—sometimes referred to as an "S" curve of diffusion because of the shape of the graph of adoption plotted over time. In some cases specific public policies were implemented to affect the timing and direction of the diffusion, and these policies changed over time to meet new conditions. In other instances, the public policies were either indirect or nonexistent.

Electricity, the automobile, telephone, and televison are among the technological innovations in the past century that have followed a path of starting on a small scale at a high price, used by those who saw value in the technology or who could afford to experiment with new technology. In each case, as the volume of use increased, the cost of providing the product decreased, with prices following. The rate of adoption by consumers varied, being shortest for television and longest for the telephone.

The circumstances of the development of each are not perfectly comparable, as the nature of the product, the regulatory regime, and the requirements for infrastructures varied somewhat. Still, the following vignettes serve as a reminder that the computer and the related information technologies may have more similarities to than differences from their historical cousins.

Telephone. In the case of the telephone, the early entrepreneurs recognized they could not afford to wire whole cities at once, so they chose first to wire affluent neighborhoods and business districts.[15] The phone companies in the United States swiftly found ways to reduce the cost to users, however, such as the introduction of metered service, pay phones for those who could not afford their own lines, and the building of minimal systems, sometimes laid down and maintained by farmers themselves. Meanwhile, government policy shifted from promoting unfettered competition to regulated monopoly. The combination of technological improvements and the public policies of universal service through nationwide cost averaging helped bring the monthly price of local service from the equivalent of 2 weeks' pay for the average worker in 1896 to about 2 hours' pay today.

Electrification. Electricity, too, was initially expensive. Again, the pattern was for the first users to be businesses and wealthy residences.

According to a 1922 account of the Edison Company, Andrew Carnegie had an electric range installed in his house in 1896. Still, this was seen as little more "than an expensive toy for the wealthy customer."[16] By 1912, less than four percent of electricity consumption was for residential use. Railroads alone accounted for 20 %.[17]

However, as has been the case with many technological innovations, the vision of the inventor or early proponent of the product or service has been a factor in the rate of diffusion. As with Henry Ford's automobile, Edison's aim was for low cost and durablity. His early light bulbs cost $1.25 to make, but he was selling them for $.40. In building up volume, he was able to bring down his average unit cost in 3 years to $.37, and then, in 1 year made up his previous years' deficits.[18]

The cost of generating and distributing electricity fell almost from the start of commercial applications until the 1970s. Still, in 1983, a resident of Hartford, Conn., paid 8.8 cents on average for a kilowatt of electricity, compared to 11 cents in 1905. Adjusting for the change in living costs, this translates into 39 minutes of work for the 1905 workers and less than 1 minute in 1983.[19] Meanwhile, the proportion of electricity consumed by residences had increased to 35%.[20]

Automobile.   Once again, the diffusion of the automobile in society went through stages, starting with adoption by wealthy urban groups, then the middle class, and ultimately the general population. In the process, the industry itself had to adjust to its customers, its labor force, and a changing industrial structure. The automobile was, at first, regarded as a plaything, certainly not a revolution. Yet it gradually changed from being a status symbol to being a useful product.

Henry Ford had a vision of the automobile for the average worker. His work in reducing manufacturing cost through production lines and the introduction of branch assembly plants led to, among other ramifications:

1. lower prices, which led to a broader market that spread beyond the United States' borders;
2. a sharp increase in labor productivity and higher wages;
3. perhaps least recognized but of substantial significance, a precipitous *decline* in the need for skilled workers and for mechanical skills among owners of automobiles.[21]

The magnitude of the decline in the price of automobiles is seen in comparing relative prices over the years. In 1908, a Buick cost about $1500, or the equivalent of more than 2.5 years' wages for a production worker. Even after mechanization, the price never fell much below $1000. Today, a comparable wage earner must work about 6 months for pay for a $10,000 automobile. Used automobiles bring the price down to a level of affordability of almost anyone.

Radio and Television.   In the mass media, history shows that the colonial press was structured for the educated elite. A series of cultural and technological developments that started to merge in the 1830s created the conditions for the mass audience penny press. The spread of newspapers, like many cultural innovations, followed an "S" curve.

In the earliest days of radio, a user had to have a modest technical bent to use the medium, tinkering with the crystal set. With improvements in the technology and the development of programming, the radio spread rapidly. Installment plans allowed households of modest means to purchase a radio. Even during the Depression, the number of radio sets grew.

Television followed a similar pattern. As with other innovations, prices came down rapidly as production volume increased. In 1950 a small black and white television cost about $3000 in 1984 dollars. Today, a larger screen color model can be had for $300 and even less.

The Present: Microcomputers in the Schools

The best data on which fears such as those expressed by Sen. Lautenberg can be based comes from a survey conducted between December 1982 and January 1983 by the Center for Social Organization of Schools.[22] Among its many findings was that two-thirds of the schools in the wealthiest school districts in the United States had microcomputers, compared to 41% in the least wealthy districts.

This information is subject to various interpretations. Sen. Lautenberg and others think the difference among districts is cause for concern. On the other hand, one could take the position that the survey was taken barely 5 years after the introduction of the basic Apple II microcomputer. Is it significant that so many schools have at least one microcomputer at such an early stage of its life? Given the reality that those with more money generally are the early adopters of technology, what significance should be be placed on the finding that at this early date the proportion of schools in the poorest school districts with microcomputers is two-thirds that of the most well-off schools?

Perhaps this says that any "gap" is moderate, that the technology is declining so rapidly in price, improving so quickly in ease of use, and is of high enough priority among educators and parents that there is no crisis and maybe not even need for concern. Or, it may be put in the broader context: poorer school districts would tend to have fewer new books, higher ratios of students to teachers, etc. The problem, if any, is not a computer hardware one.

What is the Role of Public Policy?

The assumptions by governments of the potential for a new product or service color the policies they adopt. Many of the early prognosticators on the telephone's future believed that its price would stay high and it would remain a luxury for the rich. Such prophecies could be self-fulfilling when held by those with power. In the U.S., the telegraph law was applied to telephone; thus policy, largely supportive of entrepreneurs' going into business, provided them with rights to string wires. In other countries, England and France among them, assumptions about the telephone's potential utility and its appropriate role were quite different. The restrictive policies adopted thus kept prices high and availability limited until recently. In the current debate over what should be the role of government policy regarding the newer information media, two overarching lessons seem to emerge from history.

First, there is no need to act precipitously. Technology casts a long shadow. Thus, there is time for society to see how some technology or combinations of technolgies move toward their natural markets and costs. Moreover, there is danger that jumping in too fast can lock in a technology that soon would be superseded by a better one. Examples of this abound:

- The diffusion of the telephone might have been delayed for years if some influential body had convinced the federal government in 1860 that telegraph was the personal communications medium of the future and a massive effort had been implemented to see that every household was wired and provided with a telegraph key. A similar roadblock might have been the success of a proposal for the Post Office to gain control over telecommunications—the outcome in most of the rest of the world.

- In the late 1940s, the Federal Communications Commission was about to give its blessing to a standard for color television developed by CBS that involved a cumbersome mechanical process that was incompatible with existing black-and-white broadcasting. The Korean War put the final action on hold, and by the time the FCC returned to the topic, RCA had perfected what, in retrospect, was a far more flexible and superior technology, which became the FCC's designated standard.

- It may take decades before it is clear that some technologically innovative service or product has the potential to become an actual or near necessity, worthy of some government attention for regulation, subsidy, etc. The telephone and electricity (for residential use), the automobile, radio, and television are examples of such techno-logical innovations. It is not at all clear when, if ever, personal computers and/or access to electronic information services will be perceived to be of similar value.

The second lesson is that the type of government action that might be taken, if any, is not consistent or obvious across technologies. Some examples:

- The modern steam-driven rotary printing press and the attendant publishing ventures stimulated by this technology received virtually no direct help from government. In the 19th century, the gradual spread of tax-supported public education and public libraries had a variety of indirect effects, including providing a larger body of literate customers. Near the end of the century, the subsidization of postal rates for printed material was about as targeted a program as government has enacted. (The withdrawal of these subsidies in the 1970s has had no measurable impact on magazine circulation, though some publishers had feared it would).

- The automobile was developed with virtually no direct government intervention or subsidy. However, government has played a crucial role in providing the infrastructure—the highway system—financed by taxes roughly tied to usage. In addition, rather than direct subsidy of automobile ownership, in the past three decades governments have adopted a policy of providing subsidized mass transit.

- The telephone's early years were characterized by private develop-ment. The industry has passed through eras of monopoly during the time of Bell's early patents, to a period of competition, then government-approved and regulated monopoly, and now a period of regulated competition. The role of government to encourage cross subsidies and nationwide cost averaging to promote universal service was pursued decades after telephone service began.

- For broadcasting, there have been few direct economic subsidies to users. In this case, policies involved the conditions of ownership of licenses, regulations covering broad areas of programming and the like.

- Hand-held calculators are an example of an application of technol-ogies that has had a widespread impact in a short period of time but with virtually no government role (save the funding of the space and defense research that led to the development of much of the underlying technology).

There are indeed all sorts of "gaps" in and among societies. Many are related to the state of an economy. Poorer people and societies have fewer and older automobiles than the better off. The poor eat fewer steaks, rely more heavily on public education, are less able to afford designer jeans. They are less able to subscribe to magazines or purchase books.

The issue is not one of information or knowledge gaps, any more than it is one of a protein gap or transportation gap. If there is an issue, it is: What priorities should a society have in making decisions on what are necessities, what are frills, and what falls in a debatable middle ground? A second question is: What mechanisms can be implemented to address any problems?

The matters of books, magazines and education have been addressed by public libraries and public education. Concerns about protein have been addressed with food stamps. And nothing has been done about designer jeans for reasons that need not be dwelled on. Whether cable television should fall into the book category or into the designer jeans one is still up for grabs.

Clearly there is a role for public policy to fine tune areas not adjusted by themselves. The determination that telephone service should be universal—a consensus that did not spring full grown with Bell's first call—led to policies of nationwide averaging and a two-tier pricing structure, one for businesses and one for residences. That this structure may be in the process of being dismantled (it is not a certainty) with so far barely a yawn from the majority of subscribers may be an indicator that telephone service has indeed become so cheap that the complex policies that were appropriate 40 years ago are no longer needed.

This, then, may suggest the direction for policy. There is evidence, only lightly drawn on in this article, that national economies that are growing with participation from a broad spectrum of the workforce reduce or eliminate the need for targeted programs of government subsidies. In the industrialized economies, the creation of a broad middle class has narrowed greatly the proportion of the population that *needs* subsidies (as opposed to the vast array of middle class subsidies, such as deduction of interest from taxable income, that are the perks that a wealthy economy can rationalize).

As seen in the figures representing the constant dollar price of electricity, automobiles, telephone, service and television sets, the combination of declining costs, thanks to improvements in technology, and a wealthier work force, has lessened the difference in life style between the poorer and richer in society. Today, with many manufacturing jobs being transferred to the developing industrial nations, there are signs that a similar process is taking place on a global scale.

NOTES

1. T.R. Ide, "The Information Revolution", in J. Bertirg, S.C. Mills, and H. Wintersberger, eds., *The Socio-Economic Impact of Microelectronics*, Oxford: Pergamon Press, 1980), p. 40.
2. Benjamin Disraeli, (Earl of Beaconsfield), *Endymion* (London: Longman, Green and Co. 1881), p. 155.
3. Proverbs 24:5
4. Elie Abel, "Looking Ahead from the Twentieth Century," in Robert W. Haigh, George Gerbner, and Richard B. Byrne, eds., *Communications in the Twenty-First Century* (New York: John Wiley & Sons, 1981), p. 8.
5. Herbert I. Schiller, *The Mind Managers* (Boston: Beacon Press, 1973), pp. 174-175.
6. James W. Carey and John J. Quirk, "The History of the Future," in George Gerbner, Larry P. Gross, and William H. Melody, eds., *Communications Technology and Social Policy* (New York: Wiley Interscience, 1973), p. 501.
7. For a description of the notion of a new literacy, see Chapter 5.
8. Melvin Webber, "Urbanization and Communication,"in Gerbner, p. 303.
9. Wilson P. Dizard, *The Coming Information Age* (New York: Longman, 1982), p. 119.
10. Oliver Grey, "Minorities and the New Media: Exclusion and Access," in Gerbner, p. 322.
11. Kaarle Nordenstreng, "New International Directions: Nonaligned Viewpoint," in Haigh, p. 193.
12. Herbert I. Schiller, "The Free Flow Doctrine: Will It Last Into the Twenty-First Century", in Haigh, p. 189.
13. Jane Perlez, "Computers Pose a Peril for Poor, Lautenberg Says," *The New York Times*, June 8, 1983, p. B-1.
14. David Burnham, "In Bell System Breakup, Small is Expensive," *The New York Times*, July 31, 1983, Sec. 4, p. 8.
15. Ithiel de Sola Pool, ed., *The Social Impact of the Telephone* (Cambridge, Mass.: MIT Press, 1977), pp. 28, 32, 142.
16. Thomas Commerford Martin, *Forty Years of Edison Service*, 1882-1922 (New York: Press of the New York Edison Company, 1922), p. 78.
17. Richard B. Duboff, *Electric Power in American Manufacturing*, 1889-1958 (New York: Arno Press, 1979), Table 12, p. 50.
18. John W. Oliver, *History of American Technology* (New York: The Ronald Press Company, 1956), p. 350.
19. Raymond R. Beauregard, "Memories on Energy More Myth Than Reality," *The New York Times*, July 3, 1983, Sec. 11, p. 18 (Mr. Beauregard is an economist with Northeast Utilities).

20. Calculated from *U.S. Statistical Abstract,* 1984, Table 1003, p. 586.
21. James M. Laux and Patrick Fridenson, *The Automobile Revolution: The Impact of an Industry* (Chapel Hill, N.C.: University of North Carolina Press, 1982), p. xiv.
22. "School Uses of Computers—Reports from a National Survey," No. 1, April 1983, The Johns Hopkins University: Center for Social Organization of Schools, p. 3. Some more recent statistics on computer use in schools from the same source can be found in chapter 5.

Chapter 7

Privacy and Computer-Based Information Systems

Meredith W. Mendes

Developments in information technology are widely perceived to play an expanded role in data collection.[1] Increased efficiency and decreased costs of computers and telecommunications have contributed to a growing demand for information and services from institutions and from personal users in their homes. The mechanics of information systems, their interconnection through networks and their expansion into users' homes, and the large amount of personal information being collected and retained in such systems have raised questions about the effects of information technology on individual privacy.[2]

Reactions to the growing computerization of information services, their interconnection, and the expanding use of both one-way and interactive information technology for institutional, business, and personal use range from outrage over the potential for impropriety and privacy invasion[3] to admonishments that, although the potential for such invasions exist, privacy regulations may be "premature."[4]

A study conducted by Louis Harris and Associates, Inc. in 1984 to examine people's perceptions of the impact of technology on personal privacy stated that "vast majorities of the general public and most leadership groups believe it is now possible to assemble master files from many sources. And they believe such files are an invasion of privacy."[5] Moreover, although society recognizes the computer as a "symbol of the new era and the core of much of our high technology," a majority of those polled see the present uses of computers as an "actual threat to personal privacy."[6]

This chapter explores the extent to which such privacy concerns may be warranted in light of the types of privacy invasions that may become possible as a result of changes in, and the expansion of, both information technology, and current and proposed laws regulating the information collected, transmitted, and stored by that technology.

The following designations distinguish the types of privacy violations discussed in this chapter: aggregation,[7] unauthorized access, intrusion, misuse, and piracy. Additionally, the personal data contained in any information system may be obtained by or of interest to any of the following groups of users: government executive and regulatory agencies; law enforcement officials, judges, prosecutors, and private party lawyers; private institutions, agencies, and employers; systems operators and commercial marketing organizations; and private party "hackers." Confidential information may also be disclosed by subjects of privacy violations who feel pressured or coerced into revealing such information.

Some of the forms of privacy violations described in this chapter and defined in Appendix B may have occurred in the past, and may still occur in manually stored records, while many of the presumed dangers and the potential privacy violations pointed out here may never be realized. However, this chapter is intended to raise privacy issues that might occur, and to reflect privacy concerns of users, policymakers, authors of articles or books on the subject, and others. Moreover, the changes in information technology have increased the probability that at least some violations discussed herein will occur.

The objectives of this chapter are:

1. To define privacy and personal information in a way that is useful in electronically stored one-way and interactive information technology;

2. To discuss the changes in technology that may increase the potential for privacy violations;

3. To examine existing common law and statutory provisions, measures that have been taken, and measures that are pending in response to potential privacy intrusions;

4. To discuss whether these measures are likely to be responsive to privacy concerns; and

5. To present alternatives to existing and pending legal sanctions.

Database is used in this chapter to mean a system in which a central operator provides text and sometimes graphics, on a public dial- up access basis, to a large number of subscribers or users.

DEFINING PRIVACY

The concept of *privacy* seems simple enough, but a study of the legal and philosophical literature on privacy today reveals a surprising lack of consensus on its meaning. Nevertheless, it is important to define privacy, even if this definition exceeds current limits of legal protection, because privacy allows us to achieve other values that our society considers important.[8] Privacy is important in the context of information technology because the degree to which individuals are willing to forego their privacy gives them some control over decisions that affect them, such as whether they qualify for employment, insurance, credit, loans, or government benefits. Defining privacy as a legal value may help raise awareness of its importance, deter reckless invasions, and create predictability in the law. Coming to a consensus on the meaning of privacy may aid in determining which losses are most undesirable, therefore most in need of legal protection.

Constitutional Right to Privacy

The Supreme Court expressly recognized a right to privacy under the United States Constitution in *Griswold v. Connecticut*.[9] In *Katz v. United States*[10] the Court developed a subjective "expectation of privacy" test that it has subsequently used to determine whether individual privacy expectations will be protected.[11] Three categories of privacy interests have been found to be within the constitutionally protected right to privacy: the right to make certain kinds of important (i.e., intimate) decisions independent of state interference,[12] the expectations of freedom from government intrusion into places where one's reliance on privacy is justified,[13] and, most recently, the individual's interest in avoiding disclosure of certain "personal matters" contained in stored records.[14]

Although certain records have been found to be within the procedurally protected expectation of privacy, the boundaries of this right are unclear. For example, the Supreme Court held that bank customers lacked standing to contest government access to their bank records, because the bank records were the property of the bank.[15] The Court maintained that "the depositor takes the risk, in revealing his affairs to another, that the information will be conveyed by that person to the government,"[16] and that the depositor therefore had no justifiable expectation of privacy in his bank records.[17] The Court has not recognized substantive privacy rights for individual records stored in databanks.

The Supreme Court has held that the use of an electronic system that records signals from a private home is not unconstitutional. In 1979, the Court found in *Smith v. Maryland*[18] that the use of pen registers without a warrant to record telephone numbers dialed from a private household is not an expectation of privacy "that society is prepared to recognize as reasonable."[19]

The scope of the right to privacy protected by the Constitution is unclear and, it might be asserted, largely a matter of judicial discretion. Moreover, the constitutional right to privacy does not extend to protect invasion perpetrated by private third parties, unless that invasion can be characterized as state action.[20]

Individuals' privacy may also be protected by asserting the Fifth Amendment privilege against self-incrimination when a state or the federal government has attempted or is attempting to conduct an inquiry into a person's records. The Fifth Amendment, applicable to the states through the Fourteenth, confers a privilege to be silent in an inquiry as long as an individual's answers to official questions might be employed either as evidence or as leads to evidence in a future criminal prosecution of that individual.[21] Exercise of such a privilege cannot be punished by the government as a failure to cooperate with a proper inquiry, or used as the basis for adverse treatment, including denial of a public benefit.[22]

This doctrine could be used to support the argument that unauthorized government inquiries into computer records for personal information are the equivalent of forcing individuals to testify against themselves, and as such, violate the Fifth and Fourteenth Amendments. The argument is somewhat undercut by the fact that, once an individual has been promised immunity from future prosecutorial use of compelled answers or their "fruit," refusal to answer questions pertaining to a legitimate government interest may be punished criminally and civilly.[23] Thus, the government might promise immunity and still conduct an inquiry, which would then be difficult to link to the denial of a benefit or subsequent privacy violation. The government is, however, limited in the scope of its inquiry, which cannot be of unjustifiable breadth.

Common Law Privacy[24]

The common law privacy tort affords minimal protection against potential privacy invasions in the context of modern information technology. Warren and Brandeis[25] wrote the seminal article on the creation of a legally recognizable right to privacy wherein they defined privacy as the right to be left alone.[26] Although the motivation for their article was a series of then-current technological developments including the telephone, microphone, audio recorder, and camera,[27] the right has not been subsequently expanded to deal with more modern phenomena.

The widely accepted analysis of the privacy rights covered by this tort recognizes four categories: a) unreasonable intrusion on the seclusion of another, b) appropriation of another's name or likeness, c) unreasonable publicity given to another's private life, and d) publicity that places another in the false light before the public.[28]

The law of intrusion may be violated by "one who intentionally intrudes, physically or otherwise, upon the solitude or seclusion of another, or his private affairs or concerns . . . if the intrusion would be highly offensive to a reasonable man."[29] In contrast to the other branches of the privacy tort, intrusion requires no publication or other use of the materials obtained for a defendant to be liable.[30] Actionable privacy intrusions have arisen from improper investigations of individual bank accounts,[31] tax returns,[32] and over-zealous police work.[33]

Courts have upheld actions for intrusion of privacy where eavesdropping through a wiretap or concealed microphone was used to intercept private communications.[34] However, in an action where a court ruled the information tapped was not confidential, no actionable privacy intrusion was found.[35] Intrusion is actionable only if the plaintiff can prove that the defendant's conduct was "truly intrusive" and that the intrusion was designed to elicit information unavailable through normal inquiry or observation.[36] Standards for measuring what is "truly intrusive" or "highly offensive to a reasonable man" may vary considerably and may ultimately be a matter of judicial discretion.[37]

A second branch of the privacy tort was developed to prevent unauthorized uses of people's images in photographs for commercial gain.[38] This branch is probably inapplicable to modern information technology. It could be argued that disclosure of computerized personal information can create a profile of a person perhaps more intrusive than a photograph.[39] But the argument seems misplaced since the crux of this action is the unjust enrichment a defendant gains by his gratuitous use of a plaintiff's identity.[40]

The latter two branches of the privacy tort, unreasonable publicity and false light, require plaintiffs to prove the offending disclosure was published or disseminated to the public at large. Disclosure to one person does not constitute "the public." This allowance means any file containing confidential information about a person could be disclosed without authorization, and not constitute an actionable privacy violation.[41] Thus, without creating a common law action for invasion of privacy, one who obtained a credit grantor's identifying code number could conceivably get detailed information on thousands of individuals by simply telephoning information-gathering agencies.

In addition, false light requires that any publicity be highly offensive to a "reasonable person" before damages will be awarded.[42] This reasonableness raises the same definitional problems as does the definition of an "unreasonable" intrusion.

Each category of the privacy tort is subject to common law privileges. If the defendant can show the exposure of information was in the community's interest, the victim must show the defendant's act was motivated by willful and malicious intent.[43] Consent, which may be used as a form of pressure in return for a benefit or favor, may also curtail the utility of a common law action in the computer context.[44] While a common law action for invasion of privacy could conceivably be developed as a deterrent for information privacy invasions, the current definitions and requirements for an actionable privacy invasion severely limit the privacy tort's usefulness to modern information technology.

Privacy Statutes

Congress has passed a patchwork of statutes protecting individuals against privacy invasions by the federal government and, in some areas, against informational privacy intrusions in the private sector. Surprisingly, none of these statutes attempts to define privacy. In 1974, Congress enacted the Privacy Act,[45] a general enactment of self-restraint regulating unauthorized disclosures of individual records by the federal government.[46] Specific federal statutes have been passed preventing unauthorized disclosures of the United States mail[47] and credit information,[48] regulating wiretapping[49] and the seizure of work product materials relating to the news media by government officials,[50] and prohibiting unauthorized interception of broadcast telecommunications.[51] A privacy interest has been recognized against searches or seizures by federal officials where such actions would intrude upon a "known confidential relationship," including clergyman and parishioner, lawyer and client, or doctor and patient.[52] Privacy rights are also recognized in educational records.[53]

Several states have enacted either constitutional provisions or statutes that supplement federal law and limit state governments' uses of personal data.[54] A number have adopted state fair-information practice statutes, modeled on the federal Privacy Act of 1974, that define the procedure for collection, maintenance, correction, reports, and public access to stored personal information.[55] However, many states have not adopted comprehensive privacy statutes, and those enacted are uneven. Some states have passed statutes protecting information privacy in one or perhaps a few areas.[56] While such a policy promotes state autonomy, it also creates disunity, unevenness, and unpredictability in the law, and leaves individuals largely unprotected against private business enterprises and other private sector violations—except to the extent that such businesses and private parties regulate themselves.

Thus, a grab bag of rights might be compiled under the heading *privacy*. But there seems to be no unifying concept to identify why certain types of information are legally protectable. Indeed, there are commentators who believe privacy is just a bag of unrelated goodies.[57] Those who subscribe to this concept argue privacy rhetoric in the law is misleading[58] because privacy is never protected without some other interest also being protected.[59] Hence, the argument follows, the law would be clearer if the real values at stake were identified and the term *privacy* were disregarded altogether.[60]

Moreover, because the law has strong commitments to values that may conflict with individual privacy concerns, no area of individual concern can ever be absolutely protected. Among such values are the public interest in preventing evasions of the law and promoting effective enforcement,[61] the freedom of expression protected by the First Amendment, the corresponding right of the public to be well informed, and the protection of public health. In addition to these gaps, some privacy invasions may go unreported because reporting them necessitates a further loss of privacy. Litigation costs and delays may also discourage actions for privacy invasions, unless courts award or statutes provide for victims to be awarded attorney fees. Moreover, a definition of privacy based on legally protectable rights recognized in the past may be inadequate to cover privacy violations in the context of modern information technology.

A descriptive definition of privacy constructed from remedies at law, then, will leave gaps and will afford little prescriptive guidance for future law- and policymakers. The constitutional concept of privacy is nebulous and unpredictable. The common law is outdated, has doubtful application to information technology, and is subject to privileges and immunities. Federal statutes are riddled with exceptions and holes because of competing considerations that circumscribe the right. State statutes vary in coverage, and most are modeled after the federal Privacy Act. States without specific privacy statutes rely on legislation passed in specific areas. No statute adequately defines privacy.

Types of Privacy Concerns

What seems to be needed is a prescriptive definition of privacy that will provide grounds for consensus yet be flexible enough to encompass and adapt to developments in information technology. At the same time, it must afford some limits so as not to encompass every type of information that may be disseminated about a person.

At least five types of privacy concerns may arise as a result of changes in the methods and amounts of information gathered and stored by information technology: unauthorized access, misuses, piracy, aggregation of data, and continuous or intermittent intrusion into terminal lines.[62] Changes in the methods of collecting and storing data, and how these changes may affect information privacy, are discussed in the "Legal Framework" section.

Alternative Definitions

Given the limitations of constructing a legal definition, several commentators have suggested more expansive definitions for understanding the content of the right to privacy. There is little agreement on the meaning of privacy, although there is consensus on the fact that no definition is appropriate in every context.[63] One definition in the computer context has been suggested by Dr. Alan F. Westin, who has written a number of books about privacy and information technology. Westin wrote in one of his early books,

> Privacy is the claim of individuals, groups or institutions to determine for themselves when, how, and to what extent information about them is communicated to others.[64]

Westin's definition has been influential, but certain aspects of it have received criticism.[65] For example, the dictionary[66] defines the word *claim* as an assertion of one's due. But as indicated above, claims to privacy are not absolutely protected because of changes in facts, because of conflicts between individuals' and society's needs, because of changes of circumstances or developments giving rise to new claims, and because some claims may not be asserted.

Moreover, if *claim* means a legal claim, then it implies an interest recognized by courts and legislatures. This definition is too narrow. If *claim* refers to a "moral" claim, then it assumes a preferred position in society's hierarchy of values and, equally important, by the courts. But, while most Americans esteem their privacy[67] – perhaps as much as any other value – it is freedoms of thought and speech that occupy the highest position in our courts.[68] Thus, the assertion of a broad unitary claim of privacy may imply that privacy holds, or should hold, an exalted position over other conflicting values, which is not always true.[69] A definition based on privacy as a "right" is vulnerable to the same criticisms.[70]

Privacy is defined in this study as a condition, because it carries no legal or normative connotations. The legislative process and the courts are ill-equipped to handle many privacy invasions because they are either too clumsy, too slow in responding to abuse, or because competing considerations outweigh personal privacy protection in the eyes of law- and policymakers. In many situations privacy may be better protected when legal measures are supplemented with, or replaced by, nonlegal preventive measures such as physical security precautions or market forces. Thus, the word *condition* is used herein because it implies no legal value judgment.

Another criticism that can be made of Westin's definition is that the word *information* is too broad. We constantly communicate information that is unintended, but that may not result in someone's loss of privacy. It is suggested that privacy should be equated with "personal and confidential information," and that loss of privacy should be recognized only when such personal and confidential information are disclosed without the subject's authorization. Personal and confidential information will be defined as information about oneself that one would not want disclosed without one's prior consent. This definition allows individuals substantial discretion, and individual viewpoints of what is personal are certain to vary considerably. Since the law will never afford complete protection to all private information,[71] it may be more accurate to recognize the disparity among individual viewpoints rather than to attempt to define personal information according to some external and arbitrarily imposed standard.[72] For the purposes of this analysis, however, it is presumed that certain types of information are private, including information relating to one's own financial transactions; buying habits; entertainment and information sources (books, programs, newspapers, magazines, and movie selections); medical, drug, and related data; educational and tax records; work papers and intellectual material relating to one's employment; and unpublished written and oral communications.[73] Westin's definition, then, subject to the above changes, will be used to delimit privacy in the context of information technology. In this chapter, *privacy* is defined as:

> A condition in which individuals, groups or institutions can determine for themselves, when, how and to what extent private information about them is communicated to others.

CURRENT AND PROPOSED DATABASE AND OTHER COMPUTER-BASED SYSTEMS

Historical Background

This section discusses certain information services that are currently available or proposed, including personal computers, database transmitted via cable television or telephone systems, and electronic funds transfer.

It is useful to note before discussing these technologies that technological innovations have historically been approached with trepidation which has later been considered unwarranted or premature. For example, in Warren and Brandeis' article advocating a right to privacy,[74] the authors warned that cameras and newspapers:

> Have invaded the sacred precincts of private and domestic life; and numerous mechanical devices threaten to make good the prediction that "what is whispered in the closet shall be proclaimed from the housetops."[75]

Moreover, futurists and courts have predicted privacy losses and dire consequences of technology that never materialized.[76] Thus, while it may be wise to be aware of the potential ramifications and privacy losses that could result from today's new information technology, it may also be advisable to wait to see which threats, if any, are realized, before calling for legal remedies.[77]

This policy was adopted, for example, in the development of the tort of defamation, where the courts developed a distinction between the degree of protection afforded to public and private figures. It might be argued that this policy of "wait and see" is misplaced, because it victimizes innocent individuals and results in a legal system that is unresponsive to current privacy invasions. It might also be argued that some privacy invasions may be so gross, or their harm so great, that they should be prevented before they are realized. But the counter argument is that trying to prevent even the most egregious privacy invasions with immediate legal preventives would be costly, would be likely to result in overly broad legislation, and would probably be disfavored by those who view such a policy as a hindrance to innovation. And while innovation and change may not always be beneficial, the costs, delays, inexactitude, and political conflicts inherent in the legal system might be minimized by other privacy protections such as industry self-regulation in the form of privacy codes,[78] physical security locks, or encryption codes. Local information systems such as interactive cable may be regulated by franchise agreements or private party contracts.[79] These protections would probably be more responsive to privacy dangers requiring immediate attention than would be statutory measures or litigation.

Electronic Databases

Interactive data systems, some of which are called videotex, especially when they are designed for the mass audience, may transmit information via cable television hook-ups, over the air (for at least the "down stream" part of the transmission from the head-end computer to the user's console), over the switched telephone network, or through some combination of these forms.[80] One of the first systems to offer some degree of interactivity, though not a videotex system, was the Warner Amex cable television system marketed under the name of Qube.[81] True videotex systems that have been commercially or test marketed include Cox Cable Communications INDAX, Times Mirror's Gateway, and Knight-Ridder's Viewtron.[82] In addition to receiving text and simple graphic information, users can transmit responses and request services using typewriter-like consoles linking televisions, via coaxial cable wire or the telephone network, to a central computer. Among the services that videotex systems offer or are expected to offer are:

- *newspaper-like* services—news, financial, sports, and Congressional information;
- *financial* services—market reports, routine accounting services, and electronic funds transfer;
- *shopping* services—mail order merchandising, a wide variety of ticket and reservation services, and comparative shopping information;
- *message* services—word processing and text formatting, and, eventually, electronic mail;
- *information storage;*
- *entertainment* services—schedules of events and games;
- *educational* services—instructional material and drills;
- *monitoring services—homesecurity devices to detect smoke, fire, sound, movement; energy load management; and medical oversight;*[83]
- *program* selection (when part of a cable television service)—commercial channels; premium channels (primarily movies that have not been shown on commercial channels; community channels that allow users to participate in community politics, talk shows, and interviews).[84]

Warner Amex introduced its Qube system in Columbus, Ohio. Warner has subsequently received approval for two-way cable operations in Cincinnati, Pittsburgh (a system subsequently sold), Dallas, Houston, St. Louis, suburban Chicago, and Milwaukee.[85] Qube gathers billing and response data on its computer by "polling" each subscriber's terminal every 6 seconds.[86] The information collected includes whether the set is in use, the channel selected, and the last response button touched. A separate computer performs billing and administrative services. Data is transferred from the polling computer to the information system via magnetic tape and then matched with user names and addresses in the information system. Itemized bills are kept for 9 months;[87] summary data, not containing individual names, is kept indefinitely for programming and marketing purposes.[88] Infomercials offer products for purchase and, for programming, request viewer preferences on products, pilot commercials, and serials. Infomercials are also used in other marketing functions.[89]

Some Qube systems offer subscribers a home security system. This system is comprised of ultrasonic motion detectors, pressure sensors placed under rugs, infrared photoelectric cells, doors and window sensors, and an emergency button that polls the system once every 10 seconds.[90] Once an alarm is triggered, information is conveyed manually by an operator to the appropriate authority.[91]

Videotex, transmitted via common carrier (as discussed in Richard Hooper's chapter on Prestel) is currently offered on the broadest scale in Great Britain.[92] American companies are also investing in videotex, however. An estimated $100 million had been invested nationwide by U.S. companies in the development and testing of videotex systems through 1984.[93]

Because computerized databases are capable of storing and retrieving archival records, some futurists have predicted that some information will no longer be stored in books. Instead, much may be stored as electronic data entered digitally into a computer.[94]

Futurists and other prognosticators have also speculated that electronic mail service will eventually bypass the current mail system.[95] Users may be able to send messages to general or limited (closed user group [CUG]) audiences. Confidential messages could be limited to CUGs by transmitting messages in codes known only to certain people.[96] Alternatively, computer information systems could be used to conduct business meetings without requiring all of the participants to be physically present or available for a conference call at the same time. According to this scenario, conferences could be conducted by sending prepared messages (in the form of speeches) to the meeting's participants. Recipients could respond if so inclined, and each terminal would log their responses, giving a serial number to each.[97] This way a participant could "attend" meetings while conducting other business at the same time. Travel time and expenses would be saved as well.

Computer Systems[98]

Computer systems have proliferated in business organizations and in user households. Many business' inventory and internal control procedures, communication systems, and information systems are computer operated. Computers in users' homes could provide services similar to videotex. Americans' household computers[99] are now being used to play games, control activities within the home, perform accounting functions and data analysis,[100] write letters and reports, and store confidential information. Such information may include data concerning personal and business finances, medical treatment and physical conditions, personal diaries, and work-product of substantial intellectual property value.[101] Personal computer users have also created voluntary, noncommercial networks to share common interests and information through data communication. These networks, called "bulletin-boards," send information outside users' homes and voluntarily open up the owner's data to outside access by network members.[102]

Electronic Funds Transfer

A computer network comprised of commercial financial institutions has been created by the growth of electronic funds transfer (EFT). EFT is money transferred in the form of electronic bits[103] via telephone wire, cable, satellite, or magnetic media.[104] Four types of operations are generally grouped under the heading of EFT: automated teller machines (ATM), national bank cards, automated clearing house systems (ACH), and point-of-sale (POS) transfers.

Automatic tellers are located in almost every major city in the United States and in most industrialized nations.[105] Among the services performed by ATMs are cash withdrawal, deposits, transfer of funds, and installment payments to financial institutions.[106] Customers can use their bank cards at any bank branch, and in states with less restrictive banking laws, ATMs have been installed in shopping centers, supermarkets, airports, and work places.[107] Arrangements have been made to share ATMs among different financial institutions.[108] Regional and national networks are increasingly permitting cash withdrawals from ATMs at institutions other than the user's own bank.

Another category of EFT technology is the national bank card network. The two largest credit card operations, VISA USA and Interbank Card Association (Master Card), have automated their credit operations and have also issued debit cards.[109] These access cards will authorize automatic payments nationwide without clearing first through the Federal Reserve System.[110]

A third change in the national banking system is the automatic clearing house (ACH). The ACH is a computerized center that receives payment information in electronic form.[111] The information received is sorted automatically, forwarded to the receiving bank, and posted in appropriate accounts.[112] No paper is involved other than the customer's receipt of documentation. The basic services ACH offers are direct payroll deposit, preauthorized payments of a fixed amount (mainly mortgage, insurance, loans), and bill-checking.[113] The latter allows the customer to authorize payment of a bill by signing the bill and returning it. The need for a check is thus eliminated.[114]

Finally, POS transfers allow customers to transfer funds immediately from their accounts into merchant's accounts.[115] POS terminals are located at retail stores and are operated by the debit cards (also known as cash or asset cards) discussed above. These terminals function like ATMs, verifying and guaranteeing checks, and allowing customers to make immediate deposits and withdrawals.[116]

The current trend is toward an electronically linked nationwide financial network. Commercial banks, savings and loans, merchants, the travel and entertainment industries, insurance companies, and the Federal Reserve are becoming interconnected.[117] Networks of banking institutions are also becoming internationalized. The first of these networks, Society for Worldwide Interbank Financial Transactions (SWIFT), is operated and owned by participating banks in Canada, Europe, and the United States.[118]

Developments Creating Potential Privacy Issues

The development of these and other computer-based services offer users several potential benefits, including greater choice and access to information, time and energy savings, greater efficiency, less margin for error, and potentially increased security for stored information.

Certain aspects of electronically stored information and the technology transmitting the information, however, have raised fears of possible new forms of privacy invasions, and have increased the amount of harm that could result from other intrusions. Some observers warn against potential abuses of:

Networks.   The interconnection of remote terminals via networks and the sharing of information have increased the potential for privacy invasions.[119] Networks reduce the accountability of any one organization for stored confidential information. Communications facilities are shared among many unrelated users, all of whom have access to information contained in the files of every other organization in the network, unless a particular organization installs security measures on its files. Networks have thus exponentially increased the potential for unauthorized access, misuse, and disclosure of personal information among private and government agencies,[120] commercial information providers, and "hackers."

Ease of Access.   As networking has grown, so has the "user friendliness" of accessing electronically stored data through networks.[121] Most systems use some variant of an identification code/password system to protect their information against privacy invasions. During the past few years, however, personal computers have been used to break these codes by systematically speeding up what would otherwise be a slow hit-or-miss process.[122] Thus, password codes may no longer be satisfactory security.

Increased Memory of Microchips.   Another aspect of information technology that has increased the potential for privacy violations is the use of microchips. Record keepers were once limited in the amounts of information they could retain and exchange by physical storage space. Even if information were stored, it was necessary to physically locate that information. But now the microchip compresses information so that voluminous data can be retained. Electronically stored files can be retrieved and reviewed more quickly than printed matter, and, as the price of data retrieval and systems decreases, more agencies, organizations, and individuals will have access to computer information systems.

Any stored records could be the target of the privacy violations enumerated previously — unauthorized access, misuse, interception, and aggregation of data and piracy.[123] However, the developments of networks, the need for easy access to files (user friendliness), the microchip, and price decreases of technological components that have made information storage and retrieval a growth industry have also increased the potential gravity (and perhaps the likelihood) of such privacy violations.

Detection of Privacy Abuses

Some observers fear a possible increase in the accessibility of potentially damaging and incriminating information due to unauthorized access. Computer "break ins" may be easier to execute than traditional break ins because they can be perpetrated from a remote terminal and do not require the physical presence of the violator. Currently, detecting and prosecuting such violations is difficult because there is generally no tangible evidence of the violations. Complications may also arise because, as discussed in the next section, few states have statutes directed at information privacy violations and no federal statutes address potential privacy invasions in the private sector.

Forms of Privacy Abuses

The interconnection of many computers into networks and the sharing of information among organizations may increase the incidence of voluntary transfers of information without subjects' authorization.[124] And it is possible that increased storage capacity will encourage the tendency to retain outdated and no longer accurate data about individuals.

Networking might create damaging and incriminating "psychographic profiles"[125] by aggregating information that could well be innocuous when segregated. These profiles, and projections based on them, says the Attorney General of New York, could be used by credit companies, government officials, landlords, insurance companies, investigators, marketing firms, and others for decision making.[126] In addition, the existence of large pools of stored personal information and the current low risk of detection are likely to have significant appeal to third parties.[127] Unauthorized disclosures of psychographic profiles and projections could seriously harm the personal and professional lives, and emotional and psychological well-being, of the subjects of disclosures.

For example, at least two attempts have been made to use the information maintained by Warner Amex on its Qube subscribers for purposes that might constitute invasions of subscriber privacy. In one of these incidents, the Columbus mayor's opponent in an election tried to use some information from Qube's records to damage the mayor's reputation and gain an unfair advantage in the campaign.[128] In another incident, a proprietor of a movie theater who was prosecuted for showing X-rated films sought (but did not obtain) a subpoena to acquire the names of Qube subscribers who had watched a particular X-rated film when it aired over the interactive cable television system.

Interactive technology will also create the potential for unauthorized intrusions into subscribers' homes. For instance, a cable operator providing a home security service could use the system to determine whether subscribers are home.[130] This information could be used, in turn, to jeopardize subscriber security if it was used for unauthorized purposes such as facilitating robbery. (Of course, burglars have also been able to use the telephone to ascertain that inhabitants are not at home before breaking in.) Utility companies could also monitor or regulate the energy level of homes.[131]

Electronic Protection of Information Privacy

Conversely, technology may help prevent privacy invasions and electronic information crimes. It is possible that, as the amount of personal information collected increases, privacy may also increase. Information in machine-readable form reduces access to the human eye.[132] And there may be less opportunity for leakage, mishandling, and human error, because fewer individuals may ultimately handle this information.[133] Computer security, like safes for physical goods, can be used to prevent unauthorized access to other computers, thus further reducing access to the human eye.[134]

Even if information crime may be made easier in certain respects by electronic systems, reducing the number of computers and instituting elaborate security measures may not be necessary to reduce the number of unauthorized appropriations of information. According to at least one expert, information thefts have occurred most frequently where no security precautions have been taken. Thus, implementing management policies and procedures that encourage the use of any security measure at all should provide significantly better protection.[135]

LEGAL FRAMEWORK

This section presents a framework for examining the legal protections intended to safeguard information privacy in the United States, and addresses some of the communications industry's attempts at self-regulation. The laws have been divided into the following categories: those that apply to records maintained by federal agencies and the executive branch, federal communications statutes, state penal statutes and theft laws, and state cable television laws.

This section is not intended to advocate or suggest that legislation is a necessary or even appropriate response to many privacy concerns. Indeed, certain legal enactments such as the Bank Secrecy Act[136] may actually increase the possibility of individuals' privacy violations because the information required under this Act might not otherwise have been retained.

The Privacy Right: Current Federal Legislation and Regulation of Stored Records

In 1973, the Department of Health, Education, and Welfare Secretary's Advisory Committee on Automated Personal Data Systems developed five principles for fair information practices. It recommended that:

> (1) there must be no personal data record-keeping systems whose very existence is secret; (2) there must be a way for an individual to find out what information about him is in a record and how it is used; (3) there must be a way for an individual to prevent information about him obtained for one purpose from being used or made available for other purposes without his consent; (4) there must be a way for an individual to correct or amend a record of identifiable information about him; and (5) any organization creating, maintaining, using, or disseminating records of identifiable personal data must assure the reliability of the data for its intended use and must take reasonable precautions to prevent misuse of the data.[137]

These principles were intended to guide the development of new statutes, regulations, and private sector initiatives so that privacy rights in all uses of personal data might be preserved. Congress has enacted several statutes guaranteeing the protection of privacy in specific areas: the Fair Credit Reporting Act of 1971,[138] protecting credit, insurance, and employment information; the Fair Credit Billing Act,[139] protecting privacy by mandating disclosure of finance charges and credit provisions in consumer transactions; the Freedom of Information Act of 1976 (FIOA),[140] which requires disclosure and publication of agency decision-making procedures and opinions, and affords individuals the right to examine agency records;[141] and the Family Education and Privacy Rights Act,[142] which denies federal funding to educational institutions that deny individuals the right to see their records, or that make unauthorized disclosures.

The Privacy Act of 1974.   A year after the Secretary's Advisory Committee report, Congress enacted the Privacy Act of 1974.[143] This Act prohibits, with limited exceptions,[144] federal agencies from disclosing records that identify an individual unless that individual has either requested the disclosure or has consented to it in writing.[145] The Privacy Act provides that individuals on whom records have been maintained by federal agencies may request amendment of these records. Agencies may either make the requested correction or inform individuals that they refuse to amend the record, giving the reason for the refusal and notifying them of the procedure to request a review of the refusal.[146] Individuals must be informed of the uses to which information will be put on the forms used to collect the information.[147]

The Privacy Act also states that agencies may retain only those records that are "relevant and necessary to accomplish a purpose of the agency required to be accomplished by statute or by executive order."[148] The Act does not establish criteria to determine what information is relevant and necessary under this provision. Moreover, the "routine use" exemption from the nondisclosure provision of the Act,[149] which allows disclosures for a "purpose which is compatible with the purpose for which the information was collected,"[150] has been used to circumvent other requirements of the Act.[151]

The Office of Management and Budget (OMB) has been charged by Congress with issuing guidelines and with overseeing the administration of the Privacy Act.[152] While guidelines establishing security measures for computer systems have been issued,[153] the OMB has been severely criticized for its failure to implement and enforce the Act.[154] Because the Privacy Act applies only to records maintained by federal agencies, private telecommunications companies are not subject to this Act.[155]

Privacy Protection Study Commission.   The Privacy Act established a Privacy Protection Study Commission (the Commission) comprised of Presidential and Congressional appointees.[156] The Commission was instructed to "make a study of the data banks, automated data processing programs, and information systems of governmental, regional, and private organizations to determine the standards and procedures currently in force, and to make recommendations for the protection of personal information."[157] The Commission issued its report in 1977, recommending that

> Congress provide individuals by statute with an expectation of confidentiality in a record identifiable to him main tained by a private sector record-keeper in its provision of . . . *telecommunications services.* [emphasis added][158]

The report further recommended that individuals be permitted to challenge the relevance and scope of a summons, and to assert the protections of the Fourth and Fifth Amendment in a defense against compelled production of such records.[159] Despite this recommendation, Congress has not enacted legislation to protect records identifiable to an individual maintained by a private sector record keeper in its provision of telecommunications services.[160]

Right to Financial Privacy Act.   In response to a 1976 Supreme Court decision,[161] Congress took steps to protect the privacy of data contained in financial records. The Right to Financial Privacy Act of 1978 prevents government access to individual financial records except pursuant to authorization by the customer, an administrative subpoena or summons, a search warrant, or in other limited circumstances as required by statute.[162] An individual must receive notice of an investigation of his records and may challenge access through procedures established by the Act.[163]

EFT Act.   Contemporaneous with the Right to Financial Privacy Act of 1978, Congress passed the Electronic Funds Transfer Act.[164] This statute requires financial institutions to maintain their own records; provide customers with accurate detailed records and periodic statements of all account activity;[165] promptly correct all account errors;[166] and notify customers of the terms, conditions, and disclosures respecting their accounts.[167]

Ironically, neither the EFT Act nor regulation E,[168] which was designed to answer customers' questions concerning EFT services,[169] deals with consumer privacy concerns that may be raised by electronic banking. Because banks and financial institutions are required by law[170] to retain copies of almost all financial transactions, and because so much information – credit, liabilities, mortgage payments, purchases, and salary – could be retrieved from one terminal, the incentive to intercept information may be greater when such information is stored electronically than when less information was retrievable from one place because of limitations on physical storage space.

It has been claimed that EFT will increase the amount of confidential information available to individual and institutional third parties with access to the POS network without customer consent.[171] Others have posited that consumers will have less control over, and knowledge of, their financial transactions because preauthorized payments will reduce flexibility and float, and there will be no leverage against merchants for unauthorized payments.[172]

But it might be argued that it will be easier to keep track of information and more cost-efficient to establish maximum security guards for POS terminals, since all financial information will be centrally stored in one computer terminal. Thus, financial information may be better protected and easier to control when it is stored in computers than it was when it was manually filed on hard copy. The introduction of third parties with computer terminals (for example, retail stores and supermarkets) to the POS network is unlikely to have added deleterious effect on personal privacy, however, because stores already have access to sensitive financial information, and because, if needed, customers could have receipts for transactions. All account activity will be recorded on customers' statements.

Privacy Act of 1980.   The Privacy Act of 1980 limits government officers or employees from searching for or seizing any work product materials from persons who intend to use them for public communication.[173] The Act describes a "public communication" as a newspaper, book, broadcast, or other similar form of public communication in or affecting interstate or foreign commerce.[174] The legislation's purpose is to protect the dissemination of public information by preventing overly broad searches and unnecessary seizures of such information by the federal government. The Act does not affect information maintained by the private sector.

Current Federal Legislation and Regulation of Communications Services

Privacy for communications services is protected by two federal laws: Title III of the Omnibus Crime Control and Safe Streets Act of 1968[175] and Section 605 of the Communications Act.[176]

Common Carrier.   Title III imposes criminal sanctions for the interception of wire communications by unauthorized persons. "Wire communications" are defined as transmissions provided by common carrier.[177] Title III also regulates the use of wiretapping by federal law enforcement officials.[178] Because the statute applies only to common carriers, information services that are not hooked up to telephone lines will not be covered by the Act.[179] Moreover, because the statute defines *intercept* as the "aural acquisition of the contents of any wire or oral communication," the Act will not apply to nonvideo data and transmission services provided by common carrier,[180] nor will it cover nonaural information transmitted over cable wire. Information that does not travel by wire is not covered by Title III.

The word *content* may pose still another barrier to the Omnibus Act's application to electronic telecommunications. Content, as construed by at least one court, is "information concerning the identities of the parties to [the] communication, or the existence, substance, purport or meaning of the communication."[181] Pen registers, which record numbers dialed from a telephone without intercepting verbal communications, have been found by the Supreme Court not to violate this Act because they do not overhear the substance of telephone conversations.[182] Similarly, it might be argued that billing information compiled for various information and communication services does not constitute content.

Wire Communications.   Section 605 of the Communications Act183 prohibits unauthorized interception of radio and broadcast signals. The operative provision of the Communications Act states:

> No person not being authorized by the sender shall intercept a radio communication and divulge or publish the existence, contents, substance, purport or effect or meaning of such intercepted communication to any person.[184]

This section has been interpreted in certain court decisions to apply to wire communications not covered by Title III,[185] as well as to traditional radio and broadcast signals. However, Congress amended Section 605 in 1968 to make it clear that Title III is intended for wire communications.[186]

Under this law, legal violations of communications may occur only if such communications are divulged or published. Thus, a party may intercept information without divulging it or publishing it and incur no legal liability. Divulgence by a party to a conversation, or a telephone operator eavesdropping on a conversation on demand of a lawful authority with a court order have been interpreted by courts not to violate this Act.[187]

It would appear that some accommodation may always be necessary between personal privacy and effective law enforcement. On the other hand, currently enacted federal communications statutes are based on a model developed when communications were restricted to audio transmissions via wire or radio signal, and when most information was stored as hard copy. Neither the Omnibus Act nor the Communications Act addresses privacy issues raised by hybrid forms of communications. Much information is now transmitted in the form of nonaural electronic bits and stored electronically in computer memories. Information that might not constitute content under Title III may be damaging when aggregated with other information that might not be considered substantive under this Act. And as indicated, information may be misused without being divulged or published by an unauthorized party intercepting a communication.

   FCC Regulation.   The Federal Communications Commission (FCC) has addressed consumer privacy in hybrid technology. In 1974, the FCC spoke to privacy concerns that may be raised by two-way cable television.[188] Interestingly, it did so in a warning to local franchising authorities that they were becoming too protective of the public on the issue of privacy. Fearing that two-way capability would be unduly restricted, the FCC commented that "there has been much misinformed over-reaction to this problem."[189] The FCC said it would "take any action necessary to assure system integrity[190] and urge "all governmental jurisdiction . . . [to be] on guard to guarantee that the right of privacy is maintained."[191] The FCC specifically called for a policy requiring that any activation of two-way service be at the subscriber's option.[192]
   Nonetheless, after warning the states away, the FCC has never implemented the federal privacy protections it promised in its 1974 Ruling.[193] And as yet, no Congressional act has been passed preventing disclosure or sale of subscriber billing records, or requiring corrections of inaccuracies in such records maintained by private telecommunications companies. Moreover, no federal act has been passed addressing potential privacy issues— unauthorized access; aggregration, misuse, and interception of data; and intrusions by electronic means into subscriber households[194]—that may be raised by the collection and flow of so much information into one central storage bank.

State Legislation and Regulation of Stored Records and Communications Services[195]

There is a great diversity of information privacy protection among the states. In California, for instance, the right of privacy is considered an inalienable right guaranteed by the state constitution.[196] In New York, courts have upheld a right of privacy based on public policy embodied in a statute[197] and an implied promise of confidentiality.[198] Computer fraud statutes exist in at least ten states as a general safeguard for computer information systems.[199] A number of states have also adopted broad nondisclosure statutes in the form of fair-information practice statutes.[200]

Fair Information Practice Statutes.   Fair information practice statutes require information to be collected, to the greatest extent feasible, from subjects directly, in order to promote accuracy and afford maximum notice to individuals when they are the subjects of information searches.[201] Certain state privacy statutes also place an affirmative duty on a regulatory agency or an information board to notify subjects when information is used for any purpose other than that for which it was collected, or when it is transferred to another agency without the subject's authorization.[202]

But as do the federal information privacy acts these statutes are modeled after,[203] many state statutes place an affirmative duty on the individual himself or herself to contest unauthorized uses or transfers of information regarding that individual, or to correct the information's accuracy or completeness. In most cases, however, subjects will not be apprised prior to unauthorized uses of such information. It is unlikely that people will be aware when stored information about them is being used or transferred to another agency unless agencies are affirmatively required to notify them.[204] Moreover, these statutes do not apply to records maintained by private organizations.

Larceny.   Larceny statutes[205] presently in force in many jurisdictions are based on a number of assumptions that are untenable in the context of electronic technology.[206] One assumption is the concept of unjust enrichment—that a person may gain only at another person's expense. This concept is manifest in both the Model Penal Code[207] and New York Penal Law.[208] New York, like many states, defines larceny in terms that require the defendant to intend a permanent deprivation before a larceny will be recognized.

Electronically stored information, however, can be reproduced and misappropriated without "depriving" the data owner or the subject of its use. This requirement may preclude the application of larceny statutes to prosecute unauthorized appropriations of electronically stored information. It might be argued that stored information that is disseminated or misappropriated may lose its monetary value, thus depriving the owner of its value. But the value of stored information may vary significantly depending on the person seeking the information, the person about whom the information pertains, and the number and identities of persons with knowledge of the information. Information that is valuable to one person may be valueless to another, and its disclosure might not be recognizable in a court of law. Many states define deprivation in terms that require that property be "withheld" from the owner.[209]

In addition to requiring a deprivation, larceny statutes are based on an assumption that theft requires a physical transportation of property. The term *property* appears to be based on the traditional notion of private property that can be measured by its economic market value. The Model Penal Code and the New York statute define larceny in terms of "taking, obtaining, withholding or exercising unlawful control over property."[210] Again, this assumption, that property cannot be stolen unless it is physically carried away, is incongruous when the item being apportioned is information in the form of electronic bits. A wrongful appropriation of electronically stored information would not require any physical movement. An intruder could violate a data subject's privacy simply by gaining access to information and reading it, without taking notes or physically transporting any information.

Unfair Competition.   As early as 1918, the Supreme Court recognized the potential for misappropriation of intangible property without depriving the owner of its use in the law of unfair competition. In *International News Service (INS) v. Associated Press (AP)*[211] INS charged that AP was pirating the fruit of INS's efforts by scanning bulletins and early editions of newspapers serviced by INS and selling the "pirated" news in competition with INS.

The Court refuted AP's argument that the news was uncopyrightable and, once distributed, could be used by anyone for any purpose. The Court said the plaintiff's rights against the public were different from plaintiff's rights against a competitor in business. Further, the Court said the AP's act was itself an admission that it was taking material acquired by INS "as a result of plaintiff's organization, and the expenditure of labor, skill, and money," and that by appropriating and selling such material in competition with plaintiff, the defendant was attempting to "reap where it had not sown."[212]

INS has been interpreted most liberally to stand for the proposition that it is unlawful for a business competitor to "interfere with the normal operation of a competitor's legitimate business organization."[213] The doctrine of the case has been upheld in cases before and since.[214] However, *INS* has been severely criticized and limited by subsequent case law[215] and by the federal Copyright Act. The federal Copyright Act protects works of authorship that are "fixed in a tangible medium of expression and [that] come within the subject matter of [federal copyright protection]." All other equivalent state and common law rights are preempted.[216]

Justice Brandeis' dissents in the *INS* case and subsequent cases have criticized the majority decision because of its "unwarranted" extension of the concept of property to "knowledge, truths ascertained, conceptions and ideas" that become (with a few exceptions that are patentable or copyrightable), "after voluntary communication to others, free as the air to common use."[217] Other courts have refused to accept the *INS* doctrine because of its anticompetitive implications.[218]

Because the Copyright Act invalidates all state-created "legal or equitable rights that are equivalent to any of the exclusive rights within the general scope of copyright,"[219] state-created unfair competition law is probably-preempted by the Copyright Act. The only thing that is clearly not pre-empted by the Copyright Act is state protection of works not yet "fixed in a tangible medium of expression."[220] This would include performances and broadcasts recorded without the owner's permission.[221]

It is unclear whether electronically stored information falls within the protection of the federal Copyright Act or whether such information would be protected against misappropriation if it were not eligible for copyright protection.[222] Moreover, if stored information is not within the scope of the Copyright Act, an argument could be made that states should not have the right to protect information when nondisclosure conflicts with the federal policy of disclosure and free access.[223]

Where copyright law is not applicable, however, the *INS* misappro-priation doctrine will be limited to situations involving business competi-tors. Even a liberal application of the misappropriation doctrine would not cover many privacy violations discussed in this paper that might occur where information is electronically stored.[224]

Theft of Services.   A number of states have modernized their larceny statutes and expanded the definition of property to include electronically stored or processed records.[225] Specific prohibitions against attempts to misappropriate telecommunications services, called "theft of services stat-utes," have also been legislated in many states.[226]

These statutes are intended to prevent the wrongful interception of pay and subscription cable television services. Theft of service statutes do not require physical transportation of an object or property as defined in larceny statutes, so will prevent privacy invasions to the extent that they deter invasions into subscribers' terminals and related equipment.[227] The word *services* probably would not encompass a prohibition against intru-sions into electronically stored videotex records or computer software, however.[228] Some theft of services statutes may also contain limiting provisions, as does a Massachusetts statute that requires information to be published before an appropriation of information constitutes an actionable theft.[229]

Other   Offenses. In states where computer fraud statutes do not exist, prosecutors have attempted to prosecute computer crimes by alleging various offenses involving the habitation.[230] Such offenses—burglary, for instance—require a breaking and entry into a home or business establish-ment. Prosecutors have also found that statutes prohibiting offenses against property (in addition to larceny) such as embezzlement, false pretenses, extortion, malicious mischief, and receipt of stolen property may apply to computer crimes. Successful prosecution will depend on whether the data, program, or equipment is interpreted to fall within the state's definition of property, or whether a state's statute has been amended to encompass computer crimes.[231]

Cable Television Statutes.   At least seven states have adopted cable television privacy legislation that responds to privacy concerns such as aggregation, misuse, unauthorized access and disclosure of individually identifiable data, and intrusion into subscribers' homes via interactive cable television systems.[232]

Illinois was the first state to pass a cable privacy act. The Communications Consumer Privacy Act became effective in 1982.[233] The Act prohibits a) a cable television operator from monitoring a subscriber's set or his or her selection of viewing fare without the knowledge or permission of the subscriber, b) the disclosure of subscriber lists without prior notice to the subscriber, c) the disclosure of viewing habits of any subscriber without his or her consent, and d) the use of home protection scanning devices without the written consent of the occupant.[234]

Wisconsin's cable privacy act, adopted in April 1982, requires that a subscriber's cable equipment be fitted with a device at no extra charge to prevent both the reception and transmission of all messages upon the subscriber's request.[235] A cable operator may not disclose any individually identifiable information or monitor its subscribers' terminals without written subscriber authorization.[236]

The California cable privacy bill was also enacted in 1982 as part of the State Penal Code. The California act prohibits cable operators from recording, transmitting, observing, monitoring, or listening to events or conversations that occur in a subscriber's work place,[237] and from disclosing any individually identifiable information on its subscribers.[238] The act further limits the retention of subscriber information,[239] prevents operators from making information available to government agencies without legal compulsion, and, on such event, requires prior notice when lawful to the subscriber.[240] Subscribers have the right to obtain information gathered by cable operators,[241] and must be provided with a notice from cable operators explaining their privacy rights under the act.[242]

Both the Minnesota[243] and Connecticut[244] legislatures have adopted statutes that require the agencies responsible for regulating cable communications in these states[245] to adopt and administer cable television regulations that include prohibitions against privacy invasions in two-way cable systems.[246] The Minnesota Cable Communications Board also requires that all state franchise agreements contain a provision prohibiting any signals from being transmitted from a subscriber terminal for the purpose of monitoring individual viewing patterns or practices without a subscriber's express, revokable written consent. No information obtained by monitoring the transmission of a signal from a subscriber terminal, including the subscriber's name, address, and viewing habits, may be disclosed to any third party without specific written subscriber authorization.[247]

Regulatory authorities in New York[248] and Rhode Island[249] have also adopted provisions in their cable operating rules that restrict the transmission of two-way signals.[250] Cable telecommunications privacy legislation is pending in several jurisdictions.[251]

Computer Fraud Statutes. Numerous states have proposed computer fraud statutes in response to theft and related offenses involving computers.[252] While these statutes do not specifically address the private information stored in computers, virtually all computer fraud statutes make it a crime to access, alter, damage, or destroy any data contained in a computer.[253]

A number of computer fraud statutes distinguish between crimes involving hardware and those involving software, programs, and data.[254] Many statutes also distinguish between access for the purpose of a) devising or executing any scheme or artifice to defraud, or b) obtaining money, property, or services by means of false or fraudulent pretenses, representations, or promises,[255] and intentional access, alteration, damage, or destruction of either computer hardware or the software, data, and programs.[256]

The penalties for violating computer fraud statutes range from $150[257] to $50,000.[258] It is unclear what fine within this range will be a sufficient deterrent to computer crimes. Moreover, some computer fraud statutes base the recovery of the owner on the "amount of the loss."[259] It may be particularly difficult to determine the amount of the loss to the owner, however, when the major loss is a privacy violation.

Municipal Regulation of Cable Subscriber Privacy

Electronically stored information collected and retained by cable television operators may also be regulated locally. Municipal officials may insert provisions in franchise agreements that prohibit unauthorized access to and monitoring of cable subscribers' terminals and disclosures, misuses, and aggregation of data.[260] Advocates of this type of local control over cable operations maintain it is easier for local authorities to "keep tabs" on community operators than on cable company officials who may be hundreds of miles away "behind corporate walls."[261]

Although many municipal franchise agreements do not place controls on the collection, use, and dissemination of information, subscriber privacy provisions are appearing more frequently in such agreements. Warner Amex's Cincinnati, Ohio, franchise agreement contains a section entitled "Rights of Individuals" in which Warner Amex promises to observe, protect, and ensure the privacy of all subscribers; to comply with all applicable laws, rules, and regulations respecting privacy; to keep all subscriber records in strict confidence; and to develop data specific to individual subscribers only as necessary to provide pay-per-view services.[262]

Additionally, the standard franchise agreement in Massachusetts includes a section entitled "Privacy and Rights to Information" which bars the licensee from recording or making available to any person information regarding subscriber viewing habits without subscriber consent. Any instances of recording or monitoring of the cable system must be reported by the licensee. Subscribers must receive written notice if equipment is installed to enable the recording or monitoring of viewing habits. Subscribers must take "some action to activate" transmissions from their homes, and the licensee must inform the issuing authority of the nature of any information obtained and the manner in which it is used. Finally, the subscriber is entitled to examine records pertaining to him or her upon written request. The issuing authority is not prohibited from obtaining general demographic, market, and other related data.[263]

Cable Industry Self-Regulation Industry Responses

The cable industry is generally opposed to state cable bills and restrictive franchise agreements.[264] The New York Cable Television Association opposed the New York cable privacy bill, which was introduced in 1983 and reintroduced in 1984,[265] because of its stringent authorization requirements and provisions mandating the destruction of subscriber records. Association officials object to the large fines for violations, maintaining that the cable industry should not be singled out when there are not comparable privacy laws regulating banks, telephone, and computer firms.[266]

The industry further argues that state bills and regulations will saddle cable operators with restrictions similar to those imposed on common carriers.[267] Many analysts also believe that, if there is to be legislation, it should be federal law to promote uniform rules and standards for the industry.[268] Other two-way cable promoters argue that privacy regulation is "premature," is "frightening people and giving interactive cable a bad name,"[269] and is "a cure in need of a problem."[270] Finally, industry officials point out it is in their "own best interests to protect their subscribers from privacy violations and to maintain a structure of operations which continually reassures the public regarding safety and the reasonableness of [cable's] products."[271]

Privacy Codes.   Despite protests against externally imposed regulations, cable associations and operators maintain that protecting subscriber privacy is, in fact, in their industry's best interest. Some of the major cable operators have thus introduced subscriber privacy codes.[272] Warner Amex was the first cable operator to introduce such a code (see Appendix A) for its Qube subscribers in 1981.[273] According to Warner Amex, "it is clearly possible to provide subscribers with the important benefits of interactive cable, while at the same time guarding against real or perceived infringements of their subscriber rights."[274]

The Warner code, however, allows for the disclosure of stored subscriber information to the company's own employees.[275] It includes no provisions for damages to injured parties, or penalties to punish employee violations of the Code.[276] Terms such as *adequate safeguards* and *reasonably necessary* do not specifically define the company's responsibilities to protect subscriber information, or limit the company's retention of subscriber data to any specified length of time. The Code does not specify who will enforce its provisions, and whether any subscriber data may be shared with Warner Cable Communication's parent company.[277] Finally, there has been concern that not all operators will adopt these rules, or that the rules they do adopt will not provide comprehensive subscriber privacy protection, especially where the rules threaten to diminish income from secondary uses of subscriber data.[278]

FEDERAL REGULATIONS

Cable Communications Policy Act

The multitude of state cable laws, local regulations, and rate restrictions in franchise agreements have prompted the cable industry to seek uniform regulations in the form of a federal cable telecommunications bill.

The Cable Communications Policy Act (discussed in Chapter 4) was enacted by Congress in 1984 as Title VI of the Communications Act of 1934.[279] The law was passed despite battles and lessening support in the cable industry [280] following court decisions in Miami and Nevada in 1984 limiting local regulators' control over cable,[281] and the Supreme Court's decision in the *Capital Cities*[282] case. In *Capital Cities*, the Court said that the FCC has absolute power to regulate and preempt state and local jurisdiction over cable television.[283] It appears that those who withdrew support from the bill feared that the FCC's preemption of cable television jurisdiction would loosen city regulators' hold on franchise fees, rates regulation, and program content.[284]

The Protection of Subscriber Privacy section of the cable bill [285] prohibits cable service providers from collecting personally identifiable information without the prior written or electronic consent of the subscriber, requires destruction of subscriber information collected, prevents disclosure of information except with subscriber consent or a court order, and requires notice to subscribers before disclosure of their records. Subscribers must be notified of their rights prior to entering into any agreement for cable services, and must be given access to their records.

The cable law also prohibits the interception or receipt, or assistance in the interception or receipt, of cable service without the specific authorization of a cable operator or as may specifically be required by law. [286]

The passage of a federal cable telecommunications act containing subscriber privacy provisions preempts the existing inconsistencies in state and local cable subscriber privacy laws and regulations; provides uniform practices and procedures for cable operators; and should help end the struggle among the FCC, cities, the cable industry, and the cable industry's competitors for jurisdiction over two-way cable services.

Proposed Federal Computer Legislation

The Cable Franchise Policy and Communications Act does not apply to electronic databases operated over telephone lines, nor does it apply to potential privacy invasions of privately owned computer databases. Legislators have proposed federal legislation such as the Federal Computer Systems Protection Act (FCSPA) to prevent computer crime. [287]

Federal prosecutions of computer software crimes may be based on the federal Copyright Act, patent law, trademark and service mark protection, federal statutes prohibiting fraud perpetrated through interstate communication wires, or the federal mail fraud statutes. But the Copyright Act only applies to original works of authorship, and does not extend to "ideas, procedures, processes, systems, methods of operation, concepts, principles or discovery." [288] Inventions and discoveries of processes are protected by patents, but patentable works must be useful and novel, [289] and there are expenses and delays in securing a patent. Trademarks and service marks are applicable to proprietary designations, and the federal fraud statutes will apply only where a person has devised or intends to devise a fraudulent scheme or artiface for obtaining money or property. [290] As indicated above, computer software and electronic files have not traditionally been considered property.

POLICY DECISIONS AND OPTIONS

The legal sanctions that may become available for prosecuting crimes involving computers, telecommunications services, and electronically

stored records are only touched upon in this paper. Some statutes such as the Cable Franchise Policy and Communications Act of 1984[291] and state cable privacy acts are responsive to privacy invasions that may be posed by interactive cable. Other statutes such as the Omnibus Crime Control Act[292] and the Communication Act of 1934[293] are based on the notion that communications media can be plugged into categories that, in reality, may be inapplicable to hybrid and new forms of technology.[294] Additionally, some statutes contain provisions such as the publication requirement in the Communications Act of 1934,[295] the aural content requirement in the Omnibus Act,[296] and the services requirement in theft of services statute, that limit their applicability to electronically stored data. Some states have passed theft of services statutes, some have passed computer fraud statutes, and still others have amended the definition of property in their larceny statutes to apply to services and electronic data. The purpose of this section is to examine the policy decisions reflected in the legal sanctions affecting information privacy in the United States and to present options to protect, and perhaps improve, information privacy for present and future law- and policymakers.

Policy Decisions[297]

Emphasis on Specific Areas.   The legal framework of privacy protections in the United States indicates that lawmakers have made a policy decision to focus legislative efforts on developing proposals for specific areas and specific types of information. Banking information is treated separately from information contained in medical or educational records, and interceptions of telephone messages are covered by a different statute than that which regulates radio communications. In its study on record keeping, the Privacy Protection Study Commission rejected an "omnibus approach" that would apply to any private or public agency, organization, or individual.[298]

Specific legislation is responsive to specific abuses. But in the long run, as evidenced by existing privacy statutes, specificity may lack flexibility. Information technology is evolving so rapidly that attempts to mold legal privacy protections to match fleeting developments are inefficient. Such attempts at exactitude create a blueprint for avoidance.[299] In addition, this practice of focusing on specific areas engenders a disparity in the amount of information privacy afforded to different industries in the United States.

The lack of a uniform national standard of informational privacy protection may also have detrimental effects on international data transmissions, since many countries have stricter privacy laws. Other countries may be wary of transmitting confidential information to the United States if it will be less protected here.[300] On the other hand, uniform standards may be too broad and all-inclusive in some areas, but not strict enough to protect confidential information in other areas. Privacy protection may be more effective when it is responsive to particular privacy intrusions. This type of regulation can only be done on an ad hoc basis.

Federalism.   One way to develop a more uniform set of information privacy protections would be to compromise the notion of *federalism* reflected in the current patchwork of statutes applicable to information privacy. *Federalism* is a policy of governing that elevates the value of state sovereignty above federal power.[301]

State autonomy creates flexibility but it also creates inconsistency among privacy protection laws and uncertainties among those affected by such laws. People may have difficulty learning and keeping abreast of the law in their particular state. Moreover, state autonomy may instigate struggles over the power to regulate a particular industry.[302] This policy could also lead to the development of *data havens* – areas which attract companies with unscrupulous information storage practices – because privacy laws are more lax in these states than in others.[303] But inconsistency may be less problematic than failure to adopt any protections at all, since it appears that those states with information privacy protection statutes have modeled them after the federal Privacy Act.[304] Moreover, all of these risks should be examined in light of the countervailing prospect of a federal government without adequate checks.

Balance of Interests.   Another policy decision illustrated by the afore-mentioned framework of information privacy protections is that differing rights should be weighed and balanced against competing interests.[305] This reflects the American notion of the democratic political process, in which various constituencies with differing interests compete to make themselves heard. Such a characterization of American politics may be accurate some of the time. But interest groups with the most monetary resources and/or the most effective connections may dominate the political process, or those with fewer resources or who are ignorant of political issues may not make themselves heard. Thus, privacy protection legislation is not necessarily responsive to the needs of those constituencies whose interests are not represented in the political system. However, this is a criticism of the legislative process rather than of privacy law or any other specific area of law. It would seem to be inherent in the democratic system that no legislation, whether or not it becomes law, will ever be totally responsive to every political constituency.

Respect for Private Enterprise.   American privacy protection policy has traditionally respected private enterprise and attempted to minimize the intrusiveness and burdens of government regulation. This respect is based on the assumption that business and industry will find it in their self-interest to deal with matters such as privacy invasions in a constructive way in order to avoid adverse market reaction or the imposition of government regulation.[306] Industry self-regulation may be preferable to external government regulation because industries are likely to be more familiar with their own operations and the most frequent and dangerous information abuses than external regulatory bodies would be. Industry self-regulation could lead to less stringent controls than external regulations, but it could arguably lead to regulations that will be enforced if the organizations handling personal data deem it their best interest to maintain their integrity and to avoid external regulation.

Policy Options

Because of the rapid growth and changes in information technology, a number of the laws originally passed to protect information privacy no longer appear applicable. But laws such as the Communications Act[307] and the Omnibus Act[308] could be amended to apply to electronically stored and transmitted information and to hybrid forms of telecommunications. The passage of the Cable Franchise Policy and Communications Act in 1984 and a federal computer anti-fraud statute containing user privacy provisions would together replace the multiplicity of state and local regulations in these areas, and would establish a more uniform national policy. Such uniformity would stimulate predictability and confidence in our legal system, both domestically and abroad.

   Legislation that defines certain conduct as criminal and that provides for legal sanctions cannot be effective without the means to enforce it, however. The problems of detecting electronic information abuses, enforcing existing federal and state statutes, and establishing local and industry self-regulation in the private sector have been discussed. But according to at least one source, few criminal prosecutions have failed for lack of statutory sanctions.[309] Moreover, many information violations are not being reported.[310] It would appear that resources could be productively spent to increase prevention, detection, and reporting of electronic information violations.

   Physical Security Measures.   One method of preventing electronic information crimes is to increase and enforce the use of security measures. Installing security measures may be as simple as blocking off physical access by unauthorized users to the mainframe computer, programs, data, and output, and requiring the use of passwords. Voiceprints to identify users have been used by planners for Prestel, the leading videotex system in

Britain.[311] Voiceprinting registers the authorized operator's voice on a microphone, and thereafter the system functions only if it registers that operator's voice.[312] This measure would probably reduce the number of intruders into videotex and computer systems. Restricting the circulation of operations manuals or programs that control user access could also help prevent access to computer systems by unauthorized users.

Security measures may also take the form of communications controls designed to protect data transmissions by preventing or detecting interception. Encryption, or security coding, has also been used to deter break- ins and interceptions of computer communications. The codes may be created by computer equipment or scramblers currently on the market.[313]

Black markets for descramblers of encryption codes could develop, as they have for other types of computer systems.[314] But encryption codes are extremely expensive both to create and to crack, and it is unlikely that resources would be expended on routine data transmissions. Messages extremely confidential or vulnerable to break- ins, such as foreign intelligence or financial transactions, could be protected with more complicated codes[315] or might be transmitted using other means.

Hardware controls may also be used to help control unauthorized access. Hardware controls are mechanical controls built into a system to lessen the opportunity for improper use of the computer. Examples of such controls include machine-maintained logs of individual user numbers, time records, and restrictions on acceptable programming languages.[316]

Increased prevention, detection, and reporting of electronic information crimes may ultimately depend on the willingness of three potential groups—operators, manufacturers, and outside auditors[317]—to accept these responsibilities voluntarily, or on a Congressional decision to impose such responsibilities.

Operators.[318]   The implementation and maintenance of security measures could significantly reduce the incidence of videotex and other computer crimes.[319] According to at least one study, however, most operators either fail to initiate security procedures,[320] or they delegate such jobs to analysts and programmers who may not have training in auditing and security techniques, but who are likely to be knowledgeable about systems and best able to perpetrate fraud.[321] Users may be reluctant to report incidents of computer crime because of fear of liability to shareholders for negligence, because of a desire to avoid negative publicity, and a wish to maintain public confidence.[322]

It might be possible to require licensing of individual computer systems to ensure compliance with minimum security requirements. However, standard procedures applicable to all computers would be difficult to develop,[323] and minimum security might be inadequate for certain systems.

Mandatory reporting procedures might be easier to develop, but both licensing and reporting would require government regulation.[324] Such mandatory regulation would, in all likelihood, be vehemently opposed by the industry.

Increasing public awareness of potential privacy invasions and electronic data crimes may be an alternative to mandatory security procedures for operators. Publicizing computer crimes could increase public demand for security measures.[325] Another approach to increasing prevention by users would be to create economic incentives such as government grants or tax breaks for organizational users who voluntarily implement security measures.

Manufacturers. Manufacturers currently provide only those security measures for which users pay. Computer system developers are not liable for failure to provide security features unless such developers contractually agree to provisions imposing such liability.[326] The same problems that apply to government regulation of users would appear to apply to regulation of manufacturers. It might be argued that imposition of statutory liability on manufacturers would deter organizations from remaining or becoming computer manufacturers. The result might be less progress in the computer field, or alternatively, a diversion of resources from innovations in programming, technology, and services to advancements in security technology. The latter may be desirable. Additionally, investment in security technology may be more cost justified than equal investment in attempting to enforce computer crime laws.[327]

Imposing statutory liability on computer and database system developers or operators would be complicated by additional practical difficulties of tort law such as determining whether buyers or subsequent users have tampered with an original design, and whether and how far manufacturers' liability should extend beyond the first user.[328]

Accountants. Accountants could also help detect and report privacy invasions and other computer crimes in their quarterly and year-end audits of business organizations.[329] Accountants are currently required to review clients' "internal control" systems to certify their clients' financial statements.[330] Such review specifically includes an examination of computer accounting control procedures,[331] testing the client's compliance with previously implemented procedures,[332] and evaluating the adequacy of particular computer systems' security procedures.[333]

The accountant's examination does not affect the outcome of the audit, however, and is not designed to detect computer crimes.[334] Rather, assessing the quality of a client's internal controls is intended to help the accountant determine the extent of testing that should be performed to certify that client's financial statements. Thus, the American Institute of Certified Public Accountants (AICPA) does not require auditors to state a conclusion or to determine the adequacy of a client's computer system and its vulnerability to potential computer crimes. The accountant's liability, if fraud surfaces, is determined by the degree of care exercised in conducting the audit.[335] And except in extraordinary circumstances, the accountant can avoid liability by showing conformity with Generally Accepted Auditing Principles promulgated by the AICPA (GAAP).[336]

Because accountants must review their clients' computer data processing systems, a statutory requirement that auditors report uncovered computer crime would relieve them of the decision of whether or not disclosure is necessary, and would increase the incidence of reported computer crimes.[337]

The imposition of increased liability on auditors would be likely to cause practical difficulties, however. The AICPA has traditionally been the body that sets standards for auditors, and the AICPA is not likely to be enthusiastic about increasing the liability of its members.[338] Except where there is voluntarily compliance by the accounting profession, the government has generally declined to mandate auditing standards.[339] The Securities and Exchange Commission (SEC) has in some instances required accountants to comply with different standards for reports filed with the SEC than the standards required by the AICPA or the Financial Accounting Standards Board for certification of financial statements.[340] But the SEC's regulations apply to only relatively large corporations that file with the SEC.

SUMMARY

This chapter has attempted to delimit within the sprawling concept of privacy a smaller zone of information privacy that may call for different protections than in the past because of changes in the way information is handled, transmitted, and stored. Electronics can increase efficiency and could increase access to stored personal data. Computers have also created the potential for the aggregation of hitherto harmless information that could constitute a privacy invasion when combined with other information. Many of policy- and lawmakers' assumptions about the distinctness of various media and the legal categorizations that regulate these media may be inapplicable to regulate interactive technology. Many of the assumptions that form the foundation for the criminal law also seem outdated when applied to misappropriations and misuses of information.

Still other assumptions about individuals' rights to retain their privacy and autonomy with respect to personal or sensitive information remain the basis of both general and specific privacy protection laws. Federal and state privacy acts have been passed establishing fair information procedures to notify individuals when they are the subject of information searches by the government, and of the procedures to obtain redress for privacy intrusions. Federal and state laws also prohibit collection and dissemination of certain types of information in the private sector without individuals' knowledge in industries where the collection of information by legislators and their constituents have been deemed most intrusive.

These laws do not protect individuals against the kinds of privacy abuses that may occur as a result of electronic information storage, however. Additionally, most forms of the federal communications laws are based on an outmoded notion of the separability of distinct types of communications facilities, which limits the laws' applicability to hybrid technology, and they contain certain other provisions that limit their applicability to electronically stored information.

However, recently enacted legislation such as the Cable Communications Act does not contain these restrictions and is drafted to apply to electronic information. Several states have also recognized the limited applicability of prior common law notions and federal statutes to electronic information crimes. This has resulted in amended larceny statutes in some jurisdictions, theft of service statutes, protection of pay television statutes, cable television privacy laws, and computer fraud statutes.

The passage of federal laws directed at the kinds of abuses that may be created by electronically stored information would create greater uniformity and predictability in the law. Struggles among members of the communications industry and local, state, and federal officials for jurisdiction to regulate the communications industry might also dissipate.

Nonetheless, legislative sanctions against electronic information crimes are not enforceable without preventive measures and increased detection and reporting of violations. It remains to be decided who, if any, of the various players in the communications and computer business (information collectors, providers and transmitters, computer system developers and operators) will or should be responsible for enforcement of security measures, and for reporting and detecting privacy and information abuses. Such distinctions may be less meaningful now than in the past because many of the functions and services previously performed by distinct entities such as newspapers, radios, television, electronic information retrieval, shopping, banking, and message transmission may be combined by a single information provider. It may also be necessary to determine how much and what form of security should be afforded or mandated for computer information systems.

Until now, privacy safeguards in the communications and computer industry have been largely voluntary, presumably based on the assumption that industry self-regulation will be prompted by fear of adverse market reaction or excessive government regulation. Such an assumption might be valid in light of the examples provided by the cable, broadcast, and motion picture industries. Much of the media now seems to be subject to codes of conduct that depend on voluntary self-enforcement. Privacy codes could be extremely effective if the present political power of professional and industry associations used their power to enforce privacy codes. The pressures of conformity from within an industry may be as cogent as legal restraints, and may provide more flexibility.

On the other hand, members of the communications and computer industry may not adopt voluntary regulations. It is possible that no segment or organization connected with these industries—operators, manufacturers, or independent auditors—will be willing to accept responsibility for enforcing security measures and for detecting and reporting information abuses without external compulsion or economic incentives. And, historically, Congress has been unwilling to impose such measures or to single out any one segment of the industry because of practical enforcement difficulties, and because of a policy preference for industry self-regulation.

Relatively few computer privacy violations and crimes have come to the public's attention.[341] This might indicate that widespread privacy invasions have not resulted from the growing use of computers and electronic telecommunications. However, because of the further loss of information privacy inherent in reporting violations, it is difficult to know whether the absence of public reports supports such a conclusion. Because there is no way to substantiate this conclusion, the best policy may be to come to a consensus on what we mean by information privacy, to sensitize ourselves to the ways in which electronic information storage and developments in interactive technology may affect our privacy, and to wait and see whether such invasions of information privacy are real or imagined.

NOTES

1. A. Westin, "Information Abuse and Personal Computers," Popular Computing, August 1982, at 113 to 114 [hereafter cited as Westin, *Popular Computing*]. Westin writes that 2 million personal computers are functioning in users' homes today, 5 million are expected to be purchased in 1985, and forecasts for 1990 range from lows of 8 to 10 million to highs of 15 to 25 million. *Id.*, at 114. Additionally, some form of computer-based technology is employed by virtually every major American and international business, private, and government institution. Computers have in fact become so fundamental to our society that some colleges and graduate schools require students to enroll in at least one basic computer programming course. Major business schools may either require students to purchase personal computers prior to enrollment or charge for them in the cost of tuition.

2. A. Westin, "New Eyes on Privacy," *Computerworld*, November 28, 1983, at 1 [hereafter cited as Westin, *Computerworld*], Westin, *Popular Computing, Supra*, Westin, "Home Information Systems: The Privacy Debate," *Datamation*, July 1982, at 100 [hereafter cited as Westin, *Datamation*], D. Nash & J. Smith, *Interactive Home Media and Privacy*, January 1981 (Report for the Office of Policy, Planning, Federal Trade Commission). *See also United States Information Society* (1977) [hereafter cited as P.P.S.C., *Info. Society*]; United States Privacy Protection Study Commission, *Technology And Privacy* (1977) [hereafter cited as P.P.S.C., *Technology*], A. Miller, *The Assault on Privacy, Computers, Databanks and Dossiers* (University of Michigan Press: Ann Arbor, 1971).

3. For instance, New York Attorney General Robert Abrams has testified at state assembly committee hearings that interactive cable television operators will collect "large banks of confidential, personal information about cable subscribers" that could be used to create "detailed psychographic profiles." These profiles could be used by credit companies, landlords, insurance companies, government investigators, marketing firms, and others to harass subscribers and invade their privacy. A. Breznick, "NY Attorney General Favors Cable Bill", *Multichannel News*, March 26, 1984, at 33. For two futurists' predictions, see J. Wicklein, *Electronic Nightmare* (The Viking Press: New York, 1981) and J. Martin, *Telematic Society: A Challenge For Tomorrow* (Prentice-Hall, Inc.: Englewood Cliffs, 1981). Wicklein says that although the new communications systems will create many benefits, they "will also put us in danger of losing our individual liberty." Martin, who is in general a strong proponent of telecommunications, warns, "electronics could make our lives as visible to officials as that of a goldfish in a bowl." Martin, note 2, at 199. The Privacy Protection Study Commission concluded that largely as a result of technology, reports have "never been able to affect an individual as easily, as broadly and potentially unfairly as they can today." P.P.S.C., *Info. Society*, note 2, at 60.

4. D. Nash & D. Bollier, Protecting Privacy in the Age of Hometech, 8 Tech. Rev. 67, at n.86 (1981) [hereafter cited as Nash & Bollier].

   Advocates of interactive cable television argue that privacy regulation is "premature," is "frightening people and giving interactive cable a bad name," and is "a cure in need of a problem." Remarks of New York Attorney General Robert Abrams to State Commission on Cable Television cited in Westin, *Datamation, supra* note 2, at 111. *See also* Breznick, *supra* note 3, at 33. Cable industry officials also point out it is in their "own best interests to protect their subscribers from privacy violations and to maintain a structure of operations which continually reassures the public regarding safety and the reasonableness of [cable's] products." J. Koenig, "Protecting Consumer Privacy" in *Cable TV Renewals & Refranchising* 113 (1983). *See generally* R. Neustadt, G. Skall, & M. Hammer, *The Regulation of Electronic Publishing* IV-3 (Report, 1981).

5. Louis Harris Associates, Inc., *The Road After 1984: The Impact of Technology on Society*, Presented by Southern New England Telephone (1984), at 7 [hereafter cited as *Road After 1984*].

6. *Id.*, at 13.

7. *See* Appendix B, *Definitions*.

8. R. Gavison, "Privacy and the Limits of the Law,"*Yale L. J.* 89 (1980): 421, 423. Among these values are liberty, autonomy, and intimacy. *See* S. Bok, *Secrets on the Ethics of Concealment and Revelation* (Random House: New York, 1983). Bok has written that control over secrecy (which the author says is overlapping with privacy because the purpose of both privacy and secrecy is to become "less vulnerable, more in control." *Id.*, at 11) is important to protect four values: identity, plans, action, and property. These values relate to "protection of what we are, what we intend, what we do and what we own." *Id.*, at 20. Charles Fried argues privacy is necessary for the development of trust, love, and friendship. Human relations, he suggests, are determined by personal information shared by a partner but with no one else. C. Fried, "Privacy," Yale L.J. 77 (1970): 475, at 484-485.

9. 381 U.S. 479 (1969) (right to privacy includes right of a married couple to use contraceptives). The Supreme Court found privacy to be within the "penumbra" of rights expressly granted by the Constitution. Although seven Justices concurred in the opinion, the members of the Court disagreed on the theory used to reach its opinion. Justice Douglas said the right to privacy is implicit in the Bill of Rights, protected by the First, Third, Fourth, Fifth, and Ninth Amendments. Justices Goldberg, Warren, and Brennan said the right to privacy is one of the additional fundamental rights protected by the Ninth Amendment. *Id.*, at 486. Justices Harlan and White relied on the Due Process Clause of the Fourteenth Amendment. *Id.*, at 499.

10. 389 U.S. 347 (1967) (FBI agents listened to respondent's conversations from a telephone booth with electronic eavesdropping device).

11. Katz v. United States, 389 U.S. 347, 352-53. Justice Harlan, in his concurrence, stated the two-pronged test to determine whether an individual has a right to privacy. The test requires a person to have exhibited an actual expectation of privacy, and that the expectation be one society is prepared to recognize as reasonable. *Id.*, at 361. The Katz rule has been applied in civil as well as criminal cases. Miller, 425 U.S. 435, 442-44 (1976) (bank depositor has no legitimate expectation of privacy in bank records). For criticism of the Katz rule, *see, e.g.*, A.G. Amsterdam, "Perspectives on the Fourth Amendment," *Minn. L. Rev.* 56 (1974): 349.

12. *See* Roe v. Wade, 410 U.S. 223, 152 (1973) (right to privacy includes the right of a woman to determine whether or not to have an abortion); Eisenstadt v. Baird, 405 U.S. 438, 453 (1972) (an individual has a right to privacy from government intrusion in deciding whether or not to have a child).

13. *See* Katz v. United States, 389 U.S. 347 (1967).

14. *See* Whalen v. Roe, 429 U.S. 589, 599-600 (1977). (Individuals had justifiable expectation of privacy in state records containing names and addresses of persons who have obtained a doctor's prescription for certain harmful drugs. State's retention of records did not violate individuals' right to privacy, however, because adequate safeguards were taken to protect the information.) *But see* Schulman v. New York City Health and Hospital Corporation, 38 N.Y.2d 234, 342 N.E.2d 501, 506 (1975) (court refused to uphold a constitutional challenge to the New York City Health Code requirement that names and addresses of patients obtaining abortions be recorded); Belmont v. State

Personnel Board, 36 Cal. App. 3d 518, 522-25, 111 Cal. Rptr. 607 (1974) (two psychiatric social workers employed by the State Department of Social Welfare were suspended from employment for willful disobedience of Department order calling on them to furnish confidential information on patients).

15. *See* United States v. Miller, 425 U.S. 435, 440 (1976). *But see* The Right to Financial Privacy Act of 1978 Ss1101-1122, 12 U.S.C. 3401-3422 (amended 1980 and 1982). This Act gives customers standing to challenge unauthorized government access to their bank records.

16. United States v. Miller, 425 U.S. 435, 446 (1976).

17. *But see* Charnes v. Digiacomo, 200 Colo. 94, 612 P.2d 1117 (Colo., 1980). (Respondent was served with an administrative subpoena for alleged tax evasion. The court said the Colorado constitution protects the depositor from government intrusions into bank records in the absence of judicial supervision.)

18. 442 U.S. 735 (1979).

19. 442 U.S. 735, 745 (1979).

20. *See* Civil Rights Cases, 109 U.S. 3 (1883) (parts of this case have been overruled and expanded, but the majority's holding that Congressional power does not reach private conduct under the Fourteenth Amendment still stands). G. Gunther, *Constitutional Law*, 10th ed., (The Foundation Press, Inc.: Mineola, N.Y., 1980), p. 984.

21. Mallory v. Hogan, 378 U.S. 1 (1964); Murphy v. Waterfront Commission of New York, 378 U.S. 52 (1964). *See* L. Tribe, *American Constitution Law* (The Foundation Press: Mineola, 1978), 1979 Supplement.

22. *See, e.g.*, Lefkowitz v. Turley, 414 U.S. 70 (1973) (state statute requiring public contracts to provide that existing contracts may be cancelled and contractor disqualified for five years from future transactions with state if contractor refuses to testify concerning contracts or waive immunity is unconstitutional); Spevack v. Klein, 385 U.S. 511 (1967) (failure to produce financial records and refusal to testify by attorney in disbarment proceeding cannot be used as evidence of misconduct).

23. *See* Gardener v. Broderick 392 U.S. 273, 278 (1968) (dictum): A public employee may be compelled to answer questions "specifically directly, and narrowly relating to the performance of his official duties," if his answers or the fruits thereof cannot be used in a subsequent criminal prosecuion. Tribe, *supra* note 21, at 710. The government may have broader discretion to inquire into the duties of public servants than into the affairs of those employed inside in the private sector, however.

24. For a discussion of the development of common law privacy in England, *see* D. Seipp, *English Judicial Recognition of a Right to Privacy*, Program on Information Resources Policy, Harvard University, May 1982, at 13-24, 34-44.

25. *See* S. Warren and L. Brandeis, "The Right to Privacy," *Harv. L. Rev.* 4 (1890): 193.

26. Cooley, *Torts* 29 (2d ed. 1888) cited in Warren and Brandeis, *Id.*, at 195.

27. Nash & Smith, *supra* note 3. *See* W. Prosser, *Privacy*, 48 Cal. L. Rev. 383 (1980). *But see* E.J. Bloustein, *Privacy As An Aspect of Human Dignity: An Answer to Dean Prosser*, *N.Y.U.L. Rev.* 39 (1964): 962, 1001-07.

28. Restatement (Second) of Torts §652P.
29. W. Prosser, *The Law of Torts*, §117 (4th ed., West Publishing Company: St. Paul, 1971).*Id.*
30. *Id.*
31. Zimmerman v. Wilson 81 F.2d 847, 849 (3d Cir. 1936); Brex v. Smith, 104 N.J. Eq. 386, 391-92, 146 A. 34, 36 (1929) (defendant liable for intrusion where, seeking evidence for use in civil action against plaintiff, he obtained access to plaintiff's personal bank account by using a forged court order).
32. *See* Frey v. Dixon, 141 N.J. Eq. 481, 485 58 A.2d 86, 88 (1948).
33. *See* Monroe v. Darr, 221 Kan. 281, 559 P.2d 322 (1977) (cause of action existed for nonconsensual entry by sheriff's deputies into plaintiff's apartment because entry was unsupported by probable cause or a valid search warrant).
34. *See* Fowler v. Southern Bell Tel & Tel Co., 343 F.2d 150, 156 (5th Cir. 1965) (wiretap by I.R.S. agents was sufficient to constitute tort of privacy invasion without proof of publication); Hamberger v. Eastman, 106 N.H. 107, 112, 206 A.2d 239, 242 (1964) (landlord's installation of recording and listening device in plaintiff's bedroom constituted privacy intrusion beyond the limits of decency).
35. Nader v. General Motors, 255 N.E. 2d 765, 25 N.Y. 2d 560, 565 (1970). (Nader alleged G.M. was harrassing him by a) interviewing acquaintances, b) keeping him under surveillance in public places, c) causing him to be accosted by women for illicit relations, d) making threatening phone calls to him, e) tapping his telephone, f) conducting investigations of him. Court said interviewing acquaintances did not violate privacy right since information confided to acquaintances could no longer be regarded as private. Neither harassing phone calls nor solicitations by hired women constituted privacy invasions since neither involved intrusion for the purpose of gathering information of a private and confidential nature). *Id.*, at 569.
36. *Id.*, at 567.
37. *See, e.g., Id. See also* Hamberger v. Eastman, 106 N.H. 107, 206 A.2d 239, 242 (1964) (court sympathized with plaintiff and awarded damages for emotional pain and suffering resulting from wiretap of plaintiff's bedroom activity); Sidis v. F.R. Publishing Corporation, 113 F.2d 806 (1940). (*New York Magazine* wrote a profile of math prodigy who went into seclusion. The court said the article was a "ruthless exposure" *Id.*, at 807. But Sidis did not recover any damages because the court said Sidis had been a public figure and his activities were a legitimate subject of public interest.)
38. *See* Pavesich v. New England Life Insurance Company, 120 Ga. 190, 50 S.E. 68 (1905) (unauthorized use of plaintiff's likeness for life insurance advertisement); Roberson v. Rochester Folding Box Company, 171 N.Y. 538, 64 N.E. 442 (1902) (unauthorized use of plaintiff's likeness to sell flour). For a discussion of English cases based on this branch of privacy law *see* Seipp, *supra* note 24, at n.157.
39. *See* Miller, *supra* note 2, at 174.
40. *See* R. Wacks, *The Protection of Privacy*, 165 (Sweet & Maxwell: London, 1980) [hereafter cited as Wacks].
41. *See* Miller, *supra* note 2, at 177.

42. *See* Wacks, *supra* note 40, at 170. *See also* Prosser, *supra* note 29, at §112.
43. Miller, *supra* note 2, at 180.
44. *Id.* It may be possible to argue that such pressure constitutes coercion or compelled self-incrimination.
45. 5U.S.C. §552a (1976).
46. 5 U.S.C. §552a(b) states:

> No agency shall disclose any record which is contained in a system of records by any means of communication to any person, or to another agency, except pursuant to a written request by, or with the prior consent of, the individual to whom the records pertains, unless disclosure of the record would . . . [the Act then lists 10 exceptions to this provision].

Individuals on whom records have been maintained may have access to those records and may request amendment of those records, 5 U.S.C. §552a(d). Only those records "relevant and necessary to accomplish a purpose or required by statute or by executive order may be maintained." 5 U.S.S. §552a(e)(1). Individuals must also be informed of the uses to which such information will be put on the forms used to collect such information. 5 U.S.C. §552a(e)(3).

47. 18 U.S.C. §§1701, 1702 (1909).
48. Fair Credit Reporting Act, 15 U.S.C. §1681 (1970); Equal Credit Opportunity Act, 15 U.S.C. §1691 (1978).
49. Omnibus Crime Control and Safe Streets Act, Title III, 18 U.S.C. §2510 to 2520 (1968).
50. Privacy Protection Act of 1980, Pub. L. No. 96-440, 94 Stat 1879, 42 U.S.C. §§S2000aa-2000aa-12.
51. Communications Act of 1934 c. 652, Title VI, §605, 47 U.S.C. §605 (amended 1968 and 1982).
52. Privacy Protection Act of 1980, Pub. L. No. 96-440, 94 Stat. 1879, 42 U.S.C. §2000aa-11(3).
53. Family Educational Rights and Privacy Act of 1974, P.L. 98-380, 88 Stat. 484 §513, 20 U.S.C. §1232q (1974). Federal funds are denied under this statute to any eligible agency or educational institution that denies its students or their parents the right to inspect and challenge the accuracy and completeness of educational records maintained on its students. 20 U.S.C. §1232g(a). Funds are also denied to any agency or educational institution that permits release of educational records (or personally identifiable records contained therein). 20 U.S.C. §1232g(b).
54. *See, e.g.*, Ariz. Rev. Stat. Ann.§16-802 (1977). The Arizona Information Practices statute provides for the establishment of an Information Practices-Board to implement the legislative intent set out in §16-802. The aforementioned section lays out fair information procedures for, inter alia, providing subjects with notice when information about them is used, maintaining security, updating inaccuracies, purging irrelevancies, and preventing other misuses of personal information. Data subjects' rights are defined in §16-806. Other information practice statutes, for example, the Utah statute, Utah Code

Ann. §60-50-1 (1975), provide that fair information practices shall be established and maintained by the Secretary of State. See also National Telecommunications and Information Administration, Privacy Protection Law in the United States, N.T.I.A. Report Series, Report 82-78, May 1982, at App. I5 [hereafter cited as Privacy Protection Law]. For further information see generally R. Smith, "Selected 1983 Federal Privacy and Security Legislation; Compilation of State and Federal Privacy Laws," Privacy Journal, Washington, D.C. (1981).

55. See, e.g., Ind. Cod Ann. §4-1-6-1 (West 1979); Mass. Gen. Laws Ann. ch. 66A §§1-3 (West 1976); Va. Code Ann. §§2.1-377 (1976).

56. See, e.g., Nev. Rev. Stat. §629.061 (1977); Va. Code §2.1-342 (1979).

57. See Wacks, supra note 40, at 10-23; see also R. Posner, "Privacy, Secrecy and Reputation," Buffalo L. Rev. 28 (1979): 1; R. Posner, "The Right to Privacy," Ga. L. Rev. 12 (1978): 393; J. Thomson, "The Right to Privacy," Phil & Pub. Aff. 4 (1975): 295.

58. Gavison, supra note 8, at 424.

59. Wacks separates at least eight other categories that have become "entangled" ith privacy: a) privacy and autonomy, b) privacy and other liberties including freedom from unreasonable search, freedom of association, freedom of expression, c) privacy and confidentiality, d) privacy and secrecy, e) privacy and defamation, f) privacy and property, g) privacy and computers, h) privacy and privilege. Wacks, supra note 40, at 10-22.

60. Wacks argues:

"Privacy" has become as nebulous a concept as "happiness" or "security". Except as a general abstraction of an underlying value, it should not be used as a means to describe a legal right or cause of action. Id., at 21.

61. See W. Renquist, Privacy and Effective Law Enforcement, Kansas L. Rev. 21 (1974): 1.

62. See Appendix B for explanations of these terms. See also Nash and Smith, supra note 2, at 6-9. See generally "Information Management, Locking The Electronic File Cabinet," Business Week, October 18, 1982, at 123.

63. See R. Parker, "A Definition of Privacy," Rutgers L. Rev. 27 (1974): 275, 277-78.

64. A. Westin, Privacy and Freedom (Atheneum: New York, 1967). Westin has subsequently written several articles and books on information technology and privacy. See articles cited in notes 1 and 2 supra. See also: A. Westin and M. Baker, Databanks in a Free Society, Computers, Record-Keeping and Privacy (Quadrangle Books: New York, 1972) [hereafter referred to as Databanks]. Databanks examines the conflict between society's right to know and individual privacy concerns, and is based on information gathered from visits, interviews, and surveys conducted from 1970 to 1972 at 55 leading educational and professional institutions in business, government, and welfare systems.

In Databanks Dr. Westin writes that the definition of privacy " . . . involves the social policy issues of what information should be collected at all and how much information should be assembled in one information system." Id., at

393.

According to Dr. Westin, he has not changed his basic definition of privacy. Rather, Westin claims his earlier definition in *Privacy and Freedom* is "generic," and applies to a variety of social and cultural contexts. The *Databanks* definition is "aimed at the organizational ethos and is limited. It assumes the existence of a society in which records are being kept." Conversation with Dr. Alan F. Westin, June 10, 1983.

65. *See, e.g.*, L. Lusky, "Invasion of Privacy: A Clarification of Concepts," *Colum. L. Rev.* 72 (1972): 693.

66. *American Heritage Dictionary of the English Language* (1976 ed.), p. 246.

67. More than three quarters of the public say they are "very" or "somewhat" concerned about threats to their personal privacy. *See supra* note 5, at 7.

68. *See* Palko v. Connecticut, 302 U.S. 319 (1937) (Butler, J. dissenting). Justice Cardozo noted that freedoms of thought and speech are the "matrix, the indispensable condition of nearly every other form of freedom." *Id.*, at 327. *See also* the Pentagon Papers cases, New York Times Co. v. United States, and United States v. Washington Post, 403 U.S. 713 (1971) (United States brought action to enjoin publication of certain classified material against *The New York Times* and *Washington Post*).

69. Lusky, *supra* note 65, at 706. Lusky makes this argument criticizing Professor Arthur Miller's definition of privacy as a "right," but the same criticism applies to the word "claim." Values that conflict with individual privacy are cited at note 50. *See also* Westin, *Databanks, supra* note 64.

70. Professor Miller has defined privacy as a right: "The basic attribute of an effective right of privacy is the individual's ability to control the circulation of information relating to him." Miller, *supra* note 2, at 25.

71. Because individual viewpoints vary considerably on what constitutes personal information, and because the law must take into account competing interests and considerations, it would be unrealistic and inefficient to attempt to accommodate everyone's conception of what personal information should be protected from disclosure. Private, personal, and confidential information will be used interchangeably hereafter.

72. It might be asserted that it would be most accurate and responsive to privacy concerns to let individuals define what is "personal information" themselves rather than imposing a community standard. But it has been asserted by various political theorists that the notion of a popular consensus may be somewhat idealistic, if not presumptuous. *See* J. Ely, *Democracy and Distrust* (Cambridge, Mass.: Harvard University Press, 1980), pp.63-69. In his book on the legitimacy of judicial review, Ely argues there is rarely such a thing as a popular consensus.

Moreover, the notion of a popular consensus raises definitional problems of how and whom to trust to devise the standard. Finally, the assumption of a popular will also assumes the existence of a political process that is open, or at least, representative of all citizens fairly — rich, poor, influential, and weak. This may not be an accurate portrayal of the political process, however.

73. It is recognized that certain communications and information may be more or less protected depending on whether one is a "public figure" or not. However,

because this factor is mainly relevant to defamation rather than privacy issues, the distinction will not be made in this paper. Moreover, private information may be subject to qualified disclosure when there are competing law enforcement considerations.

74. *See* Warren and Brandeis, *supra* note 25.

75. *Id.*, at 195. *See also* E.L. Godkin, "The Rights of the Citizen to His Own Reputation," *Scribner's Magazine Illustrated* 60, (July 1890): 66-67. In his article on the natural rights of citizens, Godkin warned of the dangers to privacy posed by the newspaper:

> The chief enemy of privacy in modern life is that interest in other people and their affairs known as curiosity, which in the days before newspapers created personal gossip . . . In all this the advent of the newspapers, . . . has made a great change . . . Gossip about private individuals is now printed, and makes its victim, with all its imperfections on its head, known hundreds or thousands of miles away from his place of abode . . . It thus inflicts what is, to many men, the great pain of believing that everybody he meets in the street is perfectly familiar with some folly, or misfortune, or indiscretion, or weakness, which he had previously supposed had never got beyond his domestic circle. *Id.*, at 66.

76. *See, e.g.*, Pugh v. Telephone Company (a Kentucky court upheld the telephone company's right to cut off a defendant's telephone service for "damning the telephone company" over the telephone wire). The court said:

> The inventors have a right to be protected, and have their instrument placed in a respectable light before the world, otherwise it might go out of use.

"Improper Use of Telephone," *The Legal News* 105 (1883): 6. Fears such as these are often proven unfounded after time.

Another article, written in 1882 on legal issues likely to be posed by the telephone, stipulated that whether an affiant could make an affidavit by telephone would become an "interesting question of law." "Swearing by Telephone," *The Albany Law Journal* 26 (1882): 326. The article said the answer would depend on whether telephones were "a mere carrier" or whether they "annihilate[d] space." *Id.* If the latter view were espoused by the courts, the article posited that there might be danger of "counterfeit affiants." *Id.* This question never became a legal issue raised in court.

Finally, in an article that appeared at the inception of television, the author speculated that several privacy issues might raise legal questions that would have to be resolved. For instance, the writer questioned the privacy rights of televised sports spectators, and the privacy rights of performers in old movies. The article says injecting commercials in the wrong place, which would interrupt a movie, might subject television stations to greater risks of being sued. The writer also speculated that performers might sue stations for distorted, uncomplimentary likenesses that might injure people's reputations, that camera quirks might give rise to defamation suits, and that "the television broadcaster's inability to 'cut' would present an incalculable hazard." D.M. Solinger, "Television and the Law," *Fortune Magazine*, (1948), pp.160-163.

Most of these questions never evolved into harms that were realized, however, either because the speculations were premature, or because technology improved.

77. According to Alan G. Merten, professor of computer and information systems at the University of Michigan, "the places doing the best jobs [of protecting their information] are those that have had previous problems." Thus, experience may be the best guide to protecting information, and the best policy to protect information privacy may be to wait for harms to materialize. See "Information Management, Locking the Electronic File Cabinet," in *Business Week*, October 18, 1982, at 123 [hereafter cited as "Information Management"].

78. Warner Amex Cable Communications set the industry standard in 1981 by enacting its Privacy Code. Cox Cable Communications Inc. and Storer Cable Communications have enacted less comprehensive Privacy Codes. The Cable Association of New York has also adopted a Privacy Code. The National Cable Television Association was considering adopting an industry-wide privacy code, but no further action was taken after 1983 because of the introduction in Congress of the federal cable television bills that contained privacy provisions. Telephone interview with James McElveen, Director of Public Relations, National Cable Television Association (April 9, 1984). The Cable Franchise Policy and Communication Act, 98th Cong., 2nd Sess. (1984), contains a section called subscriber privacy protections. See §631 "protection of subscriber privacy" and §634 "unauthorized reception of cable service." *Id.* See *also* Federal Regulations herein.

79. According to one source, approximately 5 million personal computers are expected to be in use in 1985 and industry forecasts for 1990 range from lows of 8 to 10 million to highs of 15 to 25 million. See Westin, *Personal Computing, supra* note 1, at 113-114.

80. Analysts' projections of a nation inundated with two-way cable have been moderated. According to Paul Kagan Associates, Inc., only 10% or fewer of the projected 53 million subscriptions to cable in 1990 will be two-way. Paul Kagan Associates, Inc, 62 Cable T.V. Technology, Dec. 14, 1983, at 1. The industry has been plagued by unexpected competition from alternative forms of technology such as DBS, STV, MDS, LFTV and microwave which can beam entertainment programs onto television screens for less money than cable (*see* J. Thomas, "Cable: The Possible Dream?" *Boston Globe*, March 23, 1984, at 70); lower-than-projected profit margins, losses of programming sources, and struggles among the cable industry, its competitors, cities, states, and the federal over the control of program content; rate regulation and general jurisdiction (*see* S. Salmans, "Cable Operators Take a Bruising," *The New York Times*, March 4, 1984, p. 22). Still, analysts anticipate that despite growing-pains, two-way services in the home, whether cable or hybrid technology, will simply be longer in coming than predicted. See comments of Ed Dooley, vice president of National Cable Television Association, and of Art Thompson, general manager of Cablevision of Boston cited in Thomas, Id., at 69, 70. See *also* comments of Dennis Leibowitz, cable analyst with Donaldson, Lufkin &

Jennrette cited in Salmans, *Id.*, at 22.

81. Although the most publicized interactive cable system is Warner Amex's Qube, other interactive systems have been or are being tested in the United States by Cox Cable Communications, Inc., Storer Cable Communications, Times Mirror Cable, and other local companies. *See* Salmans, *supra* note 80, at 22.

82. *See* J. Pearl, "The Software Channel," *Forbes Magazine*, June 18, 1984, at 158.

83. Nash & Smith, *supra* note 2, at 10.

84. See Wicklein, *supra* note 3, at 19.

85. *Times-Union*, January 12, 1983, at 2-3. Warner is proposing to reduce the scope of its two-way system in Milwaukee, however. *See* S. Cobb, "Milwaukee, Cincinnati Officials Question Cutbacks by Warner Amex," *Multichannel News*, February 6, 1983 1, at 44. The Company also hopes to sell its franchise in Pittsburgh, Pennsylvania to Telecommunications, Inc. to avoid the high costs of operating its state-of-the-art system there. "Warner Amex's Lowering Expectations," *Broadcasting*, March 19, 1984, at 37-38.

86. Wicklein, *supra* note 3, at 18, *but see* Nash and Smith *supra* note 2, at 45. They claim a poll is conducted once every 20 second.

87. Nash and Smith, *supra* note 2, at 41.

88. *Id.*

89. *Id.*

90. Nash and Smith, *supra* note 2, at 45. Not all operators, however, monitor their systems all the time. The Cox Communications System, for example, only monitors the network when the interactive cable television is in use. Conversation with Ben Compaine, Program on Information Resources Policy, Harvard University, 1982.

91. Nash and Smith, *supra* note 2, at 40.

92. The leading videotex systems outside of the United States are Prestel in Britain, Antiope in France, and Telidon in Canada. Telidon, which was developed by Bell Canada, may also be transmitted over other media such as optical fibers, cable or broadcast channels, or other link technologies that may evolve. *See generally Id.*, at 63-78.

93. Companies that have substantial investments in U.S. development of videotex or electronic databases include publishers, Knight-Ridder and Dow Jones; financial institutions, Chemical Bank, American Express, and Merrill Lynch, Pierce, Fenner & Smith; retailers, Federated Department Stores and Sears Roebuck; cable television operators, Cox Broadcasting and Warner Amex; and instrument makers, Tandy, Texas Instruments, and Zenith. *See* "Window on the World, The Home Information Revolution," *Business Week*, June 29, 1981, at 74-76.

94. *See* Martin, *supra* note 3, at 128. *See also* D. Sanger, "Technology, An Electronic O.E.D. Edition," *The New York Times*, July 5, 1984, *Id.*, at 2. The publishers of the *Oxford English Dictionary* plan to input and revise it on a database.

95. *Id.*, at 87.

96. *See* M. Tyler, "Videotex, Prestel and Teletext and the Economics and Politics of Some Electronic Publishing Media," *Telecommunications Policy* 3 (March

1979): 37, at 42.

97. See Martin, *supra* note 3, at 92.

98. Although most computer systems are not connected to an information provider, Nabu Network Corp., an Ottawa, Ontario based company, is currently test marketing software programs transmitted over cable wire. One market in Ottawa has 1,400 subscribers, or 2% of that city's cable subscribers. In Alexandria, Virginia, the service has been introduced to 20,000 cable TV subscribers through Tribune Cable System. *See* Pearl, *supra* note 82, at 157.

Subscribers get an assortment of 50 education, information, and game software for a basic charge of $14.95 per month. Additional programs, word processing, spread sheet software, and business information are available in ranges from $4.95 for a few programs to $27.95 for an entire package. Software similar to the package if purchased at retail in disks would cost approximately $2,500. *See Id.*, at 158.

99. *See* Westin, *Personal Computers, supra* note 1, at 114 for current estimates and projections of the number of computers being operated by home users.

100. *Id.*

101. *Id.*

102. *Id.*

103. *See* Martin, *supra note* 3, at 101. *See generally* P.P.S.C., *Info. Society, supra* note 2, at 101; National Commission on Electronic Funds Transfer, *EFT and the Public Interest* (Interim Report, Feb. 1977) [hereafter cited as NCEFT]; K. Colton and K. Kraemer (ed.), *Computers and Banking, Electronic Funds Transfer Systems and Public Policy* (Plenum Press: New York, 1980) [hereafter cited as *Computers & Banking*].

104. *See* Comment, *Financial Privacy in an Electronic Fund Transfer Environment: An Analysis of the Right to Financial Privacy Act of 1978 and California Financial Privacy Law*, 23 U.S.F.L. Rev. 485, 486 n.6 (1979) [hereafter cited as *San Francisco*].

105. Horan, "Outlook for EFT Technology," in *Computers & Banking, supra* note 103, at 27.

106. *Id.*

107. *Id.*

108. *Id.*

109. *Id.*

110. *Id.*

111. *Id.*, at 24.

112. *Id.*

113. *Id.*, at 35.

114. *Id.*

115. *See* San Francisco, *supra* note 104, at 487, n.6.*See* Horan, *supra* note 103, at 25.

116. *See* Horan, *supra* note 103, at 25.

117. *Id.*, at 32.

118. *See* Martin, *supra* note 3, at 79.

119. Computer Fraud and Electronic Trespass: Hearings on H.R. 3570 Before the Subcommittee on Crime, Committee on the Judiciary. U.S. House of Repre-

sentatives (November 10, 1983) (testimony by Peter C. Waal, GTE Telenet Communications Corporation), at 4 to 5 (hereafter cited as *Computer Fraud*).

120. *Id.* The federal government has almost completed arrangements for establishing 24-hour-a-day direct electronic links among approximately 100 federal agencies and 7 major private credit reporting companies. Once the links are in place, agency personnel will be able to examine the status of bank loans, liens, divorce records, and department store, oil company, and credit card accounts. *See* D. Burnham, "Agencies Creating System To Check Citizens' Credit," *The New York Times* April 8, 1984, at 17. While such information has been used by the government in the past, the combined developments of new regulations passed pursuant to the Fair Credit Reporting Act and computerized links "are expected to make such checks far more extensive." *Id.*, at col. 2. *See also* P.P.S.C., *Info. Society, supra* note 2, at 12. The Privacy Commission concluded in its report on stored records:

> the broad availability and low cost of computer and telecommunications technologies provide both the *impetus* and the *means* to perform new record-keeping functions . . . On one hand, they can give [an individual] easier access to services that make his life more comfortable or convenient. On the other, they also tempt others to demand, and make it easier for them to get access to information about him for purposes he does not expect and would not agree to if he were asked . . . The real danger is the gradual erosion of individual liberties through the automation, integration and interconnection of many small, separate record-keeping systems, each of which alone may seem innocuous, even benevolent and wholly justifiable.

121. *Computer Fraud, supra* note 119, at 5 to 6.
122. *Id.*
123. *See supra* notes 7 to 11 of text, and Appendix B.
124. In part three of *Databanks, supra* note 64, Dr. Westin describes the changes in organizational record-keeping, which many commentators assumed to be occurring as a result of increased computerization, but which were *not* observed among the organizations studied from 1970 to 1972. These assumptions were: a) agencies were collecting more sensitive information, b) there would be an increase in the intra- and inter-organizational exchange of sensitive information, and c) individuals would have less opportunity to know about what information about them was being collected.

However, Dr. Westin found some of the reasons why these phenomena had not occurred were because of high cost and software inflexibility. Spokesmen for some of the organizations interviewed said they felt more information should be retained on individuals, and that they would have collected more information if they were not prevented by technological or legal restrictions.

125. *See* Nash and Smith, *supra* note 2, at 9. The following surveillance sheet is an example of one writer's vision of the kind of projections which could be made based on information likely to be stored in electronic database systems:

> *Computers and People*, (Aug. 1979): p. 31. The amounts spent for *The Wall Street Journal*, breakfast, and gasoline have been increased to reflect more realistic prices.

NATIONAL DATA BANK
DAILY SURVEILLANCE SHEET
Confidential
July 11, 1987

SUBJECT.	Dennie Van Tasell	
	San Jose State College	
	Male	
	Age 38	
	Married	
	Programmer	
PURCHASES.	Wall Street Journal	.50
	Breakfast	2.65
	Gasoline	10.00
	Phone (328-1826)	.10
	Phone (308-7928)	.10
	Phone (421-1931)	.10
	Bank (Cash Withdrawal)	(120.00)
	Lunch	2.00
	Cocktail	1.00
	Lingerie	21.85
	Phone (369-22436)	.35
	Bourbon	8.27
	Newspaper	8.10

** COMPUTER ANALYSIS**

Owns stock (90 percent probability)
Heavy starch breakfast. Probably overweight.
Bought $10.00 gasoline. Owns VW. So far this week he has bought $40.00 worth of gas. Obviously doing something else besides just driving the 9 miles to work.

Bought gasoline at 7:57. Safe to assume he was late to work.
Phone No. 328-1826 belongs to Shady Lane. Shady was arrested for bookmaking in 1972.
Phone No. 308-7928. Expensive men's barber—specializes in bald men or hair styling.
Phone No. 421-1931. Reservations for Las Vegas (without wife). Third trip this year to Las Vegas (without wife). Will scan file to see if anyone else has gone to Las Vegas at the same time and compare to his phone call numbers.
Withdrew $120.00 cash. Very unusual since all legal purchases can be made using the National Social Security credit card. Cash usually only used for illegal purchases. It was previously recommended that all cash be outlawed as soon as it becomes politically possible.

126. See comments of New York Attorney General Robert Abrams before New York State assembly committee hearing on two-way cable privacy but reported in Breznick, "NY Attorney Gen'l Favors Cable Bill," *Multichannel News,* March 26, 1984, at 33.
127. See Westin *Popular Computing, supra* note 1, at 1.

128. Moody responded to this attack by admitting that he watches adult movies, but does so as part of his civic duty. "It's part of my job," he stated, "like going to look at the site of a flood." *See Panorama*, February 1981, at 59.
129. Although the movie theater proprietor sought specific names, the judge in the case narrowed the subpoena to limit the information disclosed to the number of viewers. *See The New York Times*, January 12, 1982, at B2.
130. *See* Nash and Smith, *supra* note 2, at 6.
131. *See* Westin, *Popular Computing, supra* note 1, at 115.
132. *See* C. Tapper, *Computer Law* (Longman: London and New York, 1978), at 120.
133. *Id.*
134. According to Herman MacDaniel, president of Management Resources International in 1982, "most frauds have been [done] by people who were not technically [sophisticated]." *See* "Information Management," *supra* note 77, at 124.
135. *Id.*
136. The Bank Secrecy Act, Pub. L. 91-508, Oct. 26, 1970, 84 Stat. 1118, 12 U.S.C. §§18296, 1951-1959. Section 1829 requires insured banks to retain records on persons having accounts and authorized to act with respect to such accounts, and to make and keep reproductions of every instrument presented for payment or deposited together with the identification of the party for whose account it is to be deposited or collected (unless the person's account is already on record). Records are not required to be kept for more than 6 years. 12 U.S.C.A. §1829b(g). Sections 1951 to 1959 contain similar record-keeping requirements applicable to uninsured banks.
137. P.P.S.C., *Info. Society, supra* note 2, at 15 n.7 *citing U.S. Department of Health, Education and Welfare, Secretary's Advisory Committee on Automated Personal Data Systems, Records, Computers, and the Rights of Citizens 41 (1973).*
138. The Fair Credit Reporting Act of 1971, Pub. L. 90-321, Title U1, §602, Oct. 26, 1970, 84 Stat. 1136, 15 U.S.C. §1681. This Act requires consumers to be notified and supplied with the names and addresses of consumer reporting agencies making adverse decisions about consumers, 15 U.S.C. §1681m; requires notification to consumers when an investigative report is being compiled on them not later than three days after the report is first requested; 15 U.S.C. §1681d (the term investigative report does not include factual information on a consumer's credit record obtained directly from a creditor of the consumer or from a consumer reporting agency when such information was obtained directly from a creditor or from the consumer) 15 U.S.C. & 1681a(e); sets forth permissible purposes for consumer reports, 15 U.S.C. §1681b; prohibits reporting of obsolete information (the Act exempts credit transactions including principal of $50,000 or more, the underwriting of life insurance for $50,000 or more, and employment decisions involving salaries expected to equal $20,000 or more, 15 U.S.C., §1681c; sets forth required reporting procedures and disclosures to consumers, 15 U.S.C. §§1681c-1681h; and establishes procedures in case of disputed accuracy §1681i.
139. 15 U.S.C. §§1601-1677. Pub L. 93-495, Title III, §302 Oct. 28, 1974, 88 Stat. 1511 (*amended* March 23, 1976). The Act was passed to mandate disclosure of

credit terms to consumers so consumers will be able to compare more readily the terms available to them, and to avoid uninformed use of credit. 15 U.S.C. §1601(a).

140. 5 U.S.C. §552, Pub. L. 89-554, Sept. 6, 1966, 80 Stat. 383 (amended Sept. 13, 1976).

141. Individuals do not have the right to examine information that is exempt from FOIA's disclosure provisions, however. These matters are essentially those that are:

1) specifically established under Executive order to be kept secret;

2) related to the personnel rules and practices of an agency;

3) specifically exempt from disclosure by statute;

4) trade secrets;

5) interagency or intraagency memorandums;

6) personnel and medical files and similar files, the disclosure of which would constitute a clearly unwarranted invasion of privacy;

7) investigatory records compiled for law enforcement;

8) contained in or related to examination, operation, or condition reports prepared by or on behalf of an agency responsible for regulating financial institutions;

9) geographical and geophysical information concerning wells.

See 5 U.S.C. §552(b)(1)-(b)(9).

142. 20 U.S.C. §1232g, Pub.L. 93-380, 88 Stat. 484, §513, Aug. 21, 1974.

143. 5 U.S.C. §552a, Pub.L. 93-579, §5 (amended June 1, 1977).

144. The disclosures authorized by the Privacy Act are essentially those that are:

1) to agency officers and employees who have a need for a record in the performance of their duties;

2) required by the Freedom of Information Act;

3) for a routine use;

4) to the Bureau of Concensus in order to conduct surveys;

5) to be used for surveys and which are to be transferred in a form that is not individually indentifiable;

6) to the National Archives for historical use;

7) to another agency for law enforcement upon written request by the head of the agency;

8) pursuant to a showing of compelling circumstances for the health or safety of an individual if notice is transmitted to that individual;

9) to either House of Congress;

10) to the Comptroller General for use in the course of his duties;

11) pursuant to a court order;

12) to a consumer reporting agency.

145. 5 U.S.C. §552a(b).

146. 5 U.S.C. §552a(d)(1).

147. 5 U.S.C. §552a(d)(2)(B).

148. 5 U.S.C. §552a(e)(B).

149. 5 U.S.C. §552a(e)(1).

150. 5 U.S.C. §552a(b)(3).

151. 5 U.S.C. §552a(a)(7).

152. P.P.S.C., *Info. Society, supra* note 2, at 517-518. For example, Subsection 3(b)(7) of the Privacy Act requires that the head of an agency request information in writing and that the legitimate law enforcement activity for which the information is desired be specified before information can be released. The "routine use" provision has been used to circumvent this requirement. *Id.*, at 517.
153. *See* §6 of Pub. L. 93-579.
154. *See* 40 Fed. Reg. 45877-8 (Oct. 3, 1975); 41 C.F.R. §§101-36000 to 361207 (1980)(regulations governing management of automatic data processing equipment used by the federal government).
155. *See* Privacy Protection Act of 1984: Hearings on H.R. 3743 Before the Committee on Government Operations, 98th Cong., 1st Sess. (1983). In the words of one witness, "OMB has 'virtually abdicated responsibility' for The Privacy Act." *Id.*, at H6344.
156. *See* definition of agency 5 U.S.C. §552a(1); 5 U.S.C. §552(e). H.R. 3743 (the Glen English Bill), which was introduced into Congress in 1983, would have established a Privacy Protection Commission as an independent agency of the executive branch. The Commission would have been responsible for pro- posing legislation to improve protection of information privacy, and for assisting in "the development and implementation of private sector data protection standards." Privacy Protection Act of 1984: Hearings on H.R. 3743 Before the Committee on Government Operations, 98th Cong., 1st Sess. (1983). The bill died in committee. Telephone interview with Robert M. Gellman, Counsel, Government Operations Committee, House of Represen- tatives, United States Congress (March 15, 1984).
157. Privacy Act of 1974, Pub. L. No. 93-579, §5, (*amended* June 1, 1977).
   The Privacy Protection Commission was not the first Presidential commis- sion to address the need to protect stored data and individual privacy. In 1974 the President established the Domestic Council Committee on the Right of Privacy, which was chaired by the Vice President. The Committee endorsed initiatives addressing military surveillance of civilian political activities, crim- inal justice information, electronic funds transfer systems, the confidentiality of taxpayer records, federal mailing lists, customer records maintained by financial institutions, federal employee rights, and security guidelines for federal computers and communications systems. The Committee and the Council of State Governments co-sponsored a 1974 seminar on privacy, which led to a resource document entitled "Privacy, A Public Concern" (K. Larsen, ed,. 1975).
158. Privacy Act of 1974, 5 U.S.C. §552a(b).
159. *P.P.S.C., Info. Society, supra* note 2, at 362 to 363. (emphasis added).
160. *Id.*
161. The Privacy Commission proposed by the Glen English Bill would have been responsible for developing principles to improve private sector data protec- tion. *See supra* note 155.
162. United States v. Miller, 425 U.S.435 (1976). *See supra* text accompanying notes 15 to 17.
163. Right to Financial Privacy Act of 1978, 12 U.S.C. §§S1101-1122, §§3401-3422

(amended 1980 and 1982).

164. Id., at §§3404(c), 3405(2), 3406(c), 3407(2), 3408(4), 3412(b), and 3410.

165. Electronic Fund Transfer Act, 15 U.S.C. §1693-1693r (1978 amended 1982).

166. Id., at 15 U.S.C. §1693d.

167. Id., at 15 U.S.C. §1693f.

168. Id., at 15 U.S.C. §1593c.

169. Id., at 15 U.S.C. §1693b, 12 C.F.R. Part 205, App. A, Supp. I & II.

170. Regulation E includes provisions on disclosure of account information and terms to customers, Id., at §205-7; procedures for error resolution Id., at §205.8; documentation of transfers, Id., at §205.11; and procedures for preauthorized transfers, Id., at §205.10.

171. See the Bank Secrecy Act, 12 U.S.C. §1829b, 1951-1959 (1970).

172. See Heller, "EFT, Privacy and the Public Good," in Computers & Banking, supra note 103, at 86.

173. See Horan, Outlook for EFT Technology, supra note 103, at 29-36.

174. Pub. L. 96-440, §§101, 105-107, 201, 202, 94 Stat. 1879-1883, Oct. 13, 1980, 42 U.S.C. §§2000aa, 2000aa-5 to aa-7, 2000aa-11, 2000aa-12.

175. Id., at 42 U.S.C. §2000aa.

176. The Omnibus Crime Control and Safe Streets Act of 1968, Title III, 18 U.S.C. §2510-2520 (1968).

177. The Communications Act of 1934, c.652, Title VI, §605, 47 U.S.C. §605 (amended 1968, 1982).

178. 18 U.S.C. §2510(1).

179. 18 U.S.C. §2511, 2516.

180. See F. Lloyd, Cable Television's Emerging Two-Way Services: A Dilemma for Federal and State Regulators, 36 Vand L. Rev. 1045 (1983) for a discussion of the FCC's attempt to impose common carrier status on two-way cable television. See Koenig, supra note 4 for an argument that cable service is a form of local utility that should be regulated like common carrier. Koenig writes

> Subscribers who sign up are not merely dealing with a commercial merchant but are obtaining basic communications services. Under this view, cable service would appear more as a right or necessity of local residents rather than a merely optional entertainment. This would be consistent with the special legal status cable systems enjoy in many jurisdictions, such as zoning exemptions, utility tax treatment, condemnation power, and entry rights into apartment houses. Id., at 108.

181. A number of companies now offer shopping services over the telephone. Teleshopping is currently provided by Comp-U-Card International, Inc. of Stamford Connecticut, Byvideo Inc. of Sunnyvale, California, and Viewdata Corporation of America, a Knight-Ridder subsidiary in Florida. Times Mirror Videotex Services and Keycom Electronic Publishing are expected to start services in Chicago and Orange County, California, in 1984. "New Video Game: Shopping, Items Offered At Home and in Stores," The New York Times, April 26, 1984, §4, at 1.

182. See United States v. Seidletz, 589 F.2d 152, 157 (4th Cir. 1978) cert. denied 99 S. Ct. 2030 (1978).

183. *See* Smith v. Maryland, 442 U.S. 735, 742 (1978) (petitioner had no legitimate expectation of privacy in the telephone numbers he dialed).
184. Communications Act of 1934, c.652 title VI, §605 47 U.S.C. §605 (*amended 1968, 1982*).
185. *Id.*, at §605 *as amended.*
186. *See* Bubis v. United States, 384 F.2d 643 (9th Cir. 1967); United States v. Russo, 250 F. Supp. 55 (E.D. Pa. 1966) and n. 289; United States v. Butenko, 494 F. 2d 593, 600 (3rd Cir.), *cert. denied,* 419 U.S. 881 (1974). United States v. Zarkin, 250 F. Supp. 728 (D.D.C. 1966). All of these cases, except Butenko, were decided prior to the amendment of §605. The original trial in Botenko concluded in 1964. Butenko, 494 F.2d at 596. Therefore, none of these cases supports the proposition that §605 continues to protect wire transmissions. Cited in R. Neustadt, G. Skall, & M. Hammer, *The Regulation of Electronic Publishing,* Fed. Com. L.J. 88 (1981): 404, at n. 287 and 289 (n. 288 omitted).
187. The Omnibus Crime Control and Safe Streets Act of 1968 Title III, *supra* note 62, S. Rep. No. 1097, 90th Cong., 2d Sess., *reprinted in* 1968 U.S. code Cong. & Ad. News 2112, 2196. *See* United States v. Seidlitz, 589 F. 2d 152 (1978).
188. *See* United States v. McGuire, 381 F.2d. 306 (1967), *cert. denied,* 389 U.S. 1053 (1968) (court said the prohibition against interception of a communication does not mean that a party to a telephone conversation may not disclose it). *See also* United States v. Butenko, 494 F.2d 593 (3rd Cir. 1974) *cert. denied* (telephone company did not violate §605 by monitoring foreign intelligence telephone conversations and turning over contents of conversations to law enforcement agencies); Coates v. United States, 307 F. Supp. 677 (D.C. No. 1970) (where a recipient of a telephone call consented to eavesdropping by a government agent unknown to the other party, there was no interception or divulgence under the Communications Act).
189. Cable Television Clarification, 46 F.C.C. 2d 175 (1974).
190. *Id.*, at 183. A similar fear was expressed by Edward P. Kearse, Executive Director of the Commission on Cable Television for New York State. "We should not be overly concerned about a problem that does not currently exist and thereby discourage the building and implementation of the interactive cable system," he stated in 1982. *Times Union,* January 12, 1982, at 2-3.
191. Cable Television Clarification, 46 F.C.C. 2d 175 (1974).
192. *Id.*, at 184.
193. *Id.*
194. Cable Television Clarification, 46 F.C.C. 2d 175 (1974). *See generally* C. Ferris, F. Lloyd, and T. Casey, "Cable Two-Way Services: An Area of Federal-State Conflict," in Cable Television Law: A Video Communications Practice Guide, ch. 14 (New York and Washington, D.C.: Mathew Bender Publications, 1983) for a discussion of the confusion over the FCC's jurisdiction over two-way cable services.
195. *See* Introduction and Appendix B: Definitions in this paper for a discussion of potential privacy concerns created by electronic technology.
196. This study is intended to be a general overview and is not intended to be comprehensive. For a more comprehensive study of state privacy statutes *See* Smith, *supra* note 54.

197. Cal. Const. Art 1 § 1. The California courts have stated that "'the right of privacy' is the right to live one's life in seclusion, without being subjected to unwarranted and undesired publicity." See Gill v. Curtis Publishing Company, 239 P.2d 630, 38 Cal.2d 273 (1952). The right, according to at least one California court, exists independent of the comon rights of property, contract, reputation and physical integrity. Id.

198. See Doe v. Roe, 400 N.Y.S.2d 668 (Sup. Ct. 1977). (Husband co-authored book with wife's psychiatrist disclosing confidential information about marriage and wife without wife's consent. The court held that husband and psychiatrist had breached an affirmative duty imposed by statute banning disclosure of confidential medical information).

199. Id., 400 N.Y.S.2d 668 at 676. (The court said every physician makes an implied promise of confidentiality to his patient. The court also said that although no case to date had recognized a common law right of privacy, it had been predicted that the New York Court of Appeals would abandon the holding of Robertson v. Rochester Folding Box Company, 171 N.Y. 538, 64 N.E. 442 (1902), that no cause of action would be recognized for invasion of privacy apart from that authorized by Civil Rights Law. Id.).

200. See Privacy Protection Law in the United States, N.T.I.A. Report Series, Report 82-78, May 1982, at 10 [hereafter cited as Privacy Protection Law].

201. See Ind. Code Ann. § 4-1-6-1 (West 1979); Mass. Gen. Laws Ann. Ch. 66A §§ 1-3 (West 1976); Va. Code Ann. §§ 2.1-377 (1976).

202. See, e.g., Ind. Code Ann. § 4-1-6-2(b) (Burns 1977); Va. Code Ann. § 2.1-382(2) (1976).

203. See, e.g., Utah Code Ann. § 63-50-7 (1975).

204. See The Privacy Act of 1974, 5 U.S.C. § 552a (1976); The Freedom of Information Act, 5 U.S.C. § 552 (1967).

205. See, e.g., Ariz. Rev. Stat. Ann. § 16-806 (1977). The Arizona statute provides that information shall not be used for any purpose other than as stated and filed in writing in accordance with subsection (a). But subsection (d) says information may be used for a purpose other than that for which it was collected if information is filed and publicly available as provided in subsection (a). Subsection (a) does not require prior notice to the data subject of the use of information. Subsection (e) says a person shall be notified when he is the subject of stored information, but excepts information which is defined by statute as confidential or records relating to medical or psychiatric treatment . . . or information compiled in reasonable anticipation of a civil action or proceeding. Id., at § 16-806(e); Hawaii Rev. Stat. §§92E-1 to 92E-13, Hawaii's Fair Information Practice Statute, requires each agency that maintains any accessible personal record to make that record available to the individual on whom it pertains. Id., at §92E-2. The statute does not provide for agencies to notify such individuals when information is being collected or maintained, however. See also Conn. Gen. Stat. Ann. § 4-193d (1977).

206. Larceny is a form of theft.

207. This conclusion based on a review of approximately 10 state theft statutes and the Model Penal Code (1974). The study is not meant to be exhaustive. The New York statute, however, together with the Model Penal Code, are assumed

to be representative of, or perhaps more progressive than, theft statutes in most states. Larceny and theft provisions vary among different jurisdictions.

208. See Model Penal Code §223.0 (1), 223.2 (1) (1974). The basic theft provisions in most jurisdictions are similar to the provisions in the Model Penal Code.
209. See N.Y. Penal Law § 155.05 (McKinney 1969).
210. See, e.g., N.Y. Penal Law § 155.00(3) (1969); Model Penal Code § 223.0(1) (1974).
211. See N.Y. Penal Law § 155.05 (McKinney 1969); Model Penal Code § 223.2(1)(1974).
212. 248 U.S. 215(1918).
213. International News Service v. Associated Press, 248 U.S. 215, 239 (1918).
214. Id.
215. See Goldstein v. California, 412 U.S. 546 (1973). (State law against record piracy not preempted merely because Congress has the power to legislate in this area. Goldstein also says Sears and Compco, infra, at note 215, did not overrule INS and the misappropriation doctrine.) See also Aronson v. Quick Point Pencil Company, 440 U.S. 257 (1979) (trade secret royalty liability of indefinite duration under state law not preempted); American Television & Communications Corporation v. Manning (Colo. App. 1982) (pirating plaintiff's exclusive right to deliver HBO programs via microwave and selling such programs in competition with plaintiff constituted misappropriation and unfair competition). See also Data Cash Systems Inc. v. JS&A Group, Inc., 480 F. Supp. 1063 (N.D. Ill. 1979), aff'd 628 F2d 1038 (1980); Adolph Coors Company v. Genderson & Sons, Inc. 486 F. Supp 131 (D. Colo 1980). See generally 2 R. Callman, The Law & Unfair Competition ch. 15, at 9 and cases cited in sS15.08 (3rd ed. and 1981 Supp).
216. See Sears, Roebuck & Company v. Stiffel Company, 376 U.S. 225 (1964). (Stiffel had been granted design and utility patents on a lamp. Sears marketed a substantially identical lamp without placing identifying labels on the lamp. The Supreme Court said the effect of a patent is a statutory monopoly; accordingly, it cannot be used to secure any monopoly beyond that inherent in the patent or in violation of the antitrust laws. The Court continued, to allow a state by use of its law of unfair competition to prevent the copying of an article that represents too slight an advance to be patented would be to permit the state to block off from the public something that federal law has said belongs to the public.) 376 U.S., at 230-232. See also Compco v. Day-Brite Lighting, Inc., 376 U.S. 234 (1964).
217. See The Copyright Revision Act of 1976, Pub. L.94-553, Title I,§101, Oct. 19, 1976, 90 Stat. 2572, 17 U.S.C. §301.
218. International News Service v. Associated Press, 248 U.S. 215, 250 (1918).
219. See Triangle Publications v. New England Newspaper Publishing Company, 46 F. Supp 198 (D. Mass. 1942). (Judge Wyzanski said Massachusetts courts do not accept INS because "I could hardly be unmindful of the probability that a majority of the present Justices of the Supreme Court of the United States would follow the dissenting opinion of Justice Brandeis . . . because they share his view that monopolies should not be readily extended . . . ." 46 F. Supp., at 204).

220. The Copyright Revision Act of 1976, 17 U.S.C.§301.
221. *Id.*
222. Such subject matter is expressly excluded from the scope of federal copyright preemption by Sections 301(a) and (b)(1). *See also* Zacehini v. Scripps-Howard Broadcasting Company, 433 U.S. 562 (1977) (performance recorded against will of the performer may be protected by state law without interference from federal law).
223. The law of unfair competition (or misappropriation) and copyright are not intended to protect to same interests, however. Copyright law is intended to foster literary and artistic creation, and prevents competition. The law of unfair competition is intended to protect the viability of a business system and to spur competition by preventing paracitism.
224. *See, e.g.,* Synercom Technology, Inc. v. University Computing Company, 474 F. Supp. 37 (N.D. Tex 1979) for an analogous argument.
225. For instance, it has been held that an unauthorized person (i.e., a customer) who attempts to benefit from pay T.V. by intercepting signals without paying for it, and anyone who assists him in doing so, is in violation of §605 of the Communication Act and there is an implied private right of action for an injunction and damages. 47 U.S.C. §605. *See* Callman, *supra* note 225, at Cumulative Supp. v. 2 at 33, n. 21 and cases cited therein.
226. *See* Mass. Gen. Laws Ann. C. 266 §30(2) (West). The term *property* includes "a security deposit received pursuant to section fifteen B of chapter one hundred and eight-six, electronically processed or stored data, either tangible or intangible, data while in transit . . . ." *Id.* Additionally, Massachusetts has amended the term "trade secret" to include "anything tangible or electronically kept or stored, which constitutes, represents, evidences or records a secret scientific, technical, merchandising, production or management information, design, process, procedure, formula, invention or improvement." *Id.,* at §30(4). *See also* N.Y. Penal Law §155.05 (McKinney 1969). *Property* is defined by the New York statute as "any money, personal property, real property, thing in action, evidence of debt or contract or any article, substance or thing of value." While this definition is broad enough to include electronically stored and processed data, much personal information retrievable from videotex or personal computers will have only "economic value" to the person about whom the information pertains.
227. *See, e.g.,* Ariz. Rev. Stat. Ann. §13-1802A6(1977); Alaska Stat. §11.46.200; Ill. Rev. Stat. c. 38 §16-10; N.Y. Penal Law §165.15 (McKinney 1967, amended 1982).
228. For instance, Illinois specifically limits its statute to "cable television services." Cable television service means any cable television system or closed circuit coaxial cable communication system, or any microwave or similar transmission service used in connection with any cable television system or similar closed coaxial communications service. Ill. Rev. Stat. c. 38 §16-10(a)(1). *See also* Mass. Gen. Laws Ann. c. 266 §37D (West); N.Y. Penal Law §165.15 (McKinney 1981).
229. *See, e.g.,* Ariz. Rev. Stat. Ann. §13-1802 A.6. (1977); N.Y. Penal Law §165-15 (McKinney 1981).

230. *See* Mass. Gen. Laws Ann. c. 266, §37D (West 1981).
231. *See* R. Couch, Note, A Suggested Legislative Approach to the Problem of Computer Crime, *Wash & Lee L. Rev.* XXXVIII (1981): n.4, 1173.
232. *Id.*
233. The following states had adopted cable television privacy acts as of July 1984: Illinois, Wisconsin, California, Minnesota, Connecticut, New York, and Rhode Island.
234. The Communications Consumer Privacy Act, Ill. Ann Stat. c. 38 §§87-1-87-3 (Smith-Hurd 1983).
235. *Id.*, at §87-3(a). Damages for violations of the act are punishable by fines of up to $10,000. *Id.*, at §87-3(b).
236. Wis. Stat. Ann. §134.45(1)(a). Although franchises in Wisconsin are granted by each municipality, the law applies a statewide standard to all Wisconsin franchises. Wis. Stat. Ann. §134.43 (West 1983). The above provision expressly excludes devices "related to security, fire and utility service." Wis. Stat. Ann. §134.45(1)(b).
237. *Id.*, at §(2). The Wisconsin act does not prohibit cable operators from collecting billing information and from conducting system sweeps to verify system integrity. Violations of this act may be assessed at fines of up to $50,000 for the first offense and up to $100,000 for a second offense. *Id.*, at §(4).
238. Cal. Penal Code §637.5(a)(1). This conduct may occur with the subscriber's express written consent or for electronic sweeps to monitor signal quality. *Id.*
239. The California Act says individually identifiable information shall include but not be limited to subscriber television viewing habits, shopping choices, interests, opinions, energy uses, medical information, banking data or information, or any other personal or private information. *Id.*, at §637.5(2). Such information may be disclosed with the subscriber's express written consent. *Id.*
240. The act states that individual subscriber viewing responses or other individually identifiable information derived from subscribers shall be retained and used by cable companies only to the extent reasonably necessary for billing purposes and internal business practices, and to monitor subscriber terminals for unauthorized reception of services. *Id.*, at §637.5(b).
241. The act provides, however, that nothing in this section shall be construed to prevent local franchising authorities from obtaining information necessary to monitor franchise compliance. *Id.*, at §637.5(c).
242. A cable operator must correct the information upon a reasonable showing by a subscriber that the information is inaccurate. *Id.*, at §637.5(d).
243. *Id.* §637.5(e). Violations of these provisions are misdemeanors punishable by fines not exceeding $3,000, and/or by imprisonment not exceeding one year. *Id.*, at §637.5(i) and (j).
244. Minn. Stat. §238.05, subd. 2(b), subd. 8.
245. State of Connecticut Cable Television Subscribers Protection of Personal Privacy, Pub. Act No 83-33 (1983) *amending* §16-331(d).
246. The Minnesota cable regulatory agency is the state Cable Communications Board. The Connecticut Department of Public Utilities has jurisdiction over cable television regulation in this state.

247. *See* 4 Minn. Code Agency R. §4.202(W); Conn. Pub. Act No. 83-33 (1983), *amending* §16-331(d).
248. *See* 4 Minn. Code Agency R, §4.202(W).
249. The New York cable regulatory authority is the New York State Commission on Cable Television.
250. Rhode Island's cable television is under the aegis of the Rhode Island Division of Public Utilities and Carriers.
251. The New York cable operating rules specify that signals may not be transmitted without a subscriber's consent, terminals must be designated to allow subscribers to prevent return signals, and subscribers who are provided with two-way terminals must receive written notice of these rights and instructions to enable them to activate and deactivate their terminals. N.Y. Admin. Code tit. 9, §596.3(e). *See also* State of New York Commission on Cable Television, In the Matter of The Establishment of Rules and Regulations Concerning Cable Television Subscriber Privacy, Notice of Proposed Rulemaking, Docket No. 90221, 83-045, Released March 3, 1983. The Commission Notice sets forth a number of findings on subscriber privacy including the following: a) two-way and interactive television subscribers risk invasion of their privacy; b) the danger of interception of subscriber-generated data exists; c) information about subscribers is now released by cable operators to outsiders, and d) cable operators do sell subscriber lists to outsiders. §11., at 3-4. The Commission invites comments, and sets forth a detailed proposal for cable subscriber privacy regulations. This Notice is currently circulating for comments.

The Rhode Island regulations provide that no signals of a Class IV CATV channel (defined in §1.9(b) of the regulations and, except for the substitution of "CATV" in the Rhode Island regulation for "cable television" in the FCC regulations, in FCC Rules and Regulations, 47 C.F.R., part 76, § 76.5(cc)) shall be transmitted from a subscriber terminal for the purposes of monitoring individual viewing patterns without the express written consent of the subscriber. Rules governing Community Antenna TV Systems, (1981) *as amended*, January 14, 1983 §1.9(b).

252. As of the date of this writing, two-way cable subscriber privacy legislation had been introduced in at least five states since the beginning of 1984: New York, A.7327 – A, 1983-1984 Reg. Sess. Cal. No. 439 (1983); New Jersey A.731, P.L. 1972, c. 186 (c. 48:5A-1 *et seq.*); Pennsylvania S.508, Printer No. 1725, *as amended*, Feb. 14, 1984, Connecticut LCO No. 1528, Gen. Ass., Committee Bill No. 5878, February Sess. 1984; Maryland H.B. 1320/83-Cal., No. 255, Introduced Jan. 11, 1984.

The New York Cable Telecommunications Privacy Act, introduced by Assemblyman Melvin Zimmer, has received considerable publicity because it would establish strict cable subscriber privacy standards in New York, and would set a precedent for other states to pass similar legislation.

The bill prohibits all persons from monitoring, observing, recording, intercepting, or transmitting any conversations or activities of a cable subscriber, A.7327 – A, 1983-1984 Reg. Sess., Cal. No. 439 (1983) §833-b; from aggregating any individually indentifiable information concerning subscriber viewing patterns or responses (except for billing and when necessary to render a service requested by the subscriber), *Id.*, at §833-c1; from conducting research or collecting identifiable information from subscriber mailing lists or other cable television company records, *Id.*, at §833-b3; and from disclosing any subscriber information absent legal compulsion without prior written authorization from the subscriber. *Id.*, at §833-f. Separate authorization is required for "each type of information collected or disclosed," and subscribers may revoke this authorization at any time. *Id.* Subscribers must be notified prior to or contemporaneous with each request to a cable operator for information, and must be given the opportunity to decline to allow disclosure of such information. *Id.*, at §833-e3. Subscribers will be able to request all information compiled on them, and require correction of information upon a reasonable showing that it is misleading or inaccurate. *Id.*, at §833-h. Information compiled on subscribers must be destroyed upon completion of the uses for which such information was collected, or upon the termination of service by a subscriber. *Id.*, at §833-d. Cable operators must also maintain adequate safeguards to protect the physical and electronic security of any individually identifiable subscriber information. *Id.*, at §833-c3.

A court may award up to $10,000 in addition to damages to each aggrieved subscriber, if it finds the violation was intentional and/or the defendant has frequently or persistently violated the Act. *Id.*, at §833-i. Section 833-j imposes criminal sanctions of $5,000 and/or imprisonment of not longer than one year for violations by an individual. Violations by a corporation are punishable by fines of up to $50,000 for each violation.

253. The conclusions of this section are based on an examination of the following state computer fraud statutes: Ariz. Rev. Stat. Ann. §13-2316; Del. Code Ann. tit. 11 §858; Fla. Stat. Ann. §815 (West); Ga. Code Ann. ss16-9-91 to 16-9-94; Minn. Stat. Ann. §§609.87 to 609.89; Mo. Ann. Stat. §§569.095 to 569.099; Mont. Rev. Codes Ann. §§45-6-310 to 45-6-311; N.M. Stat. Ann. §30-16A; R.I. Gen. Laws § 11-52-1 to 11-52-4; Utah Code Ann. §76-6-701 to 76-6-704; Wis. Stat. §943.70.

254. *See* statutes listed in note 251, *supra.*

255. *See*, e.g., Fla Stat. Ann. §815.04, offenses against intellectual property, and §815.05, offenses against computer equipment or supplies. Mo. Ann. Stat. §569.095 deals with information classified as intellectual property, and §669.096 regulates tampering with computer equipment. Wis. Stat. §943.70(2) punishes offenses against computer data and programs, and §943.70(3) punishes offenses against supplies and equipment.

256. These crimes, often called "fraud" or "fraud in the first degree," are usually punished more harshly than other computer crimes. *See*, e.g., Ariz. Rev. Stat. Ann. §13-2316C; Del. Stat. Ann. §858(a); Ga. Code Ann. §16-9-93(a).

257. The penalty for these crimes, often called "fraud in the second degree" or "misuse," is usually less harsh than for crimes involving artifice, schemes to defraud fraudulent pretenses, or misrepresentation. *See*, e.g., Ariz. Rev. Stat. Ann. §13-2316C; Del. Stat. Ann §858(b); Ga. Code Ann. §16-9-93(b).

258. *See* Mo. Rev. Stat. §569.099.2.

259. *See* Ga. Code Ann. §16-9-93(b).

260. *See* Ga. Code Ann. §16-9-93(a). The penalty for this Section is one and one-half

times the amount of the fraud, or imprisonment for not more than 15 years or both. *See also* Minn. Stat. Ann. §§609.87 to 609.89 (the penalty is based on the "loss to the owner"); Mont. Rev. Codes Ann. §45-6-311(2), is based on the value of the property lost or misused; N.M. Stat. Ann. §30-16A-4 and Utah Code Ann. §76-6-703 gauges the amount of recovery to the vlaue of the computer system. The recovery may bear no relation to the harm to the data subject, however.

261. Cable operators must obtain franchises from local governmental authorities before they can operate. Subscriber privacy protection may be a condition to the grant of a franchise.

262. "Will CATV Become a Super Snooper?" *Cablelines*, July 1974, at II.

263. A local ordinance mandates a separate penalty for violations of subscribers' privacy rights. Remarks of Richard Berman, General Counsel, Warner Amex Cable Communications, New York University School of Law Conference on Television and the Law, 1981.

264. *See* Standard Franchise Agreement, available from Massachusetts Attorney General's office, Cable Television Division, §31, at 26-27. *See also* The Boston Cablevision Franchise Agreement in Ferris, Lloyd & Casey, *supra* note 193, at Appendix C., State Forms, at C-377.

This agreement contains more comprehensive cable subscriber privacy protections than the Massachusetts Standard Agreement.

265. *See* Westin, *Datamation, supra* note 2, at 106.

266. *See* the New York Cable Telecommunications Act, A.7327 – A, 1983-1984 Reg. Sess., Cal. No. 439 (1983) §833-b.

267. *See* A. Breznick, "N.Y. Association Sets Priorities," *Multichannel News*, March 5, 1984, at 37. New York Attorney General Robert Abrams has countered this claim in New York, stating that the proposed bill covers all home information and telecommunications systems. Moreover, he argued, the legislation should not be rejected "simply because it does not solve every privacy problem immediately, or because other legislation is needed to insure that privacy abuses do not occur elsewhere." Breznick, *supra* note 3, at 33.

Cable television may be receiving more attention from regulators than other industries do because it is newer than other industries. But other industries are also regulated where danger to consumers has been perceived. For example, telephones are regulated utilities subject to the Communications Act of 1934 and FCC regulations. Banks are regulated by the Bank Secrecy Act and the Financial Right to Privacy Act, *see* text accompanying notes 161 to 170, *supra*. Banks also owe their customers a common law duty of confidentiality, *see* Peterson v. Idaho First National Bank, 83 Idaho 578, 367 F.2d 284(1961) (bank-customer relationship subject to the rules of agency law which imply a duty of the bank not to use or communicate confidential customer information, and a contractual duty to refrain from disclosure unless authorized by law): 367 F.2d, at 290. *See also* Brex v. Smith, 104 N.J. Sq. 386, 146A.34 (1929) ("there is an implied obligation . . . to keep [depositors' bank records] from scrutiny until compelled by a court of competent jurisdiction to do otherwise"): 146A 34, at 36.

At least nine states have also enacted explicit statutory obligations requiring prior notice to customers if bank records are disclosed without customer authorization, and imposing a duty of confidentiality on banks. *See* Alaska Stat. §06.05.175 (1978); Cal. Banking Code §7470 (West 1976); Conn. Gen. Stat. § 36-9j to 36-9n; Ill. Rev. Stat. Ch. 17, § 360 (1980); La. Rev. Stat. Ann Art.9 § 3571 (West 1980); Me. Rev. Stat. tit. 9-b § 163 (1977); Md. Fin. Inst. Code Ann. § 1-301 (1980); N.H. Rev. Stat Ann. 359-C (1977); Okla. Stat. Ann tit. 6 § 2201 (West 1979).

268. *See* Ferris, Lloyd, and Casey, *supra* note 193, at §§14.06-14.07. If cable operators were subject to common carrier restrictions they could be required to file applications with state commissions to be allowed to enter a market, and to file for approval of their rates and tariffs. Cable operators might also be required to use uniform systems of accounts for bookeeping, or to provide nonvideo services through a separate subsidiary.

269. *See* Westin, *Datamation, supra* note 2, at 106.

270. Remarks of New York Attorney General Robert Abrams to the New York State Commission on Cable Television in 1982, *cited in Id.*, at 111. Negative publicity may be particularly damaging to the future of two-way cable because cable operators are being hurt by higher-than-expected materials and installation costs, and competitors providing similar services for lower prices. *See* §[4] herein.

271. *See* Breznick, *supra* note 3, at 33. New York Attorney General Robert Abrams argues that "cable privacy is a problem which can be expected to arise," however. *Id.*

272. Koenig, *supra* note 4, at 113.

273. *See* Warner Amex Cable Communications, Code of Privacy (1981) reproduced at Appendix A; Cox Cable Communications, Inc. Code of Subcriber Privacy (1982); New York State Cable Association, Code of Privacy *cited in* Westin, *Datamation, supra* note 2, at 104. A committee was named by the National Cable Television Association to consider drafting an industry-wide privacy code. *See* R. Wiley & R. Neustadt, "S.66 Privacy Issues: Collection, Interception are Areas Addressed," *Cable TV Law & Finance*, March 1983, at 1. No further action has been taken on this matter, however. Telephone interview with James McElveen, Director of Public Affairs, National Cable Television Assoication (April 9, 1984). Storer Cable Communications also reported that it has a Privacy Code. Telephone interview with Pedro Policio, Coordinator of Research and Planning, Storer Cable Communications, Inc. (March 22, 1982).

274. *See* Westin, *Datamation, supra* note 2, at 104.

275. Introduction to Warner Amex Cable Communications Code of Privacy (1981).

276. Warner Amex's Chairmain in 1978 stated, "people who buy interactive service will have to accept that they give up a bit of their privacy for it. Beyond that, we'll try to protect their privacy all we can." *The New York Times*, August 8, 1978, §C, at 1.

277. Westin, *Datamation, supra* note 2, at 104.

278. Warner Amex is a wholly-owned subsidiary of American Express Company.

279. Westin, *Datamation, supra* note 2, at 104. *See also* Comments of New York Attorney General Robert Abrams *cited in* Breznick, *supra* note 3, at 33. Cox Cable Communications, Inc. has adopted a Code of Subscriber Privacy that

provides that personal information about an individual subscriber not other-wise generally available will not be disseminated to any third party except a) with the consent of the subscriber, b) under court order, or c) as required incidental to an audit. The Cox Code further provides that Cox will use its best efforts to prevent unwarranted disclosure of subscriber information, that subscribers may review their files for accuracy, and that the Code is subject to all applicable laws of the local franchising authority, the state, and federal governments.

The Cox Code does not address the issues raised in the discussion of the Warner Amex Code above, nor does it prohibit subscriber privacy violations such as aggregation and interception of data, or intrusion into subscribers' terminals using electronic monitoring devices. The Cox Code does not provide for prior notice to subscribers in the event of a court order or subpoena for a subscriber's records, and does not require Cox to maintain physical safeguards to protect subscriber data.

280. Cable Communications Policy Act of 1984, 98th Cong. 2nd Sess., P.L. 98-549 (1984).
281. Community Antenna TV Association (CATA) said it was officially reconsidering "advisability" of continuing to support the proposed bill in July 1984. See "Cable at Deregulatory Crossroads," Communications Daily, July 5, 1984, at 1-2. California Cable Television Association (CCTA), the most powerful cable television association, also determined the bill was "not in the interests of the cable TV industry or the general public," and voted to withdraw its support for the proposed bill. See "Cal. Cable TV Ass. Rejects HR-4103," Communications Daily, July 6, 1984, at 1.
282. The FCC recently affirmed its Community Cable Las Vegas decision pre-empting local rate regulation of all tiers except basic service, which it said can contain only must-carries, and deciding that an operator is free to add, delete or move around other signals. In re Community Cable TV, FCC No. 83-525 slip op. (Nov. 15, 1983). See "Disturbed By 'Timing,' FCC Affirms Cities Can Regulate Only Basic Cable Rates," Communications Daily, July 13, 1984, at 1. The FCC ruled in its Miami franchise ruling that total fees paid to cities cannot exceed 5%, that all money must be used to defray regulatory costs, and that payments for support by access must be for services available to all users. See Memorandum Opin. & Order, Daily Digest, In re City of Miami, Florida June 29, 1984, at 84,737.
283. Capital Cities Cable, Inc. v. Crisp, Director, Oklahoma Alcoholic Beverage Control Board, No. 82-1795 (U.S. June 18, 1984).
284. See Capital Cities Cable, Inc. v. Crisp, Director, Oklahoma Alcoholic Beverage Control Board, No. 82-1795 (U.S. June 18, 1984), at 12, 21 to 22, 23.
285. See "Cable at Deregulatory Crossroads," Communications Daily, July 5, 1984, at 1.
286. Cable Franchise Policy and Communications Act of 1984, 98th Cong., 2nd Sess., Report 98-934 (1984), Part IV, §631(a)-631(h).
287. Id., at §634(a).
288. See Federal Computer Systems Protection Act, (FCSPA) S. 240, 96th Cong. 2d Sess. (1980); H.R. 6192, 96th Cong. 1st Sess, 125 Cong. Rec. H. 12352 (daily

ed. Dec. 19, 1979). *See* Couch, *supra* note 230.

The FCSPA would have prohibited the use or attempted use of a computer, either as an instrument or a symbol, for any fraudulent purpose. S.240, 96th Cong., 2nd Sess. §3(a)(1980). The FCSPA would have also prohibited the unauthorized intentional damaging of a computer. *Id.*, at §3(b). The bill's prohibitions applied to any computer used by the federal government, *Id.*, at §3(a)(1)(A), or any financial institution, *Id.*, at §3(a)(1)(B), and to all computers which affect interstate commerce, *Id.*, at §3(a)(2). The authors of the FCSPA intended the term "operates in interstate commerce" to have an expansive meaning. 1978 Hearings on S. 1766 Before the Subcomm. on Criminal Law and Procedures of the Judiciary, 95th cong., 2nd Sess. 4 *cited in* Couch, *supra* note 230, at n.62, 1179.

289. 17 U.S.C. §102(b) (1976).
290. 35 U.S.C. §101 (1952).
291. *See* 18 U.S.C. §1341 (1949); 18 U.S.C. §1343 (1956).
292. Cable Franchise Policy and Communications Act, 98th Cong., 2nd Sess., Report 98-934 (1984) Part IV.
293. The Omnibus Crime Control and Safe Streets Act of 1968, Title III, 18 U.S.C. §2510-20.
294. Title VI §605, 47 U.S.C. §605 (*amended* 1968 and 1982).
295. E.g., Title III applies only to "common carrier." The Communications Act applies to radio transmissions.
296. *See* 47 U.S.C. §605.
297. *See* 18 U.S.C. §2510 (4).
298. Further discussion of the policy headings in this paper may be found in D. Marchand, "Privacy, Confidentiality and Computers: National Implications of U.S. Information Policy," *Telecommunications Policy* 3 (September 1979): 192, 197 [hereafter cited as Marchand]. Donald A. Marchand was Associate Director of the Bureau of Governmental Research and Service and Assistant Professor of Government and International Studies at the University of South Carolina, Columbia, at the time this article was published in 1979.
299. *See* P.P.S.C., *Info. Society, supra* note 2, at 15.
300. The Internal Revenue Code is a good example of this. The specificity of the Code is a map for taxpayers to avoid its provisions.
301. *See* Wicklein, supra note 2, at 208.
302. Federalism originated in the "Lockner Era." *See* Lockner v. New York, 198 U.S. 45 (1905). (Court struck down statute regulating hours of work as unnecessary infringement of contract. "Economic liberty" was the justification for suppressing government-imposed legislation that would have protected individuals from working under dangerous conditions.)
303. *See, e.g.* Ferris, Lloyd, and Casey, *supra* note 193, at ch. 14 for a discussion and the history of the struggle among the cable industry, its competitors, and municipal, state, and federal officials for jurisdiction to regulate cable television.
304. *See* M. Epperson, *Legal Aspects of the Information Order: A Forecast,* 13 (May 23, 1980) (unpublished research report). Epperson discusses datahavens in the international context, but his observations could have application to domestic

privacy policy as well.

305. *See generally Privacy Protection Law in the United States,* N.T.I.A. Report Series, Report 82-78, May, 1982, at App. I.

306. *See* Marchand, *supra* note 297, at 199.

307. The cable industry is, in fact, so opposed to externally imposed regulations that during a meeting in February 1983, the National Satellite Cable Association adopted what amounts to a bill of rights for the private cable industry or satellite master antenna television industry. This bill of rights, which was presented to the Senate Communications Subcommittee, demands: a) the right to exist and compete; b) the right to be free from unwarranted state and municipal regulation; c) the right to deal with real estate owners without government interference; d) the right to equal access to the microwave spectrum; e) the right of access to diverse program services. *See* "Bill of Rights," Broadcasting, February 21, 1983, at 10.

308. Communications Act of 1934, c.652, Title IV §605, 47 U.S.C. §605 (*amended* 1968 and 1982).

309. The Omnibus Crime Control and Safe Streets Act, Title III, 18 U.S.C. §§2510-20 (1968).

310. *See* Couch, *supra* note 230, at 1180.

311. *Id.*

312. *See* Nash and Smith *supra* note 2, at 67 to 71 for a description of Prestel.

313. *See* Wicklein, *supra* note 2, at 163.

314. According to a study concluded in 1981, encryption kits have not become widespread because: a) managers do not believe the high cost ($200 to $300 for one chip) is justifiable, and many kits also require auxiliary hardware and software development to become operational; b) managers believe that perpetrators will seek the cheapest and easiest methods to access confidential data (it may be far easier to give $50 to a terminal operator than to tap a line); c) encryption is complicated, and there is no proof that it solves data security problems; d) there are different export restrictions on cryptographic products, and exporting a device requires a license from the Office of Munitions Control at the State Department. *See* J. Ferguson, *Private Locks, Public Keys and State Secrets; New Problems in Guarding Information With Cryptography*, Report, Program on Information Resources Policy, Harvard University, 37-39, (1981).

315. Pamphlets from corporations marketing computer security contain instructions to assemble "eavesdropping kits" with readily available computer parts from electronic supply stores for approximately $500. *Id.,* at 12-13. Minicomputers can be purchased to monitor dial up communications lines. Also, groups have organized to launch massive attacks to crack the Federal Data Encryption Standard. *Id.,* at 13.

316. Different encryption codes are derived for every communication transmitted over the Washington-Moscow "hot line." *Id.,* at 1.

317. *See* Couch, *supra* note 230, at n.77, 1181.

318. *Id.*

319. The term "operator" includes videotex or database operators, and private business and organizations that use computer systems. Government computer operators are regulated by the Privacy Act, FOIA, and certain other regulations

and security procedures that do not apply to computer systems in the private sector. *See, e.g.,* 5 U.S.C. §552a(1974); 5 U.S.C. §552 (1976); 41 C.F.R. §§ 101-36.000 to 36.127 (regulations governing management of automatic data processing equipment used by the federal government).

320. *See generally* Couch, *supra* note 230, at 1181 to 1195.

321. *See* §VB(i) Physical Security Measures and accompanying notes, *supra.* No security system is foolproof and a determined thief may eventually break any security system. However, security systems will prevent most crimes. Documentation of all computer operations and controlling access to the computer system may provide a trail for audit or investigation if suspicious employee activities arise. *See* Couch, *supra* note 230, at n.86, 1182.

322. *See* Couch, *supra* note 313 for some of the reasons management may decide not to implement security codes.

323. *See* Couch, *supra* note 230, at n.86, 1183.

324. *Id.,* at n.88, 1184.

325. *Id.,* at n.90, 1184. It may be difficult to effectively adapt mandatory security measures to individual systems. Enforcement of such regulations would require the expenditure of significant resources by the federal or state governments.

326. *Id.,* at 1184.

327. *Id.,* at 1185.

328. *Id.,* at 1187.

329. *Id.*

330. Personal computer owners and small businesses and partnerships that are not professionally audited would be less affected by the imposition of increased responsibility on auditors. Videotex subscribers and other commercial computer system users would be affected because operators and manufacturers are audited.

331. Accountants must follow standard auditing procedures promulgated by the American Institute of Certified Public Accountants (AICPA). The AICPA is a national professional society of certified public accountants.

AICPA Professional Standard AU §320.01 says the term "internal controls" refers to all the measures adopted within a business to safeguard assets, ensure accuracy and reliability of financial records, and encourage operational efficiency and adherence to prescribed procedures. *Id.,* at §320.09.

332. *Id.,* at §321.24.

333. *Id.,* at §321.27.

334. *Id.,* at §321.31.

335. Couch, *supra* note 230, at 1188.

336. *Id.*

337. Irregular accounting procedures and financial statements that do not conform with GAAP must be disclosed. *See generally* AICPA Professional Standards AU sS 200 to 561. There may be substantial latitude in GAAP, however.

338. *See* Couch, *supra* note 230, at 1193.

339. *Id.,* at 1192.

340. *Id.* The SEC has considered requiring all registered companies to file a certified

report on the business' overall system of internal controls. *See* SEC Release No. 34-15772 (April 30, 1979) *published* in 17 SEC Docket 421 (May 15, 1979).

The SEC withdrew the proposed rule on June 6, 1980, because of the SEC's desire (and probably pressure from the accounting industry) to encourage the private sector to take voluntary steps toward examining internal controls and reporting weaknesses. The Commission said it would monitor voluntary efforts for three years, and might take regulatory action at that time. It recommended that companies that file with the SEC include audited reports on internal control with their other financial statements. *See* SEC Accounting Release No. 278, SEC Accounting Rules (CCH) 3282, 3802-03, 3817 *cited in* Couch, *supra* note 230, at 1190.

341. *See, e.g.,* SEC Accounting Release No. 261, SEC Accounting Rules (CCH) 3265 (accounting changes for oil and gas producers).

342. According to one study, only one out of five detected computer crimes are reported. *See* Couch, *supra* note 230, at 1176. Much publicity has been generated about the computer break-in by the 414 group in Wisconsin and the break-in to ARPANET, however. *See Computer Fraud, supra* note 119, at 6.

APPENDIX A
WARNER AMEX CABLE COMMUNICATIONS CODE OF PRIVACY

1. Warner Amex shall explain to its subscribers the information gathering functions of the cable communications services being provided.
2. Warner Amex shall maintain adequate safeguards to ensure the physical security and confidentiality of any subscriber information.
3. Warner Amex subscriber agreements shall include the following:
   A. Individual subscriber viewing or responses may be retained only where necessary to permit billing or to render a subscriber service. Any such information will be kept strictly confidential unless publication is an inherent part of the service (e.g., announcing a game show prizewinner).
   B. No other individualized information concerning viewing or responses will be developed unless the subscriber has been advised in advance and given adequate opportunity not to participate.
4. Warner Amex may develop bulk (non-individual) data concerning subscriber services for use in developing new services for improving existing services. Warner Amex will not make such bulk data available to third parties—whether affiliated or nonaffiliated with Warner Amex—without first ensuring that the identity of individuals is not ascertainable from the data provided.
5. Warner Amex will refuse requests to make any individual subscriber information available to government agencies in the absence of legal

compulsion, i.e., court order, subpoena. If requests for such information are made, Warner Amex will probptly notify the subscriber
prior to responding if permitted to do so by law.

6. Subscribers may examine and copy any information developed by
Warner Amex pertaining to them at Warner Amex premises upon
reasonable notice and during regular business hours. Copying costs
shall be borne by the subscriber. Warner Amex shall correct such
records upon a reasonable showing by the subscriber that information contained therein is accurate.

7. Any individual subscriber information will be retained for only as
long as is reasonably necessary, e.g., to verify billings.

8. Subscriber mailing lists shall not be made available to third parties—
whether affiliated or nonaffiliated with Warner Amex— without first
providing subscribers with the opportunity to have their names
removed from such lists. Warner Amex shall comply with applicable
federal, state, and local laws respecting subscriber privacy and shall
adhere to applicable industry codes of conduct which promote or
enhance subscriber privacy.

9. Third parties who participate in providing services to Warner Amex
subscribers shall be required to adhere to the Company's Code of
Privacy and all Warner Amex arrangements regarding such services
shall specifically incorporate this Code of Privacy by reference.

10. Warner Amex shall continously review and update its Code of
Privacy to keep current with technological changes and new applications.

APPENDIX B
DEFINITIONS

As used in this chapter,

1. *Access* is to approach, instruct, communicate with, store data in,
retrieve data from, intercept from, or otherwise make use of any
resources of a computer, computer system, or computer network.

2. *Aggregation* is the unauthorized collection of information that may or
may not be individually significant or identifiable to create large
banks of confidential information or "psychographic profiles" of
individuals and/or households.

3. *Compression* is the compacting of information for retention and
access into a microcomputer chip.

4. *Computer* is an electronic device or communications facility that

performs logical, arithmetic, and memory functions, and includes all input, output, processing, and software connected or related to such devices and facilities.

5. *Computer software* is a series of instructions or statements, in human- or machine-readable form, that controls, directs, or otherwise influences the functioning of a computer, computer system, or computer network.

6. *Computer system* is a set of related, connected, or unconnected computer equipment; devices that employ standard data links, software, and computer terminals (rather than converted television sets). Services are provided by software programs that access different collections of data.

7. *Database* is any data, or other information compiled, classified, processed, transmitted, received, retrieved, originated, switched, stored, manifested, measured, detected, recorded, reproduced, handled, or utilized by a computer, computer system, computer network, or computer software.

8. *Hybrid system* is any interactive system that combines more than one form of interactive technology, including, but not limited to, components of interactive cable systems, videotex systems, and computer systems; radio, broadcast, and microwave transmissions; and any service qualifying as common carrier under 47 U.S.C. subchapter II.

9. *Interactive cable system* is a cable television system that transmits signals from a central operator to users' converted television sets and consoles and from users' sets back to a central operator via cable wire. Cable operators generally employ a computer (or a group of computers) to collect billing information, to poll subscribers for marketing information and general statistics, and to monitor system integrity.

10. *Hardware* is the physical components and all associated and related components of a computer system, videotex system, interactive cable system, or hybrid communications system.

11. *Interactive technology* is any interactive cable system, videotex system, computer, computer system, or hybrid system that transmits signals "downstream" from a central computer to a user's terminal or console, and "upstream" from a user's facility to a central processor or operator.

12. *Intrusion* is repeated or continuous monitoring or surveillance of a user's terminal for purposes other than billing or checking system integrity.

13. *Misuse of data* is use of data collected about an individual for reasons other than those authorized and understood by the subject. Misuse

includes, but is not limited to, unauthorized transfer, disclosure, commercial sale, and failure to delete data that is or has become inaccurate.

14. *Network* is two or more computers or communications facilities that are interconnected.

15. *One way* information technology is computer, telephone, cable, or hybrid information communications systems that transmit information in only one direction from a center operator to a user's terminal.

16. *Piracy* is knowingly and willfully, directly or indirectly, without proper authorization, accessing, causing to be accessed, or attempting to access any computer, computer system, computer network, or communications facility for the purpose of obtaining money, property, or services for oneself or for another.

17. *Property* includes, but is not limited to, information, computer programs, and any proprietary, personal, or other information of value to the data subject; programs, data, services, and tangible and intangible items of value to a systems operator.

18. *Services* includes, but is not limited to, computer time, data programming, storage functions, banking, shopping, publications, broadcast and textual information, messages, programming, and monitoring provided by computers, videotex, interactive cable, or hybrid communications services.

19. *Videotex* is any interactive technology usually transmitting information and services over common carrier or cable line, which acts by retrieval of a specific information frame, selected and transmitted over a link such as a telephone wire. Sometimes the term *videotex* includes *teletext*, which is a system transmitting all available frames over a broadband channel, and subsequent selection, or frame-grabbing at the terminal. In contrast to typical computer systems, the display unit may be a conventional television set hooked up to a microprocessor-driven terminal adopter. Services available on videotex are transmitted to users by a central operator.

Chapter 8

THE POLITICAL IMPLICATIONS OF VIDEOCASSETTE RECORDING

Gladys D. Ganley
Oswald H. Ganley

INTRODUCTION*

By 1985, more than 60 million videocassette recorders (VCRs) had been distributed globally in the decade since 1976, when they began to be used to any extent by private individuals. This number was expected to climb to 100 million by 1986, and all indications are that it will go on growing.[1] The world market in legally sold videocassettes is more than $2.5 billion annually, and there is an illegal market of pirated and smuggled cassettes that matches or more probably exceeds this figure.

VCRs, blank tapes, prerecorded videocassette films, and TV programming are all being snapped up by people globally. Both VCRs and cassettes are now simple to use. It is easy for an amateur to record material off the air, to edit or alter it, or to produce videotapes using blank cassettes and a home camera. (Both VCR and camera are often rentable.)

Videocassette programming can presently be easily and rapidly duplicated to share with others. Whatever the programming, it can be watched in privacy, wherever a television set is available. It is not necessary to have a broadcast signal to use a VCR. VCRs and videocassettes therefore often

---

*This is a substantially abridged adaptation from Gladys D. and Oswald S. Ganley, *The Political Implications of the Global Spread of Videocassette Recorders and Videocassette Programming* (Cambridge, MA: Program on Information Resources Policy, 1985).

substitute for broadcast television. Since many sources have indicated that video impresses people much more than audio or printed material, this access makes for a possibly volatile political situation.

For several reasons, large numbers of VCRs have always been smuggled: to obtain them cheaper; to avoid taxes, registration and licensing; and to bring them into countries such as Iran, most major communist countries, and many other nations, where they are prohibited or heavily restricted. Although countries may also wish to keep out VCRs to control information, restrictions are, with some regularity, made initially on an economic basis.

Little programming for VCRs existed when they first became available. Because this medium offered the new opportunity to privately watch pornography, dealers in pirated and smuggled "blue" videocassettes quickly became active. But this underground porno route was almost immediately found also to be ideal for circumventing long waits for release and other obstacles to programming access (not the least of them copyright owner- ship). Soon, both illegal and legal cassettes with unlimited sorts of content were flooding across the world's borders. Rental dealerships mushroomed globally, offering programming for a fraction of the cost of movies, along with massive supplies of blank videocassettes.

This global blitz by VCRs and videocassettes is permitting the wholesale circumvention of government censorship of the content of film and televi- sion programming. This is no small thing, since in most of the world, media content, especially that of film, radio, and television, is strictly controlled by governments. From antiquity onward, government control of information has been the rule, not the exception. In modern times, even in democra- cies, censorship of the mass media has been only slowly and partially lifted. Says the *World Press Review:*

> Each year the International Press Institute publishes its annual World Press Freedom Review and each year the situation continues to grow worse.

> The 1983 IPI survey shows that today only a small part of the globe respects free speech. The rest of the world is "gagged." [2]

For information controls to have endured throughout the centuries and to still be in place, governments must consider that their stakes in main- taining them surpass most concerns. Examples have been surfacing that make it obvious that not all uses of VCRs and videocassettes are politically innocuous. This study was therefore undertaken to determine the political stakes of various world governments in maintaining or regaining rapidly eroding national controls over film and TV programming content. Some questions addressed were:

- What is the potential for VCRs and programming to be used for political subversion or as propa ganda tools? How much of this is already happening?
- To what extent are VCRs and videocassettes destabilizing? To what extent are they democratizing?
- Are VCRs and videocassettes different in any significant way from older, often cheaper forms of communications?
- Are governments attempting to stem this VCR and videocassette flow across their borders?
- What controls are being applied, and what is the degree of their effectiveness? If controls are not being effectively applied, then why not? What are other, perhaps higher, government priorities?

VCRs and videocassettes represent the fulfillment of some of the world's wildest fantasies. They symbolize the usurpation of control by private individuals over a mass source of information, a control that many governments consider their domain. VCRs and videocassettes offer individuals in lesser developed nations some control over a new technology. They permit easy production and dissemination of materials to wide audiences without the necessity for an official institution. Perhaps the wildest fantasy of all, VCRs and videocassettes symbolize control over Hollywood and other such dream empires. For they are breaking the monopolies on distribution long held by a few film production centers and are broadening the kinds of global materials available. That the machine making it all possible is not an American machine, nor for the most part a European machine, but is a Japanese machine, may represent another potent symbol of shift in political power.

By routinely ignoring formal bans on VCRs and videocassette programming, users in restrictive countries are striking at governmental legitimacy. *Radio Free Europe Research* says of the "major storm" of VCRs and videocassette programming now reaching the Soviet bloc countries:

> the proliferation of video recording and playback equipment and of illegally produced and procured programs have been presenting a direct challenge not only to their monopoly of power over the media but also to the strictly regulated legal order of their states.[3]

Upon seeing a videotaped movie for the first time, the elderly uncle of a Soviet journalist may have said it all by exclaiming, "'What a blow to the Bolsheviks!'"[4]

The political use of VCRs and videocassettes is still a breaking story and there must of necessity be holes and inconsistencies in the presented data.

But the new trails being broken through the forest of governmental and other controls on global information access are already becoming clearly discernible.

THE ROLE OF THE BLACK MARKET IN VCR PENETRATION

In many countries around the world, smuggling is just one arm of a fully mature black market which includes tax evasion, illegal speculation, black currency financing, and a host of other things which form an economy parallel to the official one.

In the 1940s, Guenter Reimann described black market development in countries with strictly controlled economies.[5] Black markets, he said, develop in three stages: first, they are prohibited by the state; second, they are tolerated by the state; and third, they become indispensible to the state and thus come to be "authorized" or "legalized." During short term economic difficulties in unrestricted economies, black markets usually remain within the first or second stages. But they mature to the third stage in strictly controlled economies where shortages become permanent and relief for citizens is not to be had otherwise.

The Soviet Union and the countries of Eastern Europe all have highly advanced black markets. VCRs are among the most wanted black market items. An interesting feature of the black market in Eastern Europe and the Soviet Union is the existence of so called "bursas." This name for the stock exchange, says the *Wall Street Journal*, "has come to mean secret trading in free ideas: prohibited or officially unobtainable books, magazines, records, and tape recordings ."[6] They exist in all the big cities of the Soviet Union and Eastern Europe:

> Just about every self-respecting big city east of the Berlin Wall has a bursa. To avoid police confiscation of goods, the bursas in the U.S.S.R. have no merchandise — only book titles, lists, traders' addresses and prices.[7]

In China, many peasants now have expendable income to buy luxuries like televisions and an occasional VCR. Although China claims to have controlled some of this private smuggling, it is suffering from increased smuggling by numbers of officially sanctioned organizations. During the first half of 1985, more than 1000 such instances were reported, 3.7 times more than in 1984.[8] This contraband was specifically said to include television sets and videotape recorders, as well as motor vehicles, motorcycles, and other consumer durables.[9] Noting that this was "an interesting reminder of the large hidden savings held by Chinese households" and that Hainan officials "pocketed $30m from black marketeers," *The Economist* said "the booty included 89,000 motor vehicles, 2.9 television sets and 252,000 video-recorders."[10] *Time* said that, in August 1985,

> *People's Daily* reported that Xiang Dong, an official in Yunnan province, had used state funds to buy pornographic videotapes. At the same time, China's news agency, Xinhua, revealed that some Hainan officials had jointly embezzled about $1.5 billion by importing large quantities of cars, TV sets, video recorders and motorcycles and reselling them at higher prices at government expense.[11]

Drug money has become a source of expendable income used to buy such luxuries as TVs and VCRs in many countries. Cocaine brings Bolivia $1.6 billion annually, three times the income from tin, Bolivia's biggest legal export item.

The downtown Mexico City black market center, Tepito, is described as "a quarter-mile stretch of Tenochitlan Street, crammed sidewalk to sidewalk with videotape recorders, microwave ovens, home computers, pirated videocassettes ."[12]

The quality, prices, and availability in Tepito are said to be better than for products made by the highly protected Mexican electronics firms. To get the goods

> some vendors . . . travel to the U.S. border by car or truck, or meet airplanes at clandestine landing strips . . . . And despite crackdowns, much of the merchandise comes by way of the Mexico City air port. One vendor claims he has witnessed customs agents there using calculators to count their "tips" while smugglers loaded up a truckload of color-television sets.[13]

Iran has a huge black market on which VCRs were sold in 1982 for the equivalent of $10,000.[14] Early on, the Khomeini government banned VCRs and many other luxuries for economic reasons.[15] But smuggling and black marketeering—which hindered President Carter's efforts at a trade boycott during the hostage crisis—have rendered these imports bans quite ineffective. By January 1985, the Iranian economy had become so precarious that all imports with the exception of food and arms were "unofficially halted,"[16] but it remains to be seen whether this will work any better than bans imposed previously.

In short, the world's black markets, where everything is illegal, provide the perfect conduit for VCRs to enter countries secretly and just as secretly to be transferred between private parties.

VIDEOCASSETTE DISTRIBUTION, INCLUDING THE ROLE OF ORGANIZED CRIME

The introduction of videocassettes has followed an almost uncanny pattern of uniformity worldwide. In the very beginning, a few cassettes were introduced by individual travelers, migrants, privileged elites, tourists, petty smugglers, and others. Clubs were soon formed by groups of a few people for cassette swapping and to get a little money up front to buy more titles. In most countries, these clubs were overtaken very quickly by hordes of video outlets which dealt in illegal as well as legal tapes and themselves often turned out copy after copy. The clubs then either went out of business or else converted themselves to the same types of activities. Certain aspects of this uniformity can be seen even in the most restricted countries.

There were brief efforts globally to sell videocassettes, but in most cases this proved to be too costly for patrons. Within just months, rental became the rule, giving mass distribution to all comers. Price cutting ensued, so that video rentals dropped from a beginning price of the equivalent generally of about $5 to about $1 or even as low as 50 cents for overnight, or a weekend.

The uniformity and efficiency of this global distribution is all the more remarkable, since in the beginning the big Hollywood movie types refused to distribute programming. Those who got in on the ground floor were some small independent companies and the pirates.* Some of this may be credited to widescale global communications—everybody just followed everybody else's example. But it also seems logical to conjecture that, with a suddenly popular product, and in the absence of some large legal group in control, some or several well-organized illegal groups got their hands on the ropes of videocassette distribution very early.

Everything that can be said for the penetration of VCR hardware is true—in spades—for videocassette programming. Wherever VCRs go, videocassettes follow. Videocassettes of every sort have swiftly penetrated globally, they are often introduced by migrants and other travelers, and they avail themselves of the world's black markets for distribution. They have, in addition, the attributes of being small enough to be easily smuggled, of being readily reproducible either before or after smuggling, and of being, more often than not, illegally pirated.

Through a change in labeling, or a substitution of a small portion of the tape beginning, "undesirable" material can easily pass a customs system as something innocuous. Political tapes went into the Philippines under the

---

*The word *pirate* rather indiscriminately applied both to the person or group illegally reproducing and distributing cassettes in violation of copyright and to those who actually smuggle cassettes across borders. *Pirated* should be reserved for cassettes in copyright violation.

guise of pornography,[17] and porno pours into Canada from the U.S. labeled as comedy and other materials. Canada's Revenue Minister has said that "clever methods to disguise the cassettes are used to slip them by inspectors" and that "foreign exporters often change the film titles to make them seem harmless and make it next to impossible to catch at the border."[18] In Pakistan, video outlets are said to "acquire – invariably pirated – master versions of new Indian movies released in Bombay just two or three days earlier with remarkable speed, via the smugglers' Dubai connection."[19]

Indian movies have been banned in Pakistan since 1956. In Turkey"theoretically . . . video cassettes must . . . pass through the censor to enter the country. But the cassettes are so small, so easy to declare untaped and so abundant that effective official control has so far proven impossible."[20]

Like a number of countries which are updating their legislation to take videocassettes into account, Turkey put through a copyright law, which became effective in November 1983, calling for prison terms of as much as 3 years for copyright violations. All video cassettes must have special markings to show that the distributor has the copyright.[21] However, as one Turkish official put it, "'Turks are expert at getting around official regulations. As long as there is a high demand and good profits to be made, tapes will keep coming, with or without copyright.'"[22]

In Russia, the Black Sea agricultural area of Krasnodarsky krai is a big area not only for health spas but also for smuggling. In Novorossiysk, south of Krasnodar

> smuggling is "a big problem" in the seaport used by thousands of sailors from all corners of the world . . . . more than 25 percent of those dealing in illegal goods were [said to be] foreigners. A large amount of the traffic involves scarce or un- available Western goods such as blue jeans, T-shirts, records, tapes and video tapes that command high prices on the black market.[23]

In addition to smuggled tapes, Tallinn, in Estonia, where Finnish television can be received, has become the unofficial video recording headquarters of the USSR. Here

> the best of Finnish (which can also mean American, British, Italian, German, or Brazilian) television is recorded in apartments where reception is best. Sometimes Russian-language voice-overs are added. The cassettes are distributed to Moscow, Leningrad, and other cities with no fear of border controls for those who carry them on Aeroflot planes.[24]

Such videotapes include American political debates and news of other political events, including those taking place inside Russia.

Reports of the availability of videocassettes in Russia vary. In many ways, the video business remains a primitive and costly one compared with the business in the West. The going rate for having a movie dubbed into Russian is about $40 at recent exchange rates.[25] Dubbing is nevertheless replacing the person hired for the occasion to translate while the movie is going on. Blank tapes are selling for the equivalent of $60 to $70, and western movies for the equivalent of $250 to $320 on the Soviet black market.[26]

But, despite the expense, videocassettes are spreading. There have been reports that blackmarket copies of films are available 2 weeks after their opening in the United States.[27] Illegal films are sufficiently disturbing to the Soviet government that it has opened its own videocassette rental outlets for approved films. Most of the cassettes are of films made in the Soviet Union. The cost to rent these approved cassettes is two or three rubles, or about $3.00 to $4.50.

In the new town part of Warsaw in 1984, at least one legal private dealer was quietly but openly renting a roomful of videocassettes, along with his record and music business. His tapes, all pirated, were obtained from "friends" in West Berlin and London, and probably the United States. This dealer, who stocked popular cassettes such as "Caligula" and "Last Tango in Paris," etc., was very proud to have obtained a cassette of "The Day After" before it was shown on British television. He claimed to be cutting into the Warsaw cinema business by distributing films such as "Tootsie" months before the theaters could get them. To prevent others from pirating his pirated tapes, he made a point of retaping them to the edge of fuzziness before rental. He handled the hard currency problem by paying zlotys for the support of the relatives in Poland of the Westerners who provided the cassettes to him. Cassettes rented for the equivalent of $6 or $7 a night. Variations in broadcast standards must be overcome by some commercial means, but this dealer seemed to have mastered the problem. To get past the language barrier in Poland, as was done in Russia, one person will often read all the parts in Polish. This is often put on an audiotape, to be played back with the videocassette.[28]

South of the United States, video piracy is simple because U.S. satellite signals are easily picked up in the Caribbean, Central America, and Northern South America. The feature films on Ted Turner's satellite television are pirated for cable and play 24 hours a day in Panama.* Videocassette piracy is rampant in Panama, with one duplication plant keeping 100 copying machines continuously running. Panama is said to export from

---

*Blank tapes, also globally smuggled, make it easy to record intercepted satellite signals. For instance, when South Africa was denied both participation in the 1984 Los Angeles Olympics and a live transmission, signals were intercepted illegally to watch Zola Budd run. Videocassettes of the event, probably from outside and from illegal signal interception, were also quickly supplied to rental customers.

20,000 to 30,000 pirated videocassettes a month to Latin American countries, "especially to Colombia, Ecuador, and Mexico."[29]

Prerecorded tapes are often passed off as blanks. In fall 1984, the International Federation of Phonogram and Videogram Producers (IFPI) announced the seizure of 190,000 pirated videocassettes in Benin, Africa, which were on their way from Singapore to Benin's neighbor, Nigeria.[30] They had been declared as blank tapes, not only to conceal their pirated nature, but to escape the much higher prerecorded cassette customs duty. They were hardly blank, however, and included tapes by Michael Jackson, Bob Marley, Dolly Parton, Marvin Gaye, Boney M, and ABBA.*

Lest it seem that all videocassettes are pirated, or all uses illegal, it should be stressed that there is, of course, a giant and rapidly growing legitimate videocassette market. But, while publicity usually focuses on economic factors, the main political point is that this software is frequently not susceptible even to the brakes applied by the usual market forces. Whatever type of video programming is wanted by individuals, wherever in the world it is wanted, it is either readily available or usually fairly easily obtainable—regardless of a government's wishes—under the present distribution system.

WHAT PEOPLE ARE WATCHING AROUND THE WORLD

People the world over have welcomed VCRs and cassettes in every country we have considered. Little or no thought as to whether they are legal appears to have been given, except for devising ways to get around governmental restrictions. What people are watching, in general, is whatever amuses or informs them. This includes comedies, adventure, action films, documentaries, all sorts of feature films and television programs, and kiddie fare, as well as "video nasties" and pornography.It also includes material that is subtly or not so subtly political.[31]

First-run American films and television programming are among the "best sellers." All Western films and programming, of whatever vintage, are popular. Ex-British colonials often prefer British films and programming. English-language films in general are highly sought after, since this is the language most widely comprehended. French films and programming are favored in all the French-speaking countries. The U.S. is gaining access to quite a lot of foreign films via videocassette. In mid-1984, for example, Video Movies magazine listed 69 French language films available in the U.S.

---

*IFPI is the London-based organization that acts as watchdog for the international record business, linking music and videotape businesses in 68 countries.

on video,[32] and in early 1986, in Harvard Square, Cambridge, for instance, one store was offering about 80 foreign films in its catalog of just under 1000 selections.[33] Italian and German and other European films are watched widely. Hong Kong films have a big audience beyond Chinese-speaking populations. Videocassettes have increased the access to what people prefer to watch anyway, and in most cases have greatly increased the variety.

Egypt, as the "cultural capital" of the Arab world, is the source of many films and dramas which circulate in the Middle East. Egypt make as much on videocassette rights as it does on movies. Indeed, because"in the Arab gulf and Saudi Arabia, there are no public theaters . . . videocassettes are the main method of distribution."[34] Egyptian and other Middle Eastern plays are often very political, using satirical comedy to criticize the government and society. The *Index on Censorship* reports:

> Every popular play is . . . recorded on video tapes, and many on [audio] cassettes. Villagers in Upper Egypt, Bedouins in Saudi Arabia or Dubai, fishermen in Iraq, all see Egyptian, Syrian, and Kuwaiti popular plays without having to know what a theatre looks like.[35]

In Bangladesh: "illegal VTRs of Indian movies, which are not allowed . . . and uncensored Western films some of which may be pornographic by even Western standards, are freely available."[36]

The movie "Gandhi" has not been permitted in Pakistan movie houses because it is felt that the role of Mohammed Ali Jinnah, Pakistan's founder, was badly slighted in favor of Gandhi. The film is, however, illegally available on videocassette, and private showings in homes are common.[37] Turkey has also banned "Gandhi," but, in early 1984, "Gandhi" was circulating in Turkey on videocassette, along with "Return of The Jedi," "E.T.," "Sophie's Choice," and "The Day After." It is said that these videos and much off-the-air European television programming are obtained from London, Paris, and Brussels-based pirates, and then "Turks living or traveling abroad carry them to their homeland."[38] When the United States Information Agency (USIA) offered a private screening of "The Day After" as a special treat for a selected group in Turkey, most of the guests had already seen it.

The ineffectiveness of Ayatollah Khomeini's ban on VCRs and cassettes can be seen in the following quotations:

> VCRs and cassettes are banned in Iran, but thousands have been smuggled in by wealthy Iranians.[39]

> In . . . Iran, not even the hate-America policy of current political leaders has dampened the demand for Hollywood products . . . although U.S. movies

have virtually disappeared from Iran's movie houses, American films such as "E.T." are widely available for home viewing in videocassettes.[40]

Everybody seems to have a video-recorder, and copies of American video-cassettes are easily avail able. This correspondent was the only guest at a party not to have seen Michael Jackson's *Thriller* video.[41]

Reports on what is being watched in the USSR have surfaced in many sources. Russians say that western videotapes are widely circulated in Moscow and there are underground libraries which hire out uncensored films. These tapes are often shown in private apartments by invitation to people who pay 5 or more rubles each for the privilege of seeing them. *U.S. News and World Report* says:

On the Moscow black market, a Jane Fonda workout tape sells for $372, and an original tape of an American Western movie is priced at $250 to $300. Asian entrepreneurs, especially Hong Kong, are dubbing into Russian such tapes as those of Bruce Lee karate films for the incipient Soviet market.[42]

By 1985, the Soviet black market best sellers included "Rambo," "Amadeus," and Poland's "Man of Iron," the latter a film "that sympathetically chronicles labor unrest in Gdansk, the birthplace of the Solidarity labor union movement."[43] The Soviets are also paid to enjoy movies like "April in Paris" or "Christmas in Bavaria" and James Bond films.

Group showings of videos in homes are commonplace in many countries, including the U.S. In Israel, group viewing is said to be reminiscent of the early days of television. In Egypt, groups often meet in homes, sharing expenses for food and video rental. This also happens regularly in India. In Sri Lanka, videos are usually watched by families as a whole, or with friends and neighbors, but "it is not unusual to find a fee being charged." Chinese authorities have been attempting to curb unauthorized video use. In 1975, "20,000 semi-public halls that charged entrance fees to video viewers have been closed down by CITV [China International Television Corporation]." Although communal showings were permissable, "Notices will be placed at the beginning of all imported tapes calling on audiences to report any entrance charges to the authorities."[44]

Videocassettes have become very mobile. France has put video on one coach of the main East/West Paris subway line.[45] The London to Glasgow Express train got a video viewing coach in November 1984, with "Tootsie" and "Police Academy" as the first showings.[46] Indians choose buses depending on what videocassette is being shown.[47] And in Turkey, during a price war between transit lines, intercity buses boosted ridership by showing videocassette films. These were discontinued because there were protests from the film industry and also because "passengers complained about bus drivers watching the films."[48]

VCRs are used the world over for time shifting and for taping off-the-air programming. Video cameras are widely employed to record family events like weddings. However, it is said for Jamaica that

> an increasing number of residents and organisations are now acquiring 1/2-inch cameras for use with the VHS recorders, and are making their own programmes for training, entertainment, guidance, and counselling. This opens new avenues for professional film-makers and suggests that at last the expensive communications systems of the elite are beginning to reach the masses who most need education, information and a pride in their own heritage.[49]

This would seem to go well beyond the institutional and educational uses that are, of course, being made of VCRs and cassettes in many countries, to a variety of uses by individuals.

VARIETIES OF GLOBAL POLITICAL ACTS INVOLVING VCRS

Quite a wide variety of overt political uses have been made of VCRs and videocassettes, both by citizens and by governments. While, of course, closely related to acts perpetrated through film, television, radio and print technology, and following in the footsteps of audiocassettes, these VCR-related acts give a sense of new and expanded political opportunities. Many of the acts work in tandem with or in support of other media. The ingenuity of uses and of some combinations of uses points toward an increase in such activities in the future.

Video to Circumvent Controlled Media in Times of Political Crisis

Nora Quebral, chairman of the Department of Development Communication at the University of the Philippines at Los Baños, said in a 1984 speech in Berlin:

> In the weeks after the death of Benigno Aquino, the political figure who was gunned down at the Manila International Airport upon arrival in his home country, one of the hottest items in the video rental shops in the university town where I live was a spliced-up tape of events at the airport and at the funeral which were only very sparingly reported in the mass media at that time. And so I suppose the videocassette recorder could be potentially used

to foment revolution . . . in politically unstable countries, just as audio cassettes are said to have helped bring down the last Shah of Iran.[50]

It was reported that a Japanese documentary on the assassination was smuggled into the Philippines on a cassette labeled "Playboy Lovers."[51]

This videocassette was said to be just one of many smuggled in from the U.S. and Japan in the early days after the assassination and copied and re-copied on home videocassette recorders for distribution. The cassettes were mainly made up of sections of American and Japanese network newscasts or special treatments by these broadcasters of the subject. Some of the cassettes were edited to make fairly coherent "documentaries":

> One tape producer pieced together excerpts from broadcasts by four net-works, two in Japan and two in the United States, focusing on the unexplained aspects of the Aquino killing.

> Another producer combined sequences from a documentary made by Nihon Hoso Kyokai, the Japanese Government-supported broadcasting group, and the privately operated Japanese News Network, and had a Japanese-speaking friend translate the commentaries into English. With this material he turned out an English script that can be read along with the action on the screen, and he made multiple copies for distribution.[52]

Use of Videocassettes by Salvadoran Guerrillas

In August 1984, a *New York Times* article began:

> Ayatollah Ruhollah Khomeini inspired his followers on tape cassettes. The Salvadoran guerrillas now promote their cause on Betamax . . . .

> Combining the electronic revolution with political revolution, the Salvadoran leftwing guerrilla coalition, the Farabundo Marti Front for National Liberation, has brought its cause into the plazas of El Salvador with the aid of video cassettes.[53]

The article describes the guerrillas as operating three camera teams that supply an eight-videocassette recorder "network" with propagandistic programming for local uses and make videocassettes available in the U.S. and elsewhere. These

> propaganda films give a highly partial look at the war in El Salvador. It is a war where the guerrillas never suffer battlefield defeats, where elections and political parties do not exist, and where economic chaos caused by guerrilla action is edited out.[54]

Videos of guerrilla "victories" were shown to peasants in village plazas, often with the aid of truck battery power. Training videos were also made for fighters, showing them how to erect camouflage, how to perpetrate ambushes and silent infiltration, how to resist interrogation, and how to operate unfamiliar captured weapons. To counter poor relationships with the Catholic church and religious peasants, the *Times* says, the guerrillas also made a video that "depicts scenes of armed guerrillas crossing themselves in front of a cross and taking communion from a Catholic priest."[55] The *Times* reported that video footage was being sold to CBS and various European TV networks. To gain a wider audience and influence American public opinion, the group had a video, "Time of Daring," premiered by Joseph Papp's 1984 Festival Latino en Nueva York. These guerrilla photographic activities began about 1980, and were "inspired largely by a similar film project the Sandinista guerrillas in Nicaragua started a few weeks before the war there ended."[56] Nicaraguans and Cubans are said to have given advice on setting up the Salvadoran activity.

Off-The-Air "How To" for Would-Be Assassins

John Hinkley was reportedly inspired to shoot President Reagan by the fictional movie "Taxi Driver." A group of junior Pakistani Army officers apparently sought such inspiration from reality. In an aborted 1984 coup, a videotape of an American television network's live coverage of the 1980 assassination of Egyptian leader Anwar Sadat was reportedly found at the home of a key member of the junior officers' group.[57]

The coup attempt put heavy strains on Indian–Pakistani relations, since it involved the Indian Embassy's number three man, Counselor Arun Prashad.

The Use of Videocassettes by Middle Eastern Terrorists

Tremendous television coverage was given to the activities of Shiite terrorists who hijacked TWA Flight 847 in summer 1985. In addition to press conferences which the terrorists held for the media with "their" American hostages, the terrorists also made and released to the news media their own videocassette productions. The terrorists used videotapes, along with "lectures and late-night debates" to try to indoctrinate the hostages.[58]

Within a few days after the release of the American hostages in Beirut, two car bomb attacks in Southern Lebanon killed 17 people. A Syrian-backed group claimed credit. Before embarking upon their missions, the alleged suicide drivers, a Druse woman, Ibtissam Harb, and a Syrian-born man, Khaled Azrak, made videocassettes, testifying to their devotion to the

terrorist cause and saying why they were dying for it. The videocassettes were made available by the National Syrian Socialist Party, a part of the Lebanese National Resistance Front.[59] Less than a week later, a third car, carrying a Red Cross flag, blew up at an Israeli checkpoint in Southern Lebanon, killing 10 people. The Lebanese radio proclaimed the terrorist operation "'another heroic operation by Lebanese resistance fighters'" and

> Lebanese television broadcast a prerecorded video taped message from a man who identified himself as the suicide bomber and said he was acting on behalf of a pro-Syrian group called the Baath Party Organization of Lebanon.[60]

The videocassettes were apparently an attempt to personalize the bombers and make the bombings appear like the rational acts of clean-cut people. One must take on faith, of course, that the persons shown in the videocassettes were the actual suicide drivers.

Old Vitriol in New Bottles

In the early 1980s, Eugene Terre Blanche, a 37-year old farmer and former policeman, began spreading his antisemitic message by videocassette throughout the Transvaal. Terre Blanche headed the Afrikaner Resistance Movement, which "holds that all political parties must be abolished if South Africa is to be saved as a white, Christian nation from the forces of the Antichrist."[61] A "theatrical presence on the podium," Terre Blanche had, by 1981, sold 30,000 copies of his speeches on audiocassettes. He took to videocassettes so as to reach many more people through showings at small private house meetings than he ever could meet with personally.

David Calvert Smith of the U.S. is said to be distributing copies of anti-Jewish hate films made in the heyday of Nazi Propaganda Minister Joseph Goebbels to ultra-right-wing groups in this country.[62] He is also said to be guilty of piracy. His activities came to light when Transit Films of Munich, distributor of 1926–1945 films for the Friedrich Wilhelm Murnau Stiftung (Foundation), sought to keep Smith from violating the Foundation's copyright. Smith distributes through companies with names like Kulturfilm-werks Corp., Condor Films Inc., German Film Bureau International, Edu-cational Services Administration, etc. Smith evidently obtained the prints from private collectors, some of whom may have brought them back as war booty from World War II.[63]

Videocassettes as Electronic News Releases and Other Tools to Assist in Lobbying

The newest political game in town is to have videotapes prepared which will get you TV coverage. These "electronic news releases" are delivered by mail or by satellite to local television stations and the Cable News Network.[64] A growing number of public relations firms are being paid to prepare what look like legitimate news items, but are really lobbying efforts for some specific paying client. Gray & Company of Washington D.C. came under fire from the Justice Department in spring 1985 when it prepared and distributed such materials for foreign clients without registering as a foreign agent. Prior to the meeting of President Reagan and Japanese Prime Minister Nakasone in early 1985, Gray distributed "news" reports showing U.S. produce being shipped to Japan and featuring the U.S. Ambassador to Japan, Mike Mansfield, saying that "'Japanese markets aren't as closed as we might think.'"[65] This "news item" was, however, paid for by the government of Japan, and was directed ultimately — via local U.S. television viewers — at the U.S. Congress.

These videotape packages may be sent to local TV stations by mail, or by way of communications satellites, and a package "typically includes pieces that can be run immediately as well as interviews and background shots that can be combined with a news staff's own reporting."[66] Devices used to make the pieces look like "news" rather than public relations are:

- Hiring TV personages with name recognition to do them.
- Having professional journalists using pseudonymns do them.
- Blurring the "reporter's" identity and whereabouts, or keeping the "reporter's" lines as a voice-over off camera.
- Leaving labels off the tapes so each station can insert its own typeface to make it look like its own reporting.
- Having a dark blonde "reporter" do the interview with back to camera. (" 'Every station has a reporter with dark blonde hair' " says one article.)[67]

The flooding of local TV stations with videocassettes — made easy by cheap satellite communications — is also taken advantage of by the U.S. Congress. In 1983, the Bonneville Satellite Corporation installed transmission facilities "on the edge of Capital Hill" to transmit messages. *The Washington Journalism Review* says:

> Every day Congress is in session, growing numbers of senators and representatives routinely offer news clips of their activities via satellite to stations in their home states, with the taxpayer picking up most of the tab. Advances in satellite communications in the past few years have made it simple and economical for the average member of Congress to bypass Washington reporters and beam his message to a local and often more accommodating press corps. The footage often appears on local TV newscasts with no

explanation to viewers that it was shot for and supplied by the senator or congressman it features.[68]

There are those who say that the electronic press release is no different from the ordinary print release, but the detractors of electronic news releases say the power of the picture and the deliberate tailoring to look like "real news" render these videocassettes the bearers of more powerful political messages.

Video in Lieu of Visa

Three interesting cases of the use of videocassettes when visas had been denied were discovered during the study. The first involved South African Bishop Desmond Tutu, who was denied exit from that country; the second involved United States AFL-CIO President, Lane Kirkland, who was denied entry into Poland; and the third involved two Cuban officials who were not permitted to enter the United States.

In August 1981, South African Anglican Bishop Desmond Tutu was scheduled to address the biennial meeting of the Disciples of Christ in Anaheim, California. But the South African government lifted his passport. Unable to come himself to Anaheim, Bishop Tutu instead sent a videotape to supplement the empty chair reserved for him. In the video, he twice said the same thing that provoked the government to prohibit him from leaving. That is, that "the South African government's attempt to put blocks in segregated 'homelands' is the worst travesty since Naziism."[69]

About a month after Bishop Tutu was denied exit to the United States, and 3 months before Solidarity was crushed, Lane Kirkland, president of the AFL-CIO, and other U.S. labor officials were denied visas to enter Poland. Kirkland had been invited to address the meeting of the Solidarity Congress at Gdansk. Kirkland, pledging continuing support for the Polish union, sent along a videotape of his planned speech.[70]

Also in September 1981, two Cuban officials, Alberto Betancourt Roa of the Ministry of Foreign Trade, and Marcelo Fernandez Font, advisor to the Cuban Central Planning Board, were denied visas by the U.S. State Department. However, the officials circumvented the visa denials by providing videotaped remarks to a seminar, sponsored by two local universities and the Center for Cuban Studies in New York, a private research group.[71] The officials, in their video, painted a picture of a thriving Cuban economy.

Further Uses of Videotapes by Governments

All United States Information Service (USIS) posts around the world have VCR equipment and individual libraries of cassettes suitable to support a range of issue areas from American culture and society to American policy in economic, political, and military affairs. These tapes are available for screening in USIS libraries and centers, for invitational screenings at Embassies and officers' homes, and sometimes for loan to key members of the host society. For years, CBS nightly news has been pouched to American embassies in various posts, and screening of this news, even when several days old, is said to be a major socializing event between the local press corps and USIS officers. Worldnet, the recently established USIA television feed to a large number of American posts, now sends ABC-TV news to them by satellite, for videotaping on arrival. A 72-hour wait before use is still required for business, not technical reasons, but the news is much fresher than the pouched variety. It is therefore more capable, it is said, of acting as a counter to the "news service" provided by the USSR's TASS, which is relied on by the press corps in such countries as Tanzania. Since the early 1980s, USIA has also been using "video teleconferencing." Tele-conferences between USIS posts and policymakers or cultural celebrities are supplemented by a previously taped and pouched interview or state-ment of the scheduled caller to give the phone voice—cheaply—a human dimension. The tape can also be shown prior to teleconference so partici-pants can prepare country-specific "follow-up" questions.

The U.S. and the KAL 007 incident.   When Korean Airlines Flight 007 was downed by the Russians on September 1, 1983, the television division of the United States Information Agency (USIA) hastened to put together a videocassette that discussed the incident and included recordings of the voices of the Soviet pilots. This was played to a packed Security Council Chamber at the United Nations during the heated debates following the downing. The purpose of the video was to ' "put the lie to the Soviet case.' "[72] After the showing, U.S. Ambassador Jeane Kirkpatrick told re-porters that "the airing of the tape prompted the Kremlin to admit shooting down the plane."[73]

Later, the USIA prepared a 30-minute tape that contained television news reports from six countries— Canada, New Zealand, Chile, Australia, Sweden, and Japan—to be aired at 51 U.S. embassies.[74] Embassies had also been provided, at the height of the crisis, with videotapes of the "McNeill-Lehrer Report," "ABC's Nightline," and a number of other shows, which were to be used "to keep American workers informed, to be shown to foreign government leaders and . . . [maybe] offered to local broadcasters."[75]

The Sakharov tapes.   In August 1984, *Bild Zeitung*, a West German daily newspaper, obtained a 20-minute videotape of Soviet human rights activist Andrei Sakharov and his wife Yelena Bonner. Nobel Prize-winning Sakharov, who had been banished without trial to Gorky, off-limits to foreigners, had been on a prolonged hunger strike to protest the Soviets' refusal to allow his wife to seek medical attention outside the country. At the time of the release of the video, it had been reported that Yelena Bonner had just been convicted of slandering the Soviet state and had been sentenced to 5 years of internal exile.[76]

The source of the videocassette was identified as Victor Louis, a London-based Soviet journalist who in June had supplied some still photographs of Sakharov. Other Sakharov tapes of a similar nature were released by the same sources on later occasions.

EFFORTS TO CONTROL VCRS AND VIDEOCASSETTES

If information control is as critical to governments as their hundreds of years of obsessive control efforts would imply, then the VCR medium may indeed pose a serious threat. The efforts of even very restrictive governments to control VCRs and videocassettes do not appear commensurate with such "dangers." Nor do control efforts, when exerted, seem to have much effect on VCR and cassette distribution. Any bans placed on VCRs and videocassettes by governments to date appear to have been routinely ignored by citizens. The Islamic government of Iran, for instance, in an effort to rid the country of things Western, has even imposed the death sentence in cases of videocassette possession and vending, but this has availed it very little.

Most of the Eastern European countries and the Soviet Union have taken formal steps aimed at regaining some control over what people are watching on videocassettes. They have declared their outrage and issued warnings to their people. They are also providing limited numbers of supposedly controllable VCRs and small supplies of approved videocassette programming. No evidence has been seen that this has made the slightest dent (in fact, quite the contrary) in the smuggling of Japanese and Western VCRs and banned films.

Bulgaria was among the first to take action aimed at "doing something" about the VCR/cassette invasion, *Radio Free Europe Research* reporting that the Bulgarians are very alarmed over the inroads being made by VCRs and videocassettes. Its report describes steps the Bulgarians have taken to attempt to control them, first in 1982, by setting up a state enterprise called Videofilm "to meet educational, propagandistic, ideological, advertising, official, and private demands. Among other things, Videofilm was expected to exercise some sort of control over marketing. . . ."[77] This step was apparently ineffective. In 1984, the Bulgarian Video Association was established, under the chairmanship of Georgi Nakov, a party official highly experienced in organization with a master's degree in ideological propaganda. This appointment of "a cultural Czar" who reports to a deputy prime minister indicates, a source for Eastern Europe says, the importance Bulgaria attaches to VCRs and cassettes and to getting control over them.[78] The Association reserves all rights to rent out private video equipment, and all cameras, recorders, or other video equipment, whether state owned or private, must be registered. Similar actions have now been taken by most Eastern European countries. In Poland, it is said that InterPress, the agency that maintains controls over foreign journalists, planned in spring 1985 to take over the whole business of VCR and videocassette rentals.[79] InterPress saw such a takeover not only as a means to control an independent force, but also as a means of making money. Other Eastern Europe countries are taking similar measures. According to a source for the German Democratic Republic,

> the authorities clearly intend to regulate acquisition or access to such equipment as carefully as they regulate access to all forms of information which can be controlled. VCR equipment is not available in the hard currency shops, even though the expense of such machines would guarantee only a few purchasers. Availability of VCRs for teaching purposes is tightly controlled. Some equipment is available for seminars or meetings through special offices staffed with video technicians who also maintain limited libraries of videotapes, mostly on educational subjects or tapes of GDR television programs.[80]

Remarking on the limited numbers of VCRs in the country, this source also said that "GDR controls are pervasive and effective."[81] A source for Eastern Europe has indicated, however, that the GDR is following the same pattern of VCR penetration as the rest of the countries of Eastern Europe.

The KGB is said to be deeply concerned about VCRs and the Russians are dead serious about controlling all information. All information equipment in the USSR is closely controlled. Duplicating machines are not permitted privately and within the Ministries they are locked up to prevent after-hours uses. The KGB is very actively prosecuting Soviet officials who accept VCRs from foreign businessmen. Asked why the Soviets do not control VCRs and videocassettes more rigidly than they do, a source for the USSR said that the Soviets are ambivalent about this subject and about progress in general. They are always moving in two directions. In this case, the police want to control information, but the government wants to keep up with the rest of the world.[82]

Several sources indicate that, thus far, VCRs and cassettes are still relatively few in the USSR and may therefore still be tolerable. MIT Professor Loren Graham has said that videocassettes are still well down on the list of technologies for political uses.[83] The Soviets' effort to create their own VCRs and programming are an attempt to gain some control but this has been quite unsuccessful.[84]

Many countries have been making an effort to comply with copyright claims, some in response to U.S. pressure. The U.S. Congress has made trade benefit eligibility under the Caribbean Basin Economic Recovery Act dependent in part on more vigorous protection of U.S. intellectual property. The U.S. Executive branch has also been pressuring such countries as Taiwan, Singapore, and Korea to give better protection against video and other piracy. Compliance by various countries often takes the form of anti-piracy raids, which pick up a few culprits or drive them from one base of operations to another.

> In the first half of 1984, the motion picture industry seized "more than 200,000 illegal cassettes, supervised over 2,000 investigations and obtained over 200 criminal convictions around the world."[85]

But since this is just a drop in the bucket compared to the total global illegal activity, the end result is like a drug bust that hauls in a few pounds of cocaine or a few bales of marijuana. It leaves intact the basic structure of illegal conduits through which videocassettes are distributed globally.

While several nations have upped fines for piracy, several others, including Holland, just don't want the extra bureaucratic and police work. Stiffer penalties have been recommended in the Netherlands, but cases are tried in civil, not criminal, courts. At least 50% of videocassettes in Holland were still pirated in 1984, and organized crime was specifically mentioned to be involved in this activity.[86]

Many countries have updated, and others are trying to update, their censorship laws to encompass videocassettes. Those who do so often find the workload to be overpowering. In Iceland, a country about the size of Kentucky, videocassettes come in by the "truckload."[87] The New Zealand Customs Department was pressed into service by that government to censor incoming videocassettes. These amounted to more than 11,000 tapes in a 12-month period.[88]

In Spain, all prerecorded cassettes must be licensed and that country is reportedly preparing a law both to crack down on piracy and to eliminate unauthorized viewing. But the Spaniards are not sanguine that this will make any practical difference.

Malaysia has tightened up on censorship of videocassettes and has increased checks on VCR rental centers. Burma jails offenders. But the circulation of illegal videocassettes continues.[89] For Asia in general, Reuters says: "Overwhelmed official censors complain they just cannot cope with millions of video cassettes flooding the Asian market."[90] Inadequate laws have also been cited, but, where laws exist or are implemented, they have been unable to prevent the influx.

Regarding the failure of national governments to respond to the new challenge being presented by videocassette recorders, Christine Ogan of the Indiana University School of Journalism says:

> wherever it surfaces, the discussion of policy change has focused on broadcast technology and content planned by, or under the supervision of government organizations.[91]

But policymakers have not even addressed the problem of VCRs, although this is, she says, "The greatest potential threat to the total disintegration of national communication policy."[92] One reason, she says, is that the VCR is still considered a private medium, and not a medium for mass communications.

Professor Ogan remarked on the contradictory attitudes concerning VCRs in developing countries, saying:

> for Third World countries, it is curious that in the face of the strong stand taken on the New World Information Order, and the vehement attacks levelled against the West for upsurping local cultural values with imported media, so little should be done to control this more insidious cultural invasion . . . other than establishing quotas or restricting imports to families who have lived abroad and brought back VCRs as a part of their household goods, I know of no country that has prevented VCR importation.[93]

The fact that there is, as yet, no really effective control over VCRs and cassettes in no way indicates that the desire of governments for information control has diminished. This study has uncovered no shortage of censorship of books, newspapers, radio, television—of whatever falls in the traditional framework or, especially, where the government controls the means of production and dissemination. This censorship ranges from mild to totally crippling.

Douglas Boyd explains how VCRs and videocassettes are shifting control over information from governments to their people:

> Among the many reasons that VCR ownership is increasing is that the machines are a means of gaining control over media consumption—a video equivalent of print material that is consumed at one's convenience. To some extent, the tapes are similar to books, but the consumer does not have to be literate to participate. VCRs are status symbols among all classes of people. The machines allow owners differing degrees of often forbidden fruit; pornography, banned political and religious material, uncensored western television programs, and feature films.[94]

VCRs, he says, are so popular that not even the Soviet Union, and certainly not any developing country, has the power to control them.

Part of the reason for lack of control has been attributed to the compromises made with the necessity for black markets and the need to placate migrants. Part is that illegal activities in VCRs and cassettes got in on the ground floor and it will be difficult if not impossible for governments to shake them. Part is that the world's borders have largely become sieves, letting in, not only VCRs and cassettes, but also illegal drugs, arms, and migrants. Part is due to the conflicting desires within a given nation – the necessity for the government to grant the wishes of both the most conservative and the most liberal factions to maintain political equilibrium. Partly, as in China, major control has had to be sacrificed to allow economic modernization to continue. Partly, nations are kidding themselves. Poland, for instance, and other communist countries maintain the myth that they still control the monopoly on all programming. Partly, governments were caught by surprise by this new technology, and changing laws to cover it often runs into conflicts with other priorities.

Part of the reason for lack of control also appears to be that, in some countries, the worst has happened and it doesn't seem so bad after all. Videocassettes are the new opiate of the people, and, while they are watching them, they are not out rioting.

That these various leniencies by governments may be shortsighted from their point of view is another story. *Rolling Stone* has said, in reference to VCRs,

> by the time England's infamous Luddites thought to destroy knitting machines, the Industrial Revolution had been going on for at least a hundred years, and their protests turned out to be more romantic fatalism than effective politics.[95]

But in many cases, governments believe they are doing all they can do, given the other demands they face.

NOTES

1. "U.S. Cassette Recorder Count at 13,200,00; 57,000,000 Worldwide," *Variety*, October 17, 1984, p. 2.
   Richard Klein, "Pic Assn.'s Nix Gives Antipiracy Advice to Members of AFMA," *Variety*, December 12, 1984, p. 6.
   "85 VCR Count to Tally 100-Mil, Predicts MPEA," *Variety*, February 27, 1985, p. 37.
2. "Surveying World Press Freedom. Weighing Gains and Losses of 1983," *World Press Review*, February 1984, p. 58.

3. Steven Koppany, "Unprepared Regime Scrambles to Meet Challenges of the Video Era," Situation Report, Hungary/10, *Radio Free Europe Research*, Radio Free Europe-Radio Liberty, September 4, 1985, p.17.

4. Robert Kaiser, "Russian Life: Is 'Veedeyo' A Blow to the Bolsheviks?" *The Washington Post*, September 9, 1984, p. D-10.

5. Guenter Reimann, *The Black Market. Inevitable Child of Statism*. Pamphlet No. 35, Hindsdale, Ill: Henry Regnery Co., 1948.

6. B. Jicinski, "The East Bloc's Market for Media Imports," *The Wall Street Journal*, September 19, 1984, p. 33.

7. *Ibid.*

8. "China Cracks Down on Smuggling by Organizations," *The Xinhua General Overseas News Service* August 6, 1985 (NEXIS).

9. *Ibid.*

10. "China. Beclouded by Greed," *The Economist*, August 10, 1985, p. 50.

11. Pico Iyer, "The Second Revolution. Deng's Reforms are Taking China on a Courageous if Uncharted Course," *Time*, September 23, 1985, pp. 52, 55.

12. Steve Frazier, "A Slum Black Market in Mexico Is a Part of The Establishment," *The Wall Street Journal*, March 25, 1985, p. 1.

13. Ibid.

14. Charles J. Hanley, "Today's Focus: In The Age of Khomeini, Tehran Moves at Half Step," *The Associated Press*, November 23, 1982 (NEXIS).

15. Ray Vicker, "Dubai's Traders Are Building A Thriving Trade Smuggling Goods into Iran," *The Wall Street Journal*, May 7, 1980, p. 48. Reprinted as "Dubai's Enterprising Traders Smuggle Goods Into Iran," in Burgess Laughlin, *Black Markets Around the World*, Mason, Michigan: Loompanics Unlimited, 1981, p. 36.

16. Lelia Hemmat and Philip Marfleet, "Tehran's Great Debate," *The Middle East*, April 1985, p. 51.

17. Robert Trumbull, "Videotapes of Slaying Smuggled Into Manila," *The New York Times*, September 13, 1983, p. A-9.
"U.S. Filipinos Sending Home Published Attacks on Marcos," *The New York Times*, February 7, 1984, p. A-10.

18. "Customs Cannot Stem Imports of Video Porn, Bussieres Admits," *Montreal Gazette* February 15, 1983, p. B-1.

19. Javed Jabbar, "Pakistan. A Cautious Welcome," *InterMedia*, July/September 1983, pp. 65-66.

20. Emel Anil, "Bootleg Movies Are Big Business in Turkey," *The Associated Press*, February 28, 1984 (NEXIS).

21. *Ibid.*

22. *Ibid.*

23. Anna Christensen, "The Black Sea: Prostitution and Punks," *United Press International*, August 19, 1984 (NEXIS).

24. Donald R. Shanor, *Behind the Lines. The Private War Against Soviet Censorship*. St. Martin's Press, New York, 1985, p. 154.

25. Philip Taubman, "Oh Comrade, Can I Borrow Your Rambo Cassette?" *The New York Times*, December 9, 1985, p. A-2.

26. *Ibid.*

27. "Rushin' to Their VCRs," TV Guide, Volume 33, Number 17, April 27/May 3, 1985, p. A-2.
28. Douglas Stanglin. Personal communications.
29. "Central America in Brief," Variety, March 20, 1985, p. 46.
30. "Pirate Vid Haul in West Africa Includes U.S. Tapes," Variety, October 3, 1984, p. 2.
31. Many sources, including most of the references in this chapter.
32. Matthew White and Darrell Moore, "Bastille Day Marathon. 24 Hours of French Movies," Video Movies, July 1984, pp. 35-38.
33. Personal observation. The authors.
34. Mounir B. Abboud, "Egyptian Pictures Still Pack in Arabs in Spite of Politics," Variety, October 31, 1984, p. 6.
35. "Middle Eastern Story-tellers Give Way to Videos," Index on Censorship, 14(1), February 1985, p. 53.
36. Bangladesh. Personal communications.
37. Richard Bill, "Dateline: Islamabad," The Associated Press, April 25, 1983 (NEXIS).
38. Emel Anil, "Bootleg Movies Are Big Business in Turkey," The Associated Press, February 28, 1984 (NEXIS).
39. "VCRs Go on Fast Forward. Proliferating Players and Tapes Spread Western Fare Worldwide," Time, December 13, 1982, p. 78.
40. "Out of Reach of the Curious Censors," U.S. News & World Report, July 23, 1984, p. 46.
41. "Iran. Tehran Accomodates," World Press Review, November 1984, p. 55. Reprinted from The Economist.
42. "Out of Reach of the Curious Censors," U.S. News & World Report, July 23, 1984, p. 46.
43. Philip Taubman, "Oh Comrade, Can I Borrow Your Rambo Cassette?" The New York Times, December 9, 1985, p. A-2.
44. "China Nears Agreement With Western Producers Over Video Copyrights," Variety, October 23, 1985, p. 1.
45. "Paris," Variety, August 22, 1984, p. 135.
46. "U.K.'s Vid Express," Variety, November 9, 1984, p. 47.
47. M. A. Partha Sarathy, "India. Video On The Bus," InterMedia, July/September 1983, p. 53.
48. "Early Warning. Media Beat," World Press Review, August 1984, p. 6.
49. Tess Thomas, "Jamaica. The Miami Connection," InterMedia, July/September 1983, p. 57.
50. Nora C. Quebral, The Video Recorder in Developing Countries, speech, International Institute of Communications 1984 Annual Conference, Berlin, September 22, 1984, p. 4.
51. Robert Trumbull, "Videotapes of Slaying Smuggled Into Manila," The New York Times, September 13, 1983, p. A-9.
52. Ibid.
53. James Brooke, "Salvadorans Use Video in the Propaganda War," The New York Times, August 27, 1984, p. C-17.
54. Ibid.

55. *Ibid.*
56. James Brooke, "Salvadorans Use Video in the Propaganda War," *The New York Times*, August 27, 1984, p. C-17.
57. Mary Anne Weaver, "Failed Coup Against Pakistan Leader May Have Involved India," *The Christian Science Monitor*, March 19, 1984, p. 9.
58. "Hijackers Called 'Thieves, Thugs and Murderers'," *The Boston Globe*, July 3, 1985, p. 2.
59. "15 Reported Killed in Israeli Raid on Palestinian Bases in Lebanon," *The Boston Globe*, July 11, 1985, p. 9.
60. "3rd Car Explosion in South Lebanon in A Week Kills 10. Vehicle with Red Cross Flag Blows Up in Israeli Zone – Beirut Radio Hails Act," *The New York Times*, July 16, 1985, p. A-1.
61. Joseph Lelyveld, "Extremist South African Group Arouses Concern," *The New York Times*, August 23, 1981, p. A-3.
62. Jack Kindred, "Transit Film Seeks Halt to U.S. Piracy of Nazi Propaganda Pics," *Variety*, October 31, 1984, p. 32.
63. *Ibid.*
64. Jeanne Saddler, "Public Relations Firms Offer 'News' to TV. Electronic Releases Contain Subtle Commercials for Clients," *The Wall Street Journal*, April 2, 1985, p. 6.
    Paul Harris, "JD Calls Flack On the Carpet Over TV Feeds," *Variety*, April 3, 1985, p. 49.
65. Jeanne Saddler, "Public Relations Firms Offer 'News' to TV. Electronic Releases Contain Subtle Commercials for Clients," *The Wall Street Journal*, April 2, 1985, p. 6.
66. Jeanne Saddler, "Public Relations Firms Offer 'News' to TV. Electronic Releases Contain Subtle Commercials for Clients," *The Wall Street Journal*, April 2, 1985, p. 6.
67. Paul West, "The Video Connection. Beaming It Straight to the Constituents," *Washington Journalism Review*, June 1985, pp. 48-50.
68. Paul West, "The Video Connection. Beaming It Straight to the Constituents," *Washington Journalism Review*, June 1985, pp. 48-50.
69. "Empty Chair for Tutu at Religious Gathering," *The Associated Press*, August 4, 1981 (NEXIS).
70. "Kirkland - Solidarity. Dateline: Washington," *The Associated Press*, September 26, 1981 (NEXIS).
71. George Gedda, "Cuban Officials Paint Bright Economic Picture," *The Associated Press*, September 8, 1981 (NEXIS)
72. Randolph E. Schmid, "U.S. Steps Up Broadcasts to Soviets," *The Associated Press*, September 8, 1983 (NEXIS).
73. John Usher, "UN. Dateline: United Nations," *United Press International*, September 6, 1983 (NEXIS).
74. "Dateline: Washington," *United Press International*, September 30, 1983 (NEXIS).
75. Randolph E. Schmid, "U.S. Steps Up Broadcasts to Soviets," *The Associated Press*, September 8, 1983 (NEXIS).

76. William Scally, "Sakharov-American. Dateline: Washington," *Reuters*, August 23, 1984 (NEXIS).

77. "Bulgaria Goes Into the Video Business," Situation Report, Bulgaria/13, *Radio Free Europe Research*, Radio Free Europe-Radio Liberty, October 10, 1984, p. 4.

78. Eastern Europe. Personal communications.
G. S., "Bulgaria Goes Into the Video Business," Situation Report, Bulgaria/13, Radio Free Europe Research, Radio Free Europe-Radio Liberty, October 10, 1984., p. 2.

79. Douglas Stanglin. Personal communications.

80. German Democratic Republic. Personal communications.

81. *Ibid.*

82. The Soviet Union. Personal communications.

83. Loren Graham, *Computers in the Soviet Union*, Program on Information Resources Policy Seminar, Harvard University, February 4, 1985.

84. "VCRs That Will Spout The Party Line," *Business Week*, September 3, 1984, p. 40.

85. Richard Klein, "Pic Assn.'s Nix Gives Antipiracy Advice to Members of AFMA," Variety, December 12, 1984, p. 6.

86. "Huffpuffing At Pirates By Video Trade Bodies Doesn't Do The Trick," *Variety*, October 17, 1984, p. 62.

87. "Icelandic Censors Under Full Steam," *Variety*, October 10, 1984, p. 112.

88. Mike Nicolaidi, "N.Z. Customs Dept. Wants to Lose Role as Product Censor," *Variety*, November 9, 1984, p. 47.

89. Malaysia. Personal communications.

90. Francis Daniel, "Dateline: Singapore," *Reuters*, September 24, 1983 (NEXIS).

91. Christine L. Ogan, "Media Diversity and Communications Policy. Impact of VCRs and Satellite TV," *Telecommunications Policy*, March 1985, p. 63.

92. *Ibid.*, p. 64.

93. *Ibid.*, p. 68.

94. Douglas A. Boyd, *Technology, Communication, and Development Theory: The Impact of the Home Video Cassette Recorder on Third World Countries*, speech, International Institute of Communications 1984 Annual Conference, Berlin, September 21-23, 1984, pp. 7-8.

95. Kenneth Turan, "The Art of Revolution. Video is Taking Over Popular Culture," *Rolling Stone*, December 20, 1984/January 3, 1985, p. 75.

CHAPTER 9

CONTRADICTIONS AND CONCERNS

Benjamin M. Compaine

In this volume, as in *Understanding New Media*,[1] the description and implications of the widely perceived "information revolution" remain open to questions. There is typically a time lag, of years to decades, between the introduction of a technology (or more likely the combination of several technologies) and an established pattern of effects. Technology is a necessary but not sufficient condition for many of the changes in the realm of information and communication throughout history. In the context of the debate on whether technology should be viewed as being value neutral, or deterministic, the conclusion I reach from the studies and essays in this and previous research from the Harvard Program on Information Resources Policy, as well as from others, is that reality is for the most part technology neutral.

For example, as the Mendes chapter notes, the same computer technology that makes invasion of privacy such a scary potential can also be used to secure information. The press and broadcasting, powerful technologies for propaganda in the hands of despots, are just as powerful for education and informing in a society that encourages such uses. But perhaps the most significant lesson from these studies is that information technology is becoming so cheap and easy to use that it lends itself to greater dispersion and, conversely, to greater difficulty for control for whatever ends. The Ganleys make this abundantly clear in their excerpt here and even stronger in their book.

The implications go beyond the consumption of information. For those

eed or desire, producing and distributing information is
_er, faster, and easier. Inexpensive video cameras, desktop
_ using personal computers and laser printers, computer-
_piled mailing lists and audio cassettes are among the new means of
production. The increasing connectivity and digitization of the telecommunications network provides the newer electronic pathway. But even hard
copy moves faster and cheaper. The very low tech but always available
postal services throughout the world continue to be reliable, inexpensive,
and, compared to 50 years ago, relatively fast methods of distributing
information.

PREDICTING IS A HAZARDOUS OCCUPATION . . .
ESPECIALLY WHEN IT DEALS WITH THE FUTURE

This non sequitur has been variously attributed to Confucius, Mark Twain,
and Casey Stengel, among others. For those who have been following the
technological changes in the media industry for the past decade, the futility
of prognostications is quietly told in the Appendix to the chapter by
Krasnow and Stern. Three years after it was written, the ventures and
proposals described had for the most part failed to materialize. Low power
television has gone nowhere. Neither the consumer oriented network
backed by Ralph Nader nor the rural America theme programming from
Sears has materialized. DBS? None of the 40 additional channels of video
programming have made it to themarketplace. MDS? Barely visible and not
getting brighter. STV had all the staying power of Corfam shoes (remember
them?). Teletext? Still a gleam in someone's eye. Videotex? Knight-Ridder
and Times Mirror Co. showed how much money one could lose with new
technology. Some of these or other technology-inspired services may yet
become viable. But not on the timetable predicted by an analysis of the
potential of the technology alone.

LESSONS

Lessons have their exceptions. By their very nature they are generalizations.
But they can serve as a guideline with which to examine the issue of the
moment.

Technology May Not Head in a Straight Line

If there is a single lesson that one can take away from the studies and essays
in this volume, it is that the impact of changing information technology on

individuals,institutions, and societies is unpredictable and often even counter intuitive. How else does one explain how the mechanization of the Industrial Revolution *created* tens of millions of jobs, rather than eliminated jobs?

In the first chapter of *Wealth of Nations*, Adam Smith told the story of the pin factory where a single worker could only make a few pins a day by hand. New machinery increased output to 4800 pins daily per worker. Such machinery should have created 99% unemployment among pinmakers. The opposite happened. The vast increase in productivity dramatically lowered the cost of pins, creating new uses for them, hence greatly expanding demand.

Straight-line extrapolation often leads on to outlandish (but often accepted) conclusions. In 1910, for example, the Bell System handled 7 million telephone calls with 121,310 employees, or 57 calls per employee.[2] To have handled the current call volume of more than 430 billion calls would have been impossible with the 726,000 employees of all the telephone companies (the ratio is now 592,286 calls per employee). At the 1910 productivity level we would have needed more employees than there are people on the Earth.

Reconsider Assumptions

A second lesson suggested by these chapters is to carefully examine the assumptions underlying your own analysis or that of others. The point of the "new literacy," for example, is not that it is inevitable. Rather it is that the assumptions behind current concepts of literacy are of relatively recent vintage and, like earlier notions of literacy, are subject to change. Assumptions to the effect that he who controls the broadcast tower and printing press can control the hearts and minds of the people have had to be re-evaluated in light of the "little media" such as audio and video cassettes and thephotocopying machine. Assumptions of the inevitability of Big Brother knowing all via computer terminals connected to everything by telecommunications need to contend with increasingly effective and inexpensive security devices brought about by the same computer technology.

STRATEGIC CONCERNS AND COUNTERVAILING FORCES

Players and Stakes

Strategic concerns are long term issues in which there are conflicting, hence debatable, outcomes. Individuals, organizations, and nations have their own sets of strategic concerns. A strategic concern of the librarian community, for example, is the allocation of its resources among its traditional printed products and newer online electronic information services. Newspaper publishers face a strategic issue in the resolution of their stake in the printed product and the economic and perhaps cultural forces pointing toward more electronic services. Individuals deal with strategic issues in their right to privacy and their right to know about others when it comes to illegal or unethical conduct, for example. Nations perceive their strategic issues in the information arena as involving their cultural integrity, employment, security, even pride.

Individual fears include the threat of technological unemployment. The media regularly run pieces about invasion of privacy, as described in Chapter 7, although it is less clear that most people spend much time worrying about such possibilities. At a more global level certain interests in some nations use a threat to their culture as an excuse to erect barriers to the import of ideas and information in the form of entertainment. The effect, intended or not, is to protect from competition local industries that traffic in substitute commodities.

But while some people or societies focus on defensive maneuvers as a rear guard action to threats, other are seizing on the opportunities provided by the lower cost or greater capabilities provided by the technology.

Winners vs. Losers

There is a tendency to look for a victim whenever there is change. This is implicit in the search for a growing "information gap." It need not be so, especially for a society that is adaptive. The pinmakers who were hurt by mechanization were those who refused to use the new machinery. Automation created additional jobs for telephone operators (and installers and factory hands). Semiconductor technology has created legions of winners and few big losers. Using computers, banks have been able to reduce their cost of handling transactions, making checking accounts more affordable. Computers also createdcompetition by aiding in the development of new forms of financial institutions and financial instruments such as combined brokerage, checking and credit accounts and the like pioneered by Merrill, Lynch, assisted, of course, by skillful use of legal loopholes. Newspaper publishers have been wary of electronic publishing. But they have been saved from economic disaster by using electronic publishing systems in the internal production process, keeping them viable players in the arena with direct mailers, television broadcasters, and local radio.

Losers are often those who refuse to adapt, who insist on continuing to do things "the old way." Banks that resisted installing automated teller machines (ATMs) to preserve "personal contact" soon found their economics out of whack with their competitors' and watched as many of their customers drifted away to the banks that offered ATM convenience. Typewriter manufacturers slow to recognize the impact of word processors had to scramble to recover—or never did—and had to merge themselves away.

Threats vs. Opportunities

Another way of looking at winners and losers is in terms of threats and opportunities. One may see threats to an individual's livelihood, to a specific business, to an older technology, to an industry, to a right, a privilege, a society, or to a way of life.

An example of threats to an industry include the reaction of the postal services to the telephone. In the 1880s, the Postmaster General of the United States wrote in his report to Congress that he expected telegraph and facsimile services to threaten the very existence of the Post Office. In most of the world, this fear lead to government control of telephone services by the older postal bureaucracy, forming the PTTs (Post, Telegraph, and Telephone administrations) that helped discourage telephonecompetition to the mails in the developed countries. In recent history, broadcasters feared cable operators. Newspaper publishers have feared that electronic "Yellow Pages" from the telephone companies would threaten lucrative classified advertising revenue.

Big Money vs. Little Capital

The implications of chapters 3 and 8 are that in what seems to be an era of megamergers and multimedia conglomerates, it is also true that in many ways the cost of entry into the business of providing information to users keeps decreasing and the number of players increases. It is most obvious in print, where a respectable-lookingnewsletter or newspaper can be created with computers and laser printers costing well under $10,000. The small offset presses—and even high-speed photocopying machines—make duplication a modest expense. The sophistication of computerized mailing lists makes targeting audiences for Postal Service distribution more efficient and less costly than ever.

Beyond reliance on such "old fashioned" mechanical delivery, there is the growing use of electronic distribution. The same text created on personal computers can be made available to hundreds or hundreds of thousands of individuals through electronic "bulletin boards' or mail services. With the cost of a full fledged personal computer and modem under

$1000, the cost of access is sometimes as little as the price of a telephone call.

Production and distribution costs of prime-time quality television programs or theatrical release quality motion pictures is still sizeable. But the opening up of cable television channels and video cassette outlets has created a viable outlet for more modest productions, often of a special interest nature. Like their special interest magazine counterparts, they do not get the mass audience distribution of prime time network television, but they are available to serve identifiable markets around the world.

Balance Between Government and Other Forces of Regulation

One of the ongoing debates around the world involves the degree to which law and policy is or should be the determining form of control. Alternatives to imposed regulation include market forces, self-policing professional or trade groups, collective bargaining, societal mores, and so on. Policy decisions among these alternatives rarely are made for all time and vary from nation to nation. Moreover, even a government's policy of not regulating this or that implies the wherewithal to regulate at a later date.

The practicality of one type of regulation or another changes, often as the result of technology. The widespread movement toward less governmental regulation of some sectors of the telecommunications business in the industrialized nations in the decades of the 1980s was due in some measure to the technologies that created market forces in areas of customer equipment and certain transmission services. As Krasnow and Stern point out, there remains uncertainty over the degree to which various regulatory forces are operating in the video business.

Changing Priorities of Competing Forces

In *The Future of the Mass Audience*[3] Russell Neuman of M.I.T. looks at the forces of new communications and information technology and what he sees as their potentially positive social impact. However, his research goes further by asking what other countervailing social forces might affect the march toward the adoption of new information technologies. He identifies two. One is the "political economy" of the American communications system. This encompasses the economies of scale in the production and distribution of the media and in advertising that generates pressures for mass-produced, common-denominator, mass-audience media. The second force is "the psychology of the mass audience." This is the semi-attentive, entertainment-oriented mind-set of daily media usage. (A more colloquial way to summarize this force is the "couch potato syndrome"). As confirmation of the countervailing forces Neuman mentions, the literature turns up hypotheses about the social and political implications of the new media that provides evidence to support almost any point of view.

Of the many forces that interact in determining the success or failure of some product, service, or policy, none can be considered dominant at all times. Some particular application of technology may be held back or pushed ahead by other forces. For example, cable television was held back from the growth predicted for it in some part due to restrictions placed on the industry by federal and state agencies, often at the urging of broad-casters or others who felt threatened by cable. Yet the fast track for cable still may have had to await help from the maturing of the seemingly unrelated technologies that came together in the 1970s. They provided reliable earth-circling satellites with the capacity to provide cheap transmis-sion of premium programming as well as "super" broadcast station signals to cable operators around the United States.

Similarly, the idea behind the New Literacy is that computer and video technologies will help shape cultural values and expectations. The notion of literacy will in turn be further shaped by generations brought up with electronic dissemination of information that will supplement and perhaps even replace some current applications of printed information.

Technology and economics are frequently intertwined. That which was doable but uneconomical in the past becomes feasible as costs decrease (and vice versa). Examples are plentiful. In 1964, the *New York Times* attempted to publish a West Coast edition but gave up after a short and expensive try. Today's computer, printing, and, most of all, transmission technologies have made it practical not only for the *Times* but for the *Wall Street Journal* and *USA Today*. In the late 1960s, computers attracted educators and publishers into a debacle of computer-aided instruction. Today, with a different agenda, far less expensive and more powerful computers seem to be finding a more accepted niche in the schools.

Globalization and Fragmentation

Marshall McLuhan popularized the notion that the electronic media were leading us toward a "global village," a concept that others have picked up. Under some ideological frameworks, globalization is associated with cul-tural imperialism of the West on the less developed East and South.

Paradoxically, the implications of Chapters 3, 4, and 8 support the contention that technology is splintering rather that homogenizing the streams of information. Special interest video tapes and cable channels are following the path of special interest newspapers, books, magazines and direct mail.

These trends are not mutually exclusive. The content of the U.K.'s *Financial Times* and *Economist* travel by satellite for printing in the U.S. as easily as *USA Today* or the *Wall Street Journal* are sent to Europe. The economics of video production encourage broadcasters worldwide to buy U.S. television and motion picture productions. But the declining capital cost of publishing and broadcasting facilities also makes it possible for more local production anywhere.

THE GOOD, THE BAD AND THE UNK-UNKS

The good news is that the information-intensive world has not been, and does not seem to be becoming, as terrifying a place as Orwell or several more contemporary information technology doomsayers would have us believe. The written word did not destroy memory, as King Thamus predicted. The novel did not create havoc with children, as the 19th century British librarian had feared, and television has not created a world of zombies who buy whatever they are told by the evil advertisers.

Good news should be more than the avoidance of negatives. Over the centuries, information and information technology has continued providing more substance to more people for less direct cost. The media have been controlled by individuals, corporations, institutions, and governments for noble, malicious, self-serving, or beneficent ends. But the proliferation of new processes at lower cost has historically made it more difficult for any one or a small number of entities to control all access. And this overall diversity is likely to continue growing.

The bad news? To date it remains more a potential than a reality. Misuse of personal information by third parties is always a possibility, but technology seems to strike a balance between access and protection. Copyright protection vs. fair use remains an ongoing issue but one that seems amenable to negotiation and readjustment. Governments that view it their role to control what their people read, hear and see must be looking at the information future with some trepidation, as it is becoming harder to control what passes across borders and between homes.

That leaves the unk-unks, or the unknown-unknowns. These are the variables that are so invisible we can't address them even as "what if?" Can there be some unexpected breakthrough in some technology that totally shifts the balance of other forces? Can there be some social upheaval that changes fundamental attitudes towards information-related concerns, such as the First Amendment in the United States? The concept of unk-unks is helpful for anyone speculating on the future, because it serves as a reminder that there are many factors that cannot be anticipated. The unexpected run-up of energy costs in the 1970s precipitated by geopolitical events in the Middle East, for example, had a substantial direct economic impact on publishers while barely affecting broadcasters.

John Adams observed that "All great changes are irksome to the human mind, especially those attended with dangerous and uncertain effects." The changes and potential changes associated with the rapid pace in the development of technologies of information gathering, creating, storing, and transmitting may indeed be unsettling. But they have been manageable. With reasonable foresight and an appreciation for the complexity of the forces at work we should be able to avoid being too surprised by the outcomes of the changing information landscape.

NOTES

1. Benjamin M. Compaine, ed., *Understanding New Media: Trends and Issues in Electronic Distribution of Information* (Cambridge, Mass.: Ballinger Publishing Co., 1984).
2. Bruce Bartlett, "The Luddite Answer to Unemployment, " *The Wall Street Journal*, July 18, 1983. Op-ed page.
3. W. Russell Neuman, *The Future of the Mass Audience* (Cambridge, Mass,: Harvard University Press, 1988).

Author Index

Subject Index